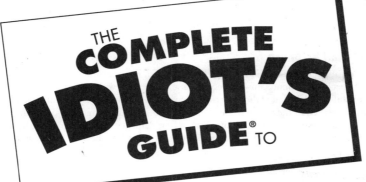

THE COMPLETE IDIOT'S GUIDE® TO

Celtic Wisdom

by Carl McColman

ALPHA

A member of Penguin Group (USA) Inc.

For John, Marcia, and BethAnn.

International Standard Book Number: 0-02-864417-4
Library of Congress Catalog Card Number: 2003100701

05   04   03   8   7   6   5   4   3   2   1

Interpretation of the printing code: The rightmost number of the first series of numbers is the year of the book's printing; the rightmost number of the second series of numbers is the number of the book's printing. For example, a printing code of 03-1 shows that the first printing occurred in 2003.

Printed in the United States of America

Note: This publication contains the opinions and ideas of its author. It is intended to provide helpful and informative material on the subject matter covered. It is sold with the understanding that the author and publisher are not engaged in rendering professional services in the book. If the reader requires personal assistance or advice, a competent professional should be consulted.

The author and publisher specifically disclaim any responsibility for any liability, loss, or risk, personal or otherwise, which is incurred as a consequence, directly or indirectly, of the use and application of any of the contents of this book.

Most Alpha books are available at special quantity discounts for bulk purchases for sales promotions, premiums, fund-raising, or educational use. Special books, or book excerpts, can also be created to fit specific needs.

For details, write: Special Markets, Alpha Books, 375 Hudson Street, New York, NY 10014.

Publisher: *Marie Butler-Knight*
Product Manager: *Phil Kitchel*
Senior Managing Editor: *Jennifer Chisholm*
Senior Acquisitions Editor: *Randy Ladenheim-Gil*
Development Editor: *Jennifer Moore*
Copy Editor: *Keith Cline*
Illustrator: *Jody Schaeffer*
Cover/Book Designer: *Trina Wurst*
Indexer: *Tonya Heard*
Layout/Proofreading: *Svetlana Dominguez, Becky Harmon, Mary Hunt, Ayanna Lacey*

Contents at a Glance

Contents

Appendixes

Foreword

On a high blanket bog in the west of Ireland, a gnarled thorn tree stands near a narrow track. Motorists use that road sometimes, cutting from one village to the next, but more commonly only thin-legged shaggy sheep traverse its rough surface. You could pass the little tree without noticing it among a cluster of granite boulders, but if you hike over to it and look carefully, you see a subtle sparkle: silver coins secreted around its roots, offerings to the spirits of the bog.

In the midlands, where a great monastic center once hid among the sharp ravines that cut the rolling landscape, another tree grows from the center of a natural spring. From it hang masses of clooties, bits of cloth torn from scarves or cut from spools of ribbon. So many offerings twist around the tree that its bark is almost invisible. Nearby, another tree—an ash, like its companion—grows beside a second holy well. Its offerings, like the bog-stunted thorn, are silver. Wood has almost closed over old English sovereigns, and bright new euros jut from the diamond-pattern bark.

On the island's southern coast, a craggy rock looks out from a heathery hillside. Steeply below, the blue ocean dances onto a thin, white strand. From a certain angle, the boulder looks like a weathered ancient face. Up close, you find that flowers and bits of bright rock fill its every wrinkle.

The ancient Celts saw nature as alive, vibrant with spirit. Even today, that consciousness has not been lost in the ancient Celtic lands. You can still find farmers who point out faery rings and artists who practice the old magic of transformation. And on certain days, in certain weathers, you feel sure the old gods still inhabit the faery mounds, coming forth to tempt mere mortals with the bliss of otherworldly love. The old Celtic lands hold magic that reveals itself to the reverent seeker.

But the wisdom of the Celtic way does not require residence in, or even visits to, the culture's traditional lands. Those who yearn for a spiritual vision that embraces the living earth feel the pull of Celtic wisdom no matter where they live. The Celts were once so rooted in place that a single word in Irish (*tuath*) meant both people and land. It is one of history's great ironies that such fiercely local tribespeople have been so scattered that today no continent lacks a Celtic presence. In their new homelands, the people of the Celtic diaspora dream of knowing their place again.

For the people of that diaspora and for "Celts of the heart," Carl McColman presents the essence of ancient Celtic culture and suggests its applications in today's world. This comprehensive but concise guide emphasizes the variations and ambiguities inherent in the Celtic way without allowing complexity to become confusion. For both new sojourners and those well traveled on the Celtic path, McColman is an excellent and sure guide.

Time's arrow flies ever forward; the Celts will continue both to scatter and to dream. And in doing so, they will share with natives of other lands their culture's special vision: that this is a world of edges as well as centers, that change is the only constant, that opposites combine to make wholeness, and that the special beauties of each moment in each place are to be embraced, for they are what sustain our souls. This book offers you a steady and steadying glimpse into that profound wisdom.

Patricia Monaghan

Patricia Monaghan is the author of *The Red-Haired Girl from the Bog: The Landscape of Celtic Myth and Spirit* and the editor of *Irish Spirit: Pagan, Celtic, Christian, Global.* She is a member of the interdisciplinary faculty at DePaul University in Chicago, where she teaches literature and environment.

Introduction

The Celtic world is a world of contradictions. On the one hand, it is a marginal realm: Only a few small regions in Western Europe are "Celtic," meaning home to those who speak a Celtic language or identify as a Celtic nation. And yet tens of millions of people throughout the world take pride in the Celtic blood coursing through their veins and look to the Celtic lands for inspiration in spiritual and cultural ways. Politically, the Celts ceased to be a major power when Caesar conquered Gaul more than 2,000 years ago, and yet to this day Celtic ideas and philosophy continue to influence countless numbers of people—a true embodiment of the proverb "The pen is mightier than the sword!" And although Celtic spirituality has often been overshadowed by the various forms of Christianity embraced by Celtic people, the heart of Celtic wisdom lies in an ancient mysticism based on reverence for the earth and devotion to the spirits of the land and the tribe.

You might have picked up this book for any number of reasons. Perhaps you feel a call to the ancient ways of Celtic shamans, druids, and pagans. Or you might simply want to learn about the inner life of this ancient and proud lineage. Whatever your motivation is for seeking Celtic wisdom, this book can help you understand the basics and appreciate the special perspective of the Celtic tradition.

How to Use This Book

Celtic wisdom is a broad subject with many unique subcategories, so this book aims to give you an overview to help you understand the big picture. In the pages to come, you'll get a taste of the many varieties of Celtic spirituality and an introduction to the vast and multifaceted realm of Celtic myth and legend. You'll also be invited to find ways to integrate Celtic wisdom into your own spiritual life, regardless of your religion—or ethnicity. Hopefully, you'll be inspired to explore the Celtic mysteries for yourself, through meditation, research, and personal ritual.

This book is divided into five parts:

Part 1, "Welcome to Celtic Wisdom," introduces you to the Celtic people, their long and proud history, and the many types of spirituality and religion that have contributed to the growth of Celtic wisdom.

Part 2, "The Three Paths," looks at the wisdomkeepers of ancient Gaul and their three orders—bards, seers, and druids—as a template for three different ways in which you can explore the Celtic path, here in the twenty-first century.

Part 3, "Mythology and Lore," celebrates the vast treasure of Celtic wonders, tales, and legends, in which gods, goddesses, heroes, faeries, and ancestral figures live forever—providing us with a glimpse into the teachings of the distant past.

Part 4, "Further Steps Along the Path," shines a light on practical ways to make the Celtic path come alive in your own world. From the spiritual practices of the ancient Celtic shamans to the philosophical quest of the druids, to the allegorical mysticism of the knights of the Holy Grail, the Celtic world provides countless doorways to inner growth.

Part 5, "Applied Celtic Wisdom," brings together a selection of real-world topics, from divination to ethics to the Celtic cycle of holy days, and explains how to integrate these practices into your own unique quest for the Celtic soul.

Extras

You'll find boxes in every chapter that provide helpful definitions, tips, cautions, and intriguing factoids to help you learn and understand more about the world of paganism.

Geasa

From an Irish word with a meaning similar to "taboo," these boxes provide cautionary notes to help you avoid pitfalls in the Celtic world.

Notes from the Otherworld

In these boxes, you'll find a variety of interesting Celtic tidbits.

Druidspeak

Here you'll find definitions of words associated with Celtic wisdom, culture, and spirituality.

The Seer Says

These tips will increase your understanding of Celtic spirituality and help you along the wisdom-seeker's path.

The Bard's Bookshelf

These boxes contain lots of Celtic-related miscellaneous info.

Acknowledgments

Many people have contributed in ways large and small to help bring this book into existence.

Linda Roghaar and Randy Ladenheim-Gil talked me into a project that I really wanted to do in the first place. Jennifer Moore has been patient about answering my silly questions and understanding above and beyond the call of duty whenever I chose to get "creative" with my deadlines. Thanks also to everyone else at Alpha who has contributed to the book's production.

Thanks goes out to Donald McColman (the technical advisor for my photography); Patricia Monaghan (who taught me more about Ireland in two or three e-mails than anything other than visiting there could do); my friends and acquaintances in Ireland, including Bob Curran, Bryan Gray, Tom Hannon Sr., Rita Minehan CSB, Dara Molloy, and Bev and Del Richardson. Various folks offered suggestions, advice, helpful hints, moral support, or hugs, including Candace Apple, Barbara Ardinger, B. J. Barrett, John Beasley, Phil Brucato, Francesca De Grandis, Phil Foster, Amy Hale, Frank Mills, Linda Sherer, Laura-Beth Straight, and Sylvia Sultenfuss. Thanks to *Atlanta Celtic Quarterly* and *Energyworks! Magazine*; portions of Chapters 4, 5, and 10 first appeared in those publications. Finally, much love to my wife, Fran McColman, and stepdaughter, Rhiannon Wilburn, for being more than understanding about my obsession with all things Celtic—an obsession which this book did nothing to assuage!

Finally, thanks to all my students, teachers, and colleagues in the Celtic spirituality community, whether Christian or pagan. There are too many of you to list by name, but you know who you are. Thanks for walking alongside me as we've explored the mysteries.

Special Thanks to the Technical Reviewers

The Complete Idiot's Guide to Celtic Wisdom was reviewed by two experts who double-checked the accuracy of what you'll learn here. This helps us ensure that this book will give you everything you need to know about the magical world of Celtic spirituality. Special thanks are extended to Frank MacEowen and Kathryn Hinds for taking on this essential task.

Frank MacEowen, MA, is a Scottish-Irish American ecopsychologist, shamanic counselor, and practitioner of ancestor-based Celtic spirituality. He is the author of *The Mist-Filled Path: Celtic Wisdom for Exiles, Wanderers and Seekers*. Kathryn Hinds has been involved in Celtic studies for 20 years, specializing in the mythical and legendary lore recorded in medieval Wales. She is the author of 18 books, including *The Celts of Northern Europe*.

Trademarks

Part 1

Welcome to Celtic Wisdom

Celtic wisdom is a broad and many-faceted topic. It covers a wide range of philosophical and spiritual perspectives that have one unifying element in common: a connection to the people called the Celts, one of the founding cultures of Europe that continues on today, not only in Europe but in the heart of men and women throughout the world whose ancestors came from this proud lineage.

The wisdom of the Celts carries deep spiritual overtones. It is a wisdom that celebrates the beauty of nature, the goodness of the human heart, and the mysterious places where the world we live in overlaps with the worlds of eternity and the gods and goddesses.

Whether your motivation is religious, spiritual, artistic, philosophical, or even political in nature, there are many treasures waiting for you to discover in the world of Celtic wisdom. This book is a guide to get you started on what can easily become a lifelong quest. Thank you for coming. Now journey on!

Chapter 1

Introducing the World of Celtic Wisdom

In This Chapter

- Welcome to a magical world
- Finding your warrior's heart
- Portals into the mystery
- Overview of a rich tradition
- The benefits of the Celtic way

Welcome to a wonderful and mysterious world—the world of Celtic (pronounced *keltic*) wisdom and spirituality.

It is a large and vast world. It is a world populated by druids and faeries and wizards. It is a world encompassing the mysticism of hermits and saints, the poetic visions of bards and *shanachies*, and the supernatural magic of folk healers and seers. It is a world full of romance, heroism, vision, and honor. The tradition of Celtic wisdom stretches back thousands of years …

… from the earliest healers ("shamans") conducting their magical rituals in the wilderness …

Druidspeak

Shanachie, which comes from an Irish word, means "story-teller" or "keeper of the old tales," specifically one who tells stories from Celtic myth, legend, and lore. The Welsh equivalent is *cyfarwyddau.*

... to the power of the druids, so mighty that even Julius Caesar considered them a force to be reckoned with ...

... to the poetic nature mysticism of early Christians who found refuge in the Celtic wilderness ...

... to the glorious chivalry of the mythic quest for the grail ...

... all the way up to the modern world, where countless people have taken a renewed interest in faeries, witchcraft, and pagan ritual.

From Christianity to belief in faeries to witchcraft, the Celtic tradition shares many elements with other forms of spirituality. It's one of humanity's many important sources of wisdom and spirituality—think of it as a stream that has flowed from its Indo-European origins near the Black Sea, then migrated to eastern and central Europe, moved eventually to the western fringes of that continent, and from there to the rest of the world. Today, people of Celtic heritage (or a "Celtic" heart) live all over the planet.

Obviously, Celtic wisdom can mean many different things to different people. This book does not provide an exhaustive study of Celtic ways—no single book could ever do that! Rather, this is an introductory guide, designed to give you a sense of the many possibilities found within the Celtic way. As you identify which streams of the Celtic tradition are the right ones for you to pursue, you'll find ideas for ways that you can put your quest for Celtic wisdom and spirituality into practice as well as suggestions for further reading and study.

The Heart of a Warrior

For your first step toward understanding the vast and many-faceted world of Celtic wisdom and spirituality, you need a basic idea of who the Celts were (and are), and what their traditions of wisdom and spirituality entail. Grasping this, however, is no easy feat.

Notice I said "traditions of wisdom and spirituality." Yes, it's plural. The first, and in many ways most important, point to remember regarding Celtic wisdom is this: There's no single "right" way to understand or master it. This isn't a simple program of mastering concept A before going on to concept B. You won't be able to reduce Celtic wisdom to a set of convenient rules, or to a series of "four spiritual laws," or anything like that. This is a wonderful, complex, many-layered tradition. Like a fine wine or a powerful symphony, its true beauty is often subtle and easy to miss.

If you're the kind of person who wants to be spoon-fed a set of simple rules and easy answers, then Celtic wisdom isn't for you. This is a path for a seeker with the heart of a spiritual warrior. But if you are the type of person who wants to think for yourself and who gets impatient when faced with meaningless rules, regulations, and dogmas—someone who wants to appreciate an ancient and proud culture and apply its long-standing wisdom to life today—then you have what it takes to walk the Celtic path!

What is the "heart of a spiritual warrior"? Ancient Celtic society included not only wisdomkeepers (druids), but artisans, farmers, and warriors (who were the heroes of many Celtic myths and legends). Warriors, naturally, sought to live a life based on inner strength, loyalty, and fearlessness. For today's seeker of Celtic wisdom, the heart of a spiritual warrior means you bring to your spiritual quest a loyalty to truth, the courage to face life's challenges, and reliance on your inner strength to guide your quest for wisdom. A spiritual warrior, incidentally, is never a warmonger, but always stands for spiritual truth and community values.

If you're not sure that you have the "heart of a spiritual warrior," read on anyway. You may find your warrior's heart in the process of learning about Celtic wisdom. Just remember that merely reading this book will not make you a master of the Celtic path, nor will reading any other book. The key to spiritual mastery cannot be found in the written word. It doesn't matter whether you live in Ireland, Scotland, Wales, or any other Celtic land. Learning a Celtic language would be a big help in mastering this tradition, but that alone won't do it either. To become wise in the ways of Celtic spirituality requires finding your warrior's heart and living a life full of honor, integrity, and hospitality. It means taking responsibility for your knowledge, your personal power, and the destiny of your life. It means living in a balanced and healthy relationship with nature, especially the land and water and air right where your home is.

Ultimately, these qualities of the heart matter more than how much you know or where you've been. Yes, as a follower of the Celtic path you'll want to be familiar with the names and personalities of the Irish gods and goddesses, and you'll want to understand the symbolism in Welsh mythology. You'll want to know the functions of the four fire festivals and understand the difference between *Annwn* and *Tir na n'Og*. Sure, this book will help you with facts like these. But as you learn the "stuff" of Celtic wisdom, remember that the larger task—finding the heart of wisdom—will require far more than merely reading a library full of books.

Druidspeak

Annwn is the Welsh name for the otherworldly realm where spirits dwell. **Tir na n'Og**, which means "Land of the Young," is an Irish name for a similar otherworldly paradise.

This book *will* give you lots of information you can use to get started on your journey toward the heart of wisdom. You can read this guide merely to learn a thing or two about Celtic wisdom, decide this path isn't for you, and then go merrily on your way. Nothing wrong with that. Or you can use this book as a starting point for a lifetime of learning and seeking. That is closer to the true path of Celtic wisdom.

As an overview of *Celtic* wisdom, this book draws on a variety of different sources in the Celtic tradition: from Irish and Welsh mythology, to druidic lore, Christian piety, and magical spirituality. Because there's no such thing as "one" Celtic wisdom, keep in mind that, especially in ancient times, Irish Celts would not have necessarily been familiar with Welsh myths (and vice versa); nor would the teachings of the druids have been espoused by Celtic Christians. Part of your job as a spiritual warrior is to find which elements in the Celtic tradition speak to you personally, and explore those elements further. You don't have to master it all to walk the path of wisdom!

Oh, one more thing before we get started: Don't be in a hurry to "master" the Celtic tradition, as if this were a three-year program with a certificate to be earned at the end. Take your time. By the time you finish this book, you'll have a basic orientation into the world of Celtic spirituality. Then, you can choose how to take your pursuit of wisdom to the next level.

What Makes a Celt Tick?

Who are the Celts? What is their history? What makes a person, or an idea, "Celtic"? What is the difference between Celtic wisdom and any other kind of wisdom?

These are all good questions, covering important information to help you nail down your understanding of Celtic spirituality. Chapters 2 and 3 address these very issues in depth. For now, let's just say that what makes wisdom and spirituality Celtic is its connection, either now or in the past, with one or more of the European languages and cultures that scholars identify as Celtic. This includes the following languages: Irish, Scots Gaelic, Welsh, Cornish, Manx, and Breton; and the cultures associated with these languages. Of course, culture and language is just the very tip of the Celtic iceberg—read on to learn more.

Entry-Points to the Celtic Tradition

As you begin your journey into the heart of Celtic spirituality and wisdom, take a minute to think about why you are attracted to this tradition. What is it about the Celts that appeals to you?

Chances are, you became interested in Celtic wisdom and spirituality through one or more of the following ways.

You Have Celtic Ancestry

Even if you live in North America or Australia, you may have ancestors who came from Scotland, Cornwall, Brittany, or another one of the traditionally Celtic lands. For you, connecting with the Celtic tradition is a way of finding your own spiritual roots.

Celtic Music and Dance

From the Chieftains to *Riverdance*, from Scottish bagpipes to Welsh choirs, one of the most popular forms of Celtic culture is music, and that extends to traditional forms of Celtic dance. From the hypnotic drone of Celtic jigs and reels to the aching sadness in traditional melodies like "Danny Boy," Celtic music conveys emotional power and sonic beauty. Traditional Celtic dance, meanwhile, can be graceful and powerful. If you love these aspects of Celtic culture, perhaps you feel drawn to the spirituality and wisdom that such artistry is built upon.

> **Notes from the Otherworld**
>
> *Riverdance* was a cultural phenomenon in the 1990s. A celebration of Irish music, dance, and culture, the show featured dozens of step dancers, rousing music, and a story line that followed the history of the Irish people from their pagan roots to the emigration of many to the New World. It's a celebration of the spirit of the Irish people and their culture. It's an excellent example of how a work of art (in this case, a performance) can be spiritual as well as entertaining.

Celtic Literature and Design

Even though music may be the most popular of Celtic art forms, many other cultural treasures hail from the Celtic world. Celtic design is known for its intricate patterns of colorful spirals and interlaced knotwork, while Celtic poetry, drama, and novels have expressed the soul of the Celtic world in powerful and moving ways. Like music, the art and writing of the Celts are lovely testimonies to the deep spiritual sensibility of its creators.

The Land Itself

You may live in a Celtic land, or you might visit one whenever you get the chance, or you may know the Celtic nations strictly as an armchair traveler. In any case, the lands where Celtic languages and cultures have existed in modern times—Ireland,

Druidspeak

A **cairn** is a pile or mound of stones, usually erected to mark a gravesite or the location of an important event, such as a battle. They can be only a foot or so high, or as large as a house.

Scotland, Wales, Cornwall, the Isle of Man, Brittany, and Galicia—have a reputation as powerful places where ancient wisdom exists literally in the air, water, and soil. From the holy wells where ancient rites are still enacted, to ancient *cairns* associated with the faeries in myth and legend, many aspects of the Celtic lands bear longstanding witness to an ancient spirituality.

"Celtic" Archaeology

Some of the most popular "symbols" of the Celtic tradition aren't actually Celtic in origin at all! People often mistakenly believe that the prehistoric monuments of the British Isles—like Stonehenge in England or Newgrange in Ireland—were built by the Celts. Actually, these ancient structures predate the Celts by many centuries! Still, the ancient stone rings or passage tombs capture our imagination because they suggest that ancient humankind had profound knowledge of engineering and astronomy; if so much scientific knowledge existed in the distant past, what other wisdom might be hidden in the mists of time? So even though such archaeological wonders are not technically Celtic, because they exist in lands where the Celts eventually would live (and were regarded as spiritually sacred sites by the ancient Celts), they still represent Celtic wisdom to many modern seekers.

Although it predates the coming of the Celts by many centuries, in the popular mind Stonehenge continues to be associated with the Celtic druids.

The Druids

Perhaps the single most common symbol associated with Celtic wisdom is that of the druids, the philosophers/scientists/priests of Gaul (roughly equivalent to modern-day France), Britain, and Ireland prior to the coming of the Roman Empire and Christianity. Although little is known about the ancient druids, many people in recent centuries have attempted to create new orders based on wisdom and spirituality patterned after this mysterious lost order. If they symbolize anything, the druids stand for the quest for, and attainment of, wisdom both mundane and spiritual.

Arthur, Merlin, and the Grail

The myths and legends associated with King Arthur, his court at Camelot, his Knights of the Round Table, and their sacred quest for the Holy Grail have inspired countless books, movies, and dreams. The Arthurian tradition arises out of a blend of Welsh myth and medieval codes of chivalry and mysticism. Today, many people see in Merlin (Arthur's mentor) a symbol of the quintessential druid, while the Holy Grail represents the ultimate goal of the ultimate quest.

The Faeries

Faeries, or nature-spirits, are not unique to the Celtic world, but they are certainly a significant part of the mythology and folklore of places like Ireland, Scotland, and Wales. Belief in the faeries pre-dates the coming of the Christian religion, and even after churches dotted the countryside, farmers and other ordinary folk continued to believe in the powerful presence of a spiritual community of faeries. Far from being an antiquated superstition, the faery faith continues to this day, and is evolving even as the complex relationship between humanity and nature evolves and changes.

Wicca and Neopaganism

Beginning in the mid-twentieth century, increasing numbers of people have turned to the spiritual paths of *Wicca* or *neopaganism* as ways to find meaning in their lives. Both of these new spiritual movements have drawn inspiration from Celtic myth and lore.

> **Druidspeak**
>
> **Wicca** is a modern religion that incorporates Goddess worship, reverence for nature, and ethical witchcraft. Wicca is part of the larger movement of **neopaganism**, which is the revival or re-creation of ancient pre-Christian beliefs of Europe in a modern context of nature mysticism.

Other Pieces of the Celtic Puzzle

Let's take it a bit deeper—here are some other, less commonly known elements that can be found in one part or another of the Celtic tradition. Which of these appeal to you?

- **Irish mythology.** In the Middle Ages, monks in Ireland recorded numerous tales of warriors, heroes and heroines, ancient gods and goddesses, and faeries. Even though centuries separate the origin of these tales from the time they were written down, they still provide a valuable glimpse into the Celtic world prior to, and just after, the coming of Christianity.

- **Welsh mythology.** Although not as extensive as the Irish myths, and less intact in their original pagan state, the Welsh tradition has its own share of mythical and magical stories, including some of the loveliest of Celtic tales (and the earliest stories of King Arthur).

- **Folktales and faery tales.** Before television, radio, and the Internet intruded into people's lives, families would entertain themselves with the telling of stories and legends. The Irish government has put tremendous effort into cataloging and recording such tales of old, recognizing that the telling of folktales is a dying art. Many strands of Celtic wisdom can be found in these simple tales of faeries and other supernatural beings, handed down from generation to generation.

> **The Bard's Bookshelf**
>
> Many modern translations of re-tellings of Irish and Welsh myth are available, such as T. W. Rolleston's *Celtic Myths and Legends* (Dover Publications, 1990). Reading these ancient tales can be a powerful doorway into the world of Celtic spirituality.

- **Folklore.** In addition to folktales, many traditional practices (such as the reciting of special prayers through the day, or ceremonies associated with the seasons of the year) have survived from ancient times to recent years or even the present day. Many of these traditions have their root in ancient spiritual wisdom that remains relevant today.

- **The Ogham.** The Ogham is an alphabet used in Ireland and other Celtic lands on tombstones or property markers; it originally consisted of 20 characters, with 5 additional characters added at a later date. Writers like Robert Graves have suggested that the Ogham could be used, like the Norse runes, as a system of divination. Each Ogham character corresponds to a tree or other plant, with magical and spiritual qualities associated with it.

◆ **The druid revivals.** While in the strictest sense of the word a "druid" was a priest of the pagan Celts prior to the Roman conquest, over the past few centuries many attempts have been made to revive the druid movement as a modern spiritual or philosophical community. Some of these druid revivals have been focused on national pride (especially in the British Isles), or on community service, or on esoteric teachings. By the second half of the twentieth century, druid revival groups were adopting a mainly pagan worldview. While we'll never know for sure just how accurate these revival groups are at capturing the spirit of the ancient druids, we can find in them, on their own terms, a path for the practice of Celtic spirituality today.

◆ **Celtic shamanism.** Like Wicca, shamanism is not technically a Celtic phenomenon—the word *shamanism* refers to magical spirituality from Siberia. Nevertheless, shamanism has come to signify tribal or primal spirituality from throughout the world. Many people interested in shamanism have noticed similarities between Celtic practices as recounted in myth and legend and the shamanic spiritual paths from other parts of the world. Thus, shamanism has become a convenient framework for understanding the Celtic way.

> **CAUTION** **Geasa**
>
> Don't assume that Celtic spirituality only belongs to one religion (such as Christianity or Wicca). The Celtic tradition crosses all faith boundaries. No matter what your religion is (or isn't), you can benefit from Celtic wisdom—and so can people whose religion is different from yours.

◆ **Celtic Christianity.** Celtic wisdom originated in the pre-Christian or pagan era. But when Christianity arrived in the British Isles, Celtic spirituality didn't just vanish. Instead, many aspects of Celtic wisdom influenced the development of the Christian religion in places like Ireland, Scotland, and Wales. Today, both Christians and non-Christians can find spiritual insight in the writings of the early monks and mystics of the Celtic church.

◆ **The *Carmina Gadelica*.** This is a massive collection of chants, prayers, spells, and other strands of folk wisdom gathered in Scotland in the mid-to-late nineteenth and early twentieth centuries by folklorist Alexander Carmichael. It demonstrates how paganism and Christianity fused within the mind of Gaelic speakers. Merely reading this anthology can give you a sense of the powerful mysticism within the Celtic tradition.

Druidspeak

The **second sight** is a form of psychic ability that enables a person to see events from far away in space or time, such as events from the future or the past. Different seers have different abilities, such as the gift of seeing spirit beings, of dreaming prophetic dreams, or divining the future.

◆ **The seer tradition.** The ability to predict the future and divine hidden wisdom is hardly unique to the Celts, but has long been a central part of Celtic spirituality. Such psychic skills are found in more than just myths and legends. People with the *second sight* are often known as seers, and their extraordinary powers can be an inspiration to all spiritual seekers.

◆ **The bardic arts.** In ancient times, bards were the historians and journalists of the Celtic tribes. Their ability to use music and poetry to tell stories was considered a magical art. For today's seeker, the bard's craft symbolizes how art and spirituality can unite to create meaning and wisdom.

◆ **Nature mysticism.** Many people think of the Celts as nature mystics. Why? Here are a few possibilities: The druids were believed to have been carriers of the wisdom of the trees; both in pagan and Christian times, the Celts have venerated wells and springs and considered water from such sources to have powerful healing properties; and the major holidays of the Celtic past were all based on events related to the turning of the seasons. Of course, we can never know whether the ancients felt that "nature" was something to be revered or worshipped, but in the modern world, where too many people feel alienated from their environment, Celtic wisdom stands for a spirituality that is connected with the earth.

◆ **Celtic reconstructionism.** A few paragraphs back I talked about the various efforts to revive the druids. Some groups have gone even further, trying to use archaeology, religious history, comparative mythology, and even the study of non-Celtic Indo-European religions in an effort to create a well-researched and scholarly "reconstruction" of the ancient Celts.

Notes from the Otherworld

It's a common stereotype to see the druids as "tree worshippers." This idea is related to the fact that all Celtic spirituality has a strong component of nature mysticism. It also stems from the fact that the ancient druids conducted their rituals in groves of sacred trees. To a modern druid, nature is certainly sacred, although different druids have different ideas about what deity is, so it's a good idea to keep an open mind about what druids (and other Celtic seekers) believe.

Obviously, there are many, many different doorways into the rich world of Celtic wisdom. No one way is right for everyone. The ancient Celts never had a single, unified spirituality that everyone practiced, but rather different people from different tribes, clans, and communities would have honored the spiritual world in their own way. So in today's world, a similar freedom applies. Find the path of Celtic wisdom that speaks to you, and follow it with all your heart.

> **The Seer Says**
>
> If all the different possibilities in Celtic spirituality seem a little overwhelming, take it slow. You don't have to become a whiz at every single element of the Celtic tradition. Just pick those parts that interest you the most, and start there.

Spirituality, Wisdom, Tradition: Understanding the Path

Up to now, you may have noticed that I am using words like *wisdom* and *spirituality* and *tradition* more or less interchangeably. Let's take a moment and look more closely at what each of these words means.

Wisdom is more than just the accumulation of knowledge. Although true wisdom implies knowledge as well, it goes beyond mere smarts to include a sense of discernment—of understanding principles, values, and intangible qualities like integrity, honor, and love. Wisdom is the guiding light that can help make life meaningful and worth living.

Celtic wisdom comes out of a *tradition* that includes much of the material that's been introduced to you in this chapter, including ancient myths, legends, folklore, and spiritual practices associated with holy wells and other sacred sites. Like all traditions, this involves the accumulated wisdom of generation after generation, as recorded in stories and lore.

And finally, what is *spirituality?* It involves everything connected with the inner world of dreams, imagination, vision, and intuition. Like most people from around the world and throughout history, the Celts believed that the magical inner world was connected to a genuine spiritual realm where gods, goddesses, ancestors, and other spirits exist. By connecting with the world of spirits, we receive guidance to grow in true wisdom.

So Celtic wisdom and spirituality are closely related, and both arise out of a long-standing tradition.

What's in It for Me: The Benefits of the Celtic Way

So what's the point? Why should you read this book, or study ancient lore, or bother learning about the wisdom and spirituality of the Celts? In other words, what are the benefits to be gained by following the path of Celtic tradition?

Just as the tradition means different things to different people, so, too, will the benefits be unique for each individual. Which of the following appeal to you?

A Deeper Connection with the Land

Our natural environment is in trouble. For many people, nature is a resource to be exploited, not a living essence that supports each of our lives. Celtic spirituality begins with the assumption that it is more natural to relate to nature as a spiritual gift rather than a material resource. When you walk the Celtic path, your natural connection to nature is honored and supported.

> **CAUTION** **Geasa**
>
> Don't let your interest in Celtic spirituality become just a "head trip." For example, having reverence for nature means more than just enjoying the great outdoors—take time to recycle or to participate in efforts to clean or protect the environment. Many such programs can be found at the state or local level.

Naturally, this includes not only loving nature, but also caring for the environment. Many people today realize we need to take better care of the environment, but feel overwhelmed or defeated by the problems we face. Those negative emotions can be counterbalanced by a simple belief in the sacredness of nature and in seeing nature as our nurturing mother—both hallmarks of the Celtic way. Thus, Celtic spirituality can inspire us to be caretakers of the earth.

A Deeper Connection with Ancestors (Including Ancestors of the Heart)

Especially in America, many people feel rootless—disconnected from their ancestors and lineage. For some people, genealogical research may be a way to reconnect; but exploring the Celtic path can provide just as powerful a sense of rootedness. Even if you aren't Celtic by blood ancestry, Celtic spirituality can put you in touch with your "ancestors of the heart."

A Meaningful Framework for Your Life, Found in the Myths and Lore

Modern life, with its obsession with making and spending money, can feel meaningless and soulless. Getting to know the magic and myth of the Celtic world can introduce you to eternal values such as honor or hospitality and can provide a sense of connection with the world through the guidance and inspiration that come from the inner realms. Through Celtic eyes, the world is not meaningless, but rather alive with love and joy.

A Spirituality That Inspires Creativity

The ancient bards were masters of creativity through their poetry, stories, songs, and music. For today's Celtic seeker, that means this is a spiritual path that honors creativity and encourages you to find your own authentic voice as an artist (of any kind). To a modern bard, artistic talent is not just a way to make money or a pleasurable hobby, but is indeed a key element in the spiritual life.

A Spirituality That Inspires Psychic or Mental Development

You don't have to be a psychic to follow the Celtic path. But unlike some spiritual systems where mental power is frowned upon, the Celtic tradition has long acknowledged the existence of seers, shamans, and others with extraordinary gifts. This is a path that encourages you to develop your skills to the fullest extent of your ability.

A Spirituality That Leads to Personal Experience of Enlightenment

Celtic spirituality isn't just a hobby like collecting stamps or learning about the Civil War. Celtic wisdom offers more than an interesting pastime. From the magical powers of ancient druids to the visionary quest of the knights in search for the Holy Grail, Celtic wisdom has pointed to *enlightenment* as the potential available to every human who sincerely pursues spiritual growth.

> **Druidspeak**
>
> **Enlightenment** literally means "to be filled with light." In spiritual terms, it suggests achieving a state of spiritual mastery, with a powerful sense of joy and peace, and/or powerful abilities to serve others, whether through magic or healing.

A Spirituality That Offers an "Alternative Way" to Mainstream Society

You may have already picked up on this theme, but it bears noting. Celtic spirituality provides a different point of view from that of mainstream society. Instead of seeing the environment as a resource, Celtic wisdom sees nature as sacred. Instead of finding meaning in money, the Celtic path finds it in our ancestors and their mythic stories. Knowing that the Celtic way is an alternative path is a powerful way to cope with a society that doesn't always seem to embody spiritual values.

A Deeper Connection with the Gods and Goddesses, and the Gifts They Offer to You

The old gods and goddesses of Ireland, Wales, and other parts of the Celtic world can be sources of inspiration, wisdom, and meaning. You'll learn more about these awe-inspiring beings in Chapters 13, 14, and 15. For now, it's helpful to remember that connecting with the old Celtic deities can be a pathway to increasing your wisdom and your sense of connection to the spiritual world.

There may be many other benefits to the Celtic path. Only you can determine the ways in which this path will make a positive difference in your life. One thing is for sure: The further you walk along the Celtic way, the more you can feel connected to nature, the spirit realm, and the treasures of the past.

The Least You Need to Know

- Celtic wisdom arises from a long tradition of spirituality and mysticism that has inspired many generations of seekers.

- Many people are drawn to Celtic spirituality through an interest in magic, mysticism, the faeries, King Arthur and the Holy Grail, or the druids.

- Other doorways into Celtic spirituality include Irish and Welsh mythology, Celtic "shamanism," Celtic Christianity, and Celtic reconstructionism.

- Just as the ancient Celts never had a unified system of spirituality, so today there is no single correct way to study Celtic wisdom; rather, you should follow your heart and learn about what interests you the most.

- There are many spiritual benefits to walking the Celtic path.

Chapter 2

A History of a Proud People

In This Chapter

- ◆ The Celts as great storytellers
- ◆ Why history is important
- ◆ Outline of the Celtic adventure
- ◆ The Celts today
- ◆ The diaspora: Celts around the world

One of the most interesting features of the Celtic identity involves storytelling. From the bards of ancient times, to the medieval minstrels with their tales of Arthur and Camelot, and including the modern era with the shanachies, or folk storytellers, who still enchant listeners in Ireland and other Celtic lands, the Celts have always been grand spinners of tales. Celtic stories run the gamut from eerie excursions into the supernatural, to humorous stories of animals or faeries, to inspiring legends of great saints or heroes from the past. In your journey to Celtic wisdom, you'll want to become familiar with the great stories in Celtic mythology, folklore, and history.

Because myth and lore take us into the realms of the imagination and the supernatural, let's start with the most basic kind of story: the story of history. After all, history at its most basic level is simply the grand story of the past. And in your Celtic quest, understanding the past is an important key to the wisdom of today (and tomorrow).

Why History Matters

You may be thinking, *Who cares about history? Sure, I'm interested in the druids or the shamans of old, but I want wisdom I can apply to my life, today.* Especially if your experience of history in school amounted to little more than a bunch of meaningless names and dates, it may be hard to see what's "wise" about history.

We know that history has been important to the Celts ever since the first bard sang a song praising the ancestors of his people. When the bards of old entertained the chieftains and kings of ancient times, they didn't just sing silly love songs! They sang (or recited) stirring epics recounting the brave deeds of heroes both from their time as well as from their past. The ancient Celts understood that history was a key to identity. Knowing who your ancestors are is a way to know who you are. In modern times, especially in places like America where many people know very little— if anything—about their ancestors, such knowledge of the past may be hard to come by. But even if you don't know the history of your personal ancestors, you can still have at least a general sense of Celtic identity by knowing the history of the Celtic people.

Geasa

Celtic spirituality and wisdom are like any other aspect of life. Don't believe everything you read (or hear). Keep an open mind, be willing to ask questions, and never stop searching for authentic answers; by doing so, you'll cultivate true and lasting wisdom.

History also matters because it contains its own measure of wisdom. You've heard the proverb, "Those who don't know history are doomed to repeat it." In other words, history can teach us wisdom simply by showing us the mistakes of the past. The Celts, like any other group of people, have their share of triumphs and defeats, wisdom of old, and historic mistakes. When we learn history, we get a head start on finding our own wisdom.

Finally, history matters because it keeps us honest. Unfortunately, in the realm of spirituality, the line separating wisdom from folly can be very blurry. Some people, both from the past and the present, have written about "Celtic wisdom" in a way that disregards actual history and instead promotes erroneous ideas. Books have been published that have insisted that the druids built Stonehenge, that Celtic wisdom came from Atlantis, or that only men were allowed to serve as spiritual leaders in the Celtic world. Such ideas are shown to be bogus when compared to the evidence of real history. It's important to remember that learning authentic Celtic history can be a way to help you recognize fantasy when you come across it.

Okay, then. It's time to take a trip down memory lane and discover the story of the Celts.

Before the Celts Were Celts

The beginning of the Celtic adventure doesn't start in Ireland, Scotland, or Wales. Rather, the story of the Celts starts among an ancient group of people whose home was probably somewhere near the Black Sea, and whose culture took shape roughly 6,000 to 8,000 years ago. For lack of a better term, historians call these people Indo-Europeans. Their ancient language eventually gave rise to the Indo-European family of languages, which includes many of the tongues that came to be spoken throughout Europe and Asia.

The Indo-Europeans were people on the move. They migrated throughout much of Europe and western Asia, settling as far east as India and as far west as Ireland. It was from the Indo-Europeans that a distinct culture emerged, sometime between 1200 *B.C.E.* and 750 B.C.E., that today we think of as Celtic.

Druidspeak

B.C.E. stands for "Before the Common Era." In western dating, the common era began approximately when Jesus Christ was believed to be born; today, the terms "Common Era" (C.E.) and "Before the Common Era" (B.C.E.) are nonreligious terms helpful for identifying dates.

Celtic Archaeology: From Hallstatt to La Tène

One of the challenges of understanding Celtic history is that the ancient Celts didn't leave a written record of who they were, what they believed, or how they lived. The earliest written accounts of the Celts come mostly from non-Celts like the Greeks and Romans, who often saw Celts as the enemy. Thus, our oldest objective record of this people comes from archaeology. One of the most important archaeological sites in Europe in which early Celtic artifacts were found is Hallstatt, Austria. Hallstatt was the site of an important cemetery dating back to 1100 B.C.E., with its golden age being approximately 750 to 450 B.C.E. It was the site of salt mines, and the salt in the area helped preserve artifacts buried in the cemetery. Because of the importance of this archaeological site, today scholars speak of the earliest era of Celtic society as the "Hallstatt period." The Hallstatt culture was an *Iron Age* society that thrived from approximately 750 to 450 B.C.E.

Characteristics of the Hallstatt Culture

The Hallstatt cemetery is the first solid evidence of a culture that eventually came to be known as Celtic. Although its origins in the *Bronze Age* suggest that Celtic culture may have existed more than 3,000 years ago, the greatest achievements of the Hallstatt culture came with the transition from Bronze Age technology to the more advanced tools and weapons of the Iron Age. The Hallstatt Celts lived in a largely agrarian society, with villages and small forts. This culture was marked by elaborate burial customs, suggesting that the society had a governing class of chieftains who were entitled to lavish funerals.

Notes from the Otherworld

In studying ancient history, such as the history of the early Celts, you'll discover three significant epochs, or "ages," named for the level of technology attained by the culture. The **Stone Age** refers to the era when weapons and tools were made of flint or other stones; this was also the era when great stone monuments (such as Stonehenge) were erected. It was followed by the **Bronze Age,** characterized by the earliest use of metal tools, ornaments, and weapons; which in turn was followed by the **Iron Age,** marked by an increase in military and technological power through the use of iron. Incidentally, there are no fixed dates for the various ages: Each culture moves through the ages at its own rate. The beginning of known Celtic history coincides with the Celts adopting Iron Age technology.

Thanks to the efficiency of iron farming tools, this was a time of prosperity and population growth, with a vigorous economy fueled by trade with outsiders such as the Greeks. Toward the end of the Hallstatt era, the center of Celtic civilization appeared to be moving west from Austria toward modern-day Switzerland, where the next major phase of Celtic culture would be discovered by archaeologists, in a site called La Tène.

As part of this westward expansion, Celtic language and culture appear to have arrived in the British Isles around 600 B.C.E.

La Tène: The Celtic Golden Age

The second great era of Celtic culture lasted from 450 B.C.E. until approximately the beginning of the common era. With the technology of the Iron Age fully defining Celtic society, the artistry of the Celts developed a distinctive curvilinear style, featuring flowing designs that combined geometric patterns with imagery from nature. The mysterious Turoe Stone from County Galway, Ireland, is carved in this distinctive La Tène style.

The La Tène period not only marked great artistic achievements for the Celts, but was also the period of their greatest military might. Indeed, the Celts were at one point a fearsome enemy to their neighbors in Greece and Rome. In 387 B.C.E., Celtic warriors attacked Rome, sacking the city and leaving only when the Romans paid them a hefty ransom. Another, less successful, military excursion into Greece at approximately 279 B.C.E. led to a thwarted attack on the sacred Greek city of Delphi.

Meanwhile, continued Celtic expansion led to the founding of a Celtic settlement in Galatia (modern-day central Turkey).

The Turoe Stone, from County Galway, Ireland, is an ancient carved stone that may have had some form of religious significance. It is an example of La Tène art as found in Ireland.

In 225 B.C.E., the Celts marched on Rome once more, only to be repelled by the Roman army. The Celts' skill and ferocity in battle made them at one point a frightening adversary to their southern neighbors, but as the Roman Empire increased its might, the fortunes of the Celts would change.

Caesar and Conquest

By the second century B.C.E., Roman traders were engaged in thriving business with the Celts of southern Gaul (a region roughly similar to modern-day France). However, the Romans never forgot the indignity of having their city sacked by the "barbarians" to the north. Unlike the Celts, who lived in tribal communities that often would fight with one another, the Romans built a mighty empire governed centrally by Rome. Regarding Gaul as an unstable region and needing a land link between Roman-controlled areas in Spain and Italy, the Romans gradually established control over the southern region of Gaul, where Roman trade was strongest. In 58 B.C.E., the ambitious governor of southern Gaul, Julius Caesar, launched a military campaign to bring the rest of the region under Roman rule. By taking advantage of intertribal conflict among the Gauls, and offering to protect the Celts from the German tribes to the north, Caesar rewarded tribes that submitted to Roman rule, and defeated those that resisted. By 55 B.C.E., Gaul was fully a province of the Roman Empire. Caesar also launched two brief campaigns into Britain, possibly to dissuade the British Celts from providing military assistance to their cousins in Gaul.

The fierce and warlike Celts didn't simply roll over and submit to Roman rule. Several uprisings challenged Roman authority, the greatest of which was led by a chieftain with a mouthful of a name, Vercingetorix. However, Caesar's superior forces defeated each uprising, and when Vercingetorix surrendered in 52 B.C.E., opposition to Roman rule was effectively crushed.

The Invasion of Britain

In Rome, the quickest way to achieve political power was through military success. Thus, the Roman conquest of most of the remaining Celtic lands was all but inevitable. Even after Gaul fell to Rome in the first century B.C.E., Roman expansion into Celtic lands wasn't complete. A century after Caesar's brief excursions into Britain, the Romans returned. Between 43 and 84 C.E., Roman authority extended over most of modern-day England and Wales. Only Ireland and northern Scotland would escape conquest.

One of the saddest chapters of the Roman conquest of Britain came around 60 C.E., when, according to the historian Tacitus, a druid college was massacred on the island of Mona (Anglesey) in Wales. Not only were all the druids killed, but their sacred groves were demolished as well.

Like their cousins on the main continent, the British Celts didn't simply submit to the Roman invasion without a fight. Several uprisings and resistance movements dogged the Romans during the nearly 40-year campaign to subdue the island. The most famous uprising was led by Boudicca, queen of the Iceni tribe. Like Vercingetorix before her, her rebellion was doomed to fail, and the queen killed herself rather than surrender.

By the end of the first century C.E. Britain, like Gaul, had become a Roman province. Only Ireland and what is now northern Scotland remained free Celtic states (although scholars believe that some areas of other regions, such as Cornwall and Wales, remained unromanized). But a new invasion was set to occur that would change all the Celtic lands forever.

The Coming of Christianity

From its birth in Jerusalem in the early years of the common era, Christianity—a monotheistic religion that regarded its leader, Jesus Christ, as the only son of God—soon spread throughout the Roman Empire. Legend holds that Joseph of Arimathea, an early follower of Christ, brought Christianity to Britain within a few years of the religion's founding. Although that legend is important to the grail tradition (which we'll take a closer look at in Chapter 22), it cannot be proven by historical evidence. What we do know is that Christianity came in the wake of the Roman conquest, and certainly by about 200 C.E. missionaries had established a Christian presence in Britain.

The Romans governed Britain for about 350 years. Early in the fifth century, Roman authorities left Britain, called back to defend other parts of their troubled empire. They left a land vulnerable to invasion from enemies like the Germanic Saxons and Angles, who would eventually give England its Anglo-Saxon identity. In this time of chaos, the only stable force seemed to be the Christian religion.

Christian missionaries soon established churches throughout the British Isles, including the Celtic regions of Cornwall, Wales, Scotland, and Ireland. Some historians marvel at how relatively easily the British Isles were converted to Christianity, and have speculated that Celtic spirituality was similar enough to Christianity to facilitate an easy conversion. Others argue that the Roman conquest had essentially destroyed the druid priesthood, leaving the Celts spiritually bereft and, therefore, vulnerable to whatever new religion came along. We'll probably never know exactly what facilitated the conversion to Christianity, but we do know that Christianity was soon flourishing throughout the British Isles, both in the Saxon and Celtic regions.

For about a 250-year period, the Christian church in the British Isles had only limited contact with Christianity in the rest of Europe, including the authority of the church in Rome. This period of relative isolation is now considered the golden age of Celtic Christianity. This was the period when now-famous saints like Patrick, Bridget, and Columba, are said to have lived. (Because the historical evidence is so sketchy, some scholars question whether saints like Patrick or Bridget ever existed, or if they are "composite" saints drawn from legends that originated with two or more historical figures.) Many other lesser-known Christian saints, mystics, and writers also date from this period, such as Brendan and Kevin of Ireland, Aidan of Scotland, David of Wales, and Piran of Cornwall.

Some Celtic Christians even made names for themselves in the wider world. Pelagius (whose Welsh name was Morgan) was a fifth-century British theologian whose ideas were attacked by Augustine and who was eventually rejected as unorthodox; a few centuries later, an Irish theologian called John Scotus Erigena wrote a number of important philosophical treatises (and fortunately, never was branded as a heretic!).

Celtic Christianity's beauty arose out of how it married pagan Celtic spirituality with the teachings of the new religion. Celtic Christianity worshipped the same God and obeyed the same Bible as Christians everywhere, but also included a deep love and reverence for nature, allowed women much more power than was possible in other corners of the Christian world (for example, St. Bridget was not only a powerful leader of a convent, but also is said to have received ordination as a bishop!), and generally stressed God's love rather than his wrath.

Alas, the unique culture of Celtic Christianity would eventually come under criticism from Rome. More and more Christians in the British Isles, especially in Saxon England, conformed to the teachings and practices of the Roman Church. Toward the end of the seventh century, the king of Northumbria (northern England) convened a council to reconcile the differences between how Christianity was practiced among Celtic Christians and Roman Christians. After hearing arguments from both sides, the king sided with the Roman faction, thus signaling the end of independent Celtic Christianity. Of course, the culture of Celtic Christianity continued to exist unofficially, and even survives to this day in such practices as the veneration of holy wells in Ireland and other Celtic lands.

> **Notes from the Otherworld**
>
> Celtic Christians had a great love for artistic beauty, as evidenced by their intricately designed hand-illuminated books, such as the *Book of Kells* (a ninth-century manuscript of the Christian Gospels, in which every page features intricate designs of animals, people, and knotwork).

Saxons and Vikings and Normans (Oh My!)

While Celtic Christianity was flourishing, historical processes were underway that would continue the erosion of Celtic political independence. The Anglo-Saxon invasion of Britain effectively replaced the Romano-Celtic culture with a new society that was the cradle of modern England. Many Celts retreated from the Saxon invasion, emigrating to places like Brittany (in modern France) or finding refuge in the far western regions, such as Cornwall, Wales, and the Isle of Man.

Other Celts resisted the Saxons with force. The greatest of these freedom fighters was Arthur. Historical information about Arthur is sketchy, and a number of different theories have been put forth to explain who Arthur may have been. He could have been a warlord who first came to power at the end of the Roman period, or he could have been a Cornish, Welsh, or British chieftain from the fifth or sixth century. We'll never know for sure, but the myths and legends that have grown around this mysterious figure depict him as a valiant Celtic warrior who did all he could to protect the sovereignty of his land from the foreign invaders.

But the invaders came, and eventually a lasting Saxon presence dominated most of southern Britain. Nor were they the last invaders of the British Isles. From the north came Vikings, who plundered the shoreline of Scotland, Ireland, and Wales (as well as much of the rest of western Europe) for several centuries, especially between 800 and 1000 C.E. Viking settlements were established in many parts of the Celtic world, including the Orkney Islands of northern Scotland, the Isle of Man, and the coast of Ireland. In 1066, Norman invaders conquered England, and shortly thereafter Anglo-Normans were settling in eastern Ireland, beginning eight centuries of struggle between the English and Irish over control of Ireland.

By the late Middle Ages, England was asserting control over Wales and Scotland; the formation of the United Kingdom in the early seventeenth century solidified English authority over these Celtic lands. It wouldn't be until the twentieth century that Celtic sovereignty would reassert herself, with the independence of southern Ireland and the formation of the Irish Republic.

From the Diaspora to Today

Much of the conflict that occurred between the English and traditional Celtic societies in the seventeenth through nineteenth centuries involved religious or economic issues. Often, such conflicts would inspire (or force) many people from the Celtic countries to leave the British Isles, moving to North America, Australia, or even more unusual destinations such as Patagonia in Argentina, where a Welsh community settled in the 1860s. From attempts to limit religious nonconformity in Wales, to the "clearances" in Scotland where poor farmers were removed from the land, to the Great Hunger in Ireland where several years of potato blight led to crop failure and economic disruption, for many people from Celtic lands, hope lay over the water. The migration of the Celts to the Americas and Australia is today known as the Celtic *diaspora*, or scattering.

Although the Celtic diaspora could be seen as a tragedy fueled by famine and political oppression, it also meant that Celtic heritage became a significant factor in the formation of nations like Australia, Canada, and the United States. Thanks to the Celtic diaspora, today millions of people throughout the world identify themselves as Celts, and look to the history and spirituality of Celtic culture for wisdom and guidance in their lives.

Druid Revivalism and the Celtic Renaissance

Although the triumph of Christianity marked the end of ancient Celtic paganism as an overt religious practice, many pagan ideas and attitudes remained part of Celtic folklore, rural customs, and popular piety. From belief in faeries to the use of prayers to mark such natural activities as the rising and the setting of the sun, Celtic spirituality (especially among the ordinary people) retained a deep connection to its pre-Christian heritage. Thus, it hardly seems surprising that, beginning in the eighteenth century, movements would begin that focused on reviving ancient Celtic wisdom for the modern age. Most of these movements, especially in the beginning, focused of reviving druidism in one form or another. Because so little is known about the ancient druids, often these druid revival groups would borrow liberally from a variety of non-Celtic sources, ranging from Christianity to *theosophy* to *ceremonial magic*. But by the twentieth century, more and more druid revivalists were attempting to make modern druidry as consistent as possible with what is known about ancient European paganism.

> **Druidspeak**
>
> **Theosophy,** a movement that began in the nineteenth century, seeks universal spiritual wisdom through integrating eastern and western religious ideas. **Ceremonial magic** is a similar spiritual movement, but draws its energy from integrating alchemy, Jewish and Christian mysticism, and Greco-Roman pagan philosophy into an elaborate system of ritual and personal growth.

Similar to the attempts to revive druidry is the Celtic Renaissance, a cultural movement of the late nineteenth and early twentieth century. Spearheaded by great literary figures like William Butler Yeats and Lady Gregory, this movement supported the Irish quest for independence through pride in the Celtic identity and heritage of the Irish people. Not only did the Celtic Renaissance lead to many wonderful new works of literature, but it also sparked an interest in folklore, wherein the common wisdom of farmers and other ordinary people was recorded and managed by the government of the newly formed Irish republic. Similar efforts to preserve Celtic folklore have been initiated in the other Celtic lands.

The Six Nations: Today's Celtic World

Celtic history is not just something that happened "back then." Millions of people alive today proudly trace their ancestry back to one or more of the Celtic nations, whether or not they themselves speak a Celtic language or live in a Celtic land. Furthermore, four Celtic languages have survived into the twenty-first century, with two others staging a comeback as people attempt to revive them.

Eire (Ireland)

After generations of Irish rebellion against British authority, independence was finally won by three fourths of the island in 1921. (Northern Ireland, where Protestant Christians historically have opposed Irish independence, remains part of the United

Kingdom; it is a land long tormented by civil unrest expressed primarily along religious lines between Catholics and Protestants.) In the Republic of Ireland, Irish Gaelic is one of the official languages of the nation, although practically speaking, only about 20,000 people, mostly in the west of the country, routinely speak the language today.

The six recognized Celtic nations, with particular attention to the state of modern Celtic language.

Alba (Scotland)

The home of bagpipes and kilts has not rebelled against British rule since the mid-eighteenth century; but small steps are being taken to increase Scottish sovereignty, including the re-establishment of a Scottish parliament that convened in 1999—the first in 300 years. The Celtic tongue of modern Scotland is Scots Gaelic, which today is spoken mostly in the islands off the northwest coast of Scotland; some 30,000 people still speak the language habitually.

Cymru (Wales)

Cymru, or Wales, is the home of the healthiest modern Celtic language, Welsh (Cymraeg). In the 1990s, over half a million people in Wales spoke Welsh, with about a third of a million people using the language on a regular basis. The numbers of regular Welsh speakers are actually increasing, especially among children. Wales is part of the United Kingdom, although as in Scotland, efforts are underway to increase Welsh home rule (including the 1998 establishment of the National Assembly for Wales).

Kernow (Cornwall)

Like Wales, Cornwall is part of the United Kingdom. Located on the most remote, southwestern region of Great Britain, the Cornwall peninsula is one of the legendary homes of King Arthur and was home to native speakers of the Cornish language until about the year 1800. In the twentieth century, efforts have been made to revive the language, not only in Cornwall but in other parts of the Celtic diaspora as well.

Mannin (The Isle of Man)

An island in the Irish Sea, the Isle of Man covers an area of about 221 square miles, with approximately 77,000 inhabitants. The island is considered a dependency of the United Kingdom, although it does have its own parliament regulating internal affairs. At one point, the Manx language was spoken here, and as recently as the 1860s, half of the inhabitants spoke Manx, but the last native speaker died in 1974. Today, efforts are underway to revive the language.

Breizh (Brittany)

This region of northwest France, like Wales or Cornwall, has no political independence but retains a thriving Celtic language, Breton, second only to Welsh in terms of numbers of living fluent speakers. Approximately a quarter of a million Bretons still spoke their Celtic tongue in the 1990s.

Although Celtic influence has been felt far beyond the "six nations," they are generally considered the heart of the modern Celtic world, for they are the lands that have had a Celtic language survive into modern times.

Real Issues Facing Real People

Today's Celtic world is not some misty dreamland where unicorns frolic and magicians exercise their power. Rather, the Celtic "nations" are places where the pressures of politics, economics, religion, and social change cause problems similar to those faced by people throughout the world. As you can see from this brief overview, different Celtic regions enjoy different levels of political independence, with the same kind of internal conflict and debate that characterizes any other society. Traditional Celtic culture, like traditional cultures all over the world, is slowly giving way to the impact of mass media (especially television) and the economics of globalization. Perhaps these cultural changes are inevitable, but if Celtic language and other forms of traditional Celtic culture simply die out, it means that our world will have lost a way of life and a source of wisdom that have guided people for thousands of years.

The moral of the story is simple: As you pursue Celtic wisdom as a way of finding your own spiritual path, remember that this is not just a fashionable mythology, but a real tradition that has shaped the lives of real people. If you can, take the time to learn a Celtic language and make a real effort to incorporate Celtic traditions into your life and the lives of your family. Do what you can to help this magnificent culture survive.

The Lessons of History

So what can we learn from the history of the Celts? What are the lessons of the past that can help us lead lives of wisdom today? Here are a few ideas. The more you study Celtic history, the more lessons you'll likely find.

- **If you live to fight, eventually you must fight to live.** At one point in time, many Celts were fearsome warriors who struck terror in the heart of Romans and Greeks. They fought not just to defend their land, but aggressively, invading the homes of other peoples. Then the tides of fortune changed, and eventually the Celts were the hunted, rather than the hunters. Moral of the story: There are limits to the glory of war.

- **Resistance is not futile.** Sure, great warriors like Vercingetorix or Boudicca lost to the might of Roman power. But for 2,000 years since the Romans destroyed the Celts as a major European power, Celtic people have clung to their culture, even while living on the fringes of Europe or struggling under hostile or unsympathetic governments. That has not always been easy, but it has meant that Celtic culture (and wisdom) has survived, even if only in limited ways. The fact that you are reading this book now validates the many centuries of Celtic resistance.

- **Remember who your enemy really is.** The Romans were able to conquer most of the Celtic world because the Celtic tribes were so busy fighting amongst themselves that they never united to successfully meet the Roman challenge. Today, this Celtic problem is echoed in Northern Ireland, where the economy suffers while Catholics and Protestants fight over their religious and political differences. Yes, sometimes there are conflicts "within the tribe," but the history of the Celts reminds us that it's a mistake to not stand united.

♦ **Spirituality is essential.** The Romans knew that the druids, as the spiritual and intellectual leaders of the Celts, were a force to be reckoned with. For the Celts, spirituality (and wisdom) were at the heart of their way of life. Caesar commented that the Celts were deeply religious—a quality that remained after the coming of Christianity. To follow the path of Celtic wisdom means to engage with the spiritual world.

♦ **Celtic wisdom and spirituality are not just something from "back then."** Sometimes, especially in non-Celtic lands like America, it's easy to think of the Celtic path as something from the past. Indeed, there are grand and glorious traditions of Celtic wisdom going back thousands of years. But we must remember that these are living traditions. Perhaps one of the responsibilities for those of us who pursue Celtic wisdom in the twenty-first century is to be aware of the political and social issues facing the remaining communities of the Celtic world.

This chapter provides only the briefest of an overview of the rich tapestry of Celtic history. You could devote a lifetime to this one topic, and as you explore more deeply the vast world of Celtic wisdom, you'll want to keep acquainting yourself with the grand story of the Celtic people. Like any other aspect of Celtic wisdom, choose those aspects of history that interest you the most.

The Least You Need to Know

♦ Celtic history goes back more than 2,000 years; at one point the Celts were the dominant culture throughout much of Europe.

♦ Beginning with Caesar's conquest of Gaul, Celtic power diminished, although Celtic culture has survived in one form or another to today.

♦ Religion (especially Christianity) has played an important role in the shaping of the modern Celtic world.

♦ Today's Celtic culture is centered on the "six nations" of Brittany, Cornwall, Ireland, the Isle of Man, Scotland, and Wales; other locations, such as Galicia and Nova Scotia, also have strong Celtic identities.

♦ Celtic history helps us understand who the Celts have been and gives us a glimpse into the foundations of Celtic wisdom.

Chapter 3

The Concept of Celticity

In This Chapter

- ◆ Your "college word" for today: Celticity
- ◆ Five ways to understand Celticity
- ◆ Celts: the "other" ones
- ◆ Traditional Celtic culture as a doorway to wisdom
- ◆ Why language is important

In Chapter 2 you encountered the story of the Celtic past, from the formidable warrior culture of ancient times to today's world, where small pockets of people in western Europe still speak Celtic languages and keep traditional culture alive, while millions of people the world over can trace their heritage back to one or more of the Celtic nations. Meanwhile, the Celtic nations themselves, like many other nations in the world, have become home to many different cultural influences and ethnic groups, not all of which are Celtic in origin.

Given this kaleidoscopic world of different cultures, ancestries, and ethnicities, what makes Celtic wisdom and spirituality, so, well … Celtic?

That's the central question of this chapter. To explore it, we'll look at a concept, that of "Celticity." Understanding this concept will help you understand just what makes Celtic spirituality distinctive and special.

Defining Celticity

What distinguishes Celtic spirituality from any other kind of spirituality? Or Celtic art from other art forms? Or Celtic philosophy from other wisdom perspectives? These questions illustrate the challenge of defining the mysterious essence that is the heart of Celtic identity.

On a superficial level, Celticity may be defined as the *quality* that makes something or someone genuinely Celtic. That's probably as useful a definition of this word as we'll get. But it's not an easy quality to pin down, as the following questions illustrate:

> **The Seer Says**
>
> This chapter may seem to be long on theory and short of practical ideas about how to embrace Celtic spirituality for yourself. However, the ideas of this chapter are important for developing the knowledge of a true Celtic wisdomkeeper.

> **Notes from the Otherworld**
>
> Modern attempts to revive druidism serve as a good example of how different people define Celticity in different ways. Some authors have speculated that druidism was a wisdom tradition that originated in Egypt or even Atlantis. Others, however, attack such theories because they seek to blend Celtic wisdom with ideas from other cultures.

- Is Celticity related to language? But if so, what about the millions of people with Celtic ancestry who speak a non-Celtic language like English or Galician?

- Is Celticity related to geography? If so, then what about immigrants from Celtic lands like Ireland or Scotland—do they stop being Celtic the minute they get on a boat or a plane? Meanwhile, do people with a non-Celtic background suddenly become Celtic when they move to a place like Cornwall or Brittany?

- Is Celticity related to participation in Celtic traditions and culture? But that's also problematic: The cultures of a Scottish fisherman, an Irish farmer, or a Welsh musician are quite different from one another. Furthermore, all Celtic cultures have been influenced by ideas, beliefs, and practices that are non-Celtic in origin, such as Christianity, the English or French languages, and American entertainment.

It's an exasperating problem with no easy, cut-and-dried way to draw a line separating what is Celtic from what isn't.

Some people might be tempted to throw up their hands in frustration and declare that Celticity must be a personal matter, and everyone gets to decide for him- or herself what it means to be Celtic. Such a subjective approach has its limits, however. If anything can be Celtic, then it is meaningless to try to understand what is unique about the Celtic tradition.

You'll find, in your journey into the world of Celtic wisdom, that different people define Celticity in many different ways. Here is a list of some of the most common qualities that people look for in assessing the Celticity of their spiritual path:

- **Language.** The firmest foundation for identifying Celticity is the languages of the modern Celtic world: Irish, Welsh, Scots Gaelic, Manx, Cornish, and Breton.

- **Lore.** The myths and legends written in Celtic languages, such as Irish or Welsh mythology, or other sources directly related to the Celtic world, such as classical Greek and Roman accounts of the druids, or modern studies of comparative mythology that explains Celtic lore through the legends of other Indo-European cultures.

> **The Seer Says**
>
> For your journey into Celtic wisdom, try to find several different sources of learning. Read books, but also try to get to know people of Celtic descent—ideally someone fluent in one of the Celtic languages. And if at all possible, visit one or more of the regions in Europe where you can experience Celtic culture as it exists today.

- **Land.** Yes, lands where Celtic languages are (or recently have been) spoken have a claim of Celticity, especially given that the Celtic world is one where spirituality begins with the relationship between people and the land. The land is especially important because of archaeological treasures, both from Celtic and pre-Celtic times.

- **People.** No one owns the copyright to Celticity. If you are of Celtic ancestry, you have a share in the Celtic tradition. Galicians, for example, assert their Celticity because of both historical and legendary evidence linking their homeland with Celtic ancestors, as well as a thriving Celtic arts community in Galicia today. And even if you are not of Celtic ancestry, you might still qualify as a "Cardiac Celt," which is explained later in this chapter.

- **Culture.** For some, Celticity has mostly to do with the music, art, literature, and folk beliefs of the Celtic-speaking world. Cultural treasures such as an Irish jig, a Scottish kilt, and a Welsh harp help many people (especially in the Celtic diaspora) to feel "Celtic." In other words, Celticity seems to be a spiritual feeling that blends nostalgia for the ancestral homelands with an appreciation for the arts from those lands.

Although I don't support the idea that Celticity is merely a subjective quality, practically speaking you will need to decide what qualities are important for you as you pursue your Celtic journey. You might be comfortable with a very general appreciation of the folklore from Celtic lands, or you may have a deep desire to learn as much as you can of traditional ways, including mastering a language and understanding the cosmology of one or more of the Celtic lands. It's up to you just how deeply you will delve into the Celtic world.

Ancestors and Mentors

Celtic paganism probably included some form of ancestor worship, and for many people today interested in walking the path of Celtic wisdom, the ancestors are a crucial element of the tradition. If you are of direct Celtic ancestry, then your ancestors represent the tradition that lives on today in your blood and DNA. But even if you are not a person of Celtic ancestry, you may see the Celts as "spiritual ancestors," mentors whose history and lore help to shape who you are. No matter which is the case, an important way for you to connect with the Celticity of your own spirituality will be to find ways to connect with your ancestors. This can include doing genealogical research, studying Celtic history or archaeology, or spiritual work such as meditation, shamanic processes, and visualization whereby you seek to connect with your ancestors.

The Idea of the Celtic: Otherness and Valor

Another challenge in identifying Celticity is the murkiness of the words "Celt" and "Celtic" themselves. Scholars are divided over the exact meaning of the word *Keltoi*, used by ancient Greeks to describe their "barbarian" neighbors to the north. According to one theory, *Keltoi* is related to the concept of "outsiders" or "others," suggesting that the Greeks (and later, the Romans) saw the Celts only in terms of how they were different from the "civilized" nations. Another theory holds that *Keltoi* translates as "the secret people" or "the hidden ones" since some Celtic tribes were forest-dwellers. Meanwhile, other scholars think that the word may be related to the concept of valor or bravery, arising from the legendary reputation the Celts enjoyed as fearsome warriors.

> **Notes from the Otherworld** _____
>
> Many people of Celtic descent living in places like America enjoy the privileges of being "white" (in other words, of European descent). America is a land where social divisions occur mostly along racial lines. But historically, ethnic Celts in Europe often were social minorities, with the political and cultural problems that such a position entails. For Americans of Celtic ancestry, one way to honor our forefathers and foremothers is to work for a society where all people, regardless of skin color and ethnicity, enjoy the same social privileges. In other words: The path of Celtic wisdom stands opposed to racism or other forms of social privilege.

Although we may never know exactly what *Keltoi* originally meant, it can be useful for us today to think of Celticity in terms of the qualities of "otherness" and "valor." Look at how each of these concepts can help you on your wisdom journey.

- **Otherness.** To be Celtic has as much to do with what we *aren't* as with what we *are*. In ancient days, the Celts were "other" than Greek or Roman or German; in more recent times, they are "other" than the English or French or Spanish. In a more global way, this concept reminds us that Celtic wisdom can function as an alternative spirituality; for example, it is a wisdom path that doesn't just settle for the American way of getting and spending (which is increasingly dominating the entire world, not just America) but rather is a path that preserves an older, more sacred, way of being in the world. To be a Celtic wisdomkeeper, therefore, is to be a carrier of a vision of the world that is "other" than the mainstream values of society.

- **Valor.** What does it mean to truly be brave? Such a quality includes standing up for what's right, being true to one's beliefs, and choosing to live according to one's principles and highest aspirations. We live in a world where conformity and "fitting in" are valued more highly than the courage to truly be ourselves and fight for our principles. Celtic valor may not be expressed on a battlefield today, but it can be useful when we need to question an unethical directive from a boss or a public policy that is harmful to the environment. The path of the Celt is the path of a warrior, who isn't afraid to fight for what's right.

> **CAUTION**
>
> **Geasa**
>
> A Celtic warrior doesn't just fight for his or her own subjective opinions of what's "right." He or she is a "spiritual warrior" who thoughtfully and carefully works to live according to the highest principles of honor and wisdom.

One more thought on understanding the meaning of the words *Celt* and *Celtic:* A subtle but important point to bear in mind is that these were words the Greeks used to describe the Celts, and may not have been words that the Celts used themselves.

From the Particular to the Universal: How the Celtic World Has Expanded Post-Diaspora

Celticity is so hard to pin down in part because the Celtic world has expanded so much in the last few centuries. Even though there is no Celtic "world power" (as the ancient Celts might have seemed to Julius Caesar), today millions of people throughout the world can claim the Celtic heritage as their own. Indeed, there are more "Celts" living in places like the United States or Australia today than in the ancestral homelands of Ireland or Brittany! But just as the Celts of Ireland think of themselves first and foremost as Irish, so, too, do the descendents of Celts in America see themselves primarily as Americans. Nowhere in the world is Celticity a people's primary identity. Instead, wherever Celts are found, their identity as Celts is linked to another identity such as Irish, Welsh, Canadian, or Australian.

So although no one carries a passport or a driver's license showing them as citizens of Celtica, anyone with a cultural or ancestral connection with the Celtic world can still rely on the qualities of otherness and valor to shape their understanding of themselves. I can be an American, a person of Scottish descent, and a courageous follower of an alternative wisdom tradition, all at the same time.

Real Celts and Cardiac Celts

On occasion I've used the terms "Cardiac Celts" or "Celts of the heart." "Cardiac Celts" was coined by British folklorist Marion Bowman, whose essay "Cardiac Celts: Images of the Celts in Paganism" explores the distinction between people who are Celtic by virtue of birth in one of the six nations, and people (usually from other parts of the world) who have little or no connection with Celtic language and culture, but who are Celtic "from the heart."

Cardiac Celts may be descended from Celtic ancestors or they may not be; what makes a person a Cardiac Celt is his or her emotional and spiritual connection to the Celtic world, rather than a connection based on language or citizenship in one of the six nations. Although "real" Celticity might be a matter of ancestry, anyone can be a Cardiac Celt. In fact, the beauty of Cardiac Celticity is the extent to which a person adopts the principles of Celtic wisdom, regardless of his or her ethnic background.

How Celts Understand Themselves

So how *do* Celts understand themselves? Here are a few ideas.

◆ People who identify themselves as Celts generally live in, or are descended from people who come from, one or more of the six nations.

◆ People who identify themselves as Celts often have a committed interest to Celtic lifestyles, including the language, religion, spirituality, history, and culture.

◆ People who identify themselves as Celts generally believe that the unique treasures of the Celtic tradition can help make the world a better place.

The Romantic Vision of Cardiac Celts

Sometimes, Cardiac Celts and the citizens of the six nations have different ideas about Celticity. To the Cardiac Celts, qualities such as paganism, nature mysticism, ancient mythology, traditional art and culture, and magic are often important; Cardiac Celts are sometimes very romantic and ethereal in their way of understanding the Celtic world. By contrast, many of the natives of the six nations prefer to understand their identity in terms of language, history, politics, economics, and the Christian religion. This is not to say that Celts by birth aren't interested in mysticism, or that Celts of the heart have no interest in practical issues. It's mainly a matter of emphasis. And because of these different emphases, sometimes the two groups have difficulty communicating.

Whether you're a Cardiac Celt from San Francisco or a Gaelic-speaking fisherman off the coast of Scotland, I hope this book will inspire you to explore both dimensions of the Celtic tradition. Take the time to get to know both the magical and the mundane dimensions of Celticity. There are treasures to be found throughout the Celtic world!

> **The Seer Says**
>
> Whether you're a dreamy Cardiac Celt or a down-to-earth Celt by birth, try to keep an open mind about the perspective of others who share your interest in Celtic ways. No one person has the Celtic path fully figured out, which means we can all learn from one another.

The Wisdom of Being a Marginal Culture

As you learned in Chapter 2, Celtic history follows a long arc in which the Celts went from being a major cultural and political force in Europe prior to the Roman conquest, to the current state of Celtic culture which is very *marginal*. In trying to understand the concept of Celticity, let's look at how this long history of being a marginal culture has affected the Celtic world.

The Celtic tradition doesn't require everyone to think the same way, believe the same things, or act in the same way. Rather, it stresses individual thought, creativity, and spiritual growth. As a culture that has suffered under different forms of political oppression, the Celtic soul tends to be fiercely dedicated to personal freedom and individual liberty. And since the Celts, in their historical moves to

> **Druidspeak**
>
> A **marginal** culture or society has relatively little power or influence on the course of world events. The Celtic cultures are marginal because other European cultures have a much more profound impact on global affairs. But just because the Celts are marginal doesn't mean they have no influence at all—just that their influence is felt in indirect or minor ways.

avoid oppression, retreated into some of the most difficult climates in Europe, Celtic wisdom has come to stress working and living in partnership with nature in order to make a living.

The Celts will always be a marginal people. Likewise, Celtic wisdom will always find its highest expression not as some sort of all-things-to-all-people philosophy that is bland in its attempts to be universal, but rather as a rich, deep, textured tradition that may only speak to a small number of people—but for that small community, it provides a lifetime of knowledge, wisdom, and meaning.

Wisdom, Language, and Celticity

The material covered in this chapter will raise more questions than it answers. So many different elements of history, culture, and tradition are woven together to create the mysterious tradition we think of as Celtic that it's nearly impossible to establish a once-and-for-all definition of Celticity.

And that's okay. Pursuing the heart of Celtic wisdom involves entering a realm where there are no cut-and-dried, black-and-white absolutes. It's important to keep an open (if discerning) mind about the many different ways in which people explore the Celtic path. By doing so, you'll be in the best position to find the path that's right for you.

Speak Your Celtic Mind!

Having said all that, I would like to make one final plug for the primacy of language. This is a controversial issue; after all, some Celtic lands (Cornwall, The Isle of Man, and Galicia) do not have living Celtic languages, and even the languages that have survived to the present day are all spoken only by a small minority of the residents of the Celtic lands. So anchoring the concept of Celticity in the languages is not a perfect solution, but language is probably the best single tool for exploring Celtic ways.

> **The Bard's Bookshelf**
>
> Want to learn a Celtic language? Try one of these books, all published by NTC Publishing Group: *Teach Yourself Gaelic* by Boyd Robertson and Iain Taylor; *Teach Yourself Irish* by Diarmuid O'Se and Joseph Sheils; or *Teach Yourself Welsh* by Julia Brake and Christine Jones. Each one can be purchased with tapes to assist in pronunciation.

Language represents not only cultural identity, but the grammar of a language reflects the philosophy and thought patterns of the people who speak it. In the names of people and places, language preserves both history and geography. And most of the lore from the Celtic lands, from mythology to folklore, was originally recorded in one of the Celtic tongues.

Especially for Cardiac Celts who live in one of the diaspora lands, learning a Celtic language may not be practical (or even possible, if no fluent speakers are available). So while I won't say that learning a language is a necessary part of studying Celtic wisdom, in an ideal setting it would be an essential step toward truly understanding Celtic wisdom—inside and out.

An Irish Speaker's Perspective

In the summer of 2002, I visited Arain (Inishmore), an island off the west coast of Ireland where Irish speakers still live in traditional ways. While there, I had a wonderful conversation with a local community activist who works to support traditional ways of farming, living, and making money. This man and his wife are raising their children in traditional ways, including speaking Irish. I asked him why he felt language was so important to the preservation of traditional Celtic ways. He spoke about cultural identity and preserving tradition; and then he said one thing that has haunted me ever since: "In Irish, every sentence is a prayer." He went on to explain how the words, idioms, and expressions of Irish continually reinforce a sense of spiritual presence in the minds and hearts of those who speak the language. I was electrified. English is a language without such a built-in spirituality. What would it be like, I thought, to not only speak but think in a way that continually reinforced spirituality? Merely asking that question brought me closer to the heart of Celtic wisdom.

Even if you never learn a Celtic language, you can still adopt many ideas and perspectives from this wonderful wisdom tradition. But if at all possible, learn one of the languages. Your wisdom will be that much deeper for it.

Of Pipes, Whistles, and Fiddles: Celtic Music

One of the best ways to encounter Celticity involves exploring the grand and glorious tradition of music from the Celtic world. Traditional music from the various Celtic lands (and from Celtic-inspired musicians all over the world) provides a lovely and powerful doorway into the spirit of Celticity; furthermore, since many traditional ballads and songs include lyrics in a Celtic language, music can be a way even for those who don't speak such a language to make a connection with the Celtic world.

You can enjoy Celtic music on many levels. At your local Irish pub, or on the radio through programs like National Public Radio's "Thistle and Shamrock," or at Celtic festivals or Scottish Highland Games, you can find plenty of music to enjoy. If your talents run along a musical line, you might enjoy playing an instrument traditionally associated with Celtic music, such as the harp, fiddle, pennywhistle, bagpipes, Uillean pipes, or bodhrán (frame drum). Or you might enjoy singing a traditional song, whether in English or a Celtic language. Many communities have clubs or other org-anizations dedicated to learning and performing traditional music from the Celtic lands. Or perhaps your interest lies in dancing—if so, you'll find that wherever tradi-tional music is performed, traditional dances are never far away.

Celtic music can be exciting and lively, filled with energizing jigs, reels, and hornpipes, or it can be contemplative and wistful, with melancholy airs and sad ballads that bring a tear to the eye. Some traditional songs, such as the Scottish ballads *Tam Lin* or *Thomas the Rhymer*, include insights into Celtic spirituality and mysticism. Furthermore, the hypnotically trancey melodies of Celtic fiddles and pipes create an otherworldly sense of magical beauty that simply cannot be put into words.

Remember, Celtic music is like any other aspect of Celtic culture—it is diverse and many-faceted. Indeed, it is mainly in North America that the term "Celtic music" is even used. Back in the old countries, musicians generally prefer more specific labels like "Irish music" or "Welsh music."

A final note on music's role in the quest for Celtic wisdom: The ancient figure of the bard combined poetry, music, and song to keep the stories and lore of the people alive. Thus, it only makes sense to make Celtic music a significant part of your spiritual life!

The Least You Need to Know

- ◆ Celticity is the quality that makes people, culture, or things authentically Celtic.
- ◆ For a variety of reasons, it's difficult to precisely define Celticity.
- ◆ Celticity can be understood in terms of language, land, lore, or legacy.
- ◆ "Otherness" is a concept helpful for understanding Celticity. The Celts have traditionally been defined by who or what they are not: not Greek, not Roman, not English. In today's world, Celticity may still involve being different from the mainstream.
- ◆ Celtic languages, music, and traditional culture can help you understand the heart of the Celtic world.

Chapter 4

The Seven Dimensions of Celtic Wisdom

In This Chapter

- ◆ Qualities of the Celtic path
- ◆ Overview of the seven dimensions
- ◆ Finding your own way

Wisdom is a complex concept, related to knowledge, spirituality, ethics, values, and ideals. To be wise, a person needs knowledge, but also a sense of how to apply that knowledge effectively; a person needs a spiritual sensibility, but also a sense of perspective that transcends mere religious dogma; a person needs a sense of ethics and integrity, but must avoid the traps of moralism or self-righteousness. In other words, it's not easy to be wise! Fortunately, over the long history of the Celtic people, at least seven different doorways into wisdom have emerged, and you can use any of them to explore your personal spiritual path. We'll find the keys to open those doors in this chapter.

A Few Basic Celtic Wisdom Principles

Before we look at the seven dimensions in detail, let's take a moment to consider some qualities of Celtic wisdom that are truly universal in their nature. These qualities define the Celtic tradition in all its manifestations.

Balance: The Story of the White and Black Sheep

One old tale recounts the story of a druid who had a vision of two pastures, one filled with white sheep, the other with black sheep. Every once in a while, one sheep would cross between the pastures. When it did, two things would happen: First, the sheep would change color (if it had been a white sheep, once it entered the black-sheep pasture, its wool would become black, and vice versa); and then, as soon as the one sheep crossed over, another sheep would cross in the opposite direction, also changing color as it crossed.

This vision speaks of the importance of balance as a quality of Celtic wisdom. The two pastures symbolize a metaphor for the spiritual and material worlds; the energies of both worlds need to be held in balance for the good of the inhabitants of both. To walk the way of wisdom is to live in service of such balance, and to conduct one's life in a way that supports the universe remaining in a healthy balance.

> **CAUTION**
>
> **Geasa**
>
> Especially on the Internet, you'll run into students of Celtic spirituality who will insist that their particular style of wisdom is the most authentic, pure, or accurate. Although such individuals might have knowledge to share, don't pick up their arrogant manner. A true wisdomkeeper doesn't need to belittle others!

> **The Seer Says**
>
> I once met a Catholic nun who dedicated her life to serving Saint Brigid. Knowing that the Christian Saint Brigid is related to the pagan goddess of the same name, I asked the nun whether she thought of Brigid more as a saint or as a goddess. She pointed to a painting of scales hanging on the wall and said, "The answer to your question is just a matter of maintaining the balance."

Liminality: Neither This Nor That

The Celts have long been a people who appreciate the mysterious nature of "in-between" times and places, the space between where one thing ends and another begins. Samhain, the sacred ritual marking the end of summer, takes place between the end of summer and the onset of winter; its opposite, Beltane, takes place between the end of winter and the start of summer. Dusk and dawn, as the magical times between day and night, are seen as points of mystical power, as are holy wells (neither earth nor water), spirits (neither alive nor dead), and myths (neither true nor false). It is in the *liminal* places where we can most easily access the wisdom of the spiritual world.

Druidspeak

Liminality comes from the Latin word *limen*, meaning "threshold." It refers to a place that is in-between two other places, such as dawn and dusk, which are in between day and night.

Three Is the Magic Number

Again and again, Celtic wisdom appears in threefold ways. One of the most popular literary forms of ancient Wales was the triad, or a poem containing three key pieces of information. It is said that Christianity succeeded in Ireland in large part due to the fact that the Irish responded to the Christian idea of the Trinity (one God with three persons or aspects). Other examples of how triplicity appears in the Celtic wisdom include the following:

◆ Many Celtic goddesses have three "faces" or aspects, such as Brigid, the goddess of healing, poetry, and fire; or the Morrígan, a war goddess who appears as Badb, Macha, and Nemain; or the Goddess of the Land herself, whose Irish faces include Ériu, Banba, and Fotla.

◆ The Celtic cosmos incorporates three realms: the celestial realm (where the gods and goddesses dwell); the earthly realm (home of mortal men and women), and the underworld realm (home of the faery people and human ancestors) or underwater realms (home of the spirits of chaos, such as the Irish Fomorians).

◆ The druids of Gaul were said to be divided into three orders, including bards (historians/minstrels), ovates (counselors/seers), and druids (priests/administrators).

Notes from the Otherworld

Technically, the Welsh triads were not poems, for classical Welsh poetry followed strict rules of compositions. The triad was a simple literary device for memorizing important information, often about history or lore. Here's an example:

Three Enchanters of the Island of Britain:

Coll son of Collfrewy,
and Menw son of Teirgwaedd,
and Drych son of Kibddar.

—Triad 27, translated by Rachel Bromwich

Modern science suggests that the human brain consists of three dimensions: the "reptilian brain" where our most basic animal impulses are governed; the "old mammalian brain," which governs basic reasoning and emotions; and the "new mammalian brain," which governs abstract thought and higher states of consciousness. Perhaps the Celtic respect for triplicity was an intuitive way of understanding how the human mind itself is constructed!

A Triskele is a popular symbol among lovers of Celtic wisdom. In combining three branches emanating from a unified center, it symbolizes the Celtic respect for triplicity.

The Awen: The Light Beyond the Gates

Awen is a concept out of the Welsh tradition that modern druids and other Celtic seekers have found to be a key to the heart of Celtic wisdom. It's a concept that applies to nearly all forms of Celtic spirituality. No one today knows for sure how Awen was understood, or accessed, in ancient times, although Welsh poetry provides a few tantalizing clues. The Awen seemed to be connected with goddess energy, specifically the energy of Ceridwen, a goddess associated with magic and the cauldron of inspiration. It also has a connection to poetry and to singing and chanting for the purpose of spiritual illumination.

Some druids of the modern era have speculated that Awen is a spiritual source of visions, enlightenment, or prophecy, and that ancient bards and druids

> **Druidspeak**
>
> **Awen** is a mysterious Welsh word that has been defined as "inspiration" or "poetic gift" but also as "flowing Spirit." It refers to a principle of sacred inspiration, which flows out of the spiritual realm to poets, bards, and wisdomkeepers.

sought the Awen for its wisdom-giving properties. Seekers of the Awen might use meditation, ritual, or shamanic techniques such as vision-questing (venturing into the wilderness to seek spiritual guidance) to try to manifest the Awen within their lives.

Awen is a mysterious energy; it symbolizes the wisdom that is available to us from the realm of the spiritual world.

Nature: The Matrix of the Spirit

Finally, Celtic spirituality and wisdom are profoundly connected to the natural world, from the powers of elemental forces like fire and water to longstanding traditions of lore associated with animals, trees, or particular locations. This is actually such an important part of the Celtic tradition that it deserves its own chapter (Chapter 5).

These five qualities appear throughout the world of Celtic spirituality in many ways. For example, the story of Taliesin (which you'll discover in Chapter 8) tells of a boy who accidentally ingests a magic potion, thus giving him the ability to shapeshift into a variety of natural objects, before undergoing an initiation in which he is reborn with the gift of poetic inspiration. This story has a triadic element (the hero goes from innocent boy to magical shapeshifter to inspired poet), is filled with imagery from nature, and culminates with the hero gifted in the ways of Awen. As you study the Celtic tradition, look for these themes of balance, liminality, triplicity, inspiration, and nature. They crop up again and again!

It might help to think of these qualities together as comprising the trunk of a massive tree—a tree representing Celtic spirituality. (Hey, we're pretty sure that the druids venerated trees, so this is an especially appropriate analogy.) These qualities are the foundation upon which all things Celtic rest.

The Seven Branches of Celtic Wisdom

If the qualities just described are the trunk of the tree of Celtic spirituality, then the seven approaches to Celtic wisdom are its branches.

No matter how different the branches may be from one another, it's important to remember that the trunk (the Celtic tradition itself) unifies the seven branches. Also, you'll notice plenty of overlap between the different approaches, which only makes sense given the underlying unity.

You can also think of these seven branches as seven primary portals, or gateways, into the realms of Celtic spirituality, wisdom, and magic. Some of these doorways are religious in nature, such as Christianity, Wicca, and neopaganism (none of which are exclusively Celtic in nature, but all include a historical or modern Celtic connection).

Other paths are not tied to any particular organized religion, but function as meaningful gateways nevertheless. From the mystical quest for the Holy Grail to the healing rituals of ancient shamans and from the philosophical rumination of modern druids to the nature-based folklore of faery belief, there's a pathway into the Celtic world for every temperament and taste. Read on, and see which of the Celtic portals speak to you!

Celtic Shamanism

Several modern writers and teachers, including John Matthews, Francesca De Grandis, and Tom Cowan, have explored the unity between primal Celtic spirituality and shamanism—earth's oldest spiritual path, practiced by tribal priests and magicians in indigenous cultures the world over. Globally speaking, shamanism is a path that links the energies of the natural and psychic worlds. With the help of spirit guides, power animals, and ancestral entities, shamans receive healing and empowerment so they in turn can help themselves and their people. And yes, in its most primal form, Celtic spirituality includes all these qualities.

> **The Bard's Bookshelf**
>
> If you're interested in Celtic forms of shamanism, get a copy of *The Druid Animal Oracle* by Philip and Stephanie Carr-Gomm (Simon & Schuster, 1994). The set includes 33 beautifully illustrated cards showing animals sacred to the Celts, and a book explaining the spiritual significance of each of the animals.

Celtic shamanism may be for you if …

- You're interested in how animals, plants, and trees were sources of wisdom and power in ancient Celtic lore and would like to access that wisdom and power for yourself.

- You're drawn to other forms of shamanism (such as Native American spirituality) but want your spirituality to have a more Celtic focus.

- You're particularly interested in spirit contact, including connecting with the spirits of your ancestors or spirits from the natural world.

If Celtic shamanism interests you, then you might consider reading the following books:

- *Fire in the Head: Shamanism and the Celtic Spirit* by Tom Cowan (HarperSanFrancisco, 1993). An introduction to the unity between the Celtic tradition and world shamanism.

- *The Mist-Filled Path: Celtic Wisdom for Exiles, Wanderers, and Seekers* by Frank MacEowen (New World Library, 2002). A personal spiritual journey from Native American wisdom into the heart of the Celtic tradition.

- *The Celtic Shaman: A Handbook* by John Matthews (Element Books, 1991). A practical guidebook covering both the theory and the practice of Celtic shamanism.

Celtic Faery Spirituality

Closely related to shamanism is the "faery faith," based on honoring the faeries—the nature entities said to be the spirits of the old gods and goddesses who were worshipped before the coming of Christianity. Scholars believe that the faeries are the last remaining vestiges of the spirituality that once was practiced by druids and seers like Merlin and Morgan LeFay. Today's faery spirituality is a "homegrown" path, still practiced in the rural areas of the Celtic world where it has existed for generations. The faery faith also survives in legends and lore, speaking to anyone who loves a good story told around the fire.

Notes from the Otherworld

Faery does not come from a Celtic language, but rather is the Old French word for "fairy." It derives from the Latin word *Fata*, for the goddess of fate. Faeries, like many other aspects of Celtic spirituality, are not unique to Celtic lands and can be found throughout the world. Incidentally, the most commonly used Irish word for faery is *sidhe*, an abbreviation of *daoine sidhe*, literally "the people of the hills," deriving from the Irish belief that the faeries lived underground in cairns or "faery mounds." In Welsh the faeries are called *Y Tylwyth Teg*, meaning "the fair family."

Celtic faery spirituality may be for you if …

♦ You enjoy the myths, legends, and folklore associated with the Celtic faery traditions.

♦ You feel a strong connection with the energies of nature and the land.

♦ You believe you have a particular connection with the Celtic faeries.

Geasa

Both Celtic shamanism and the faery faith involve contact with the spirits of the otherworld. Tradition warns us not to take such beings lightly. A faery is not an imaginary plaything, but a spirit being who should be treated with respect and courtesy.

Books for further study include the following:

♦ *The Fairy Faith in Celtic Countries* by W. Y. Evans-Wentz (Carol Publishing Group, 1994). A classic study from the early twentieth century that documents faery traditions from the six modern Celtic lands.

♦ *The Middle Kingdom: The Faerie World of Ireland* by Dermot MacManus (Colin Smythe, 1973). Written by an associate of William Butler Yeats, this is a compendium of Irish faery customs and traditions from the mid-twentieth century.

◆ *The Living World of Faery* by R. J. Stewart (Gothic Image Publications, 1995). Drawing on folklore, traditional ballads, and the personal experience of the author and others, this book explains how to establish your own contacts with the faery world. Also check out R. J. Stewart's *Earth Light* (Mercury Publishing, 1998).

Celtic Christianity

Although Christianity is a fairly recent arrival on the Celtic scene, having come to the Celtic lands between the second and sixth centuries C.E., today it is the most widely practiced religion among people with Celtic blood. Looking at the unique ways in which Christianity has been practiced in Celtic lands, one might ask, "Who converted who?" Celtic Christianity is deeply ecological, optimistic, and poetic; far more beautiful and lovely than many other expressions of the Christian religion. Today, Celtic Christianity especially appeals to Christians who want to find a way to honor nature while remaining faithful to their religious beliefs.

The Celtic Cross (also called the Iona Cross) is a powerful symbol that can be seen as representing the union of pagan and Christian spirituality. As such, the circle symbolizes the feminine, natural dimension of pagan spirituality, while the cross symbolizes the masculine, heavenly dimension of Christianity.

Celtic Christianity may be for you if …

- You are already a Christian (or feel drawn to Christian spirituality) and would like to express your faith in a Celtic way.

- You feel especially connected to great Celtic saints, like Patrick, Bridget, or Columba.

- You want to practice a spirituality that honors just one supreme God.

Books for further study include the following:

- *Celtic Christian Spirituality: An Anthology of Medieval and Modern Sources* edited by Oliver Davies and Fiona Bowie (Continuum Publishing Company, 1995). The poetic nature of Celtic Christianity shines through in this lovely collection of writings.

- *An Introduction to Celtic Christianity* edited by James P. Mackey (T&T Clark, 1989). Essays on a variety of topics, from theology to art to both Catholic and Protestant forms of Celtic Christianity.

- *Anam Cara: A Book of Celtic Wisdom* by John O'Donohue (HarperCollins, 1997). The living tradition of Irish Christianity comes alive in this lyrical book by a Catholic priest.

Modern Druidism

The ancient druid orders were wiped out first by the Roman Empire and then by Christianity. But Celts and non-Celts alike have long been fascinated by this ancient order of sages, and many attempts to revive druidism have taken place over the centuries. Today, dozens of druid organizations exist worldwide, each dedicated to reviving ancient Celtic wisdom in practical modern ways. Many modern druids view druidism more as a philosophy than a religion, and some druids also practice another religion (such as Christianity, Wicca, or even Buddhism!).

The Seer Says

Druids have established a powerful presence on the Internet. Some of the best druidic sites include the home page for these druid organizations: the Order of Bards, Ovates, and Druids (www.druidry.org), Tuatha de Brighid (www.tuathadebrighid.org), and Ár nDraíocht Féin: A Druid Fellowship (www.adf.org).

Modern druidism may be for you if …

♦ You feel particularly drawn to the druids of old, or feel interested in learning more about modern druid groups.

♦ You would like to practice a spirituality that blends Celtic wisdom with other mystical or esoteric systems, such as ceremonial magic or theosophy.

♦ You want to explore Celtic wisdom from a philosophical perspective rather than a religious or spiritual perspective.

Books for further study of druidism include the following:

♦ *The Druid Renaissance: The Voice of Druidry Today* edited by Philip Carr-Gomm (Thorsons, 1996). A collection of essays exploring the worldwide dimensions of the druid revival and how it relates to Celtic wisdom, environmentalism, and the modern quest for meaning.

♦ *The World of the Druids* by Miranda J. Green (Thames and Hudson, 1997). A superbly illustrated historical survey of druids, from ancient times to today.

♦ *Principles of Druidry* by Emma Restall Orr (Thorsons, 1998). Basics of modern druidism written by a British druid priestess.

Celtic Wicca

One of the most significant spiritual trends of recent years has been the explosion of interest in Wicca, or ethical religious witchcraft. Although Wicca is primarily based on English and Italian witchcraft, it does have some Celtic influences, notably in terms of the holidays it celebrates (four of the eight main Wiccan holidays are inspired by Gaelic and other Celtic traditions), and some of the mythology of Wicca borrows from Celtic sources. While it is important to remember that Wicca is no more inherently "Celtic" than Christianity or any other spiritual path, it (like Christianity) can be a meaningful path to Celtic wisdom when it integrates Celtic symbolism.

Notes from the Otherworld

Wicca was originally an Old English word for "witch," literally meaning a male witch. The Old English word for female witch was *Wicce*. Different theories can be found as to the original meaning of these words; some writers suggest they mean "wisdomkeepers," while others think they are related to "wicker" and have to do with bending or shaping (as in magic as a force for bending/shaping the future).

Celtic Wicca may be for you if …

◆ You are especially interested in magic and witchcraft.

◆ You are comfortable blending Celtic wisdom with ideas from other spiritual traditions from around the world.

◆ You want to practice a spirituality that honors one Goddess and one God, seeing the many gods and goddesses of Celtic tradition as aspects of the Lord and Lady.

Books for further study include the following:

◆ *An Irish Book of Shadows: Tuatha De Danaan* by Katherine Clark (Galde Press, 2001). The rituals and traditions of a Wiccan lineage based on Celtic lore.

◆ *Celtic Wicca: Ancient Wisdom for the 21st Century* by Jane Raeburn (Citadel Press, 2001). Another Wiccan lineage, this one is based on Romano-Celtic sources.

◆ *A Witches Bible: The Complete Witches' Handbook* by Janet and Stewart Farrar (Phoenix Publishing, 1984). Not a Celtic book per se, but an essential introduction to Wicca that details how Wicca has adopted Celtic holidays into its ritual cycle.

Celtic Reconstructionism

While Celtic shamanism and Celtic Wicca are popular, not all people interested in finding a nature-based expression of Celtic spirituality feel comfortable with these multicultural forms of spirituality. A small but dedicated group of people, mostly neopagans, have formed a vibrant community in recent years devoted to reconstructing ancient Celtic pagan spirituality for the modern world. Such reconstructionists are attempting, through both spiritual and scholarly means, to create as purely Celtic a spirituality as is possible. Many Celtic reconstructionists stress the importance of learning a Celtic language, like Irish or Welsh, and approach their spirituality from a polytheistic perspective, discarding the idea of a single unified spirit in favor of belief in many gods and goddesses.

Notes from the Otherworld

Celtic reconstructionists often look to other cultures outside the Celtic tradition to fill in the gaps of missing knowledge about ancient Celtic spirituality. Many reconstructionists explore the history of the ancient Indo-Europeans; others pursue comparative mythology, a field that seeks to understand the common themes in the myths of different cultures. By comparing the mythology of the Celts to that of the Norse, Greeks, or Baltic pagans, reconstructionists have been able to develop an in-depth revival of ancient wisdom.

Celtic reconstructionism may be for you if ...

◆ You would like to revive, as closely as possible, the ancient pre-Christian spirituality of the Celts, free of any modern or non-Celtic influences.

◆ You are interested in archaeology, comparative mythology, and Indo-European studies, and are willing to do the scholarly work necessary to "get it right."

◆ You want to practice a spirituality that honors the many different Celtic gods and goddesses.

Books for further study include the following:

◆ *The Sacred Isle: Belief and Religion in Pre-Christian Ireland* by Dáithí Ó hÓgáin (Boydell Press, 1999). Scholarly survey of spirituality on the Emerald Isle, from before the first Celts to the triumph of Christianity.

◆ *Myths and Symbols in Pagan Europe: Early Scandinavian and Celtic Religions* by H. R. Ellis Davidson (Syracuse University Press, 1988). Similarities between the Norse and Celtic paganism are highlighted in this academic survey.

◆ *The Gods of the Celts* by Miranda Green (Sutton Publishing, 1986). An introduction to the Celtic gods and goddesses of pagan times.

The Grail Quest

For many people, the loveliest doorway into the Celtic world involves the myths and legends of Camelot, King Arthur, and the Holy Grail. The grail itself is a curious symbol, merging pagan Celtic symbolism of a cauldron of abundance with Christian mysticism related to the cup (grail) used by Jesus at the last supper. To this day, people speculate about the location of the "real" grail, but to many spiritual seekers, the most important quality of the Holy Grail is what it symbolizes spiritually: enlightenment or union with God.

Notes from the Otherworld

The power of the grail as a symbol of spiritual yearning continues to fascinate people. This is apparent in how the grail appears as the subject of movies, whether thrill-a-minute action adventure films (*Indiana Jones and the Last Crusade*) or silly comedies (*Monty Python and the Holy Grail*). Furthermore, the word *grail* has taken on a new meaning based on the Holy Grail—it is a synonym for "ultimate prize."

The grail quest may be for you if …

- You feel drawn to Merlin, Morgan LeFay, or the other wisdomkeepers of Arthurian myth.

- You enjoy the mysteries surrounding the Holy Grail and enjoy learning about this elusive topic.

- For you, the grail is more than just a missing relic of the past—it is instead a living symbol of humankind's ultimate mystical destiny (enlightenment; union with the divine).

Books for further study include the following:

- *The Crafted Cup: Ritual Mysteries of the Goddess and the Grail* by Shadwynn (Llewellyn Publications, 1994). A lovely vision of Christian-pagan synthesis, built around the quest for the grail.

- *The Secret Tradition in Arthurian Legend* by Gareth Knight (Samuel Weiser, 1983). Eloquent introduction to the esoteric dimensions of the grail quest.

- *The Grail Seeker's Companion* by John Matthews and Marian Green (The Aquarian Press, 1986). Spiritual exercises for conducting your own inner quest.

Finding Your Path

As you've probably noticed, the seven dimensions overlap: Christianity and the grail quest share much in common, as do shamanism and faery spirituality. Perhaps one of these paths clearly beckons you to follow; or perhaps you feel drawn to two or more. The only truly "right" way to explore the Celtic way is to be true to your own heart—so follow whatever path(s) speak to you.

How, then, does one embark upon the Celtic journey? You can visit the Internet to find websites devoted to the Celtic vision, and your local metaphysical bookstore probably stocks a variety of books related to these paths. But perhaps the best way to explore Celtic spirituality is to connect with nature. After all, the Celtic path involves seeking spiritual insight within the air you breathe, the water you drink, and the land where you stand. Such reverence for nature is the heart of the Celtic way.

 Geasa

Don't limit yourself when it comes to these seven Celtic pathways. Even if you have strong religious beliefs that inspire you to identify as a Christian or a Wiccan, you can still learn from the wisdom of the "other" paths. Celtic spirituality works best with an open mind.

Activity: Keep a Journal

Chances are, by now you have begun to think about how the world of Celtic wisdom can relate to your individual life. You may have as many questions as you have answers, but at least you're beginning to see the many possibilities of the Celtic tradition. So now, how do you move forward?

If you don't already do so, you may find it useful to keep a written record of your explorations of the Celtic world. If you already keep a journal or a diary, that's wonderful; you may want to use it as a tool for documenting your progress in learning about Celtic wisdom. You don't have to be a great writer or an accomplished editor to benefit from a journal. Journal-keeping is a personal spiritual practice; you write for yourself, not anyone else. Think of keeping a journal as a gift to your future. Months or years from now, your journal will be a tool to help you reconnect with who you are today.

In your journal, you can keep the following kinds of information:

◆ Your ideas, questions, and insights about Celtic spirituality.

◆ A list of the books you're reading, and what you think of them.

◆ Notes on any classes you take or workshops or rituals you attend.

◆ Your thoughts on how you can apply Celtic wisdom to your everyday life.

◆ And whatever else you feel inspired to write down!

You don't have to limit your journal to just words. As the saying goes, a picture is worth a thousand words, so use your journal to draw pictures about your spirituality. Or use it as a scrapbook where you can keep interesting articles or photographs or downloaded articles from the web. Remember, the journal is a tool to help you keep a record of your growth in wisdom—don't be afraid to adapt it to your particular needs.

The Least You Need to Know

◆ Seven primary doorways can be used to enter the world of Celtic wisdom, including shamanism, druidism, Christianity, Wicca, reconstructionism, faery spirituality, and grail mysticism.

◆ Although there is much overlap among these seven dimensions of Celtic spirituality, there are also differences, defined by religion and history.

◆ Practically every branch of Celtic wisdom has also been influenced or shaped by non-Celtic sources.

◆ The best way to explore Celtic spirituality is by learning about the aspect(s) of it that appeal to you the most.

◆ A personal journal can be a useful tool as you explore the Celtic tradition.

Chapter 5

The Sovereignty of Nature

In This Chapter

◆ Love your Mother!

◆ Sovereignty: the land, the Goddess

◆ Stone circles and holy wells

◆ Sacred plants and sacred animals

◆ Becoming conscious of your natural place

If there's one quality that truly embodies the spirit of Celtic wisdom, it is devotion to that natural world. The Celtic path regards nature as more than just an "environment," but rather a living, breathing presence, a nurturing mother and loving partner to humanity. The further you walk along the Celtic path, the more insistent will be the call for you to honor, love, and protect your Mother—Mother Nature, Mother Earth. And even if you never wear a kilt or listen to a bagpipe, if you live a life of intentional harmony and balance with the earth, then you are truly embodying the Celtic tradition.

The Secret of Celtic Wisdom: Partnership with Nature

John Sayles's 1993 movie *The Secret of Roan Inish* is, on the surface, a charming children's story set on the rural coast of northwest Ireland. It tells the story of a family who has a special relationship to the forces of nature, from the powerful ocean to the seals that according to legend have a magical kinship to humans. After a tragedy in which the family's little boy is lost at sea, his sister finds a way to cooperate with the elements to rescue her brother, who has survived thanks to the watchful eye of seagulls and seals. A charming children's tale, or something more meaningful? For those who look a little deeper, *The Secret of Roan Inish* tells a poetic and beautiful tale of Celtic wisdom—the wisdom of living in harmony and cooperation with the natural world.

> **Notes from the Otherworld**
>
> *The Secret of Roan Inish* tells the story of a selkie—a mythical creature who is half-human and half-seal. Celtic legends abound with magical beings, including selkies, leprechauns, faeries, and banshees. Such supernatural beings represent the Celtic belief in the mystical spirituality that pervades our universe; furthermore, the selkie is a reminder of the close ties uniting humans with the nature world.

Celtic wisdomseekers in today's world can learn a lesson from this children's tale. Nature is not just some sort of backdrop to human existence, full of resources to be mined, harvested, consumed, and exploited. Yes, nature is abundant, and when we live in harmony with her, she is gracious in caring for us and providing for our needs. But our society has gotten out of balance in our way of treating our environment. Instead of loving and cherishing her, we regard nature as little more than a slave who exists solely to do our bidding with no thought for her needs. This out-of-balance way of treating the environment is in direct opposition with Celtic wisdom! Not only is it unspiritual (and unethical), but it also runs the risk of impending disaster, as humans consume nonrenewable resources (like petroleum or natural gas) and destroy the air, soil, and water with our waste.

Mother Nature Rides Again

You'll notice that I've personified nature in the previous paragraph. I refer to nature as "she" and "her." You might think of this as a charming way of acknowledging "Mother Nature." But on the path of Celtic wisdom, it points to a deeper truth. Yes, Mother Nature is real. She is indeed the spirit of nature, and to many Celts, both ancient and modern, she is a goddess, worthy of our reverence and devotion. When we stop treating nature like a slave and return to our ancestral path of regarding her as a goddess, then we will be well underway on our search for Celtic wisdom.

A Universal Love for Nature

In ancient times, and indeed throughout the modern Celtic lands until relatively recently, the vast majority of Celtic people lived in rural, rather than urban, settings. Our modern world is so oriented around cities that city dwellers sometimes think of farmers and other country dwellers as "rednecks" or "hicks." In other words, we live in a society that considers urban living to be the better, more preferred lifestyle. This is nothing new: Such attitudes go all the way back to the ancient Greeks and Romans, where great cities like Athens and Rome were considered the preferred places to live, while the rural "backwater" of places like Britannia or Gaul were dismissed as hopelessly rustic.

As you'll remember from your history lesson in Chapter 2, the Romans were able to conquer the Celts because they were governed by a centralized authority (seated in the great city of Rome), that controlled a massive and powerful military. The Celts, who had no centralized authority but lived in smaller towns, villages, or rural settings, were unable to unite to stop the Roman conquest. On one hand, it seems that the moral of the story is how much better (or at least, stronger) urban culture is than rural.

 Geasa

Love for nature should not be understood as a sentimentalized belief that nature is pure and innocent or somehow better than the grime of urban life. Celtic spirituality acknowledges the terrible side of nature: the dangers of the sea, the power of thunder, and the sheer hard work of living off the land.

But now, after 2,000 years of city-oriented societies and culture being dominant in the West, what do we have? A world that is rapidly overpopulating, with runaway pollution and waste problems, rapid deforestation, and worrisome trends of global warming. Meanwhile, the cities themselves have become festering problems of poverty, drug abuse, and crime. People with moderate amounts of money have fled to suburbs, where land is converted from farms to subdivisions full of asphalt-covered streets or ornamental lawns where no food is grown but plenty of pesticides are sprayed. The bottom line: The urban culture has spread cancer-like, to the point where it is out of balance, and nature is taking it on her chin. That's a trend that cannot go on forever.

The Celtic Alternative

Abandoning cities altogether is, of course, not a realistic option. But the Celtic tradition calls us to begin rethinking how we as individuals, and collectively as a society, relate to our environment. We can look to the long tradition of rural living in Celtic society to remind us that the Celts have lived for thousands of years by maintaining a balanced and harmonious relationship with the environment. Even though most of us in today's world live in concrete cities or asphalt-rich suburbs, we can still take steps to begin to reconnect with the heart of Mother Nature. This is an essential part of the Celtic path.

It's a mistake to romanticize the Celts, seeing ancient Celtic culture as somehow "pure" in its treatment of nature (indeed, there is archaeological evidence that the ancient Celts engaged in deforestation and other practices that today might be considered environmentally questionable). Likewise, it's important to remember that other ancient cultures, from Native Americans to Australian Aborigines, also can teach the modern world a thing or two about relating to the environment. The Celts didn't have a monopoly on environmental sensitivity, nor were they perfect! But for modern urban and suburban wisdomseekers, the Celtic tradition can be a powerful symbol calling us to a renewed commitment of living in partnership with the land, rather than seeking dominion over her.

> **The Seer Says**
>
> Remember, the Celtic tradition is a *living* tradition. Those of us who live in cities in the twenty-first century need to be finding new and innovative ways to apply Celtic spirituality to our urban lives. Doing so helps keep the tradition alive.

Nature: The Heart of Celtic Wisdom

Throughout this book, you have been (and will continue to be) introduced to many elements of the Celtic path: from mythological goddesses and gods, to faeries and heroes of old, to the lessons of history and the varied spiritual practices of the proud Celtic family. While all of this is important to the practice of Celtic wisdom, here's an essential piece of the puzzle: Nature is at the heart of the Celtic way. This means that to walk the path of Celtic wisdom, you will begin and end with reverence for Mother Nature. If you only take one thing from this book, I hope you'll remember this ultimate principle.

Here are just a few of the ways nature has been honored, revered, or incorporated into religious and spiritual wisdom throughout the long history of the Celtic tradition.

The Nemeton: The Sacred Ritual Centers of the Druids

According to classical writers such as Lucan and Tacitus, the druids of old were the outdoorsy type. They conducted at least some of their rituals outside in groves of sacred trees (usually oak), called *nemetons* in some parts of the Celtic world. Pliny, another ancient writer, speaks about the ritualistic care used in gathering sacred herbs, such as mistletoe. For the druids, it appears that nature wasn't just a backdrop to life, but rather the womb in which the sacred duties of the people were carried out.

Druidspeak

Nemeton is a Gaulish word believed to mean "sacred place" or "sacred grove" or "sanctuary." Some ancient Celtic tribes venerated a goddess of the sacred grove, Nemetona.

Stone Circles: Pre-Celtic Reverence for Nature

The ancient stone circles of prehistoric Europe also suggest a link between Celtic wisdom and the natural world. Although such circles predated the coming of Celtic language and culture by centuries, they suggest that some of the most ancient inhabitants of Europe had enough of a sense of the sacredness of place to go to the trouble of erecting huge stone circles and other monuments, many of which were associated with the burial of the dead. Although we have no solid evidence to link the druids themselves to the stone circles and other ancient sites, we do know that Celtic mythology acknowledged the spiritual power of the stone monuments, linking Newgrange with the Irish gods the Dagda and Óengus, and linking Stonehenge with Merlin. We also know that astronomical factors determined the layout of many ancient sites, suggesting that the wisdom of prehistoric Europe included knowledge of the stars.

All this points to the Celtic tradition having emerged in a land where reverence for the natural world, in some form or other, has flourished literally for 5,000 or more years. Thus, the wisdomkeepers of the Celts were simply one aspect of a venerable tradition. Just as other tribal and indigenous cultures from throughout the world have a strong element of nature mysticism in their spiritual rites, so, too, did the Celts, following in the footsteps of their pre-Celtic forebears.

Holy Wells: Honoring of Nature Up to the Present Day

Nemetons and stone circles may point to the nature connection within the Celtic world, but they are mainly relics from the past. However, in at least one significant way, Celts up to the present day, whether Christian or pagan, continue to engage in a powerful practice of honoring the spirituality of nature. This is the practice of prayer and veneration at holy wells, found throughout the traditional Celtic lands. From prayers to offerings to stylized rituals, many people seeking healing or comfort turn to the soothing waters that emerge from Mother Earth herself. We'll take a closer look at this beautiful form of Celtic spirituality later in this chapter.

Notes from the Otherworld

In modern Ireland, holy wells are usually surrounded by Christian imagery, often related to veneration of the Virgin Mary or of popular saints like Brigid or Patrick. Reverence for wells did not begin with Christianity, but dates back to the pagan past. Today, both Christians and neopagans visit sacred wells for spiritual sustenance, their religious differences overcome by a shared love for the waters of Mother Earth.

The Sovereignty of the Land

The origin of the Celtic reverence for nature lies in the ancient belief that nature is divine. The Earth Goddess, who appeared in the Celtic world as many different goddesses connected with the land, was considered in ancient times to be the source of sovereignty (freedom, liberty, and the authority to self-govern). The "sovereignty of the land" is, therefore, a central concept both for understanding the mind of the ancient Celts, as well as for putting Celtic wisdom into practice today.

The Sacred King and the Sovereign Land

Irish mythology recounts that, in ancient times, the high king of Ireland did not receive his office through inheritance, but was chosen, usually through one or more methods of divination or magical knowledge. For example, a sacred stone at the Hill of Tara, called the Lia Fail, was said to emit a loud cry when the rightful king would touch it. Other methods of selecting the king included a ritual in which a chosen druid would sleep and in his dreams would see the rightful king.

Once the king was chosen, he inaugurated his reign through a ceremonial "sacred marriage" with the Goddess herself. It was only through marrying her that he could take on the authority of kingship. Thus, temporal power (political sovereignty) was derived by virtue of a "sacred marriage" with the Goddess, who was the source of eternal, spiritual sovereignty. Furthermore, once a king assumed power, the people expected his rule to result in abundance and prosperity. A good and righteous king would maintain the balance between human and nature in such a way that the land would remain fertile and harvests would be plenty. By contrast, a bad king who did not uphold the duties of his office would be rejected by the land, and famine and hunger would result.

In today's world, none of the Celtic lands or the lands of the Celtic diaspora have such a ritual of selecting or crowning a sacred king. But no longer having a king doesn't affect the sovereignty of the land. Our physical needs are met through the abundance and bounty of the earth. No matter what our form of government, we are all dependent on the fertility of the earth. Celtic wisdom calls us to honor the earth as the true source of our freedom and liberty, as well as the true source of our very lives. Recognizing this, we can begin to move back toward living in harmony and respectful balance with the land that we've neglected for so long.

> **The Seer Says**
>
> How does the sacred king's marriage to the sovereign Goddess apply to modern life? Here's one possibility: Think of your body as the "land" and your mind as the "sacred king." When the king rules justly, the land is abundant. In other words, when your mind chooses to eat right, exercise, get proper amounts of rest, and attend to spiritual matters, your body will respond with increased health and vitality.

The Legend of Niall

One ancient Irish legend recounts the importance of the relationship between the king and the land (and also comments on how nature is not always "nice"). The story recounts how a group of brothers were engaged in an unsuccessful hunt in the Irish wilderness. Eventually tired and hungry, they came to a stream and wished to drink. But standing in front of the stream was a hideously ugly old woman. Speaking to the oldest brother, she invited him to come take a drink, but first, she added, he must kiss her. Revolted by her appearance, the eldest brother declined the offer. Each brother in turn was offered water for a kiss, and each said no. Finally the youngest brother, Niall, accepted the hag's offer. He kissed her, and she transformed in his arms to the loveliest of goddesses! For she was the sovereign goddess of the land, and since Niall had accepted her, he was rewarded not only with water, but with her love, and he became high king over all the land.

The story of Niall not only reinforces the idea that the king must be a lover of the land, but also illustrates an important principle of wisdom: that beauty (or truth or goodness) is not just a matter of appearance. Wiser than his brothers, only Niall could look past the hag's unpleasant appearance to accept her and the gift she offered him. Because of his wisdom, the goddess rewarded him with her true beauty.

A World Filled with Gods and Goddesses

The Irish tradition associates several goddesses with the land. These nature goddesses include Dana (the mother of the gods and goddesses), Ériu (for whom Ireland is named), Banba, and Fotla. But "the land" is not the only aspect of nature seen as divine. Indeed, many of the gods and goddesses of the Celtic world have strong associations with nature; these deities could be seen as symbolic of elements of nature, or (perhaps more accurately) should be seen as actual essences of the forces of nature they represent. Thus, the god Manannán can be seen as a god of the sea, or perhaps is simply the personification of the ocean. The goddess Bóand is similarly associated with the Boyne river in Ireland. Other Celtic deities have strong animal associations: The Gaulish goddess Epona is associated with horses, while the Welsh goddess Blodeuedd is associated with owls.

> **Notes from the Otherworld**
>
> The Celts didn't create images of their gods and goddesses, at least not until they came into contact with the classical civilizations of Greek and Rome. Apparently, the Celts felt that nature was enough of a "symbol" of spirit to make idols or statues unnecessary.

Even if you don't find it personally meaningful to associate nature with the old gods and goddesses of the Celtic world, try to find a way to honor and respect the natural world in a way that works for you. Don't just think of nature in abstract ways (as "the environment" or "the great outdoors"), but keep it personal. One thing is for sure: Nature is teeming with life, and with the raw materials for nurturing life. Thus, respect for nature is the equivalent of respecting life!

How to Connect with the Singing Presence

Given the nature orientation of Celtic spirituality, you may find that your interest in Celtic wisdom translates into a desire to feel more closely connected with nature. There are several steps you can take to cultivate such a connection in your life.

- ◆ **Spend time outdoors.** To connect with nature, begin by getting close to her. Visit a wilderness area if possible; if not, at least get to a park or a garden whenever you can. Put up a bird feeder where you can sit and watch for feathered visitors. If you have a suitable garden, you might even make part of it a wildlife garden. If all else fails, bring some nature into your home. Even potted plants and a pet can be a link to the natural world.

- ◆ **Slow down.** Most of us live at such a breakneck pace that we don't have time to stop and smell the flowers—or meditate by the waterfall or enjoy the view. Nature is not an entertainment program or a media extravaganza. To make a spiritual connection with nature, we need to reach out with an open heart and a quiet mind.

- ◆ **Imagine.** If the trees could talk to you, what would they say? If the sky had a nugget of wisdom to share, what would it be? Use your imagination to make a spiritual connection with the natural world. Remember, you (and your imagination) are part of nature, too, so when you have an "inner dialogue" with nature, it's as "real" as the nose on your face!

◆ **Learn.** Meditation and visualization may be helpful tools for befriending the spirit of nature, but there are other important resources at your disposal as well. Take the time to know the basics of the geography and biology of your region. Become familiar with issues related to conservation and environmental protection. Just as a doctor cannot help her patients without a solid grounding in medicine, to truly connect with nature you need scientific as well as spiritual knowledge.

◆ **Don't just sit there, do something.** One common mistake among spiritual seekers involves doing nothing: You might learn to meditate, become familiar with problems facing the environment, and even feel an urgency to work for making the world a better place, but it often stops there. Sometimes this is because the issues facing the environment are overwhelming, and sometimes it might be because you simply don't know where to begin. To avoid this pitfall, think of relating to nature on a level similar to relating to a friend or spouse. If your friend called you in a time of need, you'd be there for him or her. The same with nature. Everyone knows that the environment is under stress; fortunately, there are books, organizations, and websites to help you make choices to help preserve the natural world.

> **The Seer Says**
>
> Here are a few resources to get you started on living a life of connection to Mother Nature. Read *Save Our Planet: 750 Everyday Ways You Can Help Clean Up the Earth* by Diane MacEachern (Bantam Books, 1991), or join the Sierra Club (www.sierraclub.com). For ideas of other organizations that might interest you, check out Environmental Organizations Online (www.envorgs.com).

Later in this chapter we'll take a closer look at how to apply the Celtic tradition in practical ways regarding the environment.

Putting Spirituality in Its Place

The modern world is a world of standardization. Drive anywhere around America and you will see the same fast-food restaurants, the same programs on television, and hear the same songs on the radio. The local bookstores will all feature the same best-sellers, and the same comic strips run in all the newspapers. Worse yet, although this cultural nondiversity is mostly an American phenomenon, it is influencing other parts of the world (yes, including the Celtic lands) as more and more American corporations extend their reach around the globe.

Given this kind of bland sameness, it may be difficult to imagine one of the most important and distinctive qualities of the Celtic tradition: that spirituality is not some sort of standardized universal phenomenon, but rather is intimately tied in with locality and place. In other words, the customs and traditions of the Aran Islands off the west coast of Ireland have its own unique character, and are different from the traditions of the highlands of Scotland, or the rocky coast of Cornwall, or the mountains of Wales. The gods and goddesses of Celtic pagans were not a centralized pantheon of deities that everyone worshipped everywhere, but often were local deities, connected with a particular river, well, mountain, or rock, and honored only in the specific place associated with them.

When Christianity came along, many saints and holy men or women also became associated with particular places (such as Brigid in Kildare, Ireland, or Columba with Iona off the coast of Scotland). But many other lesser-known saints were honored in towns and villages throughout the Celtic lands. Some of these saints may well have been old pagan deities who were "Christianized" (transformed from god or goddess into the more acceptable form of saint). But even when the saints were historical persons who lived in the places where they are venerated today, the impact is the same: By honoring specific holy figures associated with a local places, Celtic spirituality retains a decentralized, multifaceted quality.

> **The Seer Says**
>
> When we think of "nature" in a big way (like "the earth" or "the universe") it tends to get lost as an abstraction. But when nature is approached in a more specific, localized way (such as this particular holy well or that particular saint's shrine), then it's easier to see the holiness inherent in nature herself.

How does this relate to nature? Quite simply: Because different places have different spiritual qualities, *place* itself has a unique spiritual value. This is important to remember. "Nature" is not an abstract quality, but always has a real place in the world of space and time.

The Land, the Sea, and the Sky

In Celtic mythology, the gods of Ireland (the Túatha Dé Danann, or peoples of the goddess Dana) came to Ireland in ships that descended from the sky. The Túatha Dé defeated a previous race of godlike beings who inhabited Ireland, only to subsequently be themselves defeated when the Milesians (the Celtic humans) came to the island at a later date. When the humans defeated the gods, the humans took control of the land above ground, while the gods retreated into a magical otherworld located underground, or over the water.

These basic elements of myth point to an understanding of the natural world as consisting of three realms: land, sea, and sky. The sky is the legendary home of the gods and goddesses, while the land is now the home of mortal men and women. The sea, which is the guardian to the magical otherworld, is the home of the old-gods-become-faeries and, in particular, of the ancestors and other heroes of the past.

The majestic Cliffs of Moher on the west coast of Ireland symbolize the union of the three great realms of nature: the land, the sea, and the sky.

Many spiritual systems from around the world understand the cosmos as consisting of three realms, usually a heavenly realm, an earthly realm, and an infernal or hellish realm. What makes the Celtic concept of land, sea, and sky so important is the assumption that no one realm is any better or more sacred than the others. Gods, goddesses, and spirits are associated with all three realms. As human beings, our job is to do our part in living a life in which the energies of all three realms—which is to say, the energies of spirit, nature, and humanity both present and past—exist in balance and harmony.

More About Holy Wells

One of the loveliest traditions found in the Celtic lands like Ireland, Scotland, and Wales is the practice of venerating holy wells—natural sources of water associated with healing or magical powers. In Ireland alone, it has been estimated that some 3,000 wells are regarded as sacred. (Exact numbers are impossible to determine, as many holy wells are small and known only in their immediate vicinity—there's that local characteristic of Celtic spirituality again.)

Why would a natural water source be considered sacred? For a number of reasons. A well represents the coming together of the three categories of land, sea, and sky. Put another way, the well (as water coming up from the Underworld to the surface of the land) can be regarded as a gateway to the spiritual otherworld. Finally, the waters of many wells have long been regarded as containing magical or healing properties.

St. Brigid's Well in Kildare, Ireland, is one of the most famous holy wells in the Celtic world. Today Celtic wisdomseekers come from the world over to pray and seek healing at this sacred natural site.

What Happens at Holy Wells

Visiting a holy well is like going on a miniature retreat. Many of the wells that are still venerated in the British Isles are set in lovely gardens with a peaceful, meditative atmosphere. Often the wells have been decorated with religious statues or outdoor altars. Many wells feature one or more trees nearby, where supplicants have tied clooties, or prayer rags, to the branches. Different traditions exist to explain the spiritual power of clooties. According to one tradition, as the clooties are destroyed by the weather, the diseases of those who have prayed at the well will be destroyed. Another idea holds that prayer rags are like time-release capsules: They hold the energy of prayer, which is then released into the spirit world over time.

When people visit wells, they often bring *votive* offerings. In modern days, such offerings often are Christian in nature: rosaries, statues of the Virgin Mary, mass cards, or other objects that symbolize reverence and devotion. Of course, coins are often offered, both directly tossed into the well or hammered into the trunk of the clootie tree. Such offerings are the modern equivalent of making sacrifices to the old gods and goddesses associated with the healing wells.

Many wells have particular rituals associated with them. For example, St. Brigid's Well in Kildare features a row of five stones leading to the well. Supplicants offer prayers at each stone, honoring spiritual virtues associated with the saint such as meditation, charity, and hospitality. For supplicants, making an offering, performing the ritual of the well, and simply praying and meditating all form part of the experience of venerating the sacred site.

Druidspeak

A **votive** object is something offered as fulfillment of a religious vow or spiritual pledge.

Venerating Your Own "Holy Well"

If you live in a traditional Celtic land, you probably have one or more actively venerated holy wells near your home. But if you are part of the Celtic diaspora living in a place like North America, chances are no such sacred site exists near you—at least, not officially. However, unless you live in the middle of the desert, there must be some sort of natural water source near you: the ocean, a lake, a river, a stream. Perhaps you have a well on your property, whether natural or man-made. Perhaps the headwaters of a river or a beautiful mountain stream are within driving distance of your home. With a little bit of investigation, you will likely find some sort of way to honor the water that flows near you.

How do you honor the flow of water in nature? Well, you don't need to do anything as elaborate as tying clooties to a tree or leaving an offering. (Indeed, unless the well you visit is actively being used as a holy site, do not leave material things, but rather make your "offerings" in a spiritual way.) Visiting the water source (if it's on private property, you'll need to get permission from the owner), taking time to meditate and pray, and thinking about the wonderful ways in which Mother Nature supports your life is all that's necessary. For "extra credit," take a trash bag and pick up any litter you find near the well.

If you don't have any way to access a natural water source, try setting up a water fountain in your home as a symbol of your love for nature. This artificial "holy well" can be a focal point for your prayers and meditation, and is simply a beautiful element for any room in your house.

Walk Your Talk

Reverence for nature is a central feature of the Celtic path, but it's important to walk your talk—which is to say, do more than just think nice thoughts about nature or tell your friends how much you love Mother Earth, but actually put some effort into living your life in accordance with your respect for the land, sea, and sky. Here are two ways you can put your spirituality into practice.

♦ **Become familiar with the unique qualities of your bioregion.** Celtic spirituality has a local dimension. Whether you live in Cornwall or California, you're part of an ecosystem that is unique to your area. Study the flora and fauna of your land; get to know the geography, weather patterns, and water sources. Make note of whatever environmental problems are facing your region as well. Acid rain? Smog? Erosion? As you learn about the issues facing your own region, figure out what you can do to help protect the natural world at your doorstep.

♦ **Get involved with environmental protection.** From picking up litter on roadsides to river cleanup projects to political activism designed to promote eco-friendly legislation, you can put your Celtic spirituality into action in many ways. Like your mother taught you, dirty dishes and dirty laundry don't clean themselves. The same goes with a heavily polluted environment. When you get involved in ecological action, not only are you helping to create a better world for our children, but you are expressing love and honor for the Celtic tradition as well.

The Least You Need to Know

♦ The single most important element of Celtic spirituality is devotion to nature.

♦ Celtic wisdom regards nature as sovereign; in other words, nature is the ultimate source of all that we need to survive.

♦ Among the pagan Celts, many gods and goddesses were simply embodiments of the forces of nature; revering the gods can be seen as a metaphor for respecting nature.

♦ Many animals, trees, and plants are sacred to the Celts.

♦ One of the best ways to respect nature is by becoming familiar with the unique features and circumstances of your own bioregion, regardless of where you live.

Chapter 6

The Otherworld: Nature's Dance Partner

In This Chapter

- ◆ The inner life of nature
- ◆ Different dimensions of the spiritual world
- ◆ How to get from here to there
- ◆ Faery demographics
- ◆ The otherworld's role in the quest for wisdom

Shamans and druids were mystics of the natural world, and Celtic Christians used plenty of nature-based imagery in their poetry and prayers. But this profound love of the material universe is more than just a precursor to modern environmentalism. The Celtic tradition reveres nature because of nature's connection to a vast and magical spiritual universe, a world of wonders that exists parallel to the material world.

This spiritual dimension has had many names over the years. It's been called Faeryland or Elfland. It (or places within it) often has lovely and romantic names in Welsh or Gaelic, like Gwlad Haf ("Summer Land") or Tir na n'Og ("Land of the Young"). But of all the names associated with this mystical realm, the simplest is probably the best: the otherworld.

In this chapter you'll learn about some of the traditions and ideas surrounding this mythical realm, as well as discover ways to make contact with the otherworld in your own life and how such contact can further you along your quest for Celtic wisdom.

What Is the Otherworld?

The otherworld is simply the spiritual dimension of the universe we live in. It is not a different world, located far away in space or time. It's not like the Christian idea of "heaven," which is somehow infinitely above us, or "hell," which is infinitely below. Rather, the Celtic otherworld exists alongside and within all parts of the manifest, physical, matter-and-energy universe in which we all live out our lives.

Understanding the Concept

Here's a way to think of the otherworld. You have two aspects to your life: a body and a soul. Your soul exists both inside and outside your body: It's inside in the sense that it's connected to your mind, which functions within your brain; but it's outside in the sense that your soul can take a flight of imagination to be literally anywhere you wish. Thanks to your soul, the "universe" inside you is far larger than your physical body could ever contain.

Notes from the Otherworld

Did you know that hell takes its name from a Norse goddess? Hel was the Scandinavian goddess of the lower regions of the otherworld. It's important to remember that, in the pagan world, just because a realm is "below" (like hell) doesn't automatically make it "bad."

The relationship between the physical universe and the otherworld functions in much the same way. The otherworld is the inner, spiritual dimension of matter and energy. Thus, every stone, every tree, every well, every person, has its inner counterpart within the otherworld. And the otherworld is not limited by the physical universe: In addition to being the inner dimension of all things, the otherworld also contains anything that can possibly be imagined, including realms of unspeakable beauty and joy (as well as realms best left alone).

Its Significance to the Celts

This magical, mystical realm is not unique to the Celtic tradition. Indeed, most (if not all) spiritual traditions speak of some sort of spiritual dimension, such as the heaven and hell of Christian mythology. Most shamanic traditions see the world in terms of three realms: an Overworld, the Middle World, and the Underworld, an understanding of cosmology echoed in the Celtic reverence for sky, land, and sea. But what is important, to the Celts, is the *immanence* of the otherworld and the possibilities of interacting with it that are available to the average person.

Celtic myth and folklore abound with stories of faeries who walk among mortals, gods and goddesses who dwell just beneath the surface of the earth or just over the ocean's horizon, and mortals who travel to the otherworld, sometimes just for a short period of time, or other times never to return to ordinary life. Within the striking imagery of the otherworld can be found symbols and ideas that can teach us about what it means to be human and what it means to be wise.

Druidspeak

Immanence literally means "remaining within." It's a theological term used to suggest that God's presence is within the world—as opposed to transcendence, which suggests that God is far away. In a similar way, Celtic ideas of the immanent otherworld suggest that the spiritual dimension is very close to the material realm.

The Interweaving: The Otherworld as Always Adjacent to the "Real" World

Celtic artwork often features intricate designs showing colorful lines woven together in spirals, knots, and braided borders. This knotwork motif has become popular in recent years among jewelers, who create earrings and pendants with a Celtic theme. While such art and design can be enjoyed on its own as visually appealing, it also is a stirring symbol of the relationship between the material and spiritual worlds. Faeryland and the mundane universe are woven together, just like the strands in a Celtic knot. After all, every human being has his or her own portal to the universe within the soul. The otherworld, linked as it is to the realm of nature, is connected to every single molecule or atom that exists. You could call the otherworld "the soul of nature."

The Physics of the Otherworld: Oisín

As described in the myths of Ireland and Wales, the realm of spirit is a strange and mysterious place, not subject to the same laws of physics that govern the physical universe. To explore this idea, consider a story from the Irish tradition.

One day a group of magical hunters and warriors known as the Fianna stood on the western shore of Eire (Ireland) and saw a remarkable vision. What appeared to be a beautiful woman riding a powerful and majestic steed came toward them, riding on the surface of the ocean as if it were solid as land. The men stood in wonder until the woman came to the shore; and upon seeing her at close range, their amazement only deepened. For this woman's loveliness ran beyond the limits of mortal beauty; her luminous skin, velvety golden hair, and delicate features suggested she was a daughter of the gods.

The faery woman introduced herself to the Fianna as Niamh, a princess of Faeryland. She explained that she had come from the land of Tir na n'Og, which means the "Land of Youth." Years before she had seen one of the Fianna, Oisín, and had fallen desperately in love with him. Finally her father had granted her permission to come to the land of mortals and ask Oisín to return with her to Tir na n'Og, where he would rule as lord of that unearthly paradise forever.

Enraptured by her beauty, Oisín agreed, and climbed behind her on her mighty horse and rode with her, over the waves to the Land of Youth. There all was as she described it: The land was a flawless paradise, where health, prosperity, and love ruled the day.

> **Notes from the Otherworld**
>
> Although the themes of Oisín's story date back to the earliest writings of Irish myth, the details of this particular story come from the eighteenth century, written by a bard named Michael Comyn. Celtic myth and legend are a living tradition, and so stories may be a thousand years old—or they may be the creation of a storyteller alive today!

After a magnificent wedding, Oisín and Niamh settled down into a perfect existence without pain, disease, or aging.

Without a sense of earthly time, Oisín could not tell if weeks, months, or years had passed. But the day arrived when he felt a heaviness in his heart for Ireland and his companions. Seeing his yearning, Niamh offered him her horse to return to Ireland for one last visit. But she warned him that the island would not be as he had left it; and that he must not under any circumstances allow his foot or any other part of his body to touch the ground. He agreed to these conditions, and rode off alone over the sea, east to the land of his birth.

When he arrived in Ireland, Oisín found a land he could scarcely recognize. The people he saw looked small and puny compared to the mighty Fianna. He came across a few men struggling to lift a boulder. He asked them of news concerning the Fianna, and one replied, "There is no such thing as the Fianna. We have legends of such a band of men from 300 years ago, that is all." Oisín realized that centuries had passed during his sojourn in Tir na n'Og.

Mindful of Niamh's warning, he made no effort to dismount his horse, but offered to help the men move the boulder while remaining in his saddle. But as he leaned over to assist, a bridle broke and he fell to the ground. Immediately he began to age, making up for the 300 years that had passed since he last set foot in Eire—his hair became brittle and gray, his skin parched and wrinkled, his strength all but left him. Alarmed at this sight, the men sent for Patrick, for this was in the era of the coming of the new religion. Patrick and Oisín spoke briefly before the aged warrior died.

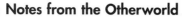

Notes from the Otherworld

A recurring motif in Celtic legend is the encounter between pagan gods or heroes (like Oisín) and Christian saints, often due to some sort of magical time warp. Since these stories were written by Christian monks, generally the pagan figures are shown as accepting the new religion. But not always: Oisín, in one version of the tale, refuses to be baptized, saying he would rather spend eternity in hell with the pagan heroes of old.

This story illustrates a number of interesting qualities associated with the otherworld:

◆ Time passes differently in the otherworld than in the physical world, and the passage of time does not have the same effect on aging there as it does here.

◆ Although there are ways to move between the worlds, there are limits to what is possible in regard to inhabiting both realms.

◆ Immortality is possible in the otherworld, but cannot be imported back to the physical universe.

◆ Although the otherworld may be filled with great joy and idyllic pleasure, it cannot fully satisfy the soul of a person who was born of the physical world.

A Geography of the Otherworld

Over the ages, many wisdomkeepers have described different realms within the otherworld. Through Oisín and Niamh you've been introduced to one of the loveliest sites in the mystical world, the Land of Youth, or Tir na n'Og. Here are some other places you might encounter as you read the myths or explore within your own inner connection to the faery realm:

◆ **Tir Taingire,** the "Land of Promise," a particularly heavenly aspect of the otherworld that appears in myth as the object of adventurers who would travel over the ocean in search of this paradise.

◆ **Tir na mBan,** the "Land of Women," is the ultimate heterosexual male fantasy: a realm full of sexy, available women, who attend to every need of the mortal men who find their realm. The myths often depict the pleasures of this place as ultimately hollow, suggesting that there's more to life than just the pursuit of sexual bliss.

◆ **Tech Duinn,** or the "House of Donn," is said to exist over the waves to the west of Ireland. This is the realm where the ancestors go after death. Donn, incidentally, is the Irish god of the dead, similar to Hades.

◆ **Gwlad Haf,** or "the Summerland." This poetic Welsh name for the paradise where souls go after death has been embraced by Wicca. Many Wiccans refer to life after death as the Summerland, even if they have no other connection to the Celtic tradition.

◆ **Annwn,** or "the Abyss" (the underworld). This was the spiritual realm located literally (or symbolically) beneath the earth. But this is not a hellish place of suffering; rather, it is a land full or marvels and joys, a magical variation on the aboveground world.

Gateways to the Otherworld

Spirituality is the process by which human beings seek knowledge, power, happiness, and healing, with assistance on "the other side." That could mean help from angels, departed loved ones, a divine being (God or Goddess), or a nature spirit. Religious and spiritual practices from around the world usually have this one theme in common: finding ways to access the spiritual realm, whether it is heaven up above or a magical realm deep within.

The Celtic wisdom tradition is no different. Celtic myth and legend contain hints about how to access the realm of the spirit; and universal spiritual principles also can help you open up to your own encounter with the otherworld.

The majestic prehistoric tomb called Newgrange, north of Dublin, has long been considered a portal to the mystic otherworld. In Celtic myth, several deities are associated with New-grange, including the Dagda (the good father god) and his son Aengus (the god of love).

Finding Our Own Apple Branch

An apple branch is sometimes used to symbolize the gateway to the otherworld in Celtic myth. The branch is offered to mythical heroes seeking spiritual enlightenment. The apple tree symbolizes eternity, beauty, and wonder, and the branch represents that magical place in eternity that is the source of all earthly beauty.

For Celtic seekers of our time, what "apple branch" can we use to find access to the otherworld? Here are a few ideas:

◆ **The imagination.** All gateways to the otherworld are ultimately symbolic and are designed to help open the one portal that truly matters: the one within your own soul. Within each of us lies the ability to visualize entry into the *imaginal* realm, where spiritual beings reside and wonders never cease. Indeed, all the symbolic gateways to the otherworld mentioned in this list are helpful in that they inspire us to make the *imaginal* connection.

> **Druidspeak**
>
> If something is **imaginal**, it comes out of the realm of imaginary or mental images.

◆ **Nature.** Gateways and portals in the natural world, such as the mouths of caves, natural springs or wells, or holes in aged tree trunks, appear as if they could lead into a faery realm. These symbols can, in the mind's eye, truly open up into a realm of mystery and magic.

◆ **Ritual symbols.** The Celts, like many other ancient cultures, revered powerful elemental symbols. Fire was sacred to the earliest Celts, as were natural sources of water, trees that symbolized the center of the cosmos, and the stones arranged in ceremonial circles and rows. Perhaps in the theatre of the mind, it is possible to swim through the water, or pass through the fire, or move around the tree or the stones to find an extraordinary world.

◆ **Ancient sites.** Stone circles, prehistoric tombs (like Newgrange), and cairns have in legend been regarded as places where the otherworld connects to mundane reality. Whether visiting such places in person or within the imagination, they can inspire a sense of connection to the spiritual world.

In the rest of this chapter (and indeed, throughout much of the rest of this book), you'll be invited to explore the otherworld for yourself. This can include encountering the otherworld through stories, myths, and legends, or in a more intimate way through meditation, visualization, and focused imagination. In this "imaginal" doorway to the realm of magic, you can encounter gods, goddesses, heroes, ancestors, and saints and interact with them (just as you do with anyone you encounter in a dream or daydream). If your religious and spiritual orientation is toward paganism, Wicca, or shamanism, such visualized interaction with the spiritual world can be a vital and enjoyable part of your spiritual life.

Are such imaginal encounters with the otherworld "real" or just a figment of our imagination? Many magic and shamanic teachers would argue that it doesn't matter—what's important is how interacting with the entities of the otherworld can put us in touch with wisdom and spiritual knowledge. Even if the otherworld exists purely in the imagination, it can be seen as a doorway into the riches of the unconscious mind.

Denizens of the Otherworld

Who lives in this fantastic realm? Again, whether it's "real" or "imaginary," the otherworld is teeming with life. All the ways of accessing the otherworld—whether through reading the myths and legends of the otherworld, journeying there yourself through dreams and visualization, or opening yourself to the experience of the otherworld through ritual—lead to encounters with the citizens of this magical land. In this section, we'll look at whom you are most likely to encounter when exploring the realm of faery.

The Seer Says

Because the normal rules of space and time don't apply to the otherworld, it's conceivable that an inner journey could lead to encountering gods and goddesses from cultures other than the Celtic nations. But if you want to work with just the Celtic beings, politely inform any non-Celts you encounter of your intentions, and keep your mind focussed on attaining contact with the Celtic deities.

Gods and Goddesses

The greatest beings in the imaginal realm are certainly the many gods and goddesses from throughout the Celtic world. Even though in history most of the Celtic deities had very specific homes (often tied to specific and localized features of the natural world), in the otherworld any deity in whom you are interested can appear. For that matter, deities in whom you have never shown an interest might pop up! Deities are identifiable by their magnificent appearance, their unmistakable power and might, and their attributes—for example, the Morrígan usually appears with a raven, while the Dagda generally carries a gigantic club, a cauldron, and/or a harp.

To learn more about the Celtic deities, see Chapters 13, 14, and 15.

Ancestors

Perhaps the most intimate and personally meaningful encounters you will experience in the magical realms involve ancestors, or beings from whom you are descended, whether biologically or spiritually. Such ancestral spirits may be close to you, such as your grandparents or great-grandparents, or distant relatives from thousands of years ago. Such beings may come to you offering wisdom, protection, or guidance; or they may be angry and want your help in seeking revenge or justice. However the ancestors approach you, treat them with respect and honor, and expect the same in return. As the living link in the family chain, you are important to your ancestors; of course, as your forebears, they should be important to you as well.

You'll explore the role of the ancestor in Celtic spirituality more deeply in Chapter 18.

Saints

Especially if you are a Christian, your "spiritual ancestors" in the Celtic tradition include the great saints of the Celtic church, such as Patrick, Columba, and Brigid. Like all ancestors, they come to us primarily through myth, lore, and the imagination. Although reverence for saints is generally considered a Catholic practice, in some remote parts of the Celtic world even Protestants express devotion to the saints who first practiced Christianity in the Celtic world, blending the teachings of the Bible with the optimism and nature mysticism of the Celtic tradition.

Faeries

By far the most common of otherworldly residents are the many types of entities known as faeries, the Good People, the Gentry, the Sidhe, or the Tylwyth Teg.

So many different theories are told of who the faeries are and where they come from. Some say they are the old gods and goddesses themselves, now banished to an underworldly/otherwordly existence; some say they are neutral angels who were cast out of heaven after God banished Lucifer and the rebel angels to hell; some see them simply as the spirits of nature, and others even speculate that they are extraterrestrials! No matter where the faeries may have originated, they appear in the otherworld as sentient beings related to the natural world in some significant way. Some faeries may have connections to the elements (especially water, earth, or sky), while others may have connections to specific plants, trees, or animals.

Perhaps the best way to approach the faeries is as if you're coming in contact with a personification of an aspect of nature. Just as nature can be wild or dangerous, faeries may be indifferent or even hostile to you. Be polite and respectful, allowing the faeries to interact with you on their own terms. Some of the Gentry are friendly, and it is those with whom you'll want to make contact.

More about the faeries can be found in Chapter 19.

From Banshees to Dragons: Magical Creatures of the Otherworld

Just as the normal laws of physics don't apply to the otherworld, the normal constraints of biology don't matter either. The inhabitants of the otherworld run the gamut of pretty much any kind of mystical, magical, mythical, marvelous, mysterious creature you can think of. From Celtic myth, we learn of spiritual entities such as the following:

◆ **Banshees** (in Irish, *bean-sidhe*), literally "woman faeries," faeries known for *keening*, or emitting wailing cries of grief at the impending death of a human being. To hear the banshee's cry often means that a death in the family could be imminent.

Druidspeak

Keening, said to have been created by Brigid, comes from the Gaelic word *caoíne*. It's a form of mourning for the dead characterized by loud wailing.

◆ **Leprechauns,** from the folk tradition, are said to be descended from the Irish god Lugh, the many-skilled one. These small entities are known for hoarding treasure, including the proverbial pot of gold at the end of the rainbow; they are also sometimes depicted as friendly, helpful spirits.

◆ **Pookas,** immortalized in the movie *Harvey*, are mischievous spirits that often appear in animal form. Although the pooka in *Harvey* was friendly, Celtic legend depicts them as unpredictable and sometimes even dangerous.

◆ **Boggarts,** from Scotland, are unpleasant spirits who can wreak havoc in a household. They are said to be dark, hairy spirits who wear ragged clothes and cause all sorts of mischief (like blowing out candles or knocking things over).

◆ **Selkies** were popularized in the film *The Secret of Roan Inish*. This folk shapeshifter is part seal, part human, suggesting an intimate link between humankind and the rest of the natural world.

◆ **Dragons** appear particularly in Arthurian folklore; as a young boy, Merlin the Magician is said to have divined the existence of two powerful subterranean dragons whose fighting made it impossible for the king to build his castle. Incidentally, a red dragon is the symbol of Wales.

Like any other inhabitant of the faery realms, these magical beings symbolize powerful forces (for example, the dragon symbolizes fire, while a banshee symbolizes the very mourning she gives voice to), and—within the theater of our minds—can be sources of wisdom and insight in our meditations and inner journeys.

Plants and Animals

Because the otherworld is said to closely resemble the "real" world, in it can be found the same trees, plants, animals, birds, and insects that also inhabit the physical earth. Many of these otherworldly creatures appear in myth and folklore, carrying meaning through what they symbolize. For example, the salmon symbolizes wisdom, the horse symbolizes freedom, and the raven symbolizes war. Some animals are connected to specific gods and goddesses: The owl is related to the Welsh goddess Blodeuedd, the hound is linked to the Irish hero Cú Chulainn, and the raven is sacred to the Morrígan, goddess of war and sexuality. Sometimes the same animal will have different characteristics in different parts of the Celtic world; for example, in Wales the raven symbolizes protection and prophecy. In your meditative excursions into the magical realm within, you may encounter animals who can serve as sources of power and wisdom. This is a universal aspect of shamanism; for the Celtic tradition, the animals of myth and legend carry a particular set of meanings based on the stories that have been told about them over the years.

As for sacred plants, probably the most useful information is connected with the Ogham, the ancient alphabet used in Ireland and Wales. Traditionally, each letter of the Ogham is related to a tree or other plant, and carries magical and spiritual energies associated with it. You'll learn more about the Ogham in Chapter 23.

The Psychology of the Otherworld

When all is said and done, what should we believe about the otherworld? Is it just an imaginary playground that exists in each of our minds? Or is it an actual place, independent of human thought, where spiritual beings dwell? Certainly traditional views support the latter theory, while a more modernist, scientific perspective might prefer the "imaginary" view. Then again, cutting-edge disciplines such as transpersonal psychology or the new physics support the view that the otherworld has an independent existence that can be accessed through altered states of consciousness.

The question of how real (or unreal) the otherworld might be is perfect fodder for late-night sojourns in an Irish pub, but it's not the purpose of this book to take sides on the question of just how the otherworld really exists. Rather, acknowledging that it is a central part of the Celtic tradition, you simply need to know that it exists *on some level*.

Some people would say the point is not what we *believe* about the otherworld, but rather what we *experience* when journeying there. In other words, what's important about the otherworld is the way it can offer you insight into spirituality, wisdom, and personal growth. Does such insight come from a place beyond, or merely from some deep part of your own unconscious that you access through the image of the other-world? If the insight truly helps you to be a better or happier person, does its source really matter?

So feel free to believe what seems right to you about the reality of the otherworld. If you are of a scientific turn of mind, it might be helpful to regard the otherworld as a metaphor. The word "metaphor" literally means "to carry over," and the otherworld is a traditional symbol that we use to carry wisdom over from the spiritual (or uncon-scious) world, to ordinary, conscious reality.

Making a Difference

The bottom line about the otherworld is this: It can make a difference in your life. If you open up to this magical and mysterious world, you can be changed in many ways. As you will see throughout the chapters to come, so much of Celtic spirituality lies in turning to the otherworld for guidance, and then applying the wisdom received in practical ways to life. Because of this, the otherworld may be thought of as the "com-mand center" for the acquisition and use of Celtic spiritual knowledge.

The Least You Need to Know

◆ A central motif in the Celtic tradition involves the existence of a magical realm called by many names, but best known to us as the otherworld.

◆ You can enter the otherworld in ways found both in nature (like caves or wells) or in the mysteries of your own mind (through meditation and visualization).

◆ Residents of the otherworld include gods, goddesses, ancestors, faeries, saints, and a wide assortment of mythical beings and spiritual animals and plants.

◆ The most important thing about the otherworld is not how "real" it is, but rather how experiencing it can make a positive impact on your life.

Part 2

The Three Paths

The depth and breadth of Celtic wisdom might best be captured by the concept of the druid. Druids were philosophers/priests of ancient times who even garnered the respect of world leaders like Julius Caesar. Druids (and druidism) have never fully died out, even after the Romans destroyed Celtic political power and Christianity converted the Celtic people away from paganism. Over the centuries, many attempts have been made to revive druidism; and because so little is known about the ancient druids, modern druidism is easily adapted to about any religious or spiritual system imaginable, from shamanism to paganism to Christianity.

The original druids may be shrouded in mystery, but thanks to classical writers, we know a little bit about this venerable order. One description of the druids of old suggests that they formed three orders: in addition to druids proper, there were bards (singers/storytellers) and ovates or seers (psychics/prophets). With the druids as philosopher/scientists, this makes for a powerful system of exploring wisdom, in which each person could pursue his or her particular gifts and talents.

Chapter 7

Singers, Seers, and Sages

In This Chapter

- ◆ The song of the first Irish druid
- ◆ Finding your unique wisdom path
- ◆ The bards and the gifts of the past
- ◆ The seers, custodians of the future
- ◆ The druids, keepers of wisdom

In this chapter you'll learn about three primary archetypes, or patterns, to follow when seeking the Celtic mysteries. These archetypes are derived from insights that classical writers had about the druids in Gaul (modern-day France) in the first century of the Common Era. They are three orders of wisdomkeepers: the bards, the ovates (seers), and the druids. In ancient times, these three archetypes may have represented three different orders into which young people would apprentice. It's also possible that the distinctions between bards, seers, and druids were less formal, and that one person might embody characteristics of two or even three of these archetypes.

However the ancients understood the roles of these three functions, for today's seeker they represent pathways of growth and development; each person can choose which path best represents her or his personal interests and abilities. Perhaps you have what it takes to be a world-class bard, finding meaning in artistic skill and meaningful stories; or maybe you are a natural psychic, embodying the gifts of a seer; or you could have the keen mind and discerning intellect of a true druid. And then again, maybe you have a little bit of all three! This chapter will introduce you to each of the archetypes, and includes a little quiz to help you find which Celtic path(s) is right for you.

"Song of Amergin"

To begin our journey into the world of bards, seers, and druids, let's begin by looking at one of the most famous of wisdomkeepers in Irish myth: Amergin.

It is said that when the Milesians (who, according to some scholars, symbolize the Celts) first came to Ireland, one of their number, Amergin, recited the following poem when he first set foot on the land of Eire (Ireland):

> I am the wind that blows upon the sea,
> I am the ocean wave;
> I am the murmur of the surges;
> I am seven battalions;
> I am a strong bull;
> I am an eagle on a rock;
> I am a ray of the sun;
> I am the most beautiful of herbs;
> I am a courageous wild boar;
> I am a salmon in the water;
> I am a lake upon a plain;
> I am a cunning artist;
> I am a gigantic, sword-wielding champion;
> I can shift my shape like a god.
>
> —Translated by Charles Squire

The Three Paths of Celtic Wisdom

In the "Song of Amergin," three distinct ways of relating to the spiritual world may be discerned:

◆ First, the song is filled with imagery from throughout the natural world, illustrating the singer's claim to be a gifted shapeshifter: a shaman. Only through the visionary skills of a shaman could Amergin have known the experience of being the wind on the sea, the eagle on a rock, a courageous wild boar, and other elements of nature. So the first path of wisdom in the "Song of Amergin" is the path of spiritual experience that seems related to the psychic adventures of medicine men and women in many cultures.

♦ The second path is encapsulated in the phrase "I am a cunning artist," testifying to the role that creativity plays in the pursuit of wisdom. The quality of "cunning" suggests that language and knowledge are as important as visual image in the life of the spiritual artist. This path of sacred creativity is related to the special role that mythology, storytelling, poetry, and other forms of sharing traditional wisdom play in spirituality.

The Seer Says

Replace every "I am" in "The Song of Amergin" with "You are," and the song becomes a powerful and beautiful prayer, suitable for venerating any of the Celtic gods.

♦ Finally, the third path of the "Song of Amergin" is found in the last line, "I can shift my shape like a god," raising the stakes of spiritual experience expressed in the song: This is not merely about becoming one with nature or accessing the words of knowledge, but this song culminates in finding union with the divine. This speaks to the role of priests in spiritual traditions, who intercede with gods and goddesses (or the primal energies of the land) on behalf of the people they serve.

Psychic experience, cunning creativity, and priestly interaction with the gods: These are three essential roles of wisdom that can be found throughout the Celtic tradition.

What the Classical Writers Had to Say About the Druids

One of the most succinct comments made about Celtic wisdomkeepers in ancient times came from the pen of a Greek geographer named Strabo, who said that among the Gauls "there are generally three classes to whom special honor is paid: the bards, the ovates, and the druids." (*Geographica*, IV, 4) This tripartite division of the Gaulish wisdomkeepers has captured the imagination of Celtic seekers—today, many druidic orders use the "grades" of bards, ovates, and druids to signify the stages of acquiring spiritual wisdom, while others see in these three types of wisdomkeeper a central idea of Celtic spirituality: That psychic development, historical information, and priestly leadership are different, but complementary, doorways into the mysteries of the Celtic tradition.

CAUTION

Geasa

Remember that Celtic culture covered a wide terrain and involved many different tribes and peoples. No one model of Celtic spirituality necessarily applied to all the Celts.

Celtic Quiz: Which Path Is Right for You?

The following quiz is designed to match your personal interests and inclinations with the spirituality of the three branches of druid wisdom. Please note: This is not a scientific test, but rather a tool for you to use to discover where you might fit in within the world of Celtic wisdom. Just because you score highest in one area or another doesn't mean you couldn't also enjoy learning about the other branches.

Directions: Select the best choice for each question. This quiz is looking for your preference, so even if more than one answer appeals to you, go for the one that seems most right for you. There is no time limit, but try not to agonize over the questions; simply trust your intuition as you answer each question. Instructions for scoring the test follow the questions.

1. Which of the following subjects is most appealing to you?

    a. History

    b. Psychology

2. Which of the following bothers you the most?

    a. Famous musicians who destroy their talent with drug abuse

    b. Scientists who insist that spirituality is just a load of bunk

    c. Fraudulent psychics, because they give real psychics a bad name

3. Which of the following most accurately describes you?

    a. I like to keep my spirituality as unstructured as possible

    b. I enjoy rituals and ceremonies in my spiritual life

4. A friend of yours says she can communicate with spirits. What do you do?

    a. Ask her questions to see if she's for real

    b. Ask her to teach you how to do it

    c. Secretly think that she'd make a colorful character in a story

5. Which word most clearly describes you?

    a. Creative

    b. Thoughtful

6. If you knew you couldn't fail, which career path would you choose?

    a. Quantum physicist

    b. Novelist

    c. Parapsychologist

7. Which of the following are you more comfortable with?

    a. Speaking in front of an audience

    b. Singing, dancing, or playing music in front of an audience

8. If you could talk to the president, what would you suggest to him as a means to guide his actions?

    a. You'd tell him he should trust his intuition

    b. You'd tell him he should keep his highest principles in mind

    c. You'd say he should follow the example of the great leaders of the past

9. Which of the following statements most closely reflects your beliefs?

    a. Truth is stranger than fiction

    b. Imagination is more important than knowledge

10. What do you think is the best way to teach a child important truths or values?

    a. Help the child learn to trust his or her inner guidance—after all, truth ultimately comes from within

    b. Tell the child a story with a moral that illustrates the principle

    c. Encourage the child to develop abstract reasoning skills so that he or she can mentally grasp the principle

11. Who impresses you more?

    a. A clairvoyant who successfully predicts the future

    b. A musician who holds an audience spellbound

12. Which party would you be most interested in attending?

    a. A gathering of musicians, storytellers, and artists

    b. A gathering of counselors, astrologers, and *dowsers*

    c. A gathering of ecologists, politicians, and college professors

13. Are you more of a talker or a listener?

    a. More of a talker

    b. More of a listener

Druidspeak

A **dowser** is a person who uses psychic means to locate water or lost objects, or uses tools such as a pendulum to seek spiritual guidance.

14. If you were a member of a nonprofit organization, where could your volunteer efforts be best put to use?

    a. Public relations

    b. Administration

    c. Research and development

15. Which word most clearly describes you?

    a. Intuitive

    b. Intelligent

16. Which "eternal value" is most important to you?

    a. Goodness

    b. Truth

    c. Beauty

17. Would you rather be a lawyer or a professional artist?

    a. Professional artist

    b. Lawyer

18. Which tool for predicting the future appeals to you the most?

    a. Astrology

    b. Tarot

    c. Neither

19. Which of the following is more important to safeguarding liberty?

    a. An independent judicial system

    b. Freedom of the press

20. Which pair of movies do you like the most (or are most interested in seeing)?

    a. *The Sixth Sense* and *2001: A Space Odyssey*

    b. *A Beautiful Mind* and *Gandhi*

    c. *What Dreams May Come* and *The Wizard of Oz*

21. What's the best way to approach the future?

    a. Plan carefully

    b. Simply embrace it

22. What, for you, would be the easiest way to achieve an altered state of consciousness?

    a. Meditation

    b. Listening to a steady drumbeat or some other droning sound

    c. Focusing your attention on a challenging mental puzzle

23. Which word most closely describes you?

    a. Visionary

    b. Entertaining

24. Which famous person from history would you most like to meet?

    a. William Shakespeare

    b. Nostradamus

    c. Winston Churchill

Your Score

In the Bard column in the following table, give yourself one point for each of the following answers:

1: A; 2: A; 4: C; 5: A; 6: B; 7: B; 8: C; 10: B; 11: B; 12: A; 13: A; 14: A; 16: C; 17: A; 18: B; 19: B; 20: C; 22: B; 23: B; 24: A

In Seer column, give yourself one point for each of the following answers:

1: B; 2: C; 3: A; 4: B; 6: C; 8: A; 9: B; 10: A; 11: A; 12: B; 13: B; 14: C; 15: A; 16: B; 18: C; 20: A; 21: B; 22: A; 23: A; 24: B

In Druid column, give yourself one point for each of the following answers:

2: B; 3: B; 4: A; 5: B; 6: A; 7: A; 8: B; 9: A; 10: C; 12: C; 14: B; 15: B; 16: A; 17: B; 18: A; 19: A; 20: B; 21: A; 22: C; 24: C

Now, tally your scores:

	Bard	**Seer**	**Druid**
Score	_____	_____	_____

Your score should range between 0 and 20 in each category. The higher the score, the higher your interest in that particular branch of Celtic wisdom. As a general rule, a score of 12 or higher indicates a strong interest in that path; a score of 6 to 11 indicates a moderate interest; while a score of 5 or less indicates little interest. Of course, a low score doesn't mean you can't benefit from studying that particular branch, but it may mean that you would need to make an extra effort to master the skills of that particular category.

If all your scores are "moderate," this suggests one of two possibilities: Either you are a generalist who will find pleasure in learning as much as you can about each of the different ways to express Celtic spirituality, or else you may not yet have a clear sense of which of the three paths is the best for you. If that's the case, learning more about Celtic wisdom may help you identify which branch is right for you.

> **CAUTION**
>
> **Geasa**
>
> This quiz isn't meant to lock you into only one way of experiencing Celtic spirituality, but to help you assess which path may be *most* interesting/ appealing to you. Whatever your results, take time to learn and enjoy the spiritual lessons of the other paths.

Even if you clearly prefer one path over the others, be sure to read about all three paths in the following chapters. The different paths of Celtic spirituality complement one another beautifully, and even if you are the most dedicated of bards or the most visionary of seers, you'll still benefit from understanding the qualities associated with the other paths.

One final note: Some druid organizations, such as the Order of Bards, Ovates, and Druids, present these three branches of Celtic spirituality as a hierarchical program of study. You have to complete the Bardic grade before moving on to the Ovate grade, which in turn must be mastered before studying at the Druidic level. Although this can be a useful way to organize a comprehensive study program, it does not necessarily reflect how the ancient Celts understood the relations between bards, seers, and druids. In other words, think of each path as equal to the others in terms of importance and value. No branch is "higher" or "lower" than the others.

The Bards: Keepers of the Past

Traditionally, a bard was a poet or a minstrel. Myths depict some bards as itinerant troubadours who traveled from place to place, sharing news and reciting their songs for every new audience. Other bards were attached to specific kings or chieftains, and made a career out of singing the praises of their patrons. The words of a bard were considered to be magical—they could enchant their listeners, and could even cause physical harm with their satires! Bards were the journalists, historians, critics, and performing artists of the ancient Celtic world. Today's bard would embody similar qualities, using literary or perhaps even artistic skills to weave a spell of enchantment around their listeners or readers. But a bard doesn't write poetry or sing songs just to entertain—he or she recognizes that the ultimate role of magic is to foster spiritual transformation, and so uses his or her skill to help others in their quest for spiritual growth. (For more about the bards, see Chapter 8.)

The Ovates: Keepers of the Future

Perhaps the most mysterious of the three orders, the ovate can be seen as the spiritual descendent of the earliest shamans and an ancestor of modern day psychics, diviners, counselors, and visionaries. The word "ovate" is related to the Indo-European word for mental agitation and prophecy, implying that this skill is related to entering altered states of consciousness, through which spiritual information from the otherworld may be retrieved. This is the classic job description for a shaman of any culture; an ovate, as a Gaulish shaman, would work primarily with the energies, deities, and ancestors of the Celtic peoples and lands to gain the desired spiritual knowledge, wisdom, and prophecy. The ovates would have been responsible for initiatory (death-rebirth) processes, of rites of passage, and rituals of transformation. Ovates were healers and psychopomps (shamans who aided people in the death process). In today's world, an ovate would be anyone dedicated to increasing psychic or shamanic ability and developing spiritual skills such as divination, prophecy, and trance. (For more about the ovates, see Chapter 9.)

The Druids: Keepers of the Present

The average person on the street may dismiss druids as ancient tree worshippers, but historical evidence points to this order as being far more than the world's first New Agers. The druids were the intellectuals of Celtic society; they were the scientists, philosophers, lawyers, judges, mediators, psychologists, and theologians. Just as warriors were the muscles of a society, so the druids were the brains.

Although it's reasonable to see the druids as priests (because in ancient times, there wasn't a distinction between "religion" and "science" such as exists in the modern world), it's important to think of them as intellectuals who also were spiritual leaders, rather than the other way around. Druids were often depicted as serving kings and chieftains, and Caesar regarded the druids as a serious obstacle in his quest for military victory over the Celts. Even though the free Celts of Gaul and the British Isles lived in tribes without any central government, druids had authority that extended across tribal/communal boundaries. Caesar certainly saw the druids as a large threat, because they were the only members of Celtic society who might have united the various tribes to resist Roman rule. These points remind us that, in ancient times, the druids carried much authority in their communities, not only spiritually but politically as well.

Of course, today's druid orders are small, private organizations with little or no direct influence in the outside world. But this doesn't mean that today's druids have no power. They just have to exercise their power in unofficial ways. Today's druids can include anyone who seeks to develop their mind to the fullest capacity possible, and then use that skill in service of others. (For more about the druids, see Chapter 10.)

The Least You Need to Know

- In the first century, Celtic intellectuals were described as having three different functions: bards, seers (ovates), and druids.

- The path of the bard is especially appropriate for people who love language and creativity, find meaning in the past, or enjoy the enchanting powers of music.

- The path of the seer is especially appropriate for people with intuitive or psychic abilities, or who have what it takes to be a gifted counselor.

- The path of the druid is the path of rigorous learning, covering science, law, politics and philosophy, as well as spirituality. This is the path for the person who seeks wisdom through knowledge.

- Today's wisdom seeker can follow one, two, or all three of these paths.

Songs and Stories: The Path of the Bard

In This Chapter

- ◆ Creativity: the heart of the bard
- ◆ Great bards of yesterday and today
- ◆ Beyond poetry and music: other ways to be a bard
- ◆ Giving birth to your own spiritual genius

For many people, the word *bard* means nothing more than a nickname given to William Shakespeare. But in the world of Celtic wisdom, the path of the bard is as old and honorable as the path of the druid. Indeed, from the ecstatic musicians of old, to the many performing artists, writers, and storytellers who have kept the Celtic fires burning up to the present day, the tradition of the bard is central to this wisdom tradition. This chapter will explore the history of the bard, look at some great bards over the ages, and help you to find your own bardic path.

The Quest for the Imbas: Fire in the Head

In Chapter 4, you learned about Awen, the Welsh concept of "flowing spirit" or "poetic knowledge." As you explore the bardic path, remember that the bard is dedicated to allowing the Awen to flow through him or her. And now it's time to learn another important Celtic concept: the notion of *imbas*, or "poetic knowledge."

Imbas is that mysterious place where knowledge and talent convene. It's more than just raw talent, for it implies a depth of spiritual insight and awareness that even the most talented poets in the world might never achieve. But it's also more than just otherworldly intelligence. Imbas is related to a method of divination called *imbas forosnai* (see Chapter 23 for more about this and other methods of Celtic divination), but the medieval writer Cormac noted that imbas forosnai was practiced by an Irish order of psychic poets called the filid.

Imbas for Today

How can a seeker of Celtic ways find the talent/knowledge of imbas in today's world? Alas, the ancient authorities didn't leave detailed information about the pursuit of imbas, but in our day, we can walk the path of the bard—which is the path of imbas— by doing two essential things:

- ◆ Dedicating ourselves to the pursuit of artistic excellence, in whatever our chosen media may be.

- ◆ Dedicating our creativity and artistic work to our spiritual goals; in other words, we create as a way of showing devotion to the divine, the ancestors, and the land, and by doing so seek to keep the Celtic vision alive.

This, then, is the heart of the bard: the performing artist (or some other creative person) whose art celebrates the wisdom of the Celts. Especially among modern neopagans, many students of the bardic tradition focus specifically on the poetic or musical qualities of the bard's path, following in the tradition of the bards of old who expressed their creative magic through poetry or music. But another way of approaching the bardic path today could include a more inclusive approach to the relationship between spirituality and artistic creativity. Thus, today's "bard" might dedicate any artistic endeavor to spiritual purposes. After all, not everyone is a gifted musician or poet, but everyone has some sort of talent. That talent can be used for purely selfish means or can be offered up to the spiritual betterment of all. It is in that "offering up" that the heart of the bard may be found.

Keepers of the Vision

On a stormy day in June 2002 I visited the windswept island of Arainn (Inishmore), off the west coast of Ireland. There I met with a man who is an activist dedicated to preserving the Irish language and traditional Gaelic culture. We spoke for most of the afternoon about the spiritual heart of traditional Celtic ways. At one point I asked him how he would define a bard. He said, "A bard is the custodian of an alternative vision. He or she helps us to see that the world is not just the way that the government or the church or big business wants us to think it is."

Such an alternative vision cannot be captured in the pages of a book, or even in any one work of art. But true bards, both through their artistry and (even more importantly) in the spiritual and wise manner in which they conduct their lives, are dedicated to seeing the possibilities for a better world, and communicating those possibilities to others.

Taliesin: The Quintessential Bard

In your journey to understand the soul of the Celtic bard, there's no better way to begin than with the story of Taliesin, who has been called the primary or chief bard of Britain. Taliesin's story can be found in some versions of the *Mabinogion*, the great anthology of Welsh myth. What follows is my retelling of this ancient tale.

The Story of Gwion Bach and Ceridwen

Once upon a time, a powerful sorceress named Ceridwen, who was part witch and part goddess, had a son named Afagddu who was hideously ugly. Ceridwen loved her son and wanted to give him a gift to compensate for his grotesque appearance. So she began gathering herbs from all over the world to brew a special potion that would bestow all the wisdom of the world. The recipe called for the brew to be stirred constantly for a year and a day, so Ceridwen commanded a servant boy named Gwion Bach to stand at the cauldron, ceaselessly stirring the boiling liquid within.

It was the very last day before the potion would be ready, and as Gwion stirred, a few drops bubbled up and singed his thumb. Without thinking, he put his thumb in his mouth to soothe it, and so ingested the wisdom of the world! Because the potion could only be used once, the cauldron exploded, the rest of the liquid within it now a noxious poison. Gwion, now gifted with supernatural vision, could see Ceridwen, far away gathering her herbs. She, gifted with her own psychic powers, realized what had happened and returned in haste to punish the boy.

Fearing for his life, Gwion used his newfound knowledge to shapeshift into a hare, so that he might escape Ceridwen more quickly. But she used her own skill to transform into a greyhound and pursued him. He then morphed into a fish and dove into a nearby river; she turned into an otter, still vigorously pursuing the boy. The fish swam to the surface and shapeshifted again, now becoming a bird that flew away. But the otter became a hawk, seeking the bird relentlessly. Gwion, now tiring, landed in a farmyard and transformed himself into a single grain of wheat. But Ceridwen landed on the yard and turned into a hen, and ate her fill of the wheat, swallowing the boy in the process.

But Gwion Bach was not dead. Soon Ceridwen realized she was pregnant, and resolved to kill the child as soon as he was born. But when the birth occurred and she saw what a lovely child he was, her maternal instincts overpowered her anger and she couldn't bear to destroy him. So instead, she put him in a leather sack and cast him into the river, leaving his fate to the forces of the elements.

Down the river was a poor fisherman and his wife who had almost nothing to their name. One day the fisherman found a leather bag floating in the water, and on pulling it out, saw the baby with a radiant face within. Taking the child to his wife, they decided to name him Tal Iesin, which means "radiant brow." From that day on, their fortunes changed, and as the boy grew up, his beauty only increased. He always had a faraway look in his eyes and always sang songs and composed the most spellbinding poetry. And when Taliesin came of age, he went to the court of King Arthur, winning fame throughout the land for the enchanting beauty of his words and songs.

> ### The Bard's Bookshelf
>
> John Matthews's *The Song of Taliesin: Tales from King Arthur's Bard* (Quest Publishing, 2001) is a collection of mythic stories and poems from Celtic lore, some of which are attributed to the bard himself.

> ### Notes from the Otherworld
>
> Although Ceridwen may seem to come across badly in the story of Taliesin, she is regarded as a powerful, if dark, goddess. Her cauldron is the cauldron of rebirth, and for all her fearsomeness, she is a loyal mother (after all, she was making her potion for her son, and despite her anger at Gwion Bach, she couldn't bear to kill him once he

The Lessons of Taliesin

What can we learn about the path of the bard from Taliesin? Here are a few ideas:

- **Talent and wisdom are gifts.** Gwion Bach did not ask to be the servant boy responsible for stirring Ceridwen's cauldron, but his fate put him in position to receive the wisdom contained in the drops of burning liquid. Likewise, he didn't ask for the shapeshifting powers that he used while trying to escape Ceridwen—his skills were given to him. In a similar way, each of us has gifts and talents that are given to us, just by virtue of being alive.

◆ **If you don't use your talents, you could die.** Obviously, with the anger of Ceridwen impelling him on, Gwion knew that he must exercise his abilities or else he would be killed. Your situation (hopefully) isn't nearly so dramatic, but the message is a universal one: Our skills and abilities aren't just for show; they are intended to better our lives. Likewise, spirituality isn't just a hobby, but is a tool for healing and for preserving the earth and her children.

◆ **There's a relationship between art and magic.** Taliesin didn't just write nice poems and sing catchy tunes; he could enchant his listeners, leaving them spellbound by his performance. In other words, as a bard, there was a distinctive magical element to his artistry. Magic, of course, is the spiritual tool for creating changes in life. (You'll learn more about magic in Chapter 21.) In other words, what separates a bard from any other artist, poet, or musician is that the bard uses his or her skill not just to entertain, but literally to change the world.

Other Elements of the Bardic Tradition

In addition to the legendary bard born of Ceridwen, there was a historical Welsh figure named Taliesin who lived in the sixth century. But whether historical or mythical, Taliesin was hardly the last of the bards. Both Ireland and Wales have had living bardic traditions, surviving into the modern era and even up to the present day. Less formally, many poets, writers, and musicians have continued to embody the magic of the bards, even if they did not consider themselves to be bards.

The Filid: Survival of the Bardic Arts in Ireland

Medieval Ireland was the home of an order of psychic poets known as the filid. The filid were not just literary figures, but practiced divination and prophecy as well as their poetic arts. Many scholars believe the filid represent the survival of pre-Celtic spirituality into the Christian era.

Bards Among the Modern Druids

One of the loveliest features of druidism as revived in the seventeenth and eighteenth centuries is the revival of interest in the bardic arts. Especially in modern Cornwall and Wales, modern druids have embraced the literary and artistic dimension

Notes from the Otherworld

Columba (or Colum Kille), one of the greatest of the Irish Christian saints who founded the great monastery on the island of Iona off the coast of Scotland, was said to have been one of the filid.

of their craft. Two concepts illustrate the depth of the bardic revival: The *gorsedd*, which means "throne" or "assembly place," refers to the practice among modern druids of gathering to share the artistic skill. When a gorsedd convenes, often the bards will engage in a competition called an eisteddfodd, from a Welsh word meaning "session." To this day, Wales sponsors an annual National Eisteddfodd, where Welsh musicians, poets, and other artists compete for prizes. This event combines respect for the ancient bardic path with modern national pride.

Bards of the Modern World: Harpists, Poets, Novelists, and Musicians

Finally, let's take a look at several figures from the Celtic lands over the last few centuries who truly embody the spirit of the bard. Whether or not these individuals would ever have thought of themselves as "bards" isn't the point—no matter what their self-concept may have been, the mystical dimension of their created work speaks for itself, placing them squarely in this ancient tradition:

◆ **Turlough O'Carolan.** A plaque in St. Patrick's Cathedral in Dublin calls Turlough O'Carolan (1670–1738) "the last of the Irish bards." Born in the heart of Ireland, O'Carolan was an intelligent boy whose promising future was devastated when he was blinded at age 18 by smallpox. In his day, few career options existed for the visually impaired, so his family arranged for him to learn music; after three years of lessons he began a career as an itinerant harpist, following in the footsteps of bards since the dawn of Celtic society. Fortunately, the upper class of his day patronized musicians like O'Carolan, who would receive food and lodging in exchange for entertainment or even a tune composed in the host's honor. In the mansions of the wealthy, O'Carolan became exposed to the European baroque music popular in his day; it influenced his compositions, which blended classical and folk elements to create a uniquely Irish sound. Like other folk musicians, O'Carolan never wrote down his music; fortunately, other harpists kept his melodies alive, and today more than 200 tunes attributed to O'Carolan have been documented. Much folklore has grown up around the harpist: It is said that he received much of his inspiration from the faeries, and that some of his more unusual melodies (like the haunting "Planxty Burke") were taught to O'Carolan by the Good People.

Notes from the Otherworld

In the last decades of the twentieth century, many popular and traditional Irish or other Celtic musicians have recorded O'Carolan's melodies, making his music widely accessible to a new generation of Celtophiles. Some of O'Carolan's modern interpreters include the Chieftains, Joemy Wilson, and Shelley Phillips.

◆ **Lady Gregory.** Lady Isabella Augusta Gregory (1852–1932) was the young wife of an aristocrat who was widowed at age 40; after her husband's death she launched a remarkable career as a playwright and folklorist. She was at the center of the Irish literary revival, which also included such notable figures as George Bernard Shaw and William Butler Yeats. But to the student of Celtic wisdom, Lady Gregory's greatest contribution is her numerous collections and translations of Irish legends, myths, and folk tales.

◆ **W. B. Yeats.** William Butler Yeats (1865–1939) came from a family of artists, but as a young man chose to pursue a literary career instead. He distinguished himself as an editor of the poetry of William Blake and a patron of the Irish theater, but his ultimate renown came as a poet, whose works such as "The Stolen Child," "Easter, 1916," and "The Song of Wandering Aengus" combine a deep Irish sensibility with a world-class poetic genius. His interests ranged from mysticism (he was a member of the famous magical Order of the Golden Dawn) to patriotism (a long-time Irish nationalist, he served in the Irish senate after the country won independence) to preserving Celtic culture and folklore, especially the mythology and faery tradition.

◆ **Dylan Thomas.** Thomas (1914–1953), a Welsh poet, did not speak the Celtic language of his homeland, but in works such as *A Child's Christmas in Wales* and *Under Milk Wood* brought a Welsh sensibility to his English readers (and listeners, he was a popular radio entertainer). His work covers a wide emotional terrain, from unabashed romanticism to ironic humor, while his virtuoso use of language marks how the legacy of the bards lived on in his work.

◆ **James Joyce.** Born in Dublin, Joyce (1882–1941) is celebrated as one of the towering figures in twentieth-century literature, and many scholars insist he alone stands next to Shakespeare as the greatest English-language writer of all time. But many others find his work so dense, idiosyncratic, neurotic, and self-absorbed that they cannot even read him, let alone consider him important. Indeed, his two final books, *Ulysses* and *Finnegans Wake*, are both challenging and intellectually demanding. These are not casual reads for a summer afternoon at the beach!

Right away, this points to Joyce's relationship to the Celtic tradition: As druids were the custodians of knowledge, so has Joyce made knowledge a prerequisite to understanding and appreciating his writing.

Joyce never embraced the Celtic renaissance that was championed by his older contemporaries Lady Gregory and William Butler Yeats. Instead, he criticized their embrace of Celtic mythology and folklore as a politically motivated stance that actually could undermine the place of Ireland (and Irish writers) in the world at large. But this doesn't mean that Joyce had no use for Celtic myth (or mythology in general). On the contrary, *Ulysses* explores how the ordinary activities of citizens in Dublin echo the universal themes from Homer's *Odyssey*, while *Finnegans Wake* explores a similar mythic world, only using themes directly from Irish folk songs and legends.

To Joyce, merely praising the past of Irish literature was narrow minded and ultimately did not serve Irish (or Celtic) interests. Instead, Joyce's writings explore how modern Ireland fits in with the larger world, using myth as a tool to illuminate universal truth. In that sense, Joyce deserves to be regarded as one of the greatest of modern bards (in the magical sense of the word), even though he himself would probably reject such praise.

> ### The Bard's Bookshelf
>
> Joyce's final masterpiece, *Finnegans Wake*, is based on Celtic myth but is extremely difficult to read. To get started with it, you'll want one or more guidebooks, like Joseph Campbell's *A Skeleton Key to Finnegans Wake* (Faber and Faber, 1947) or William York Tindall's *A Reader's Guide to Finnegans Wake* (Thames and Hudson, 1969).

Other Bardic Voices

Other Celtic artists deserve to be celebrated as embodiments of the bardic spirit in modern (and postmodern) times. Here's a sampling of the greatest of bards from the recent past up to the present:

- **The Incredible String Band (TSB).** This Scottish folk-rock outfit's music was steeped in pagan imagery, and their concerts were renowned as ritualistic communal events. Best-known albums include *The Hangman's Beautiful Daughter* (1968) and *The 5000 Spirits or The Layers of the Onion* (1967). Even after the ISB disbanded, one of its founding members, harpist Robin Williamson, has continued to embody the spirit of the Celtic bard through recordings and concerts that feature music, poetry, song, and story, much of which are based on traditional lore.

- **Seamus Heaney.** Perhaps the best-known Irish poet since Yeats, Heaney won the Nobel Prize for Literature in 1995. Imagery of nature and the environment feature strongly in his work.

- **Morgan Llywelyn.** A popular novelist whose work explores key points in Celtic history and myth, such as *Bard: The Odyssey of the Irish* (1989), which tells the story of Amergin; *Druids* (1991), recounting the story of Vercingetorix's final stand against Caesar; and *Red Branch* (1989), celebrating the exploits of the great Irish warrior-god, Cú Chulainn.

- **Van Morrison.** An Irishman whose bluesy music pairs a truly powerful and beautiful voice with lyrics that explore transcendental mysticism. Standout recordings include *Astral Weeks* (1968) and *Into the Music* (1979).

- *Riverdance.* One of the biggest hits of the 1990s, *Riverdance* combined Irish music and dance in a rousing celebration of the Celtic spirit. Featuring the music of Bill Whelan, *Riverdance* tells the story of the Irish people, beginning with the earthy paganism of the ancient past and leading up the diaspora that brought the Irish to every corner of the earth.

Samildánach: To Be Talented in Many Ways

According to a Celtic myth, a god named Lugh once approached the encampment of the Túatha Dé Danann, the primary tribe of gods and goddesses in ancient Ireland. At the gate of the camp, the guards asked Lugh who he was and what he brought to the encampment. Lugh introduced himself, and said he was a fierce and strong warrior. "We already have great warriors," said the unimpressed guard. Lugh added that he was also a gifted poet. "We already have eloquent poets," the guard replied. Lugh went on to list a number of other talents; each time, the guard noted that someone within the community already was a master of that particular art. Finally, Lugh said, "Do you have anyone who is a master of all that I am a master of?" To that, the guard had no answer, and so allowed Lugh to enter; he went on to become one of the greatest of the Túatha Dé.

Because of his many talents, Lugh was given the name *Samildánach.* As a many-talented god, today he is sometimes looked upon as a patron of the bards and the bardic tradition. Bards of old may have been poets or musicians, but today, following the example of Lugh, many talents may qualify as "bardic" skills.

Druidspeak

Samildánach means "possessor of many talents."

Traditional Bardic Arts ...

Here's an overview of some of the ways you can get in touch with your "inner bard." And remember, even if you're not a poet, storyteller, or musician yourself, you can still experience and support the bardic arts as a reader, listener, or audience member.

- **Music.** From Turlough O'Carolan to Van Morrison, music has always been the heart of the bard's art. To create song and melody is to weave a spell of enchantment where listeners can be lulled to sleep, roused to war, or seduced to lovemaking. Truly, music is a doorway into magic!

Gwen Knighton, harpist for the folk trio Three Weird Sisters, sings traditional ballads and modern compositions in the tradition of the ancient bards.

◆ **Poetry.** Perhaps poetry is just another form of music, where the words form the melody. The poetry of the bards was originally an oral poetry, and today's bards would do well not only to write poetry, but also find venues where it may be recited. Like music, poetry can weave a spell of enchantment and tell a story of remembering, helping the listeners to know their history and identity. Also, whether you write poetry or not, make an effort to read poetry or attend live readings by poets. Poetry is an underappreciated art form, so your support can make a real difference!

◆ **Storytelling.** We'll look at this art form more closely in Chapter 12. For now, let's just say that this folk practice of recounting legends and tales is the art form where oral tradition has survived to the present day, and it's the best hope for reviving a truly bardic tradition for the future.

... And Other Bardic Arts

Traditionally, bards were poets, musicians, and/or storytellers, who used words or music to weave spells of enchantment over their listeners and who were the historians of their people. Today's seeker of the bardic arts, however, might explore other forms of creativity besides those associated with the bards of old. After all, any creative art form can be "enchanting" or can convey spiritual or mythic truths. Thus, while not entirely traditional, here are a few other ways to enter into the world of the bard for our time.

◆ **Art.** Stunning visual imagery can be as enchanting as the most ethereal of music. Think of art as an illustrated doorway to the otherworld. This could include not only drawings and paintings, but also pottery, jewelry, quilting, or any other form of visual artistry. Celtic art was traditionally highly ornate and filled with intricate design elements such as knots, spirals, and whimsical depictions of animals—all elements still used by Celtic-inspired artists today.

◆ **Literature.** The earliest bards may have been oral artists, but that doesn't mean that writing doesn't have its own bardic element. Like James Joyce or W. B. Yeats, great magic can come to life in novels, short stories, or other written works.

◆ **Dance.** The thundering feet of the step-dancers in *Riverdance* were ecstatic to behold, but other forms of dance, both Celtic and non-Celtic, can also tell a story: from the graceful turns of a solo ballerina to the sensuous moves of a belly-dancer or the elegant simplicity of Scottish country dancing, this art form uses the human body itself to enchant.

◆ **Drama.** Drama is the place where literature and performance converge. There's one reason why Shakespeare was considered a bard: The stage is a setting for magic. (Of course, Shakespeare was truly a bard in the oldest sense of the word, for he was indeed a master of language as well as of the stage.)

◆ **History.** Maybe not an "art form," history is bardic because the ancient bards used their songs and poems to recount the story of the great kings and warriors of their people. Today, history reminds us of who we are.

◆ **Journalism.** Journalism is like history, only more immediate. The travelling bards kept people up to date on what was happening in the world. A journalist does the same today.

◆ **Genealogy.** The bards of old were the genealogists of their tribes, recounting the lineage of great kings, chieftains, and warriors. So when you climb your family tree here in the twenty-first century, you're helping to keep the bardic spirit alive.

◆ **Public speaking and teaching.** Because the bards were great storytellers, they were schooled in the art of public speaking; today's speakers (especially those who teach) embody a similar spirit of enchanting entertainment as a doorway to imparting wisdom.

> **The Seer Says**
>
> Look over these lists of the bardic arts. Which ones appeal the most to you? If you don't already take time to develop your personal creativity, begin doing so! Remember, you don't have to be a Mozart or a Shakespeare to enjoy expressing your own creativity. And don't just create your own artistry—support other artists and performers, too.

◆ **Library science.** Librarians may be quiet, behind-the-scenes kinds of people, but the work they do is vital to preserving the memory of the culture. In that sense, they are truly modern manifestations of the bard.

Nine Steps Toward Becoming a Bard

Do you think the bardic path might be for you? If so, then read on. Here are a number of steps you can take to begin fostering the spirit of enchanting creativity within your own life. Of course, as a spiritual pursuit, the way of the bard could never be codified in a simple step-by-step formula; so think of the following ideas as brainstorms to help you find you own unique path.

1. Make the Pursuit of Wisdom and Spirituality a Priority in Your Life

Pursuing the bardic arts doesn't excuse you from mastering the demands of Celtic wisdom and spirituality in general. I recommend you refer to Chapter 10 for insight into what it takes to walk the druid path. Skills such as study, meditation, spiritual discipline, and community building are all important parts of the druid way. As a bard, you'll incorporate these qualities into your path as well.

In ancient days, bards (like druids) were expected to study for up to 20 years before they were considered masters of their arts! So just because you're interested in the bardic path doesn't mean you can immediately proclaim to the world, "I am a bard!" Sure, you could call yourself an *aspiring* bard, meaning one who hopes someday to master the challenges of this spiritual path. But keep your ego in perspective. If you ever become a true bard, others will tell you so. Don't claim the name for yourself in the meantime.

2. Befriend Your Inner Genius

Perhaps the single most important quality of the bardic path today is creativity. A bard creates, whether that means creating beautiful works of art, telling creative stories, creating a particular feeling in the hearts of an audience, or creating closer bonds between the realm of the gods and the realm of humanity through his or her bardic skill. If this seems a little intimidating, that's understandable. We all have that little voice inside ourselves that whispers, "Who am I to dare to be a creator?" But we also have another voice within—the one that just needs to be set free. This is the voice that says, "Yes, I do have something to say." This is the voice of your inner genius.

You don't have to be a Mozart or a Michelangelo to be a genius (although who says you *aren't* the next Mozart? Always keep the possibility open). Think of your inner genius as that part of yourself that is naturally creative and expressive. Yes, there will always be the inner critic and the inner nay-sayer. But for now, let those negative voices take a vacation so that you can set the inner creator free!

Geasa

Don't let self-criticism or negative thoughts about your talent hold you back. Remember that practice makes perfect—no matter how humble your skills may be, if you love a type of artistry, do it and you'll get better at it.

3. Claim Your Gifts and Take Them Further

One of the most important steps on the path of the bard involves getting to know your unique creative talents. In days of yore, being a bard involved music, poetry, and storytelling, and certainly those are qualities every aspiring bard will want to explore at least on some level (see steps 4 and 7 for more on that). But a twenty-first-century bard might want to explore other forms of creativity and expression beyond just those traditional bardic art forms. Perhaps you are a gifted visual artist, with a hand for drawing, painting, or sculpture. Or perhaps you have an eye for sewing and clothing design. Maybe your skills tend toward dance or theater. Or you might even have one or more talents in areas not considered to be a "fine art" at all, but involve creatively nonetheless, such as interior or garden design, cooking, or event planning. What's important is not what kinds of talents you have, but rather your willingness to embrace them.

Although in its strictest sense, a bard is a storyteller/historian/musician/poet; the spirit of the bardic path is present whenever a person uses creative abilities of any form in the service of wisdom and spirituality.

Knowing your skills is only the first part of this step, however. Just knowing you are good at singing or storytelling (or some other form of creativity) means nothing without the discipline and commitment to hone your skills and take your talents as far as you can. Give yourself the gift of focus: Invest time in cultivating your talents so that they can truly blossom. (This helps explain why bards of old needed to prepare for up to 20 years: Any artistic skill requires years of dedicated practice and study in order for the artist to achieve his or her full potential.)

4. Play at Least One Kind of Musical Instrument

Okay, okay, I just said that a modern bard doesn't necessarily need to limit himself or herself to song and story. But that doesn't mean you should just ignore music. On a spiritual level, music is an integral part of life: The beauty and vibration of sound and song can support any spiritual seeker in his or her rituals or devotions. And if you participate in a druid or other spiritual group, you may find that your musical abilities can play an important role in the group's ceremonies.

Druidspeak

A **bodhrán** is a frame drum often used in Celtic traditional music. Celtic shamans may use bodhráns as a tool for creating a hypnotic beat for inducing trance states.

Again, don't compare yourself to Beethoven; just find an instrument that works for you and become a master at it. Even if you're intimidated by the intricate rhythms of the *bodhrán*, that doesn't mean you can't play a mean tambourine! Even just being able to keep a beat can be a powerful bardic skill!

5. Get to Know the History of Your People

Bards are keepers of the people's memory and custodians of the past. Traditionally, the role they played was similar to the role of historians and journalists. They were responsible for recounting the noble deeds of heroes and warriors and memorializing the noble dead. As a modern bard, you can carry on the great tradition of your bardic forebears by developing an in-depth knowledge of the Celts (or whoever your ancestors may be) and trying to understand the issues facing today's world in light of the lessons of the past.

As a bard, you'll want to do more than just learn the lessons of history. You can use history as a source of "raw material" for your artistic work, no matter what media you may use. You can write songs about history, or poems or stories; or you might paint historical murals or create a New Year's feast based on the foods that your ancestors ate in ancient times. Taking time to chart the genealogy of your family can be in itself a powerful bardic discipline. The possibilities are endless, limited only by your (bardic) imagination.

6. Get to Know the Myths That Shape Your Path

This is just an extension of step 5. History may be the realm of important names and dates from the past, but there's another realm that's equally (if not even more) important: the realm of imagination, spiritual fable, and myth. Although we can never "prove" any historical facts connected to gods, goddesses, and mythical heroes, we can find in their stories powerful spiritual lessons that can inspire our wisdom path today. Especially in druidic ceremonies or rituals, stories of the gods and heroes can be a powerful source of entertainment and spiritual insight.

As with history, learning the myths is not just an exercise for your own edification, but a valuable source to inspire your poetry and other creativity. Remember, when you spread the myths and legends to your audience, you are participating in a grand bardic tradition that goes back thousands of years.

7. Master the Art of Storytelling

Whether your particular style of bard is as a singer/harpist, a poet, an interpretive dancer, or a straight-ahead storyteller, you'll find that the skills of a storyteller will serve you well in your bardic practice. Storytelling is more than just being able to recount a beginning, middle, and end in the correct sequence. It is its own art form, which involves timing, diction, expression, and the ability to communicate suspense, humor, or other emotions. Organizations exist to help people learn the skills associated with storytelling, and storytelling conventions and festivals are places where you can meet the pros. Become accomplished at this art, and you will quickly develop a reputation as a master bard.

Related to this is a skill every bard needs: a disciplined, powerful memory. Ancient bards didn't write down their poems, songs, and stories, but memorized them all—by the hundreds! Sharpening your abilities to memorize will improve both your confidence and the quality of your bardic artistry.

> **The Seer Says**
>
> Want to sharpen your memory? Begin with a poem (a traditional rhymed and/or metered poem, that is). Poetry is the easiest literary form to commit to memory. Choose a favorite poem, memorize it, and then recite it (even to yourself); the reciting will help you evaluate how well you've memorized the poem, and, more importantly, recitation connects you with the bardic importance of utterance—the spoken word.

8. Ask for Divine Help

Remember, all of this developing creativity and finding your inner confidence as an artist is not just an exercise in personal gratification. What separates a bard from all the other talented artists in the world is her or his commitment to using artistic skill for spiritual purposes. Thus, an important element in the bardic path is maintaining a sense of connection to the spiritual world, including a sense of gratitude that your imbas is ultimately of divine origin.

How you do this will be a personal matter: You might meditate daily, or perform regular rituals, or make symbolic offerings to Celtic deities who are known as patrons of the bards (such as Brigid, the goddess of poetry). What matters is that in some way or another you keep the pipeline between your creativity and the spiritual world open; for as a bard, you'll come to see ever more clearly just how important otherworldly inspiration is to your creativity.

9. Put Yourself Out There

Finally, the day will come when you will need to share your creativity with others. This can mean reciting your poetry or singing your songs to a group of fellow Celtic seekers; or using your sculpture in a public druid ritual, or displaying your painting where it can be appreciated by others. Sometimes, this is the hardest step on the creative journey, and when the creativity is applied to spiritual topics, it doesn't get any easier. Once again, listen to your inner genius rather than your inner nay-sayer. You'll know intuitively when your creativity is ready to be shared. When you reach that point, don't be shy.

For many bards, the culmination of their spiritual discipline lies in helping lead public worship services or communal rituals. For Celtic Christians, this could mean singing in a church choir or performing a musical solo during a service. Celtic pagans might provide musical or poetic leadership in rituals for druidic, Wiccan, or other Celtic spiritual communities. This can be daunting at first, but it can also be a deeply rewarding experience as you see how your creativity (intended to honor the gods and goddesses of the Celts) can also help others in their spiritual journeys. Remember, this is not something you have to do all by yourself. If you are part of a spiritual community, simply volunteer to assist the group leaders in putting on ritual. As a bard, you don't have to be the star of the entire ceremony, but can play a part in the overall experience.

> **The Seer Says**
>
> Remember the lessons of childhood: "Say 'please' and 'thank you.'" In other words, always ask for spiritual guidance in your creativity, and always be gracious in offering thanks for the spiritual and creative gifts given to you.

The Least You Need to Know

- ◆ In the Celtic world, the bards were the custodians of the imbas, the knowledge and talent that comes from the spiritual world.

- ◆ Traditionally, bards were poets, musicians and storytellers/historians. Today, however, many people feel that any kind of artist can embody the spirit of the bard.

- ◆ Bardic inspiration can be seen in modern writers and musicians, such as W. B. Yeats and Van Morrison.

- ◆ The path of the bard can be seen as a path where you find spiritual meaning through developing your own unique creative talents and using them to share spiritual wisdom and knowledge with others.

Chapter 9

Psychic Development: The Path of the Seer

In This Chapter

- ◆ Contacting the spiritual realm
- ◆ The history of the ovate
- ◆ Some famous seers
- ◆ The fine art of spiritual self-defense
- ◆ Steps to awaken the seer within

For many people, the spiritual journey begins with the quest for knowledge. Such knowledge can take many forms including knowledge of the future, knowledge of the will of God (or of the Goddess), knowledge of one's soul purpose in life, knowledge to make sense out of life's trials and tragedies. Knowledge of this nature cannot be gleaned from a book (the realm of the druid) or a song (the realm of the bard). This spiritual knowledge can only be attained through direct contact with the spiritual world, seeking answers from beyond, answers from guides or messengers who come to us from the otherworld. In other words, this kind of spiritual knowledge requires the skill of a seer, shaman, or prophet.

There is nothing uniquely Celtic about this perennial quest for spiritual knowledge. Cultures and religions the world over include some form of quest for hidden information. But the Celtic world has long recognized that some people are naturally more gifted at the mystical pursuit of knowledge (in contrast to finding spiritual wisdom through scholarship or artistry)—thus, the path of the seer, the subject of this chapter. In the pages to come you'll learn about different kinds of seers throughout Celtic history, along with some insights into how you can cultivate the skills of a seer to benefit your life today.

What Is an Ovate?

Like most other elements of Celtic tradition, the ovate/seer's role has grown and evolved throughout history. In the following sections I outline a few ways of understanding the *vatic* function within the Celtic tradition. Incidentally, the word *ovates* is often translated into English simply as "vates," and these words mean essentially the same thing.

> **Druidspeak**
>
> **Vatic** means "concerning psychic ability," that is to say, concerning the abilities of an ovate or seer.

Classical Concepts

According to the classical writer Strabo, the ovates were students of nature and were diviners who interpreted the spiritual meaning of sacrifices. (*Geography*, IV, 4) In other words, Celtic seers found inspiration in two primary settings: in ritual and in the natural world. According to Caesar, druids presided over the sacrifices (rituals); Caesar may have been thinking of ovates as a subcategory of druids, or it may be that druids performed the function of high priest at rituals, while the seers supported the druids by providing prophetic and divinatory input into rituals. Although we'll never know the exact nature of the role of ovates and druids in the ancient world, one way to think of druids and ovates as complementary would be to see druids as the ones who speak on behalf of humanity to the gods in ritual, while ovates would be the ones who speak on behalf of gods to humanity. Thus, both roles are necessary for a ritual to be complete—which is to say, to fully express what needs to be communicated between mortals and gods.

The Seer in Myth

Many characters in Irish, Welsh, and Arthurian mythology function as prophets, psychics, or diviners. Many of these figures are not even necessarily identified as ovates, but by function we can identify them as such. Some of the best known of mythic seers include …

- **Merlin,** who functioned as a prophet at Camelot.

- **Cathbad,** an Irish druid who could accurately predict the destiny of a newborn baby.

- **Taliesin,** the Welsh bard whose story is told in Chapter 8. The transformation of Gwion Bach into Taliesin was a type of shamanic initiation that left him with godlike powers of wisdom and vision.

> **" " The Seer Says**
>
> Reading the myths helps the aspiring seer on several levels. Not only do myths recount the stories of great seers from the past, but as stories filled with wonders and marvels, they program the mind to envision the magic of the otherworld.

- **Fionn mac Cumaill** (sometimes spelled as Fionn McCool or Finn mac Cumaill or Fionn Mac Cumhail), a figure of Irish and Scottish lore who combined the visionary skill of Taliesin with the warrior prowess of King Arthur.

The Seer in Folklore

Unlike Celtic myths (which were preserved in manuscript form in the Middle Ages), Celtic folklore is a living tradition of tales passed down orally, many of which have been written down only in the last 200 years. The legends and stories from Celtic folklore are filled with tales of predictions, psychic dreams, and visions from the other side. Many folktales revolve around local heroes, Christian saints, fools who mess unwisely with the faeries, and legends that develop around historical figures, like Biddy Early or the Brahan Seer. Many folk tales don't have the same level of spiritual intensity as the older myths, but they still depict a world where the natural and super-natural worlds coexist and interpenetrate. This magical place where the worlds meet is the natural habitat of the Celtic seer.

The Seer Today

With the explosion of interest in Celtic shamanism, druidism, the mystical aspects of Celtic Christianity, and Celtic forms of Wicca, the ovate/seer is perhaps more popu-lar today than ever before. A person doesn't have to be a world-famous psychic or the graduate of an in-depth shamanic training program in order to walk the path of the seer. Indeed, anyone who opens his or her heart to listen to the spiritual wisdom that lies dormant within our bodies and souls, or that can be heard whispered on the wind among the trees, or that can be divined through extraordinary natural events or the casting of Ogham sticks, is walking along the seer's path.

The Elements of the Seer's Craft

So what, exactly, does a seer do? Of the three orders of Gaulish druids, the seer/ovate function is the one most directly connected with accessing wisdom from the otherworld. Bards gain their wisdom through history, while druids gain wisdom through philosophy and science; but seers appeal directly to the spirit world for the knowledge they seek. Thus, the tools of the seer's trade are all connected with ways of obtaining spiritual knowledge. These tools include shamanistic techniques such as trance, psychic exercises such as the second sight, and divination.

The Seer as Shaman

From Taoism to Native American spirituality to many African religions, shamanism is perhaps the oldest, core spiritual practice that forms the foundation of wisdom traditions around the globe. For Celtic seekers, shamanism represents the earliest forms of Celtic spirituality that can be discerned through archaeology and myth, but also is a key to understanding the role of the seer alongside the classical druids. Seers could almost be thought of as "religious" shamans—religious in the sense that they did not act alone, but performed their spiritual duties within the context of rituals and ceremonies presided over by the druid priests.

Notes from the Otherworld

Shamans usually practice their arts in tribal or indigenous cultures that have no organized religion. Scholars are divided in their opinion on how "organized" the ancient druids were. Some feel that druids may have been no more institutionalized than shamans in other tribal societies, while others see the druids as wielding significant social and political power, suggesting that they participated in an influential order within Celtic society. Either way, the seer function within druidry is the clearest survival of the shamanic origins of Celtic spirituality.

A number of contemporary writers, including Tom Cowan, Francesca De Grandis, Frank MacEowen, and John Matthews, have written about the profound shamanic qualities that lie at the heart of the Celtic tradition. Meanwhile, other Celtic teachers resist using the word "shamanism" to describe Celtic spirituality, since it is a Siberian term and may not accurately describe all the qualities of the Celtic path. On one level, this is a semantic issue; but it is important to remember that the idea of "Celtic shamanism" is essentially a twentieth-century way to explain the powerful themes within the Celtic tradition that are at least similar to primal spirituality from around the world. Trance, spirit contact, psychic healing, otherworld journeying, and powerful initiation experiences are all elements of shamanism the world over and figure prominently in Celtic tradition, as well. But what people in our time call shamanism may well have been thought of merely as the experience of the ovate or seer in an earlier age.

The Seer as Shapeshifter

Shapeshifting appears in a number of places in the Celtic tradition. In Chapter 7 you learned about Amergin, the druid poet whose immortal song speaks of his shapeshifting experiences. Likewise, the Welsh bard Taliesin exhibited the ability to shapeshift as he escaped the wrath of Ceridwen, turning into a hare, trout, sparrow, and even a grain of wheat!

One of the most remarkable examples of Celtic shapeshifting involved the warrior Cú Chulainn. As the mightiest of Irish warriors, Cú Chulainn would go into an altered state of being before battle that would bring about powerful mental and physiological changes in his body (among other things, one eye would shrink into his head while the other one would either grow massively large or else would pop out of his head, and blood would magically spout from the top of his head!), while focusing his mind into the fury of a finely honed killing machine. While in this state, Cú Chulainn was practically invincible, and deadly dangerous to anyone who got in his way, friend or foe.

> **The Seer Says**
>
> Taliesin was renowned as a bard, not a seer. He's an example of figures from Celtic myth who blur together the functions of bard, seer, and druid. Just a reminder that you can draw from all three of these traditions in charting your own course along the Celtic wisdom path.

It might seem odd to regard Cú Chulainn's fierce metamorphosis as an example of shamanic shapeshifting, but it reveals the depth of magical possibility that existed in the Celtic mind. Cú Chulainn's shapeshifting could be a metaphor for adrenaline-soaked rage, or it could be the dim memory of a warrior-hero whose prowess in battle was so awesome that to bystanders it seemed as if he really did transform into a monstrous killing machine. Cú Chulainn symbolizes the power of personal transformation—a power that enables him to access a level of skill beyond his normal abilities. In a similar way, seers are able to access transformational power in order to exercise their gifts of prophecy, divination, and spiritual healing.

The Seer as Psychic

Perhaps less frightening than Cú Chulainn's battle frenzy and less fantastic than Taliesin's metamorphoses is the long-standing Celtic recognition that psychic ability could transform ordinary people into extraordinary visionaries. Among rural Celts, the term for psychic prowess was "the second sight" or merely "the sight." A person with the second sight could have a variety of abilities. He or she might be able to predict death or other calamities, or might be able to converse with the dead. Although, as its name implies, the sight was understood to involve images (similar to what is commonly called *clairvoyance*), a seer might also receive information in other ways, through auditory cues or even just intuitive hunches.

Given that the word "ovate" seems to derive from the Indo-European root word for trance and prophecy, one of the qualities long associated with seership is the ability to prophesy, or predict the future. Such prophetic ability would extend not only to predictions about individual people, but also to large-scale prophecies about entire communities or regions. The Brahan Seer, for example, is said to have predicted the coming of such technological innovations as plumbing, gas lines, and the railroad—even though he lived in the seventeenth century!

> **Druidspeak**
>
> **Clairvoyance** literally means "clear seeing." A clairvoyant is a person who receives psychic information through visual images.

Examples of Famous Seers

Here are some of the better known seers, both in the Celtic tradition and in the world at large.

Merlin and Morgan Le Fay

The chief magicians of Arthurian legend include Merlin, the druid/prophet who mentored Arthur as a youth, and Morgan Le Fay, Arthur's half-sister who is variously depicted as a witch, a sorceress, a faery woman, or a priestess of the Goddess. Both figures were said to possess extraordinary powers; Merlin, for example, had the ability to conjure shapeshifting in another person, while Morgan could (in some versions of the legend) enchant Arthur so that she could seduce him.

The Brahan Seer

A well-known prophet from seventeenth-century Scotland, Coinneach Odhar made a series of startlingly accurate predictions involving technology, politics, war, and the fate of individuals. When he informed a local countess that her husband was unfaithful, she had him killed for witchcraft; he predicted the demise of her family line, which indeed ended as he had described.

Biddy Early

From County Clare in western Ireland, Biddy Early lived in the nineteenth century and developed a wide-ranging reputation as a healer and magician. She claimed to have received power to see into the future from a small blue bottle given to her by a dead relative from the otherworld; upon her death, the bottle was cast into a lake and has never been retrieved. She also had powers to deal with the faeries and to reverse curses or bad luck associated with otherworldly beings. A well on her property was said to have curative powers.

> **The Bard's Bookshelf**
>
> Information about the Brahan Seer, and many other examples of Scottish visionaries, can be found in *Ravens and Black Rain: The Story of Highland Second Sight* by Elizabeth Sutherland (Constable and Company, 1985).

Edgar Cayce

An American, Cayce is an excellent modern example of a seer. An ordinary businessman who from an early age developed remarkable clairvoyant skills, Cayce (1877–1945) could enter into a profound trance in which he could provide remarkable medical advice, even for people physically located far away from him; he also was a prophet who spoke on a wide range of spiritual topics and made numerous predictions for the future.

Although not all seers have the reputation (or depth of skill) of the Brahan Seer, Biddy Early, or Edgar Cayce, anyone who has the intuitive ability and who seeks to develop their psychic gifts is walking the seer's path.

The Lorica: A Key to Psychic Self-Defense

With all this talk about psychic skill and contacting spirits on the other side, you may be wondering, "Is this safe?" The spiritual realm, just like the physical realm, is populated with beings and entities who vary in their intelligence and trustworthiness. If you want to walk the path of the seer, you'll also want to make sure that you feel safe and secure journeying into the mysteries of the otherworld *and* the mysteries deep within your unconscious mind.

In the Celtic world, the tradition of the *lorica* addresses the need for psychic protection and

> **Druidspeak**
>
> **Lorica** is a Latin word for "breastplate." It's a protective piece of armor that was worn by Roman soldiers; in the Celtic tradition, it refers to a charm or spell recited for spiritual protection.

self-defense. This was made famous because of a lorica used by St. Patrick, but the tradition appears to have predated him. A Lorica is a charm (poetic incantation) used to invoke a spirit of protection and safety. It can be used for ordinary protection (asking for safety while driving, for example) as well as for spiritual protection while journeying into the faery realms.

Patrick's Breastplate

Patrick's lorica was said to have been inscribed on a breastplate that he wore (from which the lorica takes its name). According to legend, Patrick was traveling through a dangerous part of Ireland and was in danger from enemies. He recited his charm of protection, and he and his company shapeshifted into deer and were thus able to move quickly through the wilderness and escape the notice of their adversaries.

Here's an excerpt from Patrick's lorica:

> I bind unto myself today
> The virtues of the starlit heaven
> The glorious sun's life-giving rays
> The whiteness of the moon at even,
> The flashing of the lightning free,
> The whirling wind's tempestuous shocks,
> The stable earth, the deep salt sea,
> Around the old eternal rocks.
>
> —Translated by Cecil Frances Humphreys Alexander

In other words, here Patrick is invoking the powers of nature herself to guard and protect him. The lorica goes on to invoke Spirit in the form of Christ (which makes sense as Patrick was a Christian): "Christ be with me, Christ within me, Christ before me, Christ beside me, Christ to win me, Christ to comfort and restore me, Christ beneath me, Christ above me, Christ in quiet, Christ in danger, Christ in hearts of all that love me, Christ in mouth of friend and stranger." In reciting this, Patrick was literally invoking the protecting powers of sacred energy in all these ways.

Writing Your Own Lorica

If you are a Christian, you might find Patrick's lorica is itself a wonderful tool to use for invoking a sense of spiritual safety. But no matter what your religious path, you can use a lorica to call for protection. Here, for example, is the same lorica of Patrick's rewritten for the goddess Brigid:

Brigid be with me, Brigid within me,
Brigid before me, Brigid beside me,
Brigid to win me, Brigid to comfort and restore me,
Brigid beneath me, Brigid above me,
Brigid in quiet, Brigid in danger,
Brigid in hearts of all that love me,
Brigid in mouth of friend and stranger.

Here is a way to combine the talents of the bard and the seer: The bard's skill as a poet is effective for putting into the words the request for divine protection and aid. Then, the seer's skill at visualization can make those words "come alive" when recited with heartfelt feeling. What the Celtic tradition promises is that such appeals for spiritual aid will not go unrewarded!

> **The Bard's Bookshelf**
>
> For a lovely book of spiritual reflections and exercises based on Patrick's breastplate, check out *The Cry of the Deer: Meditations on the Hymn of St. Patrick* by David Adam (Morehouse Publishing, 1989).

Safety Guidelines for the Beginning Seer

The lorica is a practical tool for finding a sense of personal safety when exploring the inner life. But it's not the only precaution worth taking when you decide to plumb the depths of the spiritual realms. Here are a few other important principles to keep in mind as you begin to explore the seer's path.

◆ **Stay sober.** Drug and alcohol use does not benefit the spiritual life. If you feel you need mind-altering substances to get in touch with your intuition or psychic ability, consider learning meditation or visualization skills instead. Just as you can't effectively drive a car while inebriated, any spiritual work done under the influence of a mind-altering substance is unreliable.

◆ **Trust your gut.** Some spiritual experiences can be beautiful and awe-inspiring, but others can be boring, frightening, or anger-inducing. Learn to listen to your feelings and pay attention how spiritual experiences make you feel. If your intuition says "don't go there" or "leave this alone," don't argue. Also, allow yourself to take baby-steps in your spiritual work: You don't have to be the world's best meditator or most gifted psychic! Spirituality is not a race, so take your time with your inner explorations.

◆ **Keep it real.** The mind is a tricky thing indeed, and we can sometimes delude ourselves into thinking we are of godlike importance, or totally worthless, or some other distorted idea. The best antidote to such inaccurate ideas is a trusted friend or teacher with whom we can share our spiritual experiences—and who will let us know when our inner guidance seems to be off kilter.

◆ **Get help when you need it.** Deep inner work can reveal areas in our lives that are wounded, dysfunctional, or self-sabotaging. Psychological counseling or therapy isn't a crutch; it's a means of achieving maximum mental health. If you encounter a persistent problem or painful situation in your inner world, do what it takes to heal and grow.

Nine Steps to Becoming a Seer

If the way of the seer calls to you, here's a series of steps you can take to begin cultivating your own vatic gifts. This is not a hard-and-fast program, but rather a set of guidelines that you can use as a general map of the vatic path.

1. Make a Spiritual Path a Central Part of Your Life

As you saw in Chapter 1, the Celtic wisdom tradition is essentially a spiritual tradition. This is especially true for seers, whose skills involve dealing with profound matters pertaining to the mysteries of the otherworld. Ultimately, it doesn't matter if your chosen path is Christian, neopagan, or some combination of the two. What matters is that you make the spiritual life a central part of your journey.

Regardless of your spiritual or religious identity, refer to Chapter 10 for insight into what it takes to walk the druid path. Skills such as study, meditation, spiritual discipline, and community building are all important parts of the druid way. As a seer, you'll incorporate these qualities into your path as well. Modern druidism can be expressed as a pagan spirituality, but it can also be expressed as a philosophical path compatible with Christianity (or any other ethical religion).

Becoming a seer is not about some sort of gee-whiz psychic ability that's meant for entertainment purposes only. Your gifts of envisioning the future or the wisdom of the spiritual world are meant not just for yourself, but for others as well. Your job will involve developing your skills and then finding ways to use them for the service of the larger community. This can be challenging, because as soon as you share your skills with other people, many things can happen: You can be rejected or scorned; you can be laughed at or ignored. Or what is spiritually more dangerous, you can be seen as someone "special" or "gifted," giving your ego a big treat but not necessarily supporting your continued spiritual growth. The bottom line: As you share your seer skills with others, you will need to take good and proper care of your ego, making sure that it doesn't get bruised (or overinflated) by others.

Incidentally, in talking about "others," I don't just mean anyone you run into on the street. Actually, it makes good sense to be discreet about psychic or intuitive abilities, as many people either don't understand them, are afraid of them, or are openly skeptical and scornful. The "others" you'll want to share your seer skills with are mainly other seekers of Celtic wisdom or some other form of spirituality.

Geasa

Spirituality can be as intimate as sexuality. Therefore, it's simply not polite to discuss it indiscriminately: It can make people feel uncomfortable and awkward. Share your spiritual life with only a few trusted souls.

2. Befriend Your Dreams and Your Intuition

Perhaps you are interested in the path of the seer because you already have a sense of your own intuitive skill or psychic ability. But just as likely, you may feel a tug toward this path, but aren't sure where to begin, and you aren't even sure if you "qualify" as a psychic or an intuitive. Not to worry. A psychic is not a special kind of person, but each person is a special kind of psychic. Your job is to find your unique connection to the spiritual world, and not worry about whether it is as dramatic or accurate as someone like Edgar Cayce or the Brahan Seer.

But how do you go about developing the skills of a seer? Begin by accessing your subconscious mind. You can do this best through meditation (see step 3), but even before you work at the technical skills of meditation, get to know your dreams, daydreams, hunches, and intuition. These are all natural parts of human consciousness in which the unconscious or subconscious mind communicates with normal waking consciousness. Because it's through the unconscious that the spiritual world usually communicates with us, getting to know these portals into the mysteries is an important step along your own psychic development. Take the time to write down your dreams in the morning; doing so will facilitate remembering them more clearly. Also, notice your hunches; notice what happens when you follow a hunch, as well as what happens when you ignore it. (If you're like me, you may well find that hunches are far more often right than wrong!) Record your dealings with your unconscious mind in your journal, to keep a record of your exploration of the seer's realm.

3. Master Different Forms of Meditation

I recommend meditation as an important step on the path to becoming a druid. For a seer, the meditative stakes are higher, since a seer is a specialist of the inner world. Would-be seers need to understand different styles of meditation, from Zen silence to shamanic trance to the imaginative world of visualization (see step 5). Not every style of meditation will appeal to any one seer, but if you want to be a seasoned traveler within the psychic realms, you need to know about the many different ways to get there. Of course, in addition to learning the many different types of meditation, you also need to be a dedicated practitioner of the particular style of meditation that's best for you.

4. Believe in Your Psychic Potential

Meditation and recording your dreams are spiritual disciplines that anyone can benefit from. For a seer, however, they are tools to a higher purpose: to gain direct access to spiritual knowledge and insight that can be shared with others. Just as a professional athlete must continually train to ensure that his or her body remains in top physical form, the dedicated seer needs to continually sharpen his or her connection with the spiritual realm.

This begins with simply believing in the process. Business leaders love to say "what you believe, you can achieve." This applies equally well to the spiritual realm. By believing in your potential for making significant and powerful contact with the psychic realm, you actually set in motion the mental and spiritual processes necessary for such a connection to occur. Believe in your ability as a seer, and then use meditation, visualization, and dreamwork to make it happen.

5. Visualize, Visualize, Visualize

If you want to be a seer, you gotta learn how to see. In other words, you need to sharpen your skills at visualizing the landscape of the inner world: that realm where your imagination deepens into a spiritual reality beyond the limits of your finite mind. Visualization is an acquired skill.

Becoming adept at visualization means developing your inner landscape to the point where you not only visualize (see with your inner eye), but experience other sensory data on an inner plane (such as taste, touch, and hearing). Using your imagination to create this sensory data also means strengthening your "inner muscles" that you use to enter into a vivid and realistic inner world accessed through meditation, trance, and ritual. It is in this inner world that you will encounter your spirit guides and receive much of the wisdom and knowledge available to you as a seer.

The Bard's Bookshelf
Many of the books on the market dealing with visualization are concerned with manifestation—envisioning something as a spiritual way to "make it real." Although that's slightly different from the goal of a Celtic seer, the techniques of visualization are useful whether you're working on achieving goals or simply improving your psychic skill. One useful title for beginners is *Teach Yourself Visualization* by Pauline Wills (NTC Publishing Group, 1997).

6. Master at Least One Form of Divination

Many of the most popular divination tools available are not specifically Celtic—but can still be used by Celtic wisdomseekers. Such tools include astrology, tarot, the *I Ching*, and the runes. One divination tool, the Ogham, is based on an ancient Celtic alphabet. (For more information on the Ogham, see Chapter 23.) Divination tools, whether Celtic or non-Celtic, are useful in that they are easy to understand, are familiar to people who are seeking guidance, and in their use can actually help you sharpen and hone your natural psychic abilities.

7. Learn to Read the Wisdom of Nature

Back before there were tarot cards or astrological symbolism, a shaman might use the pattern of birds in flight or of leaves falling from a tree to divine spiritual guidance and wisdom. Indeed, the ancient Greek writer Diodorus Siculus wrote of diviners in Celtic Gaul who could foretell the future by means of bird calls or flying patterns. This kind of divination is more difficult to learn than a system like the runes, which depends on a specific set of meanings; when learning to read the wisdom of the natural world, you will learn to rely even more heavily on the guidance of your intuition. It's a skill worth developing, though, for two reasons: First, it puts you in the long tradition of Celtic shamans and seers who could access wisdom simply through the signs of nature; and second, once mastered, using nature to access inner wisdom means the entire world becomes your divination tool.

8. Keep Your Ego in Check

One of the dangers of pursuing the seer's path is that it can foster an unhealthy ego. Experiencing powerful intuitive or psychic experiences can lead to ego inflation ("I must be so special for the Spirit to use me in this way") and sometimes can also lead to

The Bard's Bookshelf

Two more books on the subject of ovates: *The Celtic Seers' Sourcebook: Vision and Magic in the Druid Tradition* edited by John Matthews (Blandford, 1999), and *The Seer in Celtic and Other Traditions* edited by Hilda Ellis Davidson (John Donald Publishers, 1989).

unhealthy ego deflation ("I'm not a very good psychic; therefore I must be a worthless person"). Either of these routes is unhealthy. The further you walk along the path of the seer, the more essential it will be for you to learn the fine art of balancing your sense of self: honoring your worthiness and specialness without becoming enmeshed in the arrogance of ego inflation. This is not always an easy thing to do by yourself; having a trusted soul friend is an essential way to keep the ego in perspective. (See Chapter 10 for more on the soul friend, or *anamchara*.)

9. Be Willing to Serve Others as a Counselor and a Guide

One of the qualities of a true wisdomkeeper is a willingness to live in service to others, including service to the clan or tribe (the community as a whole) as well as service to individuals within the community. As a seer, much of your work may be on an individual, one-on-one basis. You may have a gift for counseling that would lend itself well to a career as a counselor or psychotherapist; or you may simply be a trusted soul to whom people turn for help with spiritual problems. Either way, you'll need to approach helping others from a position of love, respect, ethics, and compassion. The further along you travel on your spiritual path, the more likely that others will come to you for guidance. Be prepared to receive such seekers with hospitality and grace.

The Least You Need to Know

- The ovate, or seer, in Celtic tradition seeks direct spiritual wisdom and knowledge through psychic and shamanic exercises.

- Seers access spiritual experience through trance, meditation, visualization, divination, and the use of intuition.

- Seers have existed throughout Celtic history, from the time of the classical druids up to the present day.

- Spiritual protection and psychic self-defense are important considerations for aspiring seers; the lorica tradition involves reciting a poem asking the forces of nature and the divine for protection.

- The true role of a seer is to help others as a counselor, healer, and guide.

Devotion to the Ways of Wisdom: The Path of the Druid

In This Chapter

- ◆ The heart of the tradition
- ◆ The three ages of the druids
- ◆ The advice of the anamchara
- ◆ The spirit of sacrifice
- ◆ Walking the druid path

If any one image in the Celtic tradition has captured the imagination of generations of seekers, it is the druid. Druids have been depicted as tree worshippers, evil sorcerers, mystic priests descended from the initiates of Atlantis, dark lords of human sacrifice, primitive herbalists/healers, ancient astronomers, pagan philosophers, and precursors to Christianity! So many different images have been used to depict druids over the years because, frankly, we know so little about who they were. Only a handful of ancient writings exist to describe druids, none of which were written by the druids themselves. (They practiced an oral tradition and refused to write down their sacred teachings.)

Just What Is a Druid?

Because we know so little about druidic history, one could say that druidism (as a concept) is a "blank screen" on which all sorts of ideas about Celtic wisdom can (and have) been projected. We'll never know if the druids really came from Atlantis or if they accepted Christianity with open arms, but based on what little evidence we do have, we can make the following generalizations:

- Druids were key intellectual figures of the ancient Celtic world.

- Druids enjoyed tremendous social prestige and political influence.

- Druids were considered, at least by outsiders, to be accomplished magicians.

- To become a druid one underwent a rigorous training program that lasted many years.

Not a lot of information to go on, admittedly. But this lack of data can actually be a blessing. Those of us who want to study the ancient Celtic lore found in myth and legend can freely adapt it to the needs of the modern world, without worrying about whether our quest for knowledge is "correct" from a druidic perspective. In fact, even though studying Indo-European archaeology or reading Irish myth might provide interesting insights into ancient Celtic spirituality, it's important to remember that any and all modern "druid" practices are to a certain extent based on speculation. For this reason, it's wise to keep an open mind and a spirit of humility when exploring how the druid path can be revived for the modern world.

> **Notes from the Otherworld**
>
> The French movie *Druids* (2000) features Max Von Sydow as the counselor to the Gaulish warlord Vercingetorix. The movie depicts druids as monk-ish shaman counselors—as good a guess as any as to what the original druids were actually like.

The Three Ages of the Druids

A prominent modern druid, Isaac Bonewits, has suggested that druidism can be divided into three ages: the *paleopagan*, *mesopagan*, and *neopagan* eras.

Paleopagan Druids

These are the druids of old, the ones that classical writers like Caesar and Pliny described in their ancient texts. According to Caesar, they were religious teachers and officiants at Celtic rituals; they were judges involved in both public and private conflict resolution; they had the power to banish criminals and other transgressors from their rituals, which was tantamount to banishing them from society. Druids were exempt from military service and did not have to pay taxes. Among other things, they believed in reincarnation and studied astronomy. Other writers, like Cicero and Diodorus Siculus, added that the druids were gifted at the art of divination.

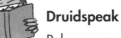

Druidspeak _____

Paleopagan means "ancient pagan," **mesopagan** means "middle pagan," and **neopagan** means "new pagan."

One of the most famous of ancient descriptions of the druids came from the Roman writer Pliny, who described druids harvesting mistletoe in a precisely enacted ritual according to the phases of the moon. On a more somber note, the historian Tacitus described a slaughter of druids during the Roman conquest of Britain.

Given that the druids themselves didn't document their teachings or beliefs, can we believe these descriptions by non-Celtic writers, some of whom were openly hostile to the very idea of druidism? It's a valid question, and one that can never be answered definitively. Some of the material written was obviously propaganda (Caesar, for example, wrote at length about how the druids presided at massive human sacrifices), but many of the details appear to be accurate. At any rate, the mere handful of writings from classical writers like Caesar are the only source we have for describing the paleopagan druids, so imperfect as it may be, this material is our only glimpse into the earliest age of these Celtic wisdomkeepers.

Mesopagan Druids

With the coming of Christianity, druidism died out, perhaps persisting in folklore and rural wisdom among Celtic farmers, or even among bardic figures like the filid, but with no real political or social power. Beginning in the seventeenth century, however, a new form of druidism began to grow. Especially in England, France, and Wales, people with an interest in ancient Celtic society began to look for ways to revive druidism as a modern cultural/philosophical movement. This is what Bonewits calls the mesopagan era: In between the ancient paganism of pre-Christian Europe and the modern efforts to revive an authentic pagan spirituality, the druids of the seventeenth through early twentieth century saw druidism more as a symbol of national pride or natural wisdom than as anything truly religious or spiritual in nature. Many of these druids formed associations that functioned as fraternal service organizations. The mesopagan druids created the image by which modern druidry is commonly recognized: that of men in white robes, chanting their rituals at Stonehenge at dawn.

Notes from the Otherworld

The mesopagan druids believed that Stonehenge and other stone circles in the British Isles had been built by the ancient druids, so naturally, they incorporated stone circles into the modern re-enactment of "druid rituals." We now realize that the stone circles actually predated the Celts by hundreds, if not thousands, of years, but the Stonehenge-druid connection still exists in the popular mind, even if it's an erroneous connection.

According to legend, in 1717 a British man named John Toland gathered together a meeting of "surviving druid groups" to hold an autumn equinox ceremony at Primrose Hill in London. This was supposed to have been the first gathering of modern druids; but today, most scholars believe this is a legendary, rather than historical, event.

The first documented formation of a mesopagan druid order occurred in 1781. By 1834 this group had split into two orders: the Ancient Order of Druids, and the United Ancient Order of Druids. Meanwhile, in 1792 Edward Williams, who also was known as Iolo Morgannwg, convened the first gorsedd, or gathering, of the Bards of the Isle of Britain at Primrose Hill in London. By early the following century, the Gorsedd had moved to Wales. Welsh bards and druids continue to hold a gorsedd every year. By 1861 the eisteddfod (or "session") was established as an annual bardic competition in Wales.

Geasa

Iolo's contributions to the revival of druidry was overshadowed by the fact that he was a fraud. He forged a number of documents, passing them off as medieval Welsh manuscripts.

Over the years that followed, various druid groups formed, sometimes splintering off from existing groups to form new organizations. Two of the most famous people associated with druid groups include William Blake (a poet/artist who lived in the late eighteenth and early nineteenth centuries, who refused to take an oath in court because he said it conflicted with his druid beliefs) and the twentieth-century British prime minister Winston Churchill (who was initiated into the Ancient Order of Druids in 1908).

Neopagan Druidry

In the mid-twentieth century, several different people on both sides of the Atlantic were exploring druidism, but with a new agenda: to study the ancient pagan druids and thereby re-create an authentic "new" paganism. This neopagan form of druidry does away with the social/cultural aspects of mesopagan druidry and instead tries to re-create, as closely as possible, a religious/spiritual system based on the paganism of ancient times.

Some of the leaders of this modern druidry include Nicholas Ross and Philip Carr-Gomm (of the Order of Bards, Ovates, and Druids), Isaac Bonewits (the founder of Ár nDraíocht Féin: A Druid Fellowship [ADF]) and Emma Restall Orr and Philip Shallcrass (of the British Druid Order). Other neopagan druid groups currently in existence include the Reformed Druids of North America, Keltria (an offshoot of ADF), and the Tuatha De Brighid (which stresses friendliness toward other religions, especially Christianity).

> **The Bard's Bookshelf**
>
> John Matthews's *The Druid Source Book* (Blandford, 1996) provides a fascinating glimpse of druidism through history. From classical writers like Julius Caesar to the voices of the druid revivals of the last 200 years, this book provides an overview of druidic ideas in the words of the authors who've written about this mysterious order.

More Than Just Priests: The Wisdom Aspect of Druidry

By now you realize that druids are far more than just psychics or mystics. (Although from the classical writers on, druids have been regarded as gifted magicians.) What other areas of knowledge are appropriate for druids, whether ancient or modern, to pursue? Keep reading to find out:

◆ **Science.** Science was once called "natural philosophy," a name that suits the druid interest in the physical world. The ancient druids were said to debate the movement of the stars and were knowledgeable about the natural world. Sounds like astronomy and biology to me! Indeed, druidism suggests that there is no real difference between the spiritual and physical worlds, so a true wisdomseeker will try to learn as much as possible about both realms.

◆ **Law.** Once upon a time, druids were involved in solving legal disputes and counseling kings and chieftains in times of war. These were not just some airy-faery New Age idealists: They were hard-nosed policymakers and consultants, respected by every level of society.

◆ **Philosophy.** More than one ancient writer commented on the druids as "Pythagoreans," seeing them as disciples of the famous Greek philosopher/mathematician. Considering that philosophy literally means "the love of wisdom"

> **The Seer Says**
>
> As the chief intellectuals of their time, ancient druids naturally had to be well versed in all the disciplines mentioned here. Modern druidism is primarily a spiritual pursuit. But in the spirit of the ancient druids, modern druids also try to be as intellectually well rounded as possible.

and druid is said to mean "the wisdom of an oak tree," it only makes sense that druids would master this most challenging of intellectual disciplines. Druids were also described as "moral philosophers," suggesting that they were concerned with ethics as well as other philosophical issues.

♦ **Psychology.** As you'll see in the next section, druids have a long history as counselors and spiritual guides. One could argue that they were among the earliest of psychologists, mastering the mysteries of the human mind so that they could more effectively serve their kings and chiefs.

♦ **Medicine.** The classical image of the druid gathering mistletoe was related to the idea that druids were gifted healers. Today, healing is a natural place where spirituality and wisdom converge, and modern druids would stand in a long tradition of serving humankind, whether as mainstream doctors or as "alternative" caregivers.

> **The Seer Says**
>
> Today, two of the most prestigious professions are doctors and lawyers. Ancient druids probably had to master both disciplines.

Druids as Counselors: The Anamchara

If you wish to find a simple and lovely way to integrate Celtic wisdom and spirituality into your life, the tradition of the *anamchara* may be for you. It's a way in which the spiritual-counselor functions of ancient druids survived in the Christian world, up to the present day. And now it's a strand of the tradition that any Celtic wisdomseeker, regardless of religious affiliation, can embrace.

Anamchara (pronounced *ahn-im-KAR-uh*) is a Gaelic word that means "soul friend." *Anam* means "soul" or "spirit," while *chara* means "friend." The plural is anamchairde (*ahn-im-KAR-juh*). A soul friend is a person who provides another with down-to-earth coaching, support, and guidance as he or she progresses along his or her unique spiritual path. From the ancient druids (who served as counselors to their kings and chieftains) to the saints of Celtic Christianity who insisted that "anyone without a soul friend is like a body without a head," this unique form of personal spiritual guidance has been at the heart of Celtic spirituality.

About the Anamchara

Anyone can have (or be) a soul friend. In its simplest form, a soul friend is one who provides spiritual support to another, no matter how humble or "ordinary." Indeed, given the quality of friendship, perhaps the best anamchairde are those who offer this support to another in very practical, un-self-conscious ways. Nevertheless, soul friendship can function in a more formalized way. In such a scenario, an anamchara can be a mentor or a coach—a person who shares his or her knowledge or expertise with others, usually in a structured way. Such an anamchara may provide his or her services as part of a religious community (such as a Christian minister or a Wiccan priestess) or may work independently (such as a spiritual counselor or professional psychic).

We live in a time of great social change. In a mere two centuries, our culture has transitioned from agrarian to industrial to information/service-based economy. Meanwhile, the role of the family and of traditional religion has changed drastically; the rise of new communication tools (from television to the Internet) has changed the way we learn and process data. Problems from the arms race to environmental crises to the rise of terrorism have created uncertainty and anxiety in our world. Many people yearn for a deeper sense of spirituality and a closer connection with the divine. It is precisely this yearning to which the anamchara speaks. When two or more people come together in the shared intimacy of soul friendship, we discover that spirituality is not something that only happens in a formal setting such as a church or classroom, but rather through the loving and nurturing interaction of souls who come together to share their lives and spiritual yearning with one another.

For some, merely having a friend with whom spiritual topics can be discussed is a profound blessing. Others may look for guidance or direction from a mentor, one who is engaged in a mature and disciplined life of meditation and contemplation. Such a spiritual friend need not be a priest, a monk, or a nun, although obviously many religious professionals can and do exercise a ministry of spiritual guidance.

> ### The Bard's Bookshelf
>
> For a Christian perspective on the anamchara, check out Edward Sellner's *The Celtic Soul Friend: A Trusted Guide for Today* (Ave Maria Press, 2002).

Roles of the Anamchara

The anamchara can be an important part of the spiritual quest in the following ways:

- **An anamchara represents personal, one-on-one guidance in the spiritual life.** This goes counter to the alienating and depersonalizing values of our society, where everything is mass produced and mass consumed. Against the conformist tendencies of much "assembly-line" spirituality, the soul friend stands for uniqueness and individuality in relationship to the Sacred.

The Seer Says

St. Brigid is said to have remarked, "Anyone without a soul friend [anamchara] is like a body without a head."

Notes from the Otherworld

Julian of Norwich (c. 1342–1420) and Francis of Assisi (c. 1181–1226) were mystics, Christian figures renowned for their personal experience of union with God. The twentieth century writers Thomas Merton (1915–1968) and Simone Weil (1909–1943) were also mystics. The Celtic tradition of soul friendship has survived within the Christian world primarily among those who seek and experience mystical spirituality.

◆ **An anamchara stands not for "immediate gratification" but rather for the slow and steady development of spiritual maturity over time.** A soul friend knows that our culture's insistence on immediate results is not useful in the realm of relationship with the holy. The Spirit is not interested in results, but rather is interested in relationship. An anamchara helps a person to nurture a meaningful relationship with the Great Mystery.

◆ **An anamchara stands in a great tradition.** This is the tradition of the ancient druids and European shamans, as well as the tradition of the Christian mystics, from the desert fathers and mothers all the way down to twentieth-century spiritual leaders like Thomas Merton and Simone Weil. This is the tradition of the Celtic saints like Brigid and Columba, as well as of the medieval mystics from non-Celtic regions, like the English mystic Julian of Norwich or the Italian mystic Francis of Assisi. By standing in a great tradition, the anamchara avoids the danger of faddishness or rootlessness. The deep mysticism of soul-friend spirituality is historic and grounded, yet powerful and excitingly relevant to today.

Dimensions of the Soul Friend

The concept of Celtic spirituality means different things to different people. For some, it points to the tradition of earth-based shamanism that existed in old Europe for thousands of years and that is being revived in such modern religious movements as Wicca and neopaganism. For many others, of course, Celtic spirituality is part of their core identity as Christians, whether Protestant or Catholic. Where does the anamchara fit in with this diverse understanding of Celtic mysticism?

As pointed out earlier, the soul friend has roots in the ancient culture of the druids, but the practice has also flourished in Celtic Christianity. Although the modern renaissance of the soul-friend ministry began in the last quarter of the twentieth century with Christians like Kenneth Leech and Edward Sellner, at its heart the ministry of the anamchara transcends the barriers and boundaries between "pagan" and "Christian." As a Celtic spiritual practice, it is universal.

Indeed, the ministry of the anamchara can support the search for creative and positive dialog between people of different spiritual traditions. As a universal Celtic ministry, soul friendship "belongs" to no one, neither pagan nor Christian, neither Catholic nor Protestant, neither druid nor Wiccan. Rather, it represents the deep hospitality and compassion characterized by Celtic spirituality at its best. This is a hospitality and compassion that breaks down barriers. A true soul friend honors the unique beauty of every person and every path. He or she understands that we live in a pluralistic world, and that interfaith encounters are normal and need to be approached positively, honestly, and with a spirit of openness and nondefensiveness. The spirituality of the anamchara is a spirituality that honors the deep roots of each specific mystical tradition, balanced with an attitude of good will and openness toward all other compassionate traditions.

The anamchara can be a deeply important figure in any individual's personal spiritual journey. A person does not need to be Celtic—or even particularly interested in Celtic spirituality or culture—to benefit from this lovely spiritual practice. All that is needed to benefit from a soul friend is the desire to grow spiritually and the willingness to work one-on-one with a companion or mentor who can help foster such interior growth.

> **Notes from the Otherworld**
>
> The Christian ministry of spiritual direction has its roots in the anamchara tradition. Christian theologian Kenneth Leech, in his book *Soul Friend: Spiritual Direction in the Modern World* (Morehouse Publishing, 2001), provides an overview of this rapidly growing aspect of Christian spirituality.

How to Be an Anamchara Today

So how does today's seeker of Celtic wisdom find (or become) an anamchara? To find a formal spiritual guide, look for spiritual teachers who you enjoy studying with; such guides can be found through spiritual bookstores, churches, or pagan groups. But in its less-structured form, soul friendship simply requires two or more people to be willing to come together in a sacred and honoring way, viewing their friendship as an arena where spiritual growth may occur. Given this informality, all it takes to find or be a soul friend is finding or being a friend to another, and giving that friendship an intentional, spiritual dimension. From there, every soul friendship is unique. It's not a program to follow: It's a relationship to live. And in living this relationship, you and your soul friend(s) will be participating in a grand tradition—one with druidic roots.

Other Pieces of the Druid Puzzle

In your journey toward understanding druidry and possibly applying its wisdom principles to your life today, you'll quickly run into one of the most controversial aspects connected to the druids: the fact that ancient druids practiced human sacrifice. I mentioned earlier in this chapter how Caesar (among others) attacked the druids for their grisly sacrificial practices. Although scholars today believe Caesar was probably exaggerating, evidence does suggest that druids performed ritual killings.

Presiding Over Sacrifice

According to Caesar, the druids presided over the sacrifices. Is this to say that the druids were the ones in charge of making blood offerings to their pagan gods?

The truth is probably quite complex. Sacrifice means more than just the spilling of blood; it involves any kind of offering made to spiritual beings. So while in its most primitive form it can include killing, it can also include any kind of offering made to the spiritual world. This is the key to the role that druids played in ancient times and can still play in today's world.

If the ancient druids presided over sacrifices, this means they were the priests who officiated at rituals and ceremonies where offerings were made. At their most extreme, these rituals of ancient times included bloodshed.

While some archaeological evidence does point to human sacrifice in some parts of the ancient Celtic world, the evidence doesn't suggest that ritual bloodshed was a universal or common practice. It appears that druidic human sacrifice was performed only in the most extreme circumstances, such as in appealing to the spirit world to fend off an invading army.

> **The Bard's Bookshelf**
>
> An out-of-print book that's well worth tracking down is *The Life and Death of a Druid Prince* by Anne Ross and Don Robins (Summit Books, 1989). This book explores the evidence that exists for druid human sacrifice, and explains why sacrifice would have made sense to the ancient Celts.

It's important to remember that many cultures have performed animal and human sacrifice; the Bible unapologetically records how even the earliest monotheists made such offerings to God, and how Christians believed that Jesus' death on the cross was a form of human sacrifice. Just because the druids of old may have done such extreme acts doesn't mean that it is a necessary part of Celtic spirituality. Indeed, many modern druids are staunch pacifists and vegetarians, and even those who aren't recognize that sacrificial killing is no longer permissible or desirable.

Spirituality in the modern world (whether druid or otherwise) has evolved far beyond the need to ever shed blood. Thus, today's druids never offer living creatures in their rituals; but that's not to say that they never make offerings. Modern sacrifices involve the offering of artistic praise (songs and poems written to honor the old gods and goddesses), or token offerings of fruit, butter, or flowers as a symbol of love and devotion for the spiritual world. In this sense, druids of today still preside over sacrifices, but in a way wholly consistent with modern spiritual values.

> **CAUTION**
>
> **Geasa**
>
> Sacrifice is easily misunderstood. In modern druidry, sacrifice is *not* about pleasing an angry god, but rather is a gift offered to the spiritual world to foster harmony and friendly relations.

Religious Balance: Druids as Ambassadors Between Paganism and Christianity

Here's one more point worth making about modern druids. With all the talk about how druids of the last 50 years embody an increasingly pagan spirituality, you might think that druids are practicing a religious perspective that puts them at odds with other religions (especially Christianity). But actually, some druids are playing an important role in bringing modern pagans and Christians together. Druids can fill a unique role as "religious ambassadors," especially between Christianity and neopagan religions such as Wicca.

This perspective emphasizes the mesopagan idea that druidry is a philosophy, not a religion, so individuals can be druids and also practice whatever religion(s) they wish. At the same time, druids of different religious persuasions can come together, united by their common commitment to Celtic wisdom, even if expressed in different religious ways. One druid order, OBOD (the Order of Bards, Ovates, and Druids), has even sponsored conferences in which Christian druids and pagan druids have come together to discuss their shared unity despite religious differences!

> **Notes from the Otherworld**
>
> In 2002, a minor uproar ensued when the future Archbishop of Canterbury, Rowan Williams (a Welshman and a fluent speaker of Welsh), was made a druid of the Welsh Gorsedd of Bards. There was much speculation that the archbishop had participated in a pagan rite. Not exactly: The Welsh Gorsedd of Bards is a cultural organization, not a spiritual one; and none of the activities involved in the archbishop becoming a druid were in any way pagan. One would hope, however, that this could be seen as an example of how druidism can serve as a bridge between the Christian and pagan worlds.

Nine Steps to Becoming a Druid

An aspiring druid must master a variety of disciplines. He or she needs to become knowledgeable about Celtic history and today's Celtic cultures; needs to know the myths and develop the spiritual skills necessary to forge a personal relationship with the gods and goddesses; and perhaps most important of all, needs to have a solid understanding of the natural world and humanity's place within the ecosystem (that's important because of the role that nature plays in Celtic spirituality, as well as the longstanding tradition of druids as priests of nature).

If you just want to get naked and dance around a bonfire, you're probably not seeking to be a druid (not that there's anything wrong with dancing naked in the woods, but druidism is far more than that!). If your goal is to sharpen your psychic or intuitive skills, perhaps you are meant to be a seer. And if your primary interest is in casting spells or cross-cultural paganism, maybe you should study Wicca. There's nothing wrong with any of these spiritual paths! Better to find the right path for you than to be miserable training for a goal that doesn't fit.

How to know if the druid path is right for you? Here's a simple way: Read the following nine steps. Does the thought of doing this work excite you, intrigue you, or otherwise call to you? If so, then the intellectually rigorous world of the druid may be right for you. If, however, these nine steps feel like a drudge, then maybe your spiritual journey will take you in a direction other than druidry. That's perfectly okay, and I wish you blessings on your quest.

Remember that a druid is like a doctor or a lawyer. He or she is a spiritual professional. You can be a pagan just by saying "I am a pagan." Likewise, you can become a Wiccan fairly quickly. (Many covens offer initiation after only a year and a day of training.) But druidism is more of a long-term commitment. Classical writers said that the process of becoming a druid (at least in Gaul) took a student 20 years. Can we expect any less of ourselves?

1. Become Environmentally Aware

Druidism is a form of nature mysticism, so it begins not with books or rituals, but with the environment in which we live. Understanding nature is more than just walking into your backyard and communing with your favorite tree. Yes, do get into the habit of spending time outdoors and getting to know the subtle shifts of the seasons and the rhythms of the plants and animals in your bioregion. But you also need to have a solid understanding of your connection with the environment. What is the soil quality in your region? Where does your trash go after you dump it? Where does your tap water come from, and your waste water go? How much precipitation is there in your region, and is it currently above or below average? What species are endangered in your region? What grasses or wildflowers are native to your area? Where does your electricity come from, and how much of it is nuclear generated? What are the critical ecological issues facing your community? Do you have a problem with smog? Acid rain? Erosion? Lack of water? What are the best ways for citizens to become involved with environmental protection in your region?

 **The Seer Says**

To test your knowledge of environmental issues in your community, take the Environmental Awareness Quiz. Several different versions exist; you can find one in *The Complete Idiot's Guide to Paganism* (Alpha Books, 2002) or online at www.draknet.com/proteus/Touch.htm.

2. Read All You Can

Since you're reading this book, I'm going to assume that you basically like to read. This will tremendously help you along your path to becoming a druid. Alas, we live in a culture where the slow and steady accumulation of knowledge is often disregarded in favor of the latest blockbuster movie, television show, or video game. Not that there's anything wrong with entertainment, but it's important to keep things in balance. As a seeker of Celtic wisdom, you'll want to devote time on a regular basis to sharpening your knowledge, not only of Celtic culture and spirituality, but of general science and the humanities as well.

The ancient druids were often depicted as scientists, philosophers, and intellectuals. For this reason, today's seeker of the druid path needs to make a similar commitment to the acquisition of knowledge. Even though in ancient times the druids shared their knowledge through oral tradition, today's world relies almost entirely on the written word as the main tool for the dissemination of information. Therefore, the aspiring druid's quest for knowledge is best served by a sustained, lifelong commitment to reading and study.

What should you read? Why, a variety of topics. Obviously, the history of the Celts, from prehistoric times to the present day is a good place to start. Irish and Welsh mythology are important. Indo-European studies will help you understand Celtic paganism in its larger context. Knowing world religion and philosophy is important. Expose yourself to today's most controversial theorists in fields like science, economics, political science, and philosophy, so that you can join in the process of wrestling with the most pressing intellectual issues facing our world. And that's just a start!

3. Meditate

Meditation isn't just for Buddhists or Hindus or New Agers. It is a core spiritual discipline that is essential to developing a disciplined mind and a heart grounded in wisdom. Meditation is a treat for your body: It lowers blood pressure, reduces stress and anxiety, and fosters a sense of inner peace and well-being. The physical benefits alone are reason enough to do it, but for aspiring druids, there's another benefit: It is the "basic training" for all subsequent spiritual practice. Magic and mysticism are both built on visualization and heightened consciousness. The doorway to such mental skill is opened by a regular (read: daily) practice of meditation.

> **The Seer Says**
>
> Support your body (and your meditation practice) by getting proper exercise, enough sleep and rest, and by eating a healthy diet.

4. Take Responsibility for Your Life

One of the most important aspects of spiritual maturity—indeed, of maturity in general terms—is learning to assume 100 percent responsibility for our lives. No less, and no more. This means that aspiring druids refrain from blaming others for life's problems (but also, refuse to accept the blame for anyone else's "stuff"). Sure, you have problems. Doesn't everyone? If you talk to people about the problems they face, pretty soon they all start sounding the same. Problems with love, problems with money, problems with abusive or neglectful family members or employers, problems with addiction or self-deception. And on it goes.

I don't mean to make light of the real problems people face, but I do believe that studying the path of druidry means choosing to rise above the temptation to whine and complain about this or that problem. Aspiring druids take responsibility for their lives. Rather than spending time complaining about problems, they work to solve them. If you want to write a book, then stop talking and start writing. If you're in an unhappy marriage, then either get the support you need to turn it around, or get out. If you're stuck in a bad situation, then find a creative solution to help make the best of it. Even if you're in prison or living in a paralyzed body, you still have control over your attitude. Keep it positive, and your life will flow accordingly. Don't give your power away: Don't blame others, and don't wait for your knight in shining armor to rescue you—*you* are your knight in shining armor.

5. Make Contact with Other Aspiring Druids

Even if you see yourself as living the druid life as a solitary (i.e., not involved with a druid organization), it still behooves you to connect with others on the same path.

The benefits include learning from others, networking, and even making a friend or three along the way. Plus, as you go further down the path, you'll have opportunities to mentor others (that's part of fulfilling step 9). Although the Internet is an excellent tool for pagan networking, look for druid organizations in your area. Join (or at least visit) a group if there is one. If not, consider starting one. You don't have to be a teacher. Start a Celtic spirituality discussion group that meets at the local New Age bookstore or other friendly venue. Even that can be a tremendous pooling of resources.

To get started on this process, try connecting with Ár nDraíocht Féin if you live in the United States or Canada; if you live in the British Isles, contact the British Druid Order.

> **The Seer Says**
>
> Here are URLs for major druid organizations' websites. In North America: www.adf.org (Ár nDraíocht Féin), www.keltria.org (Keltria), www.tuathadebrighid.org (Tuatha De Brighid); in the British Isles: www.druidry.org (Order of Bards, Ovates, and Druids) and www.druidorder.demon.co.uk (the British Druid Order).

6. Engage with the Spiritual World

Step 1 required you to become more engaged with the physical environment; this step asks you to do the same, but now with the "otherworld," or the abode of the spirits. Set up an altar to the gods and goddesses, and perhaps another one to your ancestors. (See Chapter 11 for information on setting up an altar and performing rituals.) Keep a candle burning (safely) in honor of Brigid. Use your developing meditation skills to seek out contact with the spirits of the otherworld. Pay attention to your dreams, making note of the patterns that arise out of your subconscious. Learn how to perform a basic ritual for each of the four fire festivals (see Chapter 24), as well as other times you may feel the need to connect with the spirits. If you're interested in magic or psychic development, this is the time to begin seriously cultivating such skills. Learn some of the prayers or charms from the *Carmina Gadelica* or Caitlin Matthews's *A Celtic Devotional* and adapt them so that you can begin honoring the gods and goddesses in your life on a regular, ongoing basis. Seek to fill your life with a daily sense of mystical presence. This will be empowering and transformational.

7. Let Go of Your Cherished Illusions

Sooner or later, we all have to do it, so it's time that you do, too. Following the druid path is no shortcut to bliss; it's not a magical way to automatically get more sex than you can handle or a million-dollar income with a minimum-wage set of responsibilities.

It just doesn't work that way. For that matter, let go of whatever romantic notions you may have about the Celts or druidry. Like it or not, Celtic warriors from the Iron Age were not particularly nice people. They were headhunters and their druids practiced human sacrifice.

If you're like some wannabe druids with a romanticized notion of the past, remember this: Glorifying warrior cultures is no substitute for real spiritual values like love, compassion, and care for nature (all of which are just as much part of Celtic culture as were the Iron Age warriors). Also, make a commitment to learn authentic history: Stonehenge was more than a thousand years old when the first Celts arrived in Britain, and *The Book of Fferyllt* doesn't exist. Meanwhile, don't expect to go to Ireland or Wales or Scotland and find the locals embracing you because you're a pagan. In fact, the average person living in the Celtic lands today is a devout Christian who thinks that Americans in search of their pagan roots are, well, stupid.

Notes from the Otherworld

Early manuscripts of the tale of Gwion Bach and Ceridwen refer to a mysterious *Book of Fferyllt*, which purportedly contained ancient druidic lore concerning herbs, spells, and alchemy. This mysterious book has captured the imagination of Celtic wisdom-seekers throughout the centuries; at least one best-selling book on druidism in the late twentieth century claimed to be based on the *Book of Fferyllt*. The problem is, this book never existed (and given that the ancient druids didn't write down their teachings, this is hardly surprising)! In fact, scholars have determined that the Welsh word *fferyllt* actually comes from the name "Virgil," implying that Ceridwen was actually reading a book by a Roman author when she cast her spell—not a book of druid lore at all!

Speaking of Christianity, here's a special note for pagan-oriented aspiring druids: Make sure that your interest in druidism doesn't extend to Christian bashing. After all, it was Christians who wrote down the myths, Christians who collected the folklore, and Christians who preserved at least some of the ancient *sheela-na-gigs* and other pre-Christians motifs and artifacts. Yes, druidism has pagan roots and many modern druids identify themselves as pagans, but that doesn't justify religious intolerance. Pagan druids need to treat Christianity with the same basic hospitality and respect that they would offer to any other religion. Most druids would think it is extremely bad form to walk around always criticizing Buddhism or Hinduism or Judaism; well, it's just as bad form to be a Christian basher. It's better to have a mature, adult understanding of what is both bad and good about Christianity, and be clear about the values and choices that you have made to pursue the pagan path instead. You can take a stand without getting emotional about it—and better yet, you can follow the example of OBOD and work for positive relations between Christians and pagans.

8. Become Well Rounded

Don't make the mistake of becoming a scholar of Celtic esoterica who knows nothing else. In step 4, I pointed out the necessity of learning about subjects other than Celtic spirituality; here let's look at the necessity of living a life that is balanced. Balance your mental and spiritual work with taking good care of your body, whether that means exercise, or a spiritually oriented physical practice like tai chi or yoga (just because something wasn't invented in Ireland doesn't mean that you, as an aspiring druid, can't do it!). If you're so inclined, you might also enjoy a discipline that involves energy work, such as the Japanese healing practice of Reiki. Meanwhile, if you're struggling with substance abuse, depression, or other emotional issues (like rage or paranoia) that are interfering with your life or relationships, get the help you need. Being a spiritual seeker doesn't exempt you from the benefits of good old-fashioned counseling.

And unless you already do so, I heartily encourage you to *learn a Celtic language.* Repeat: Learn a Celtic language. This is important, for several reasons. First of all, if you are so committed to Celtic spirituality, then it's important for you to become aware of traditional Celtic culture, and the best way to foster such an awareness (short of actually moving to a traditional community) is by learning a language. When you learn a language, you don't just pick up a set of foreign words, you become immersed in syntax, in the grammar that shapes the minds and thoughts of a people. Furthermore, you bring yourself closer to the gods and goddesses, as well as closer to your ancestors, by speaking in their tongue. Not only that, you learn how to pronounce the names of the deities and other figures of the Celtic myth properly!

You may also want to support efforts to keep the language alive in the Celtic lands: All the Celtic languages are endangered, both by declining numbers of native speakers (with the exception of Welsh) as well as by the nefarious influence of television and radio. When the language dies, the culture loses an essential part of its soul. Even in North America or Australia, learning a Celtic language is an act of solidarity with those who would preserve these ancient and proud cultures.

> **CAUTION**
>
> **Geasa**
>
> No matter how much you are drawn to Celtic wisdom, and no matter how long you study it, avoid referring to yourself as a druid. Better to call yourself an "aspiring druid." (Unless, of course, you have received the title of druid through membership in with an order such as OBOD). Like with other spiritual titles (such as "shaman" or "saint"), if you use it to describe yourself, others might see it as a sign of a big ego.

9. Serve Your Clan

If your reason for becoming a druid has to do with wanting to dress in long robes and look "cool," or just because you want the ego gratification of mastering a complex system, well, you're wasting your time. To be a druid means to serve others. Just as the ancient druids functioned as counselors and advisors to their kings and chieftains, today's druid needs to be available to provide spiritual service to those who seek it. Share your wisdom, whether by working to protect the environment, to preserve Celtic culture, or to teach the next generation of spiritual seekers.

The Least You Need to Know

- ◆ Of all the many representatives of Celtic wisdom, druids remain the most well known (and most misunderstood).

- ◆ The word *druid* describes the ancient philosophers/shamans/priests of the Celts, romanticized but often-inaccurate attempts to revive Celtic religion in the seventeenth through the nineteenth centuries, and sincere efforts in recent years to revive authentic Celtic paganism.

- ◆ One of the loveliest of druidic functions is the anamchara, or soul friend, who provides one-on-one spiritual guidance to others.

- ◆ Walking the druid path requires a lifelong commitment to learning and leadership.

Rituals and Tools: Supplies for the Celtic Wisdomseeker

In This Chapter

◆ What are spiritual tools, and why do they matter?

◆ The four treasures

◆ Other ceremonial implements

◆ The purpose and function of ritual

◆ Ideas for performing your own rituals

Whether you feel more drawn to the path of the seer, the bard, or the druid (or maybe even feel drawn to all three!), part of the beauty of Celtic spirituality is finding ways to honor your connection with the sacred in your own home or daily life. One of the best ways to do this is by setting up an altar, performing rituals at specific times, and using symbolic tools in the ritual. This chapter will go over these elements of spirituality, giving you the information you need to get started.

Note: The information presented in this chapter approaches the Celtic tradition from a neopagan/modern druid perspective. If you are a Christian, you might wish to adapt the material presented here to conform with your religious identity—for example, you might wish to include Christian symbolism on your altar or ritual. Always remember that there is no one "correct" way to express your devotion to the Celtic path; therefore, feel free to adapt this material (or any material presented throughout this book) to your personal spiritual needs.

Your Personal Altar

One of the easiest and yet most meaningful ways to make Celtic spirituality come alive in your life is by setting up an *altar*. This is a special place in your home or yard that has been *consecrated* for spiritual use only. Your altar will be the site where you keep spiritually meaningful objects, and it can function as the focal point of your prayers, meditations, and rituals.

What goes on an altar? Some spiritual or religious groups (especially practitioners of Wicca or some other forms of neopaganism) have precise instructions on setting up a personal altar. Your altar can be almost anything you want it to be, as long as it is spiritually meaningful for you and helps you on your spiritual journey. Some general guidelines are helpful to keep in mind:

Druidspeak

An **altar** is a place set aside for exclusive spiritual use. **Consecration** is the process for setting the altar (or the implements on it) for spiritual use.

The Seer Says

Want to put a statue of a Celtic god or goddess on your altar? Visit www.mythicimages.com or www.sacredsource.com. These two companies sell altar-friendly statues of deities from around the world, with several excellent Celtic choices in their catalogs.

- An altar ought to be uncluttered and attractive (at least to you).

- As a Celtic altar, it makes sense to have something with a Celtic connection on it: a tartan altar cloth, water from a Welsh holy well, a piece of Connemara marble, or a statue of Celtic gods or goddesses.

- Many people like to put natural objects and symbols on their altars, such as stones, seashells, feathers, or leaves. Living plants are a graceful addition to altars as well.

- Fire is such a universal symbol for spirituality that altars hardly seem complete without one or more candles.

This altar features a candle (to symbolize the sacred fire of inspiration), a bowl of water (to symbolize holy wells as portals to the otherworld), a circle of stones (symbolizing the ancient stone circles of the ancestors), a plant (symbolizing the spirits of nature), and statues of Celtic deities.

Setting Up and Consecrating Your Altar

Finding the right objects for an altar can be seen as a spiritual adventure in itself. You might find just a few special items that will grace your altar for years to come. Or you might be like me, continually refreshing your altar with new items that seem spiritually appropriate.

To help crystallize the spiritual intent of the altar and the objects on it, you'll want to consecrate them (ceremonially set them aside for sacred use). This doesn't have to be fancy. Even just saying a prayer asking for Spirit's blessing on your altar and its components is enough. Again, some neopagan traditions have ritual instructions for consecration.

> **The Seer Says**
>
> Although there's no right or wrong way to create a personal altar, you might find it useful to place the following elements on yours: symbols of nature, symbols of Spirit (god, goddess, and so forth), symbols of your ancestors, and any item that reminds you of your spiritual quest.

The Four Treasures

One of the best ways to organize a Celtic altar is around four central sacred treasures of Irish myth: the four treasures of the Túatha Dé Danann.

According to myth, the Túatha Dé Danann, or peoples of the Goddess Danu, descended to the land of Ireland from the sky, where they had flown from four mythical mystical cities said to be in the northern islands of the world: Falias, Gorias, Murias, and Findias. From each of these legendary cities came a sacred treasure that the people of Danu brought to their new home:

◆ From Falias came the *Lía Fáil* (Stone of Destiny), a stone said to emit a loud roar whenever the rightful king of Ireland touched it.

◆ From Gorias came the mighty *spear* that belonged to the many-talented god Lugh. It was said that no warrior could prevail against this spear.

◆ From Murias came the *Cauldron of Plenty*, from which the great god known as the Dagda could feed an entire army.

◆ From Findias came the mighty *sword* wielded by Núadu, a great warrior among the Túatha Dé Danann.

Notes from the Otherworld

If you're familiar with ceremonial magic or the tarot, you'll notice a similarity between the four treasures of the Irish gods and the four tools of magic: The Spear of Lugh corresponds to the wand, the Sword of Núadu corresponds to the sword, the Stone of Destiny corresponds to the coin or pentacle, and the Cauldron of the Dagda corresponds to the cup or chalice. Although the lore surrounding the Irish treasures is somewhat different from the teachings of ceremonial magic, the tools are similar enough to be used in both settings.

Why are the treasures of the Túatha Dé Danann so important? Not only do they symbolize the gods and goddesses themselves, but they also stand for important and powerful wisdom principles. The Sword of Núadu symbolizes courage and fearlessness in battle; even if you're not a warrior in today's world, it represents the fortitude necessary to stand up to whatever conflicts come your way. The Spear of Lugh symbolizes knowledge and mental skill, and represents the skills necessary to learn and eventually become wise. The Stone of Destiny symbolizes sovereignty and freedom, and represents the qualities necessary to be truly free. And the Cauldron of Plenty represents prosperity and abundance, and symbolizes the blessings we receive from the bounty of Mother Earth.

Having tools on your altar that symbolize the four treasures not only connects you to the Túatha Dé Danaan, but also creates a material connection to the energies of courage, freedom, wisdom, and abundance—energies important for leading a good and happy life.

The Bachall, the Sickle, and the Egg

Although we know very little about the ancient druids, we do have a few tantalizing hints from ancient writers. Some Celtic wisdomseekers like to adorn their altar with objects that, at least symbolically, connect them with the druids of old. Here are a few possibilities:

♦ **The bachall.** This Gaelic word means "staff" and is roughly equivalent to a magic wand. For druids, a bachall would be the primary tool used in magic and ritual. While we have no solid information about how druids would have made or used bachalls, some Celtic seekers turn to more modern magical spiritual paths (like Wicca) for guidance or simply have a wand for its beauty.

♦ **The egg.** According to the first-century author Pliny, ancient druids used a magical tool called the anguinum, which was an egg-shape object said to be made from snake secretions. Although there's no evidence that such a thing ever existed, it has caught the imagination of some modern druids, who see the egg as a symbol of Goddess energy or of abundance. An egg made of marble or quartz for your altar would add a touch of beauty as well as symbolize the magic of ancient times.

♦ **The sickle.** One of the best-known tools associated with druids is the sickle, or crescent-shape knife, said to have been used in the harvest of mistletoe and other herbs. Even as an ornamental object, it can symbolize the energies of the moon as well as druid's classic role as herbalist and healer.

> **The Seer Says**
>
> Besides tantalizing hints in myth and legend, we know very little about the magical practices of ancient Celtic shamans and druids. Many people interested in Celtic spirituality in our day turn to modern schools of occultism for training in magical arts. Modern magic can help you set up an altar, find appropriate tools, and master the principles of ritual.

Fire and Water: The Key Elements

Two items that you may want to represent on your altar are fire and water, both of which have long associations as gateways to the otherworld. Fire was often regarded as holy and kept in sacred temples, such as one at Kildare in Ireland, which was sacred first to the goddess Brigid and later, to the Christian Saint Brigid. Water signifies the energies of holy wells, as well as the power of the ocean. You can keep a dish filled with rainwater or, if possible, well water, as well as a candle or oil lamp lit in honor of Spirit. If you have the means to do it safely, you might even want to keep a votive light burning on the altar as an ongoing reminder of divine presence.

This votive flame is lit in honor of Brigid, the Celtic goddess of fire, healing, and inspiration.

The Virtue of Asking

Welsh mythology tells the tale of Pwyll, a prince who saw a remarkable vision of a woman on a horse. He sent one of his men after her, but no matter how fast the man rode, the woman on the horse always outpaced him. The next day, Pwyll rode after the woman himself, but even he, on his finest horse, couldn't overtake her. Finally, on the third day, he saw her again, and riding after her, called out, "Lady, would you please stop and speak with me?" Immediately she reined in her horse, and turned to Pwyll and said, "Gladly, lord, because you had the courtesy to ask. Indeed, it would have been better for your horse if you had asked earlier!" The lady turned out to be Rhiannon, the great queen of the faery realm.

> **The Bard's Bookshelf**
>
> Want to learn more about Pwyll and Rhiannon? One of the loveliest modern versions of Welsh mythology is *The Mabinogion Tetralogy* by Evangeline Walton (Overlook Press, 2002), a novelization of the major Welsh tales.

The story of Pwyll and Rhiannon illustrates a basic principle of communication: It is a good thing to ask for what you need. This means, on a spiritual level, that when we seek contact with the inhabitants of the otherworld, we need to be in the habit of expressing what we want and need. Friendly spirits are eager to help us reach our goals, but will wait until we ask for their assistance.

But how do we ask for help from the spirit world? Whether the help we seek is something practical (like healing or blessings for prosperity) or something entirely mystical (like a deeper, more profound sense of spiritual guidance in our lives), the lesson of Pwyll is clear: Ask for what you want. For seekers of Celtic wisdom, the easiest and most direct way to ask for spiritual help is through the practice of ritual.

What Is Ritual?

For the purposes of this book, "ritual" encompasses a wide variety of spiritual activities, all of which can foster that place where we can seek wisdom, knowledge, guidance, healing, and blessing from the spirit world. The traditional concept of prayer is a ritualistic act in its simplest form—going within the quiet places of the mind and seeking spiritual contact. On the other extreme, an intricate religious ceremony such as a Catholic high mass or a Wiccan sabbat, complete with candles, bells, incense, holy oil, robed priests (and priestesses), chanting, and other elements, fosters an altered state of consciousness where spirit contact is more possible.

> **The Bard's Bookshelf**
>
> Not sure where to begin on your quest for Celtic ritual? Try reading Emma Restall Orr's *Ritual: A Guide to Life, Love and Inspiration* (Thorsons, 2000).

Ritual Defined

The word *ritual* might come from an Indo-European root word for "joining." A ritual is a way of joining together the material and spiritual world for the purpose of improving relations between humankind and our spiritual relations, whether ancestors, spirit guides, faeries, or deities. To do this, a ritual involves a set of formalized acts designed to help foster the connection between the worlds.

How to Do It

As a seeker of Celtic ways, you'll want to have some form of ritual activity in your life. If you are a religious person, chances are that ritual is already provided for you by your religious community. You can supplement the services of your religion with private prayer and simple ceremonies such as the one described in this chapter.

If you don't participate in an organized religious group, it's totally up to you to create and enact whatever rituals you need to reach out to the spiritual world. You can choose to keep things simple, or you can join forces with other seekers to create a more elaborate ceremony. The choice is yours. Remember, the point behind a ritual, no matter how simple or complex, is to foster a sense of connection with the spirit world. The only criteria for judging a ritual's effectiveness is this connection. For some people, a few minutes of meditation may be all they need to establish a link with the ancestors. Others may need a full-blown ceremony filled with sensuous objects, sounds, and smells. And then there are others who enjoy both simple and ornate ways of doing ritual. (I fall into this camp!) Don't be judgmental toward ritual styles that don't work for you, but do take the time to find the best way for you to make the spiritual connection you seek.

> **The Seer Says**
>
> Lots of great ritual ideas can be found online. Visit the websites of Ár nDraíocht Féin (www.adf.org) and Tuatha De Brighid (www.tuathadebrighid.org). These druid organizations have filled their websites with information about rituals as well as informative essays about Celtic ceremony.

Here are a few ideas for getting started on your own rituals:

- **Meditate.** No matter how simple or complex, the spiritual connection we seek in ritual will always "happen" in our minds. Some people believe that rituals are always effective, and even if we don't feel a connection with Spirit consciously, it still has occurred subconsciously. Others feel that a ritual needs to make a real difference in their awareness before the ritual has "worked." I personally lean more toward the former position, but I still seek to have a positive, heartfelt experience in every ritual I perform. In meditation, you can open your mind (conscious and unconscious) to the spiritual world, making contact easier and more effective.

- **Prayer.** If meditation is the process of establishing a link, then prayer is the process of transmitting information through that link. Contrary to popular belief, prayer is not just "talking to God." It's a two-way street that involves both asking/speaking to Spirit, and listening for a reply, which often comes simply as a whisper in our hearts.

Prayer and meditation are really the heart of ritual, and as such can be done without any "window dressing." But if you want to add a ritualistic touch to your spiritual life, here are a few possibilities:

◆ **Simple ceremonies.** Light a candle or incense before meditation or prayer. Begin and end prayer and meditation with a recited poem, such as the "Song of Amergin."

◆ **More complex ceremonies.** Arrange symbols of the four treasures in your room, saying prayers to invoke the energies of each one. (See the ritual discussed later in this chapter for an example of this.) Or write a series of prayers, one each to your favorite Celtic gods and goddesses. You can perform these more in-depth ceremonies whenever you pray or meditate, or at specific times of the year, such as the eight holidays (also discussed later in this chapter).

◆ **Make an offering.** In Chapter 10, you learned about how the druids presided over sacrifice. Remember, for modern Celtic wisdomseekers, sacrifice isn't a matter of trying to please an angry God or shed blood as a way of atoning for sins! Rather, think of sacrifice as a present for your spiritual guides. This is why the word "offering" may seem more appropriate than "sacrifice." Like young lovers who exchange candies or flowers, an offering made to your spiritual guides, ancestors, or patron deities is a way to strengthen the bonds of relationship.

> **The Seer Says**
>
> Looking for ideas of offerings to make at your altar? Lit candles, incense, flowers, oils, or token amounts of food and drink are lovely ways to express your spiritual devotion on your altar. Remember never to leave flame unattended.

Why Do Ritual

So what are the benefits of ritual? Here are a few points to keep in mind:

◆ Ritual keeps you feeling connected to the otherworld. It reminds us that there's more to life than meets the eye.

◆ Ritual can help us pray or meditate more effectively. It's like a turbo-charged engine to make our spiritual work more powerful.

◆ Ritual can strengthen our ties with the Celtic world. Especially if your ritual is filled with Celtic art or music, or you recite poetry about Celtic deities, or tell stories from the myths and legends, all this can make your ritual a way to deepen your ties with this particular spiritual path.

◆ Ritual is enjoyable on its own terms. Most spiritually minded people enjoy ritual just for itself!

When to Do It

When is the best time to perform rituals? On one level, whenever you feel the need to connect with the otherworld. But in terms of life's rhythms, their are eight particular holidays associated with Celtic wisdom. Four of these are ancient Celtic festival days that have been revived in our time. The other four are the key turning points of the year: the solstices and the equinoxes.

To learn more about the Celtic holidays, see Chapter 24.

How Can We Create an Authentic Celtic Ritual

Many people, especially in the neopagan and Wiccan communities, want to find ways to perform as "authentic" a Celtic ritual as possible. By "authentic" people usually mean faithful to the practices and values of the ancient Celts, such as those who lived in pre-Christian times. To this end, many modern druids and Celtic-focussed neopagans do research into archaeology, comparative mythology, anthropology, and religious studies to try to nail down the most accurate possible ritual.

If this appeals to you, go for it and enjoy the quest. However, you don't have to be a scholar to reach out in a heartfelt way to the otherworld. Remember, even in ancient times, great diversity existed among the Celts, with different gods and goddesses and spiritual practices popular among different segments of the population. In other words, there was never a "standard" form of Celtic ritual (like the Catholic Church has a standard way of doing mass).

> **CAUTION**
>
> **Geasa**
>
> It's a good thing to try to make your ritual as Celtic as possible. But don't get so caught up in the externals that you forget to make a sincere effort to connect with the gods.

For modern purposes, the best way to bring an authentic feel to your Celtic ritual is to make sure that you perform the ritual with Celtic themes in mind. Seek contact with Irish or Welsh gods and goddesses, or recite excerpts from Celtic myths as part of your ritual. Play Celtic music to get in the mood for ritual and wear Celtic knotwork jewelry or a robe emblazoned with Celtic designs. Seek a heartfelt spiritual experience—that's your shortest route to "authenticity"!

A Sample Ritual

Here is a simple ritual to give you an idea of how ritual can be a meaningful part of your spirituality. It's an entirely new ritual that I wrote for a winter solstice celebration in my community. You'll notice that parts of the ritual were adapted from traditional sources: the "Song of Amergin" and prayers from the Scottish anthology *Carmina Gadelica* were adapted for use in this ceremony. Although we have no idea what ancient Celts may have done to celebrate the winter solstice, we do know that the ancient site of Newgrange in Ireland features a dramatic event every winter solstice, when the sun rises at the precise angle to shine into the burial chamber. This is mentioned in the ceremony as well, to further connect it to Celtic (or pre-Celtic) spirituality.

To perform the ritual, all you need is an altar with two candles set on it, a candle for each point of the compass (north, east, west, and south), a gift for an offering (canned goods or toys that can then be given to charity), a votive candle for each person in the ritual, and spiced cider and cookies. Optional items include a bell or chime, and symbols of the four treasures of the Túatha Dé Danann.

The ritual can be performed alone or in a small group. Groups should divide the spoken parts so each person can participate. It may be performed indoors or out. If outside, be sure to dress appropriately for the temperature! The best time to perform the ritual is just after sundown on the longest night of the year.

Set up the space where the ritual is to be performed by placing an altar in the center. Mark each of the four directions (north, east, south, and west) with a candle. Optionally, you can also place a symbol of the four treasures at the appropriate direction.

Begin the ritual with a few moments of silence. Reflect on the blessings of the sun and its importance to all life. If the ritual is being performed by a group, one member can provide soft background music with a harp, flute, pennywhistle, or frame drum.

Pagans can direct this ritual to the Dagda and Brigid. Christians may prefer to direct it to God and to Saint Bridget. Either way, you will be invoking the presence of Spirit into your life. Use whatever language is most comfortable for you.

The Seer Says

Give your ritual a nice touch by decorating your altar with a lovely tablecloth and symbols of the season. Incense can add a dimension of beauty; most spiritual traditions see incense as symbolic of prayer rising to heaven. (However, if you are doing your ritual with a group, make sure beforehand that no one has asthma or allergies that could be triggered by the incense.) An extra taper is handy, too: Rather than using matches or a lighter to light the candles in the ceremony, carrying a lit taper to each of the candles is an elegant touch.

To mark the ritual's beginning, strike a bell three times, or simply take three deep, centering breaths. Then say:

I/we perform this ritual in your honor, Brigid, font of blessing.

Brigid above us, Brigid below us, Brigid in the very air about us,

Brigid in our truest heart!

Light the candles at each of the four directions, and then on the altar. Say the following at lighting each candle:

Candle in the north:

To the North, I/we honor the Sword of Núadu, symbol of strength and of the limitless sky. May I/we receive the blessing of courage on this solstice night.

Candle in the east:

To the East, I/we honor the Cauldron of the Dagda, symbol of abundance and of the waters of life. May I/we receive the blessing of prosperity on this solstice night.

Candle in the south:

To the South, I/we honor the Stone of Destiny, symbol of harmony and of the sovereign earth. May I/we receive the blessing of freedom on this solstice night.

Candle in the west:

To the West, I/we honor the Spear of Lugh, symbol of knowledge and of the sacred fire. May I/we receive the blessing of wisdom on this solstice night.

Candle on right side of altar:

Good Father God, You are the wind that blows upon the sea, You are the ocean wave, You are the murmur of the surges, You are seven battalions, You are a strong bull, You are an eagle on a rock, You are a ray of the sun, You are the most beautiful of herbs, You are a courageous wild boar, You are a salmon in the water, You are a lake upon a plain, You are a cunning artist, You are a gigantic champion, You are the god who bestows the Imbas.

—Adapted from the "Song of Amergin"

Candle on left side of altar:

Brigid of the mantles, Brigid of the hearth fire, Brigid of the twining hair, Brigid of the augury, Brigid of the white feet, Brigid of the calmness, Brigid of the fair palms, Brigid of the kine, Brigid, friend of women, Brigid of the hearth fire, Brigid, helper of women, Brigid, woman mild, each day and each night I call the descent of Brigid. I am under the keeping of blessed Brigid, my companion beloved is Brigid.

—Adapted from the *Carmina Gadelica*

Meditation and Offering

Now that the candles are lit, take time to meditate on the winter solstice, darkest night of the year. Make an offering: canned goods or toys, which you will then donate to a food bank or charity. Set your offering on the altar, saying in your own words that this is your gift to Spirit for the solstice season.

Then each person takes a votive candle and lights it from the candle to the south. As each person lights his or her candle, he or she might make a prayer or express a wish for the coming year.

After the candles are lit, share some spiced cider and cookies. Put a small amount of food on the altar as offering to the spirits. If performing the ritual alone, still do this: You are sharing an intimate meal with the divine! If in a group, this is a relaxed time when people can enjoy each other's company as well as the food. A group might also enjoy singing carols or other songs appropriate to the season.

The Seer Says

Rituals do not need to be elaborate or fancy affairs. In many ways, they work best when done simply and from the heart. Try to write your own rituals, in which you express in your own words the connection you'd like to establish with friendly spirits from the otherworld.

After the meal, extinguish each of the candles. (Use your fingers or a snuffer; do not blow out the candles.) Say the following as each candle is extinguished:

Candle in the north:

To the North, I/we acknowledge the Sword of Núada and the gift of courage. Thank you for blessing me/us this solstice night.

Candle in the east:

To the East, I/we acknowledge the Cauldron of the Dagda and the gift of prosperity. Thank you for blessing me/us this solstice night.

Candle in the south:

To the South, I/we acknowledge the Stone of Destiny and the gift of freedom. Thank you for blessing me/us this solstice night.

Candle in the west:

> To the West, I/we acknowledge the Spear of Lugh and the gift of wisdom. Thank you for blessing me/us this solstice night.

Candle on right side of altar:

> Father God, thank you for your presence at this ritual.

Candle on right side of altar:

> Sacred Brigid, thank you for your presence at this ritual.

Final Blessing

If alone, you may recite this aloud or silently; if in a group, recite it aloud so that each person may share in the blessing:

> **The Seer Says**
>
> Take the time to memorize the words you use in a ritual—unless you're more comfortable speaking extemporaneously. Having scripts or "cheat sheets" to read in a ritual can be distracting, whether you're doing it alone or in a group.

As the sun shines in Newgrange on the winter solstice morning, so we know that the promise of winter is a new spring, and the promise of death is a new life. Go forth into the winter months and live a life of promise. May blessings abound wherever you go! So be it.

The ritual is finished. Be sure to clean up the ritual space. Food offered to Spirit ought to be disposed of in a reverent manner, perhaps left outside where wild animals could enjoy it. Remember to take the canned goods and toys to an appropriate agency.

The Least You Need to Know

- Tools are ceremonial items that help focus your spiritual journey in practical ways.

- Four of the greatest of Celtic tools are based on the treasures of the Irish deities: the sword, the spear, the cauldron, and the stone.

- Other tools symbolize powerful elements (fire and water) or the spiritual authority of the druids (the wand and the egg).

- Ritual is a formal process for communicating with the spiritual realm, requesting aid and blessings, and offering gifts to the spirits.

Part  3

Mythology and Lore

The Celts have long been great storytellers. From famous Irish novelists like James Joyce to the many anonymous farmers and fishermen who kept the art of storytelling alive over the centuries, the Celts have used stories and legends to remember who they are, where they come from, and how they as a people fit into our strange, mysterious, and wonderful universe. Celtic stories are not mere recollections of yesterday or yesteryear. They are filled with mystical images of gods, goddesses, heroes, and ancestors, opening a door to the magical otherworld where the faeries dwell (and where our souls will someday venture, after life has ended here on earth).

In your search for Celtic wisdom, you can spend a lifetime poring through learned tomes at great university libraries, but you might enjoy yourself better (and find wisdom faster!) simply by availing yourself to the rich traditions of myth and folklore. Thankfully, many Celtic stories have been written down, meaning that countless doorways into Celtic myth and lore are available today, even for those of us who live far away from the ancestral Celtic lands.

Chapter 12

Storytelling: The Waltz of Remembering

In This Chapter

◆ A glimpse into the shanachie's world

◆ How oral tradition became written literature

◆ The difference between myth and folklore

◆ Why storytelling is important

◆ Getting started on your own adventure with the Celtic myths

For many people, one of the most enjoyable aspects of Celtic spirituality is the vast and ancient tradition of myths, stories, legends, and folk tales that have originated in the Celtic lands. Many of these stories were passed from generation to generation as part of the oral tradition, but beginning with Christian monks in the Middle Ages and continuing with folklore collectors in recent decades, efforts have been made to record these traditional tales. Indeed, with the rise of mass media like radio and television, storytelling now seems to be a dying art, although even today, traditional yarn-spinners can be found in places like the west of Ireland or the highlands of Scotland.

The Role of the Shanachie in Celtic Wisdom

Our society has been dominated for centuries by an intellectual model based on the great universities. This means that philosophy, theology, science, and other disciplines of the mind have all been influenced and shaped by learned men (and, recently, women) affiliated with academic institutions.

The Celtic tradition has long been marginal and outside the mainstream of society and culture—including outside the mainstream of academia. Sure, fine institutions of higher learning have been established in the Celtic lands, but these schools traditionally have taught curricula based on mainstream ideas of philosophy and theology. Meanwhile, the traditional, indigenous wisdom of the Celtic people has existed beneath the radar of the academic world, passed down orally from generation to generation through the tales and legends of storytellers and folk poets.

So the shanachie, or storyteller, is a wisdomkeeper, but not in any official or institutionally recognized sense. You don't go to college to get a diploma in storytelling. (Well, maybe some colleges offer degrees in storytelling nowadays, but traditionally that wasn't an option.) Think of the world of powerful universities and internationally influential religious bodies as the "mainstream." By contrast, the humble, people-oriented tradition of storytelling that has survived in the remote corners of the Celtic world has preserved an alternative vision of life, of spirituality, of values, and of ethics. It is this alternative vision that is the true legacy of the druids and the bards, and that survived in written form in Celtic myth and folklore, and can still be heard in out-of-the-way places in the Celtic world.

> **Notes from the Otherworld**
>
> In the movie version of *The Wizard of Oz*, the Wizard helps the Scarecrow to see that he has a brain by giving him a diploma. The joke, of course, is that the scarecrow has a level of street smarts that eludes many college professors! But joke or not, our culture really does have a bias where a diploma equals intelligence, which in turn equals wisdom.

> **The Seer Says**
>
> Remember, you don't have to earn a college degree to be wise in the Celtic ways. Rather, Celtic wisdom is learned through living life fully and honorably, being connected with nature, and cultivating a deep and meaningful spirituality.

The Storyteller's Natural Environment

In their classic study of myth titled *Celtic Heritage: Ancient Tradition in Ireland and Wales*, Alwyn and Brinley Rees describe how a traditional Celtic storyteller from County Galway or the Scottish islands might have appeared, in the not too distant past, and might yet appear in some places where modern entertainment has not totally destroyed traditional ways. These shanachies are usually old men or women who have been interested in the stories of yore since their youth, and have been collecting stories, adding to and refining their repertoire, all their life. Like generations before them, they would entertain their listeners around a fire in a cozy farmhouse on a cold winter's night.

The best stories, like a classic movie or hit song, would get told again and again over the years, but both storyteller and listener know that it is not the facts of the story, but the artistry in the telling, that is of lasting importance. Indeed, many listeners would know the best stories by heart, but that would hardly stop them from asking to hear the good ones again and again. (After all, some of the younger listeners might themselves aspire to be traditional storytellers someday!)

Imagine this scene of a Scottish crofter's (tenant farmer) home in the late nineteenth or early twentieth century: The small house, with a peat fire burning in the middle of the room, was full of activity, as the family who lived there might be engaged in a craft such as sewing or rope-making, with lively conversation filling the air. Everyone would busy themselves completing the chores of the day: sweeping the floor, lighting the oil lamp, bringing the turf in for the fire, and even chasing a stray chicken or two who happened to wander into the house from outside. All would be working to prepare the home for a *céilidh* that would occur that evening.

Druidspeak

Céilidh is a Gaelic word meaning gathering or celebration. It refers to a traditional get-together where music, dance, poetry, singing, and storytelling are shared.

Eventually the chores would be done, and people from around the village, friends and neighbors and relatives, would start to appear, dropping by for the céilidh. Some might bring their musical instruments, others just a listening ear. If by chance there were a visitor in the home, a stranger from some other town or village, he or she would be invited to sit nearest to the host or hostess and would likely be the first to ask for a story. Once the request was made, silence would descend as the storyteller would begin to weave his or her spell, telling perhaps a tale or two about the faeries, or an adventure involving a commoner who bested a foreign king, or a story about the adventures of this or that Christian saint.

The story might last 10 minutes or it might last an hour, but however long it took, time seemed to stand still beneath the shanachie's enchantment. Everyone listened raptly and silently, except for an occasional burst of laughter or applause at appropriate moments. When finally the story reached its end, the audience acknowledged the storyteller with simple compliments and murmurs of appreciation, flowing into renewed conversation—until perhaps a child or some other member of the audience would ask for another tale, perhaps even requesting an old favorite, and after a modest declamation or two, the storyteller would weave another doorway into a magical world filled with extraordinary beasts, otherworldly beauties, and valorous heroes.

A traditional storyteller freely acknowledged that he or she did not write or create the stories recounted, but merely passed on tales that have been told for uncounted years to a new generation of appreciative listeners. The best storytellers are said to have such extensive repertoires that they can tell a different story every night from Samhain (the end of October) to Beltaine (the beginning of May).

> **The Bard's Bookshelf**
>
> *Celtic Heritage* by Alwyn and Brinley Rees (Thames and Hudson, 1961), from which these descriptions of traditional storytellers have been adapted, is considered a preeminent study of Celtic myth and folklore. It belongs in the library of every seeker of Celtic wisdom.

From Oral Tradition to the Written Word

As mentioned several times already, this ancient and venerable practice of oral storytelling is, like the Celtic languages the shanachies speak, a dying art. Even though storytelling may be the final surviving link to the great ancient bards who recounted glorious deeds of kings and warriors, in today's world of movie blockbusters, fast-action video games, and television sitcoms, fewer and fewer people are taking the time to listen to, or learn, the stories of yesteryear, even in the remote corners of the Celtic world. And certainly among the Celts of the diaspora, storytelling is a largely forgotten art. For this reason, one of the most precious resources available to the modern seeker of Celtic ways is the written tradition of myths and legends, which began with Christian monks in the Middle Ages and extended to folklorists who have collected information over the past two centuries that otherwise might have been lost with the passing of the oral tradition.

During my visit to Ireland in 2002, I had the rare good fortune to spend a day in the company of an 81-year-old retired farmer from County Galway who is a gifted storyteller. Over the course of most of a day, he never tired and never told the same tale twice. When giving me a tour of his farmhouse, he commented that his children had moved to America and none of them wanted to come home and tend the family farm, so he and his wife had no choice but to rent the land. He had no idea what would happen to the farm after they died. He spoke without a hint of self-pity, and yet I could hear in his matter-of-fact words not only the loss of a traditional family livelihood, but the loss of an entire way of life, as well.

The Monks and the Myths: Preserving the Stories

You might not be able to halt the wheels of change that are bringing to an end an ancient way of life, but as a wisdomseeker, you'll want to find some sort of appropriate and meaningful way to bring the grand tradition of Celtic myth and story into your life. And, unless you happen to be so fortunate as to know a living shanachie or two from whom you can learn your repertoire, your best bet is to explore the vast amount of myth and legend that has been documented and published. Even if you don't know one word of Irish or any of the other Celtic languages, you'll find a wealth of material translated into English.

Notes from the Otherworld

Much of the legends and lore that have been written over the years remain untranslated from their original tongue. The Irish Folklore Commission, for example, collected thousands of stories in the early years of the twentieth century that are now archived in Dublin, most of which were told and recorded in Irish and have never been rendered in English, let alone published. Who knows what treasures of ancient lore remain hidden in those files?

What's Good About the Written Myths ...

Basically, as a seeker of Celtic wisdom, you have a thousand years of written material available for you to explore: from the writings of medieval scribes who felt it was their Christian duty to document the native traditions of their homeland, to various poets and authors whose works explore mythology (and in some cases, contribute to the tradition) over the centuries, up to the vast collections of unpublished and published folklore collected especially in the last 150 years. Today, you can find actual translations of original Celtic stories, and (more often) various anthologies of Celtic tales retold for the modern mind. At the end of this chapter, nine books are listed to get you started on the vast subject of Celtic literature.

We have much to be thankful for, now that this material has been documented. Given that the Celts have long survived in a world that felt they were the descendents of barbarians and that the only "real" mythology worth studying came from Greece and Rome, it's a wonder that the medieval Christians bothered to write down the Celtic tales at all. In Celtic myth and legend, we learn much of the basic material presented in this book: information about Celtic gods and goddesses, about ideas regarding the otherworld, and about the nature and behavior of faeries and other spiritual beings. The Celtic legends give us insight into ancient spiritual practices, such as the great festivals like Samhain and Beltaine (which will be discussed in greater depth in Chapter 24).

Most of all, in a world where the scientific method and the Christian Bible dominate what most people believe about the world we live in, the Celtic myths quietly insist that there are other ways to understand the cosmos.

... And What's Not So Good

Unfortunately, though, Celtic myth and lore are not without their problems. The most obvious problem is that the lore preserved both in myth and folk tales is fragmentary and incomplete. Working with the Celtic tradition is like trying to assemble a huge puzzle, with many pieces sadly missing. Another problem is the confusion of pagan and Christian perspectives throughout the tradition. The Celtic wisdom tradition dates back to pagan times, when gods and goddesses were worshipped and ancestors revered. But by the time the lore was written down, the Celtic lands were largely Christianized, and those writing the myths were adherents of the new religion. At times, stories appear to have been altered or censored to make them more acceptable within the bounds of the new religion; or the scribes may have simply used Christian imagery when recounting pagan tales, because that was the familiar culture of their day. Whatever their motivations, this resulted in a body of myth and legend that is messy and inconsistent, with both pagan and Christian ideas and values sloppily thrown together. To the modern seeker, whether Christian, neopagan, or nonreligious, working with the stories of the tradition means trying to sort out the pagan and Christian themes, to discern what the original ideas may have been that were encoded in the stories.

> **The Bard's Bookshelf**
>
> Some students of Celtic ways believe that comparative mythology—a field of study that seeks common themes in different Indo-European systems of mythology—can help us find the missing pieces of the Celtic puzzle. If you're interested in this topic, check out C. Scott Littleton's *The New Comparative Mythology* (University of California Press, 1982) and Jaan Puhvel's *Comparative Mythology* (Johns Hopkins University Press, 1987).

Today, many seekers of the Celtic ways are working with the myths and legends to do just that. Christians have published material from Celtic lore that speaks to the Christian religion, while neopagans have attempted to retell the old myths in ways that are more sympathetic to the gods and goddesses. Rather than worry about which religion is "right," your job as a wisdomseeker is to find which elements of the Celtic tradition speak most clearly to you.

It's a Living Tradition

Some people might think it's scandalous to take old stories and legends and rewrite or recast them in ways that make them more relevant to the modern world or more consistent with one particular religious viewpoint. On the surface, that might seem to be a dishonoring of the ancient stories and the bards who created them. But it's important to remember that, even in oral traditions where stories are carefully memorized and preserved, it is natural for tales to evolve and change over the passing of time. That evolutionary process is in some ways slowed down by written literature, since a text preserved on paper never changes. But even a written story can be retold, and retold again, and therefore evolve in its various retellings. This is a natural process, and should not be seen as a violation of Celtic wisdom.

We're blessed to have many medieval manuscripts filled with ancient Celtic myths and legends. But (as mentioned earlier) even those ancient writings indicate that myths were being retold and revised in accordance with the changing needs of the Celtic world. For this reason, it's important not to treat the written myths as some sort of holy scripture which can never be altered, but rather as important documents in a constantly evolving tradition.

 Geasa _____

It can be a waste of time to worry about which of two slightly different tellings of a myth is the "more authentic" version. Instead, look for which stories are the most meaningful, or carry the most useful message.

Indeed, we could argue that one reason the ancient druids refused to write down their teachings is that they knew that written texts could be taken too literally. (Think of the problem of religious fundamentalism, which begins with people who insist on reading the Bible or the Koran literally.) By keeping their tradition oral, the druids allowed it to evolve in natural, organic ways. Even though we by necessity must engage with myths and lore through the medium of the written word, we need to allow a similar leeway in allowing the tradition to evolve. Otherwise, we run the risk of becoming "fundamentalists" in a tradition without even a sacred scripture!

Overview of the Mythic Sources

In this section, let's look at the basic sources of Celtic myth, nearly all of which comes out of Irish or Welsh manuscripts from the twelfth through the fourteenth centuries. For the purposes of this book, Celtic "myth" is defined as the body of stories derived from these medieval sources, most of which involved heroes and gods and goddesses that appear to date back to pre-Christian times. Celtic "lore" refers to the body of stories, legends, and folk tales that have evolved to the modern era, and have been documented by folklorists in recent decades. Unlike myth, lore is often less concerned with gods and heroes, and more concerned with fairies, ghosts, Christian saints, and ordinary people caught up in exceptional circumstances. But even though these stories may not have a "mythic" quality to them, they still often contain profound insights into the wisdom of the Celtic people.

The Irish Tradition

Irish scribes in the Middle Ages created huge manuscripts, filled with all sorts of material: religious sermons; excerpts from the Bible or other texts; historical data and genealogies; and various stories, myths, and legends. Here are the main Irish manuscripts where Celtic myths can be found:

- ◆ *Book of the Dun Cow* **(before 1106).** The name comes from the cow whose hide was used for the vellum on which the manuscript was written. Includes some 37 stories and legends.

- ◆ *Book of Leinster* **(approximately 1160).** More than a hundred stories, including one of the fullest versions of the great Irish epic known as "The *Táin.*"

- ◆ *The Speckled Book* **(late twelfth century).** Mostly religious stories involving the adventures of Christian saints, as well as lovely poetry expressing the wonders of Christian mysticism.

- ◆ *Book of Ballymote* **(approximately 1391).** Contains hundreds of pages of legends and other documents.

- ◆ *Yellow Book of Lecan* **(approximately 1390).** Another extensive collection of stories and history, including a lovely tale called *The Wooing of Étain.*

What is today thought of as Irish mythology has been culled from the various legends and stories contained in these medieval anthologies.

Among the filid of medieval Ireland, the mythic tales were categorized by topic (such as tales of voyages, of wooings, of raids, and so forth). Modern scholars, however, have identified four "cycles" or branches of Irish mythology:

- ◆ **The Mythological Cycle,** dealing with the earliest history of Ireland and the history of the gods and goddesses, especially the Peoples of Danu, or Túatha Dé Danann. Most of the familiar Irish deities, such as the Dagda (the "good" god) and Lugh (the many-skilled sky god) come from this cycle. Main text: *Lebor Gabála Érenn* (*Book of Invasions*, literally "Book of the Taking of Ireland").

- ◆ **The Ulster Cycle,** primarily dealing with the exploits of Cú Chulainn, the greatest of Irish heroes. This cycle features deities such as the Morrígan, the goddess of love and death. Main text: *Táin Bó Cuailnge* ("The Cattle Raid of Cooley," also called "The Táin").

> **Notes from the Otherworld**
>
> *Táin* is an Irish word meaning "raid," and is the common shorthand name for *Táin Bó Cuailnge* ("The Cattle-Raid of Cooley"). Many ancient Irish stories involved raiding, but the *Táin Bó Cuailnge* is often considered the greatest of such stories—a true Irish epic.

- **The Fenian or Heroic Cycle,** primarily dealing with Fionn mac Cumhaill (a semi-divine figure who was a guardian of the land) and his band of hunters/warriors, the Fiana or Fenians. This cycle is less supernatural and more adventurous. No single text, but many stories involve the Fenian heroes.

- **The Historic Cycle,** dealing with kings and other figures of historical record, although often with legendary or mythological elements. This cycle forms the bridge between the realm of myth and the realm of documented history. Again, there's no single primary text, but many tales and legends.

Notes from the Otherworld

King Niall (whose encounter with the sovereign Goddess was recounted in Chapter 5) is one of the quasi-historical figures who appears in the Irish Historic Cycle.

The Welsh Tradition

Although not as vast as Irish literature, and less coherent thanks to the corrupting influence of medieval courtly perspectives, the mythology of the Welsh tongue nevertheless includes many beautiful stories. Primary sources include the following:

- *The Book of Aneirin,* a manuscript dating back to approximately 1250, although the central story it recounts (in a historical war poem called "Y Gododdin") concerns events that occurred in the late sixth century.

- *The White Book of Rhydderch* (approximately 1300) and *The Red Book of Hergest* (around 1375–1425). These manuscripts contain 11 tales, including the 4 first translated in the nineteenth century as the Four Branches of the *Mabinogi* (*Mabinogion*), along with the earliest Arthurian legends and other Welsh tales.

- *The Black Book of Carmarthen* (ca. 1250) contains poems attributed to both Taliesin and Merlin (Myrddin in Welsh), some very beautiful nature poetry, the "Triads of the Horses," and the "Stanzas of the Graves" (which ends, famously, "The grave of Arthur is a mystery"). Mythological, historical, legendary, and Arthurian characters make appearances in this manuscript.

- Welsh bardic sources include the *Triads of the Island of Britain* and *The Book of Taliesin* (approximately 1250–1325), a collection of poems attributed to a great sixth-century bard who had become legendary by the thirteenth century.

The primary text of Welsh myth is the *Mabinogi* (or *Mabinogion*). Some of the themes and characters of the Welsh tradition were exported to Brittany, where they combined with Christian mysticism and medieval ideas of chivalry and courtly love to eventually become today's most familiar legends of King Arthur, Camelot, and the quest for the Holy Grail.

Common Themes and Motifs in Celtic Myth and Legend

Many of the tales of Celtic lore explore similar themes and ideas. As you explore this body of wisdom, you'll discover stories related to war and battle; feasts and adventures; love, courtship, and elopements; expeditions and invasions; visions and voyages; and magical births as well as tragic deaths. In other words, the grand sweep of Celtic myth explores the major themes of life in general. But the lore explores such themes in a way that imparts wisdom and insight to the listener/reader. By interacting with the stories of this tradition, you can find insight into living a rich spiritual life, as well as finding keys to your own happiness and well-being.

Why Bother with Myths and Legends?

You might be thinking, *Gee. Are you saying that Celtic spirituality amounts to nothing more than a bunch of stories and folk tales?* Well, yes and no. In terms of the wisdom that has been conveyed from generation to generation, the best source we have available is the tradition of myth and folklore. But keep in mind that there's more to Celtic spirituality than learning the wisdom of our forebears. This is a tradition of psychic development, of communion with nature, of connecting with spiritual beings and forming relationships with them. Obviously, the tradition of Celtic stories is only one part of the overall picture. And in many cases, the stories and myths contain important insights regarding how to connect with spiritual beings or honor the land!

But why are stories such an important source of wisdom? Why should we bother with them? Can't we just learn the wisdom of the Celts through intuition or ritual or meditation? Well, I suppose that's possible, but on the other hand, why reinvent the wheel? If the wisdom of those who have gone before us can be found in a legend or a myth, why not avail ourselves of that knowledge?

> **The Seer Says**
>
> Remember the importance of balance in the Celtic tradition. Don't get so caught up in books and stories that you lose sight of nature and experience—and likewise, don't become so focused on your personal experience that you neglect the wisdom principles found in myth, legend, and tradition. Both acquired knowledge and inner experience matter.

Here are three reasons why stories are so important to the Celtic wisdom path:

- ◆ **They're fun and entertaining.** Have you ever tried to read a book of theology or philosophy? Unless you are the rare intellectual who actually enjoys such mind-stretching prose, you probably find such high-minded literature to be, well, supremely boring. But the Celts, like other great wisdomkeepers throughout the world, found that they didn't need to convey their wisdom through learned treatises or voluminous tomes. Simple, entertaining, enjoyable stories could convey wisdom in a way that is pleasurable, easy to understand, and memorable.

◆ **The stories explain many aspects of the human condition.** For example, the tale of the children of Lir tells of a jealous stepmother who cursed her children, turning them into swans and banishing them to 900 years of life in exile. Not only does this story convey a profound sense of loss and sorrow, but it also conveys a sense of the Irish people's sorrow at having spent 900 years fighting against the English for the right of self-governance.

This beautiful statue of the Children of Lir is located in a memorial garden in Dublin.

◆ **They really do convey wisdom, even if in subtle or hidden ways.** Check out the following box for one example of how this works.

Notes from the Otherworld

Here's a very simple example of how Celtic legends can contain wisdom and lessons encoded in the story. In the first branch of the *Mabinogi*, a human prince named Pwyll unwittingly offends the lord of the underworld, Arawn. To make amends, Pwyll agrees to travel to the underworld disguised as Arawn, where he fights and defeats one of Arawn's enemies. After completing this task, Pwyll returns home and Arawn, now his fast friend, returns to his otherworldly abode. The story concludes by noting that the two continually exchanged gifts between their respective kingdoms in this world and the otherworld.

On its surface, this is a simple adventure tale. But on a deeper level, it contains a spiritual truth: The beings who populate the spiritual realm are not just psychic puppets there to do our bidding. They are beings in their own right, with needs and requests of their own. Their friendship, like any relationship, needs to be earned. And finally, once a relationship is established with an entity in the spiritual realm, it is appropriate to offer that being gifts, as a way of cultivating the ongoing friendship.

This is the key to Celtic wisdom: to explore the stories of the tradition not only for their entertainment value (even though it's perfectly appropriate to be entertained by Celtic lore), but to dig beneath the surface action to find hidden or subtle spiritual truths contained within.

Making Your Own Connection with the Lore

As stated previously, unless you happen to be fortunate enough to know a genuine storyteller of the Celtic tradition, you'll probably need to enter the world of Celtic wisdom through books. Be sure to read Appendix A to find a number of books worth exploring. Here are a few others you'll want to get to know:

The Seer Says

Looking for books that are out of print or hard to find? Check out www.abebooks.com or www.alibris.com. These websites feature a database of thousands of used and rare books, all for sale by independent and antiquarian booksellers.

◆ *Irish Myths and Legends* by Lady Gregory (Running Press, 1998)

◆ *Early Irish Myths and Sagas* translated and introduced by Jeffrey Gantz (Penguin Books, 1981)

◆ *Visions and Beliefs in the West of Ireland* by Lady Gregory (Colin Smythe, 1970)

◆ *Scottish Folk-Tales and Legends* by Barbara Ker Wilson (Oxford University Press, 1954)

◆ *The Mabinogi and Other Medieval Welsh Tales* translated and edited with an introduction by Patrick K. Ford (University of California Press, 1977)

- *Celtic Myths, Celtic Legends* by R. J. Stewart (Blandford, 1994)

- *Irish Folk Tales* edited by Henrie Glassie (Pantheon Books, 1985)

- *The Tain* translated by Thomas Kinsella (University of Pennsylvania Press, 1985)

- *The Chronicles of the Celts: New Tellings of their Myths and Legends* by Peter Berresford Ellis (Carroll & Graf Publishers, Inc., 1999). This collection is remarkable for including lore from all six Celtic nations.

Many other books are available, including out-of-print collections on the folklore of Cornwall and the Isle of Man. It's best to try to read several different anthologies of Celtic lore; because so many of the books feature retellings of the stories, different authors can give considerably different perspectives on the tradition.

Storytelling for the Future

Reading and learning the rich tradition of Celtic stories is only part of the way to make the tradition your own. To really enter into the tradition, consider becoming a storyteller and sharing the myths and legends of the Celts with your family and friends.

Storytelling is undergoing a revival in our time, thanks to more and more people who feel that we need alternatives to the canned entertainment that comes out of Hollywood and Madison Avenue.

As a modern storyteller, you don't need to limit yourself to tales of King Arthur, or the Túatha Dé Danann, or the faeries of yore. Sure, old myths and folk tales can be an important source of stories to share. But you can also draw from sources, such as the following:

> **The Bard's Bookshelf**
>
> Here's a book to help you learn the craft of spinning yarns: *The Art of Storytelling: Creative Ideas for Preparation and Performance* by Marsh Cassady (Meriwether Publishing Ltd., 1994). It reviews the skills you'll want to master to make your stories entertaining and fun.

- **Tell your own stories.** Look at your own life. What misadventures are good for a laugh? Or what important lessons have you learned that can be offered to others in an entertaining way?

- **Tell your ancestors' stories.** Reverence for ancestors is an important part of Celtic tradition. You can do your part by remembering humorous or powerful events from the lives of your predecessors. Here's an idea: If you are part of the Celtic diaspora, research the circumstances surrounding your ancestors' emigration from the old country. Bet there's a story in there somewhere!

The Seer Says

If you're interested in the professional aspect of storytelling, visit the website of the National Storytelling Network, www.storynet.org. It features information on the modern storytelling movement, where to find professional storytellers, and how to develop your own storytelling skills, for fun or profit.

◆ **Tell stories about nature.** You can honor the sovereign Goddess in a simple way, by sharing folk wisdom (and humor) through stories about animals, or tales that explore the delicate balance of relationship between humans and environment.

◆ **Read your favorite stories to others.** If you don't want to memorize stories or learn the intricacies of dramatic storytelling, you can still share your love for Celtic lore with others, even if just by reading out of a book (this works especially well with youngsters!).

Storytelling is first and foremost a bardic function, and if you don't feel called to walk the path of the bard, it may not be for you. But even if you don't think you've got what it takes to stand up in front of a dozen or more people and spin a yarn, it's worth it to learn a story or two. Knowing what it takes to actually tell a story will deepen your appreciation of the tales you read for your own enjoyment, whether myths from long ago or an Irish ghost story from the twenty-first century!

The Least You Need to Know

◆ From ancient bards, to medieval scribes, to rural shanachies and modern storytellers, Celtic wisdom has always been passed down through the simple practice of sharing stories with others.

◆ Generally speaking, Celtic myths date from antiquity and were recorded in the Middle Ages, thus containing both ancient pagan and medieval Christian elements.

◆ Several key manuscripts from Ireland and Wales contain an imperfect but valuable anthology of Celtic myths.

◆ The stories of Celtic lore are important because they entertain us, help us feel connected to the Celtic tradition, and teach us principles of Celtic wisdom.

◆ You can make the mythic tradition your own by reading and learning the legends and tales, and even learning the art of storytelling so that you can share Celtic lore with others.

Chapter 13

The Irish Tradition

In This Chapter

- ◆ The four dimensions of Irish lore
- ◆ Key themes in Irish myth
- ◆ A who's who of gods, goddesses, and heroes
- ◆ Where to study the tradition further

The myths and legends of Ireland extend back into the hidden past, took written form first under the watch of Christian monks, and have been embellished and expanded ever since by each succeeding generation of poets, bards, shanachies, and seers. For many people, the grand legends of the godly race known as the Túatha Dé Danann, or of heroes like Cú Chulainn or Fionn mac Cumhaill, stand close to the very heart of the Celtic tradition. To many wisdomseekers, the figures of Irish tradition are legendary symbols of Celtic virtues such as valor or hospitality. For others, especially pagans, the heroes, gods, and goddesses of Irish myth are beings worthy of honor, veneration, and worship. Whether or not you embrace the mythic beings as the center of your religion, you can find enjoyment in their stories and learn much about the ways of wisdom from their adventures and misadventures.

The Bard's Bookshelf

For a lovely short introduction to the themes of Irish myth (placing those themes in the larger context of pan-Celtic spirituality), check out Marie-Louise Sjoestedt's *Celtic Gods and Heroes* (Dover Publications, 2000).

This chapter will give you an overview of some of the themes and characters of Irish myth. There's no way that a chapter like this (or even this entire book) could provide an in-depth study of the myths. Hopefully, the information in the pages to come will be enough of a "teaser" to inspire you to study further. (For ideas on how to do that, check out the end of the chapter.)

The Four Cycles of Irish Myth

Irish myth isn't contained in a neat little book, like the Bible or the Koran. Rather, it consists of countless stories, legends, and poems that are found in a number of different manuscripts that date back to the Middle Ages. (For an overview of the textual sources of Irish myth, see Chapter 12.)

However, scholars have organized the myths into four primary categories or "cycles." Each of the cycles opens a different doorway into the magic of the Irish tradition.

The Mythological Cycle

Irish lore doesn't include a creation myth. Scholars don't know whether this is because the Christian monks who recorded the myths simply preferred the creation stories in the Bible (indeed, the medieval scribes attempted to make Irish myth into an "historical" saga that conformed to history as recorded in the Bible; for example, references are made to Noah's flood), or if in fact there never was a creation story to begin with. Either way, the legends and lore of the Irish don't include some sort of cosmic beginning, but rather detail a history of the various peoples and gods who came to live in Ireland over a series of succeeding "invasions."

The invaders include several different groups of humans and at least one tribe or community of gods. The Mythological Cycle also includes a mysterious group of gods who don't appear as "invaders," but whom some of the invading groups had to fight in order to win Ireland for their own. The humans had exotic names like the Partholonians, the Nemedians, and the Fir Bolg. The Fomorians (or Fomoire), who were the mysterious gods that aren't counted among the various invading groups, were similar to the Titans of Greek myth—they were primal, chaotic, and untrustworthy forces. The other tribe of gods, the Túatha Dé Danann, were members of the tribe of the goddess Dana and were the "stars" of the Mythological Cycle.

The main action of the Mythological Cycle involves the conflicts between the various races of gods and men as they fight for the right to rule Ireland. The Túatha Dé triumph over both the Fir Bolg and the Fomorians, only to eventually yield to the final invasion—that of the Milesians (the Celts), the humans who became the final mythical invaders of Ireland.

> **Notes from the Otherworld** _____
>
> It's important to remember that the gods and goddesses in Irish lore differ in many ways from the single God of monotheistic religion, as well as from the gods/goddesses of other cultures (like the Greeks or the Romans). Irish deities don't have limited "functions," in which this deity is the "god of war" or that deity is the "goddess of sexuality"—rather, each deity has a variety of interests and characteristics, and such functions often overlap among more than one deity. Likewise, the Irish (and other Celtic) deities are not to be understood as omnipotent, omniscient, or morally perfect, such as monotheism depicts the One God. Rather, Celtic deities are more properly seen as spirits advanced beyond humans, but not in any sense "perfect."

Key figures in the Mythological Cycle include gods like Lugh, the Dagda, and Núadu; and goddesses like Dana, Ériu, and the Morrígan. Incidentally, not all of the Túatha Dé Danann are necessarily "gods" or "goddesses"—some members of the tribe would be considered beings of the otherworld, yet not necessarily divine. These are the beings who, according to folklore, became the faeries (see Chapter 19). Likewise, different traditions from rural Ireland and Scotland interpret the Túatha Dé in different ways: They've been described as ancient gods and faeries, but also as fallen angels or even a lost race of magical and spiritually advanced humans.

The Ulster Cycle

Perhaps the most dramatic of the four cycles of Irish myth, the Ulster Cycle recounts the adventures of the great heroes of the northern province of Ireland, known as Ulster in English (or Ulaid in Irish). Chief among these heroes is Cú Chulainn, the fierce and supernaturally gifted warrior who single-handedly defends Ulster from the attack of Queen Medb's forces, in the action that forms the central plot of *The Táin*, the great Irish epic.

Other important figures in the Ulster Cycle include Derdriu (a tragic heroine whose beauty inspires strife and jealousy among the Ulstermen), Cathbad the Druid, and King Conchobar. Although gods and goddesses don't figure nearly as prominently in the Ulster Cycle as in the Mythological Cycle, they do appear, such as the goddess of war (the Morrígan) and the god of the sea (Manannán).

The Heroic Cycle

Next to Cú Chulainn, perhaps the most colorful and storied of Irish heroes Fionn mac Cumhaill (or Finn McCool). Fionn has been compared to several figures—from the Welsh tradition, such as Taliesin (the possessor of magically induced wisdom) and Arthur (the supreme guardian of the land). Indeed, the Heroic Cycle has been called the Irish equivalent to Arthurian legend.

> **Notes from the Otherworld**
>
> Irish nationalists have long been known as "Fenians," both by their supporters and detractors. This name is derived from Fionn mac Cumhaill, as the archetypal guardian of Irish freedom and sovereignty.

Fionn is the leader of a band of hunters/warriors called the Fianna. These heroic figures are responsible for protecting the independence of Ireland. Their stories include many adventures involving hunting, fighting, and interacting with the otherworld, but compared to the first two cycles, deities and magic play a much smaller role in the course of this cycle.

The Historic Cycle

The fourth cycle of Irish myth occupies that misty place where myth and history intermingle. The Historic Cycle tells of the adventures of kings and warriors who have more of an actual basis in history. For example, the king Niall of the Nine Hostages appears in the Historic Cycle, and Niall likely was an actual king of Ireland sometime during the third or fourth century C.E. The Historic Cycle still is considered "mythical" because some of the stories include elements of magic or the supernatural.

Key Themes in the Myths

Looking at the Irish lore as a whole, several key elements emerge that can help you understand the meaning hidden in the myths:

◆ **The Power of Magic.** Again and again, the myths describe magic or superhuman abilities. From the treasures of the Túatha Dé Danann with their extraordinary powers, to the superhuman abilities of the warrior Cú Chulainn, to the comings and goings between the earth and the otherworld seen in all the cycles, the myths of Ireland invite us to see the world as a place where anything is possible and wonders never cease.

◆ **The Glory (and Limitations) of the Warrior.** Irish myth is filled with epic battles, one-on-one combat, and various deeds of heroic valor. Indeed, one gets the impression after reading these tales that the Celts were a bloodthirsty and violent race. There are two ways to interpret the prominence of such heroic themes. First, the myths celebrate virtues such as courage, honor, and defense of one's homeland—virtues any society needs to foster if it is to remain free. At the same time, tragic warrior figures like Cú Chulainn (who kills his only son and dies before his thirtieth birthday) suggest that Celtic myth not only celebrates the warrior ideal, but also is realistic about the limitations of a life lived strictly by the sword.

- **The Importance of the Land.** Irish myths tend to emphasize gods more than goddesses; and female deities tend to be more associated with the natural world than with the heroic deeds of legendary beings. But what few goddesses do appear in the myths usually have some sort of connection with the land (as in Ériu or Dana) or with an aspect of the land (as in Bóand, goddess of the Boyne River). Goddesses are often closely associated with magic (which they use to protect the land) and shapeshifting. Meanwhile, the heroic exploits of warriors like Lugh, Cú Chulainn, or Fionn all center on protecting their homeland. Overall, the myths celebrate the land as an essential part of the life and prosperity of the tribe.

The Seer Says _____

The magic in Irish myth (or myth in general) isn't meant to be interpreted literally. Celtic wisdom is not going to teach you how to forge weapons that never miss their mark or how to predict the future with 100 percent accuracy. But likewise, don't discount the myths as foolishness, because they have a magical element. The best approach is to read the myths as imaginative tales that remind us that many things are possible in our world, and that our abilities are usually far greater than we give ourselves credit for.

Meet the Characters of Irish Myth

The best way to meet the many colorful figures who appear in the myths and legends is to read (or hear) the stories firsthand. For the purposes of this introductory book, I've included a list of many of the more memorable figures from throughout the various cycles.

As you read the list, try to keep the following points in mind. First, the lines separating "gods and goddesses" from "heroes" and "mortals" is a very thin line indeed. Some figures, like Cú Chulainn, are semi-mortal, semi-divine. Others exhibit both godly and humanlike characteristics. (Many of the deities are just as mortal as humans are.) The myths were committed to writing hundreds of years after their stories were first told, and at a time when Christianity had replaced paganism in much, if not most, of Ireland. Therefore, the ultimate nature of the mythic figures (human? divine? a bit of both?) will always be ambiguous.

The second point to remember is that these figures are not meant to be worshipped and adored the way monotheistic religions treat their One God. Rather, the gods and goddesses are meant to entertain us, inspire us, teach us, and provide us spiritual help. We, in turn, offer them our energy through devotion, ritual, and sacrifice. The relationship between gods and humans is less one-sided than what is found in the mainstream monotheistic religions.

CAUTION

Geasa

The gods and goddesses of Irish or any other Celtic tradition are not to be obeyed or worshipped in any kind of self-negating sense. Remember, the Celtic tradition is one of honor and valor, not of self-denigration or submission to spiritual entities. You can show proper respect and devotion to your spiritual guides (even those you acknowledge as deities) without surrendering your autonomy.

Who's Who in Irish Myth

- **Ailill.** The king of Connacht (the western province of Ireland) and husband of Medb. Medb, who had a voracious sexual appetite, praises her husband for his lack of jealousy. Unfortunately, she doesn't match his emotional maturity: When she learns that he owns a magnificent bull and she doesn't (which means that his wealth was greater than hers, and according to ancient Irish law would have made him the head of their household instead of her), her envy sets into motion the series of tragic events that form the basis of the great Irish epic *The Cattle Raid of Cooley*.

- **Áine.** Daughter of the sea god Manannán and granddaughter of Donn; a goddess with connections to fertility and love. Many of the tales about Áine depict her engaging in trysts with mortals.

- **Amergin.** A druid, judge, and poet-warrior who according to the legend was the first Milesian (Celt) to set foot on the Irish soil. When he did so, he spoke a visionary poem full of shamanic imagery (see Chapter 7).

- **Anu.** Irish mother goddess, sometimes seen as equivalent to Dana. Two breast-shaped mountains in southwest Ireland are called "the Paps of Anu," showing her status as a goddess of the land.

- **Badb.** One of the aspects of the Morrígan, Badb is a goddess of death and battles who appears as a crow. She is shown perching on the famous statue of the death of Cú Chulainn, which is located at the Dublin post office.

- **Balor of the Evil Eye.** The biggest, meanest, and nastiest of the Fomorians—the gods of chaos and discord who had control of Ireland until the tribes of the goddess Dana (Túatha Dé Danann) defeated them. Balor's eye could kill anyone who gazed into it; he was killed by Lugh, who was also his grandson.

◆ **Banba.** A goddess of the land; one of the three goddesses who asked the Milesians to name Ireland after them.

◆ **Bécuma.** Faery goddess who lived in the Land of Promise; after having an affair with a god, she was banished to the human world where she married the king Conn of the Hundred Battles.

◆ **Bíle.** Ancestral god associated with trees and virility. In neopagan tradition he is sometimes regarded as a god of death whose duties included escorting the souls of the departed to the otherworld.

> **Notes from the Otherworld**
>
> Lugh's destruction of Balor (his own grandfather) not only identifies Lugh as a god of salvation and protection, but also highlights a function of the Túatha Dé Danann as a whole: They are figures who preserve and protect the world by maintaining a delicate balance between order and the forces of chaos. When wisdomseekers honor the Túatha Dé Danann, they honor a world where order triumphs over chaos.

◆ **Blathnát.** A tragic figure; she was abducted by an Irish regional king and carried off to his castle; the hero Cú Chulainn attempted to rescue her, killing the king in the process; but before he could escape with Blathnát, she was killed by the king's bard.

◆ **Bóand.** Goddess of the river Boyne in Ireland; in some traditions she was married to the water god Nechtan; other sources say she was the wife of the magician Elcmar. When she breaks a geis (taboo) keeping her from one of Nechtan's wells, the water overflows and forms the river that bears her name. She was the Dagda's lover and bore him a son, Óengus.

◆ **Bodb the Red.** Son of the Dagda who succeeded his father as chief of the gods. His daughter was the mother of Fionn mac Cumhaill's son Oisín.

◆ **Brendan the Navigator.** Although there was a historical Christian saint Brendan, he also deserves a place in Irish myth because of his legendary sea voyage. The story of Brendan's voyage to a mythical otherworld over the western waters appears to be based on earlier Celtic myths that explore similar themes, although some historians have conjectured that he plausibly could have sailed all the way from Ireland to America, even in the sixth century C.E.! Also see the entry for Maelduin later in this section.

◆ **Brigid.** Her name means "exalted one," and truly Brigid is one of the loveliest and most honored of Celtic deities. Originally she was a triple goddess of healing, smithcraft, and poetry. Cows and milk were sacred to her, and a sacred fire

Notes from the Otherworld

In 1976 and 1977, the English explorer Timothy Severin and three others successfully sailed from Ireland to Newfoundland in primitive boats similar to those that would have been used in the sixth century. Although it doesn't prove that Brendan would have made it to America, Severin's daring deed showed that it was at least *possible*.

was perpetually tended in her honor. A daughter of the Dagda, she is also portrayed as a variation of Dana. Her festival day was Imbolc (February 1), celebrated about when the pregnant ewes began lactating; it marked the beginning of spring. Brigid is also the name of a Christian saint from the town of Kildare in Ireland, who shares many of the goddess's attributes. St. Brigid is second only to St. Patrick in popularity in Ireland; like her namesake goddess, she is associated with milk and cows and the beginning of spring; her Christian feast day is February 1. Some scholars question whether St. Brigid ever existed: They see her as merely as a version of the goddess that was slightly altered to be acceptable to Christians.

A handmade, equal-armed cross is associated with Brigid; it may have originally been a pagan symbol for the sun, but eventually became a symbol of a Christian cross. Such crosses are made out of rushes and are traditionally made and displayed at Imbolc.

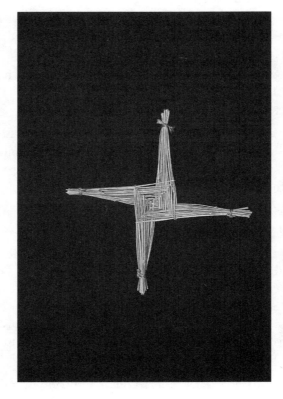

- **King Conchobhar.** A prominent figure in the Ulster Cycle of Irish myth, Conchobhar was the ruler of the northern province of Ireland during the life of the great hero-warrior Cú Chulainn. Several of the stories involving Conchobhar depict him in an unfavorable light—for example, he ignores the counsel of his druid regarding Derdriu (who is prophesied to be the cause of great sorrow among the Ulstermen) and sets into motion a series of events that nearly tear his kingdom apart.

- **Cormac Mac Airt.** Legendary high king of Ireland in the third century C.E. He was Fionn mac Cumhaill's patron. Among other exploits, he journeyed to the otherworld.

- **Cú Chulainn.** The greatest of Irish mythic heroes, *Cú Chulainn* was born of a mortal mother and divine father (Lugh). He represents both the glory of, and limitations inherent in, the warrior ethos. He is a powerful and complex figure, and ultimately tragic: Among other misfortunes, he kills his only son, and eventually dies in battle while still a young man. Although his life may have been short, it was glorious, as he single-handedly defended Ulster from the invading army of Connacht during the Cattle Raid of Cooley.

Druidspeak

Cú Chulainn's name literally means "Hound of Culann." His childhood name was Sétanta, but as a boy one of his remarkable deeds was to kill a ferocious hound that belonged to Culann the blacksmith. Although he killed the dog in self-defense, Sétanta graciously offered to perform the dog's duties until Culann could raise and train a replacement. Thus, the boy became known as Culann's hound, or Cú Chulainn.

- **The Dagda.** The father of many of the Túatha Dé Danann; his name literally means "the good god," not so much in a moral sense but in the sense of being excellent at many skills. Some traditions portray him as equivalent to Cernunnos (the Horned God), but others see him as a solar deity, in contrast to Cernunnos who ruled the Underworld. His tools include the great cauldron (one of the four treasures of the Túatha Dé Danann), a great club with which he could kill nine people in a single blow (but the club could also be used as a healing tool to revive the dead), and a magic harp that would obey his spoken commands. The Dagda is something of a "Santa Claus" figure: a source of abundance and goodness, and yet a bit of an overweight buffoon. He had a voracious appetite both for food and for sex. When the Milesians (the Celts) conquered Ireland and defeated the gods, the Dagda divided up the Underworld regions where the various gods and goddesses would henceforth dwell.

- **Dana.** Mother of the gods and goddesses, who among many neopagans is thought to be identical with Anu. The Túatha Dé Danann are literally "the peoples of the goddess Dana," showing her primacy among the deities. She is an earth goddess, representing the power and sovereignty of the land.

- **Derdriu.** The tragic heroine of a story in which beauty, jealousy, and violence converge with horrific consequences. A druid foretold at her birth that Derdriu would be the fairest of women and would cause great sorrow; the rest of her story describes how this dire prophecy came to pass. Derdriu died of a broken heart (another tradition holds she committed suicide) when she realized the destruction that came out of the rivalry between the men who loved her.

- **Dian Cécht.** One of the physicians of the Túatha Dé; among the others are his son Míach and his daughter Airmedh. Dian Cécht could perform magical acts of medical healing. Indeed, he boasted that only if someone's head were severed or their brain irreparably damaged would he be unable to heal them!

- **Donn.** A god of death. Donn was the brother of Míl, the legendary father of the Milesians (Celts). Donn refused to honor the goddesses of the land in Ireland. For this, he was cursed, and drowned. He came to dwell on an island to the southwest of Ireland known as the "House of Donn," where the dead would first go on their journey to the otherworld.

- **Emer.** The wife of Cú Chulainn, who insisted that he meet a series of demanding conditions before she would consent to marry him. She was a very patient wife who generally tolerated Cú Chulainn's frequent infidelity, although she did draw the line at his relationship with the goddess Fand. Fand, on realizing how deep Emer's love was for Cú Chulainn, renounced her liaison with him.

Notes from the Otherworld

When the goddess Fand decided to stop her affair with Cú Chulainn, her husband Manannán magically enchanted the lovers that they would never meet again. This left Cú Chulainn heartsick, and his wife Emer distraught over his pining. They turned to a druid who gave them both a drink of forgetfulness; after drinking it, neither one remembered that the affair had ever occurred.

- **Ériu.** One of the goddesses of the land who the Milesians agreed to name Ireland after; the Irish name for Ireland (Eire) reflects this ancient promise.

- **Fionn mac Cumhaill.** Fionn has been called the Irish King Arthur. Unlike Cú Chulainn who fought on behalf of a single province of Ireland, Fionn and his followers protected the entire island. He was a possessor of great wisdom, following a magical transformation similar to that of the Welsh bard Taliesin. The exploits of Fionn and his followers constitute the Heroic Cycle.

◆ **Goibniu.** A magical smith (his name comes from the Irish *goba*, meaning "smith") who forged powerful weapons for the warriors of the Túatha Dé. Goibniu was also a master brewer, and whoever drank his magical ale would achieve immortality through it.

◆ **Gráinne.** The daughter of the high king Cormac, she was betrothed to Fionn mac Cumhaill, but instead fell in love with (and seduced) one of Fionn's most loyal followers, Diarmuid. The love triangle that ensued is similar to that of Tristan, Iseult, and March, or of Arthur, Guinevere, and Lancelot.

◆ **Lir.** An ocean god and the father of Manannán.

◆ **Lugh.** A god of heroism, leadership in battle, and artistic talent. In neopagan circles he is considered a god of light and the sun. Lugh's epithet was *Samildánach* (possessor of many talents). He was a grandson of the Fomorian monster Balor on his mother's side, and of the Túatha Dé physician Dian Cécht on his father's side. He allied himself with the Túatha Dé. He was accepted into the tribe because of his skills in many different areas, including both artistic and warrior functions. He is Cú Chulainn's father.

◆ **Macha.** Several different goddesses and heroines in the Irish tradition are named Macha, including one of the war-goddess aspects of the Morrígan (also depicted as a sister of the Morrígan), and a faery woman who married an Ulsterman. The Ulsterman boasted to his fellow warriors that Macha could run faster than any horse, and when the king demanded proof, the husband insisted that Macha participate in a race, even though she was pregnant. She won the race but gave birth at the finish line; angrily, she cursed the men of Ulster that they would suffer the pangs of childbirth at their hour of greatest peril. The fulfillment of this curse is one of the themes of the epic story of the Cattle Raid of Cooley.

◆ **Maelduin.** Like Brendan, Maelduin was a navigator. The story of Maelduin's voyage is older than that of Brendan's and may be more strictly mythological. On his sea voyage, Maelduin and his crew discover a series of wondrous and magical islands, which some people have interpreted as a symbolic template showing what happens to the soul after death.

◆ **Manannán.** The major sea god of Irish myth, apparently equivalent to the Welsh god Manawydan. He was Lugh's foster father and the husband of Fand (who had a month-long affair with Cú Chulainn). He is said to preside at an otherworldly feast where he entertains the noble dead.

The hill of Emhain Macha (Navan Fort), named after the goddess who cursed the Ulster warriors. This was the legendary home of the main characters of the Ulster Cycle.

◆ **Medb.** A major character in *The Táin Bó Cuailnge*, Queen Medb (also spelled Maeve) was a sexually voracious, proud figure who launched a deadly war, just to steal a single powerful bull (she needed the bull to maintain her position as wealthier than her husband and, therefore, head of the household). She may have originally been a goddess of the land. Her name means "the intoxicating one." In later folklore, her character evolved into Mab, a queen of the faeries.

Notes from the Otherworld

Queen Medb was hardly a figure of sexual submission: She was said to always have one man in her bed with another one waiting in the wings. She was proud of her erotic appetite, hiding it from no one, not even her husband, Ailill. In fact, she praised Ailill for his lack of jealousy and his generosity.

◆ **Midir.** A son of the Dagda and the foster father of Óengus. Midir led a faction of the Dé Danaan against another faction, fighting for power after his father stepped down from his role as chief of the gods. This war was inconclusive but contributed to the gods diminishing into their eventual status as subterranean faeries.

◆ **The Morrígan.** The name means "great queen" or "phantom queen." The Morrígan was one of the fiercest and most frightening of Irish goddesses; she presided over death, war, and battle, but was also a goddess of powerful sexuality. One time she offered her love to Cú Chulainn prior to a battle; the war-mad hero rejected her advances, angering her so that she fought against him. She is sometimes regarded as a triple goddess, incorporating Macha, Badb, and Nemain.

◆ **Nemain.** A war goddess, who appears similar to (if not identical to) Macha and is sometimes seen as an aspect of the Morrígan.

◆ **Niall of the Nine Hostages.** A major figure of the Historic Cycle, Niall ruled as high king from 379 to 405 C.E. He is the ancestor of the Uí Néill (the O'Neills), a dynasty of Irish kings. He demonstrated his fitness as a king when he kissed the goddess of sovereignty, even though she appeared as an ugly hag.

◆ **Núadu.** Major hero of the Mythological Cycle, whose sword was one of the four treasures of the Túatha Dé Danann. He was a king of the gods, but after losing his hand (which was replaced by a silver prosthesis made by Dian Cécht) in battle he had to abdicate the throne, as tradition forbade a maimed figure from being king. Eventually, though, Dian Cécht's son Míach forged for Núadu a flesh-and-blood hand, enabling him to regain the throne.

◆ **Óengus Mac Óc.** A god associated with youth and love; a son of the goddess Bóand and the god called the Dagda. His legendary home was Newgrange, which originally belonged to the Dagda, but Óengus tricked his father into giving it to him. One of the loveliest of Irish myths, "The Dream of Óengus," recounts how Óengus dreamt of a beautiful woman with whom he fell deeply in love; he searched throughout the countryside for her, only to find that she was under a curse that forced her to spend part of her life as a swan. Undeterred, Óengus transformed himself into a swan so that he could fly away with his beloved.

◆ **Ogma.** A brother of the Dagda and a champion of the Túatha Dé; he is sometimes said to be a god of eloquence and literature. Ogma is said to be the creator of the Ogham script (see Chapter 23).

◆ **Tailtu.** Lugh's foster mother. A town not far from the Hill of Tara was named for her; it was the legendary seat of a month-long festival to celebrate the beginning of harvest, which became known as Lughnasadh.

Where to Go for Further Study

Irish myth, like the legends of King Arthur, have been told and retold in many different anthologies and collections of myths and stories. Relatively few actual translations of original texts exist; rather, you're more likely to find retellings of the myths. If you want to read actual translations of original texts, two good books to start with are Thomas Kinsella's translation of *The Tain* (Oxford University Press, 2002) and Jeffrey Gantz's *Early Irish Myths and Sagas* (Penguin Books, 1981), and if you want to dig deeper, you can look for these hard-to-find books from the Irish Texts Society: *Lebor Gabála Érenn* (*The Book of the Invasions of Ireland*), volumes I through V, edited and translated by R. A. S. Macalister (Irish Texts Society, 1938–1956) and *Cath Maige Tuired* (*The Battle of Moytura*), edited by E. A. Gray (Irish Texts Society, 1982). These books cover much of the material included in the Mythological Cycle.

The Seer Says

When reading the Irish myths (or any myths from any culture), don't just seek entertainment from the stories. Ask yourself what lessons may be hidden in the tales. This will not only make the myths come alive for you, but will take you further on your wisdom journey.

As for retellings of the Irish myths, one of the earliest and still among the best of interpreters is Lady Gregory, whose *Gods and Fighting Men* and *Cuchulainn of Muirthelme* remain excellent sources of the myths. *Gods and Fighting Men* was recently republished in an attractive and inexpensive edition under the title *Irish Myths and Legends* (Running Press, 1998).

Another widely praised collection is Tom Peete Cross and C. H. Slover's *Ancient Irish Tales*, which was first published by Henry Holt in 1936. Barnes and Noble reprinted it in the 1990s, but their edition is out of print now; copies sell at a premium on used-book websites. Hopefully, a publisher will see fit to bring out a new edition, for it is one of the few collections of Irish myths to include stories from all four cycles.

Finally, in terms of interpreting the myths and legends, few books for the general reader can compare to *Celtic Heritage* by Alwyn and Brinley Rees (Grove Press, 1961). This study explores the cross-cultural mythic themes to be found in the Irish (and Welsh) tradition, describes the various types of stories that are found in the myths, and considers how these different categories of stories contribute to the overall tradition. It's one of the most widely recommended books among modern followers of Celtic wisdom, as it offers tremendous insight into the hidden secrets of the mythic stories.

The Least You Need to Know

◆ Irish myth includes a great variety of legends and stories, organized into four primary cycles or categories.

◆ When reading the myths, it's important to remember that the lines separating gods, goddesses, heroes, and humans are indistinct.

◆ Some of the greatest figures in the myths include the gods Lugh, Manannán, and the Dagda; the goddesses Brigid, Dana, and the Morrígan; and heroes like Cú Chulainn and Fionn mac Cumhaill.

◆ The purpose behind learning the myths isn't to obey them, but rather learn from them, especially about such themes as magic, valor, and respect for the land.

Chapter 14

The Welsh Tradition

In This Chapter

- Heroic tales of the mythic youth
- The landscape of Welsh bardic poetry
- The Wales-Arthur connection
- An overview of the characters of Welsh myth
- Where to go to learn more

The mythic lore of Wales forms an interesting counterpart to the larger collection of myths that were recorded in Ireland. In some ways, Welsh myth echoes that of Ireland—for example, the Irish deities Manannán and Lugh appear in the Welsh tradition as Manawydan and Lleu Llaw Gyffes. This could be evidence that the Irish and Welsh traditions both developed out of a single source of wisdom and lore; and it could also indicate that the Irish and Welsh wisdomkeepers at times shared their sacred stories with one another. However, many elements of each tradition are uniquely their own. When you study Irish and Welsh myth side by side, you can begin to appreciate how some common themes are universal within the Celtic tradition, and you'll also see clearly how much diversity there is in the world of Celtic wisdom.

The Main Stories and Themes of Welsh Tradition

While Irish myth involves a collection of many different stories and tales that are only loosely related to each other, the Welsh tradition that has survived is much more compact. In terms of medieval sources (the oldest surviving manuscripts), the Welsh tradition consists primarily of several collections of poems and triads and one significant anthology of stories commonly referred to as *The Mabinogion. The Mabinogion* includes 11 (in some editions 12) mythic tales, 4 of which are collectively called the *Mabinogi.*

Druidspeak

The meaning of the medieval Welsh word *mabinogi* is unclear; some scholars speculate that it means "tales of the god Mabon." Mabon itself is a title that means "youth" or "son." Pryderi, one of the main characters of the Mabinogi, is believed to be this youth-god. Incidentally, the word *mabinogion* is actually a misspelling of mabinogi, but it was used as the title of the first major English translation of *The Mabinogion*, and so has become a common title for this collection of Welsh myths.

The Four Branches of the Mabinogi

The Mabinogi is the heart of Welsh tradition, recounting the story of the great hero Pryderi and other mythic figures. The four branches include these tales:

◆ **Pwyll, Prince of Dyfed.** The story of Pryderi's father (and his mother, Rhiannon). This branch recounts Pwyll's first adventures in the Underworld of Annwn, his courtship and marriage to the goddess Rhiannon, and the mysterious disappearance and return of their baby Pryderi.

◆ **Branwen the Daughter of Llŷr.** A tragic story of a marriage between the sister of the king of Britain and the king of Ireland, in which Branwen's jealous half-brother insults the Irish king, setting in motion a chain of events that results in a terrible war in which only seven warriors from Britain survive (Pryderi among them). Llŷr, incidentally, is the Welsh sea god, probably equivalent to the Irish Lir.

◆ **Manawyddan Son of Llŷr.** The story of Pwyll, his wife Cigfa, and Rhiannon (who is now married to Manawydan) whose land falls under a wasting spell; further enchantment causes the disappearance of Rhiannon and Pwyll, leaving Manawydan and Cigfa to solve the mystery behind the magic and so undo the spells.

◆ **Math Son of Mathonwy.** The most magical branch of the Mabinogi tells the story of the trickster druid Gwydion, his uncle Math, sister Arianhrod, and her son Lleu. Pryderi makes a cameo appearance when Gwydion tricks him out of a herd of magical pigs.

> **The Bard's Bookshelf**
>
> *Arianrhod: A Welsh Myth Retold* by Barbara Donley (Stone Circle Press, 1987) is a novelization of episodes from the fourth branch of the Mabinogi. It's hard to find, but worth the search.

The Other Tales of the Mabinogion

Aside from the Four Branches of the Mabinogi, several other tales make up the anthology called *The Mabinogion*. Each is an independent tale that reveals a different side of the Welsh mythological or literary tradition.

◆ **The Dream of Macsen Wledig.** Macsen Wledig was a legendary figure based on a fourth-century historical figure who launched an unsuccessful bid to become Roman emperor. This story tells of Macsen's vision while on a hunt with a number of other kings and rulers.

◆ **Lludd and Lleuelys.** A tale of two brothers, one the king of Britain, the other the ruler of Gaul, who join forces to rid Britain of three supernatural plagues.

◆ **Culhwch and Olwen.** A quest adventure in which Culwych performs a series of heroic feats in order to win the hand of his beloved, the beautiful Olwen. Culhwch, incidentally, is Arthur's nephew, who makes his first literary appearance in this tale!

◆ **The Dream of Rhonabwy.** One night while quelling a rebellion, the warrior Rhonabwy has a wonderful dream in which he sees Arthur and his knights on the eve of their battle at Mount Badon.

◆ **The Lady of the Fountain.** This Arthurian romance tells the story of Owein, a knight of Arthur's court who slays the dangerous Knight of the Fountain and marries his widow, only to treat her discourteously; but a series of adventures and the help of the Lady of the Fountain's handmaiden enable Owein to regain his honor.

◆ **Peredur Son of Efrawg.** A mysterious tale believed to contain some of the earliest symbolism that eventually came to be associated with the quest for the grail.

◆ **Gereint Son of Erbin.** The tale of Gereint, who questions the loyalty of his beloved, Enid, who wants him to fulfill his potential as a knight.

◆ **Taliesin.** The story of Gwion Bach, the child who served Ceridwen and tasted her spell of wisdom, which transformed him into the bard Taliesin, or "radiant brow."

The Poetry and Triads of Wales

The bardic tradition survived well in the Welsh cycle of mythic literature, particularly in two collections of medieval literature, *The Triads of the Island of Britain* and *The Book of Taliesin*. These triads and poems are filled with magical imagery and hints about the teachings and lore of the ancients.

Notes from the Otherworld

Triads are short, formulaic literary devices, and there are numerous examples in the Welsh tradition. It appears that triads were originally created as a handy way to memorize information. Given that the druids didn't write down their teachings, the triads may truly represent an ancient tool for passing down wisdom.

The Triads

The triad is a special type of literary form, in which information is shared in a group of three. To modern eyes it looks like a free-verse poem, but technically speaking the triad is not a type of poetry. Here's an example—triad #87 of the *Trioedd Ynys Prydein:*

> Three Skilful Bards were at Arthur's Court:
> Myrddin son of Morfryn,
> Myrddin Emrys,
> and Taliesin.

In this triad we learn that Taliesin had a legendary relationship with King Arthur, and that Merlin (Myrddin) was at least two different figures (more on Merlin later in this chapter).

The Taliesin Tradition

As its name suggests, *The Book of Taliesin* is purportedly a collection of works by the greatest of Welsh bards. Because it dates from the Middle Ages, some 750 years after the real Taliesin would have lived (if he were ever an historical figure), scholars believe that only a few of the poems contained within it could truly be attributed to the Radiant Brow. Even so, the less-ancient poetry still contains a wealth of information about the ancient Celtic world.

The Legacy of the Welsh Tradition: The Arthurian Cycle

You'll notice that several of the stories from the Mabinogion involve Arthur or the quest for the grail. Some scholars believe that these Welsh tales mark the earliest appearances of what would eventually become one of the loveliest and most poetic of world myths, the story of King Arthur. But what most people think of as "Arthurian" legend dates from *romances* written in French by figures like Marie de France and Chrétien de Troyes, which in turn influenced the English writer Thomas Malory, whose epic work *Le Morte D'Arthur* is the supreme expression of the Arthurian myth.

By contrast, the stories in *The Mabinogion* depict Arthur not as the glorious king of shining Camelot (which has more to do with Hollywood than history), but rather as a Celtic chieftain, engaged in a desperate struggle to keep Britain free from the invading Saxons. One theory even holds that Arthur was originally a Celtic bear-god, from whom the anti-Saxon chieftain took his name (and who, in turn, was the inspiration for the legendary king of Camelot fame).

Today, many people think of Arthurian legends as "Celtic." Well, that's partially true. In its earliest form, Arthurian myth was a part of the British tradition, and Arthur (born in Cornwall and dedicated to protecting Celtic Britain from Saxon invaders) is certainly a Celtic personality. But the full flowering of the legends associated with Arthur is a literary body of work that owes as much to medieval France (by way of Brittany) as to ancient Wales. As in so many aspects of the Celtic tradition, the Arthurian legends are a blend of Celtic and non-Celtic material.

Druidspeak

In the world of King Arthur, a **romance** isn't an inexpensive paperback novel telling the story of a passionate affair, but rather an epic poem concerning themes of knights, chivalry, magic, and courtly love, originally written in a Romance language, which means a language derived from Latin (like Italian or French).

Who's Who in Welsh Myth

As with Irish myth, there are just too many interesting stories and characters in the Welsh tradition to fit them all in an introductory book like this. Here are just a few of the key characters, to give you a sense of the many rich personalities that await you when you explore this tradition for yourself.

- **Arawn.** The enigmatic king of Annwn (the Underworld), one of the first characters to appear in the four branches of the Mabinogi. Among his powers is the ability to shapeshift, a power he can use to alter the appearance of another. He uses this skill to enable himself and the Welsh prince Pwyll to exchange places for a year.

- **Arianhrod.** Daughter of Dôn and sister of Gwydion. She is the mother of Dylan (god associated with the sea) and Lleu Llaw Gyffes (more about him below); the circumstances surrounding the birth of her sons were embarrassing to her, and so she placed a number of curses on Lleu Llaw Gyffes; but through Gwydion's trickery, each of the curses was overcome. Her name is also spelled Aranrhod.

◆ **Arthur.** The single greatest figure of Celtic mythology, who probably was based on an historical war chieftain but who over the ages grew into the archetypal British king, defender of the sovereignty of the land. Arthur's earliest appearances are in the Welsh tales that were collected in *The Mabinogion*, although the most familiar legends concerning Arthur and his court come from medieval Breton and French sources.

◆ **Beli Mawr.** Considered to be the ancestral god of the early Welsh rulers, and said to be husband to Dôn. Similar to the continental deity Bellenos. He is the father of many figures in Welsh myth, including Caswallawn, Lludd, and Lleuelys.

◆ **Blodeuedd.** The most beautiful of goddesses; her name means "flower maiden" and she was created by Gwydion and Math to be a bride for Lleu Llaw Gyffes. Unhappy in her marriage, she takes a lover with whom she plots to kill her husband; after the plot failed she is turned into an owl, cursed to hunt only by night. Also spelled Blodeuwedd.

Notes from the Otherworld

The story of Blodeuedd and Lleu has interesting correspondences with birds of prey. When Lleu is near-mortally wounded by Blodeuedd's lover, he turns into an eagle and flies to safety. When Gwydion learns of her treachery, he punishes Blodeuedd by turning her into an owl. This suggests that one way of understanding Lleu and Blodeuedd is as a balance between day and night.

◆ **Bran.** "The blessed," Bran (or Bendigeidfran) was a son of the sea god Llŷr and a king of the Island of the Mighty (Britain). A giant, he was too big to fit into a normal-size house or boat. While he was king, his sister Bran became betrothed to the Irish king Matholwych; but a series of tragic events ensued in which war erupted and many British and Irish warriors were killed. Bran himself was wounded in the heel by a poisoned spear and instructed the few survivors to behead him. His head, separated from his poisoned body, continued to live for many years. When he finally died, his head was buried under what is now Tower Hill in London, as a talisman to protect Britain from invasion. The name Bran means "raven."

◆ **Branwen.** Daughter of Llŷr and sister to Bran the Blessed; her unhappy marriage to the king of Ireland resulted in a devastating war. When she realized the extent of the destruction that had been caused by the circumstances of her life, she died of a broken heart. Her story forms the Second Branch of the Mabinogi. Her name has been interpreted to mean "White Raven." She possessed the ability to communicate with birds (while in Ireland, she trained a starling to carry a message to Bran from her).

- **Caswallawn.** Son of Beli who becomes the king of Britain after Bran goes to Ireland to avenge Branwen's mistreatment.

- **Cigfa.** The wife of Pryderi, who remained devoted to her husband even after his magical disappearance in the Third Branch of the Mabinogi.

- **Culhwch.** Heroic figure from the earliest legends of King Arthur's court. A curse placed on Culhwch required him to only marry Olwen, the fabulously beautiful daughter of a violent and treacherous giant. In order to win her hand, the giant demands that Culhwch perform a series of heroic deeds. Culhwch fulfills all that is asked of him and he and Olwen are married.

- **Dôn.** Goddess who is likely the equivalent of the Irish Danu. Not to be confused with Donn, the Irish god of death. She is a sister to Math and mother of Arianrhod and Gwydion; other mythic figures said to be her children include Gofannon the smith god and Amaethon, god of agriculture.

- **Gwydion.** Trickster figure who plays a prominent role in the Fourth Branch of the Mabinogi. Gwydion was renowned as a magician and a reciter of lore. Sometimes seen as similar to the Norse god Odin. Gwydion tricks Pryderi into trading precious pigs for some enchanted mushrooms, and performs a series of tricks to help Lleu Llaw Gyffes against the anger of his mother Arianhrod.

- **Gwyn ap Nudd.** An otherworld king whom Culhwch asks to help him in his quest to win the hand of fair Olwen. In Welsh folklore, Gwynn ap Nudd became identified as a king of the faeries.

- **Llŷr.** His name means "sea" suggesting that he could be a god associated with the sea, equivalent to the Irish god Lir. He was the father of Manawydan, Bran, and Branwen, and seen as a legendary ancestor to Arthur and other kings.

- **Lleu Llaw Gyffes.** His name literally means "the light one with the skillful hand." Not quite as prominent in the Welsh tradition as his counterpart Lugh is in Irish myth, Lleu Llaw Gyffes nonetheless is a key figure in the Fourth Branch of the Mabinogi. The son of Arianrhod, he is the object of her wrath because his birth was an embarrassment to her, but his uncle Gwydion helps him to be named, to take up his arms as a warrior, and to marry. Lleu Llaw Gyffes is eventually near-mortally wounded by Gronw Pebyr, a rival for his wife, Blodeuedd. Some scholars see the fight between him and Gronw as a metaphor for the eternal struggle between the light and the dark.

- **Mabon.** A mysterious figure who appears in "The Tale of Culhwch and Olwen," Mabon is the son of Modron; their names mean "son" and "mother," respectively. They are seen as archetypal figures representing the ultimate expression

Notes from the Otherworld

As you'll learn in Chapter 24, the fall equinox is referred to as Mabon by some neopagans. The equinox represents a turning point from light to dark (after the fall equinox, nights are longer than days), which is symbolized by Mabon's disappearance after his birth.

of the divine mother and child; Rhiannon and Pryderi of the Mabinogi have been compared to Mabon and Modron, because Mabon, like Pryderi, was taken from his mother when only an infant. In Culhwch's day, Mabon was said to be the oldest of all living beings.

♦ **Manawydan.** Welsh god who is likely the equivalent of the Irish Manannán, although with some differences: The Irish god is clearly a sea god, whereas Manawydan is depicted more as a skilled craftsman.

♦ **Math.** Lord of a northern region in Wales and one of the main figures of the Fourth Branch of the Mabinogi. He was a powerful wizard and Gwydion's uncle. Math's reign as a king depends on his feet resting in the lap of a virgin, unless prevented by the outbreak of war. This can be interpreted as saying that the king's role as keeper of the peace depends largely on the support of the sovereign goddess of the land (symbolized by the virgin). Chaos ensues when the king's virgin is raped, and another woman who applies for the job is disqualified because she gives birth to twins. That woman is Arianrhod, and her twins are Dylan, the god of the waves, and Lleu Llaw Gyffes. Incidentally, the two men responsible for raping the virgin are turned into a series of different animals— one male and one female—and consequently mating with each other as only animals do. (Now *that* sounds like a fitting punishment!)

♦ **Morfran.** The hideous son of Ceridwen; his name means "great crow" but he also was called Afagddu, or "utter darkness." Ceridwen tries to compensate for his ugliness by brewing him a potion that will give him ultimate knowledge; but the brew is ingested by Gwion Bach, the boy who eventually becomes Taliesin (see Chapter 8).

♦ **Myrddin.** A poet/prophet said to live in the sixth century; many myths and legends surround this figure. Some believe "Myrddin" was a title rather than a name and that more than one Myrddin lived. The medieval writer Geoffrey of Monmouth translated Myrddin into a Latinized name, Merlinus, from which the familiar name Merlin is derived—Merlin being the figure who is probably the supreme archetype of the magician in Western culture. (Figures as diverse as J.R.R. Tolkien's Gandalf and J. K. Rowling's Albus Dumbledore are patterned after the Merlin archetype.) One tradition depicts Myrddin as a madman who lives in the forest of Scotland from where he prophesizes; another, more familiar tradition associated with him depicts Myrddin as the counselor/druid to King Arthur.

◆ **Olwen.** The exquisitely beautiful heroine of "The Tale of Culhwch and Olwen," her name means "White Track" because beautiful white flowers would spring up wherever she walked. (Now is that romantic or is that romantic?)

◆ **Owein.** An Arthurian knight who is featured in both "The Lady at the Fountain" and "The Dream of Rhonabwy." Like his father Urien, Owein was a renowned sixth-century north British warrior; the historical Taliesin was a bard at their court.

◆ **Pryderi.** A recurring character of the Mabinogi and the only figure to appear in each of the Four Branches; commonly seen as a mythical representation of the Mabon, the "young god." The son of Rhiannon and Pwyll and one of the few survivors of the horrific battle between Britain and Ireland over the mistreatment of Branwen, daughter of Llŷr.

> **Notes from the Otherworld**
>
> Culhwch really must have had the hots for Olwen. Among other things, the tasks he needed to complete in order to win her hand in marriage were finding honey nine times sweeter than a bee's, drawing blood from a wicked sorceress, and retrieving a comb and razor from an evil king who had been magically transformed into a vicious and deadly boar.

◆ **Pwyll.** Well-meaning but rather dimwitted Welsh prince whose adventures comprise the First Branch of the Mabinogi. Among other things he insults the lord of the Underworld and nearly loses his beloved Rhiannon due to his bumbling mistakes. All ends well, though, and he and Rhiannon have a child, Pryderi. His name, ironically, means "Reason" or "Understanding"!

◆ **Rhiannon.** A major figure in the Mabinogi, this goddess's name means "great queen," possibly meaning she is the queen of Annwn. Because of her connection with horses, she is seen as a possible Welsh version of the continental horse goddess Epona. Shortly after the birth of her son, Pryderi, the baby vanishes and her ladies-in-waiting, fearing that they will be blamed for the child's disappearance, accuse Rhiannon of eating the infant. She accepts blame and punishment until Pryderi is restored to her years later; for this she is seen as the goddess of sorrowful mothers—and of patience and fortitude in difficult situations. She is sometimes depicted in the myths accompanied by three birds whose song is said to rouse the dead and lull the living to sleep.

◆ **Taliesin.** "Radiant brow" is described as the chief of poets in the tale of "Culhwch and Olwen." In one of the Welsh triads, Taliesin is depicted as Arthur's bard. The story of Taliesin's birth is recounted in Chapter 9.

Where to Go for Further Study

Naturally, the best place to start studying the Welsh tradition is with the Mabinogi and the other works that comprise *The Mabinogion*. Perhaps the most highly praised modern translation is by Patrick Ford, published by the University of California Press (1977).

If you want to explore Welsh lore more deeply, a wonderful (although difficult to find) book is *Trioedd Ynys Prydein: The Welsh Triads*, translated and edited by Rachel Bromwich (University of Wales Press, 1978). This scholarly volume includes almost a hundred ancient triads, with pages and pages of detailed notes.

For a more accessible glimpse into the bardic mysteries of Wales, consider John Matthews's *Taliesin: The Last Celtic Shaman* (Inner Traditions, 2001), which collects poems attributed to the great Welsh bard, along with Matthews's commentary.

To understand the themes of the Mabinogi and its related tales, consult these interpretive commentaries by Caitlín Matthews: *Mabon and the Guardians of Celtic Britain: Hero Myths in the Mabinogion* (Inner Traditions, 2002) and *King Arthur and the Goddess of the Land: The Divine Feminine in the Mabinogion* (Inner Traditions, 2002).

Regarding the Arthurian tradition, many sources are available, including countless retellings of the stories. Certainly a good place to start is Thomas Malory's *Le Morte D'Arthur*, available in many editions. Also check out *The Quest of the Holy Grail* edited by Pauline Maud Matarasso (Penguin Books, 1969). Finally, among the many contemporary retellings of the Arthurian story, one stands tall: Marion Zimmer Bradley's majestic and lovely *The Mists of Avalon* (Del Rey, 1982).

The Least You Need to Know

- The central body of Welsh myth is the Mabinogi, four stories loosely related because of the hero Pryderi.

- A number of other medieval Welsh tales, which explore stories of gods, goddesses, and heroes, are often published with the Mabinogi in collections called *The Mabinogion*.

- Several of the Welsh myths explore themes and tell of characters who later appear in the Arthurian cycle of legends.

- The Welsh tradition also includes a number of bardic poems, many of which are attributed to Taliesin.

- One of the most distinctive forms of Welsh literature is the triad, which may have originally been a literary form used for memorizing information.

Chapter 15

Archaeology, Folklore, and the Living Tradition

In This Chapter

- ◆ The archaeological record
- ◆ Folklore: the hidden tradition
- ◆ Putting the gods and goddesses in their place
- ◆ Contemporary concepts for Celtic deities
- ◆ Comparative mythology: tying it all together

The Irish and Welsh myths are priceless treasures of Celtic spirituality, filled with personalities and perspectives that any seeker of Celtic wisdom will want to get to know. But it's important to remember that the ancient Celtic world stretched far beyond the borders of Cymru and Eire; also, the rich tradition of spiritual wisdom didn't turn to stone when the last myth was committed to paper.

This chapter will take a brief look at Celtic deities and heroes from sources other than the mythic traditions you explored in the previous two chapters. From archaeological images of Celtic gods and goddesses found in continental Europe, to modern reinterpretations of Celtic deities embraced by Wiccans and other neopagans, this chapter will help you grasp the variety of Celtic lore, as well as its continuing vitality as a living tradition.

Archaeology: Every Picture (and Artifact) Tells a Story

When it comes to our knowledge about the druids and seers of old, we face a giant obstacle: The druids intentionally refused to commit their spiritual teachings to writing. Although this might have been a way of protecting advanced knowledge, it also meant that we'll never know just what was lost in terms of wisdom concerning science, law, spirituality, or healing.

Fortunately, the lack of a written record is at least somewhat compensated by the many sites and objects from ancient times that archaeologists have recovered and studied. Many of the treasures of the past provide fascinating glimpses into the spiritual treasures of the ancient Celts.

Notes from the Otherworld

Although Irish and Welsh medieval manuscripts reveal the Celtic traditions of Ireland and Wales, archaeological finds have occurred mainly in areas occupied by the Romans, including Britain and, especially, Gaul. Thus, archaeology provides insight into the spirituality of the mainland Celts.

Druidspeak

Insular means "of the island(s)." The insular Celts were those who dwelled in the British Isles, as opposed to the mainland, or continental, Celts.

Much of the archaeological evidence dates from the period of Roman control over the Celtic lands. The Roman conquest brought with it a new era of artistic and religious expression, resulting in many temples and statues devoted to gods and goddesses. Although the Roman citizens brought their own deities with them, Roman religion tolerated local spirituality, and many of the gods and goddesses venerated during this time were "hybrid" figures with Roman-Celtic names. For example, Apollo Belenus was a fusion of Roman and Celtic solar deities, while Mars Rigonemetis merged the Roman war god with a Celtic god of the sacred grove.

Unlike the written myths, which are exclusively *insular* in origin, archaeological evidence of ancient spirituality can be found throughout the Celtic world, from the British Isles to everywhere in Europe where Celts once lived. For example, statues of the horse goddess Epona or the hammer god Sucellus have been found in many different sites.

Most of the archaeological evidence indicates that a few "famous" deities were venerated throughout much of the Celtic world, but also that many different local divinities were only known and honored in their home region. Celtic religion wasn't some monolithic, corporatelike venture where everyone everywhere thought and worshipped alike. On the contrary, it was a spirituality that celebrated diversity, with many regional variations in the gods worshipped and the themes stressed in the religious observance.

Folklore as a Source of Wisdom

Folklore is the hidden underbelly of culture. Unlike published works of great literature or academic scholarship, folk tales and folklore pass from generation to generation orally, with little notice from the elite members of society. In terms of the Celtic lands, folklore often thrived in the areas where the Celtic languages were spoken, away from the sterilizing influence of the English language (and English education).

How Folklore Came to Be Taken Seriously

It was only in the nineteenth century that Celtic folk tales began to be taken seriously by scholars. The first important collection of Irish folklore, Thomas Croker's *Fairy Legends and Traditions of the South of Ireland*, was published in 1825. Croker lived at the same time as the Grimm brothers, well known for their collection of European fairy tales. (In fact, the Grimms translated the German edition of Croker's book.) Croker published several other collections of Irish folklore, and another significant early collection, *The Fairy Mythology*, was published by Thomas Keightley in 1828. Croker and the Grimms also published folklore from Scotland and Wales.

At the time Croker and the brothers Grimm were alive, folk tales were regarded as little more than entertainment told by the peasant farmers; but its popularity among readers is evident in the numerous anthologies that were published in the 1830s. By the 1860s, folklore was appearing in ever larger and more thoroughly researched anthologies, including John Francis Campbell's *Popular Tales of the West Highlands* (1860) and Patrick Kennedy's *Legendary Fictions of the Irish Celts* (1866).

> ### The Bard's Bookshelf
>
> Sean O'Sullivan's *Folktales of Ireland* (University of Chicago Press, 1966) is not only a fine collection of traditional tales, but also includes an interesting history of the efforts to preserve folklore over the last 200 years.

Throughout the rest of the nineteenth century the study of folklore expanded. By the end of the century, the two figures best known for their championship of Celtic folklore—Lady Augusta Gregory and William Butler Yeats—were publishing anthologies of material they had collected. For Yeats and Lady Gregory, folklore wasn't just an interesting segment of popular culture—it was the continuation of the Celtic wisdom tradition first recorded in medieval manuscripts.

In 1926, An Cumann le Béaloideas Éireann (the Folklore of Ireland Society) was created to collect Irish folklore in a systematic manner. This organization became the government-supported Coimisiún Béaloideasa Éireann (Irish Folklore Commission) in 1935, with full-time employees dedicated to recording the vanishing folklore of rural and Gaelic-speaking Ireland. Their results are impressive: Within 30 years, the commission had an archive of more than 1.5 million pages of folk tales and folk wisdom! These tales represent a living link between the bardic wisdom of the past, the folk wisdom of the present, and the ongoing survival of Celtic wisdom into the future.

Why Folklore Matters

What does folklore have to say about the Celtic approach to life?

In many ways folk songs and folk tales are simply meant for whiling away the hours on cold winter nights. Stories and songs of heroes and saints figure prominently in the folk tradition. But there are also plenty of tales about faeries and other magical beings, like banshees, pookas, leprechauns, and selkies—mysterious spirits and mythical beasts who live in that misty place where imagination meets the otherworld. Some of the ancient gods and goddesses appear in folklore, although sometimes they are demoted from their divine status to the role of mere heroes. One folk tale recounts the story of Lugh defeating Balor (which had originally appeared in the Mythological Cycle—see Chapter 13), but instead of the clash of gods, this is merely a story of a boy blinding an abusive blacksmith.

Folklore doesn't provide a tidy program of spirituality or philosophy. Rather, it reveals the worldview of people who live close to the earth and speak the old language, often carrying a rich spiritual blend of pagan and Christian perspectives. It shows how the faeries and the otherworld continued to matter to the Celts, long after the coming of an imported religion from another part of the world. For today's wisdomseekers, reading folk tales (or better yet, hearing a traditional storyteller recount his or her yarns) is both entertaining and a way to be connected to the riches of the Celtic world.

To explore Celtic folk wisdom deeper, you'll want to become familiar with the massive collection of Scottish charms, prayers, and invocations recorded by Alexander Carmichael in the *Carmina Gadelica*. This anthology is invaluable because it's more than just a collection of narrative tales, but actually a compendium of folk practices. Alas, such material is far too rare. Some folklorists have attempted to record their research into folk traditions; one relatively recent example is Trefor M. Owen's *The Customs and Traditions of Wales* (University of Wales Press, 1991).

The Power of Place

Some of the most interesting lore related to the goddesses and gods of old doesn't involve myth, but place names (which often reveal which deities were revered in a particular locale, and in what ways). In a twelfth-century Irish manuscript called the *Dinnsenchas* ("the lore of prominent places"), many tales are recounted about how different places throughout the country got their names. In this compendium of lore, many goddesses and gods are discussed, and as in the case of archaeology, many of the figures mentioned have only regional or local followings.

Unlike the myths, which tend to be dominated by gods and heroes, the *Dinnsenchas* prominently features goddesses. This suggests that the Celts saw goddesses as more related to land and place (which befits the primal idea of the goddess as one with the earth), while the gods seem more connected with conflict and heroism as recounted in the myths. Another way of seeing this: The goddesses are related to the land and the soil, while the gods are related to the tribe and the people. The goddess represents nature, while the god represents culture. A harmonious relationship between humankind and its environment is, therefore, mirrored by a loving relationship between the goddess and the god.

Deities Connected with the Land

Here are just a few spirits with a legendary connection to the land.

- ◆ **Anu.** Associated with two mountain peaks in southwest Ireland known as "the Paps of Anu."

- ◆ **Bóand.** Goddess of the river Boyne in Ireland.

- ◆ **Coventina.** The spirit of a holy well near Hadrian's Wall on the Scottish border.

- ◆ **Fionn mac Cumhaill.** The star of the Heroic Cycle of Irish myth (see Chapter 13) is associated with many sites, most especially the Giant's Causeway in Northern Ireland, said to have been built by Fionn as a (now submerged) bridge to Scotland, and a series of standing stones in County Cavan, Ireland, called "Fionn mac Cumhaill's fingers."

- ◆ **Sequana.** Goddess of the source of the Seine River (France).

- ◆ **Vagdavercustis.** Goddess venerated in the Rhineland area, near modern-day Cologne.

> **Notes from the Otherworld**
>
> Anna Livia Plurabelle, James Joyce's personification of the River Liffey, which flows through Dublin, is a prominent goddesslike figure in Joyce's mysterious novel *Finnegans Wake*.

The Giant's Causeway, which according to legend was built by Fionn mac Cumhaill.

Modern Interpretations of Celtic Deity

This chapter, and the two preceding it, focuses on ancient writings, stories, and archaeology as doorways into the wisdom of the past. It's human nature to want to know what our ancestors believed and thought—which is why ancient sites like Stonehenge or the Egyptian pyramids or Macchu Picchu remain so popular to today's spiritual seekers.

But in researching the wisdom of the past, it's important not to fall into the trap of thinking something must be old in order to be good or wise. Just as folklore has evolved (and will continue to evolve, even in a world dominated by television and the Internet), so, too, has the content of Celtic spirituality and wisdom continued to grow, change, and evolve over the generations. In this section, we'll look at some distinctly modern concepts of the spiritual world that arise from, or are connected with, the Celtic tradition. Although some people might dismiss these modern expressions of spirituality as "not Celtic enough," other wisdomseekers will remember that every spiritual idea or practice was new at some point or another; and the fact that the tradition continues to evolve shows that it is a vital, living tradition.

These concepts—the Lord and Lady, the dark and light god, the horned god, and the triple goddess—all have their roots in ancient tradition. It is the manner in which they are honored and venerated in today's world that makes them new.

The Lord and the Lady

In the modern religion of Wicca (neopagan witchcraft), the nature of divinity is often depicted as duotheistic—in other words, as consisting of a fundamental polarity between a cosmic God and cosmic Goddess. This pairing of divinity as a Lord and a Lady suggests that all of the world's various mythological gods and goddesses, regardless of cultural background, can be seen as aspects of the supreme Mother Goddess and Father God.

While this concept is mostly a modern idea (Wicca, as you'll learn in Chapter 21, only dates back to the mid-twentieth century), it does have an interesting link to Celtic spirituality. As the Celtic scholar Miranda Green notes in her book *The Gods of the Celts*, "What is very interesting is the Celtic fondness for divine couples, alien to the Mediterranean world." In other words, Celtic religion differed from Greek and Roman religion in how the Celts often depict their deities as couples. In this way, Wiccan duotheism can be seen as a modern expression of the ancient Celtic tendency to "match up" their goddesses and gods.

Dark God/Light God

In the classic tradition, some gods (like the Irish Donn or the Welsh Arawn) are gods of death, the Underworld, and darkness. Others, such as Lugh or Ogma, are connected to light, the sun, summer, and abundance. The myths of old hint that the lords of light and darkness were locked in eternal combat, as in the case of Arawn's annual conflict with the summer god Hafgan in the Mabinogi.

The modern, neopagan worldview sometimes regards the lords of light and darkness as competing for the love of the Goddess. Over the course of a year, each one is triumphant for a time, before being defeated by his rival. Some traditions see the solstices as the times when the gods do battle; thus the god of light triumphs at the winter solstice, when the days begin to lengthen, while the god of darkness triumphs at the summer solstice with the coming of ever-shorter days. Another view sees the god of darkness triumphing at Samhain (the end of summer), marking the onset of the cold season, while the god of light regains the ascendancy six months later, at Beltane (May 1, the beginning of summer).

> **CAUTION** **Geasa** _____
>
> Always remember that the dark god and light god are not to be interpreted as one being good and the other evil. Dark and light are regarded as two halves of a single whole, which require one another in order to maintain cosmic balance in the universe.

Horned God

Horned gods are popular in many European traditions; in the Celtic lands it is Cernunnos (whose name literally means "horned one") who sports antlers or horns that seem to link his humanly appearance with the world of animals. Thanks to the Wiccan movement, much has been written about the old horned gods, how they were maligned unfairly as "devils" under Christianity, but today are making a comeback as pagan symbols of vibrant, nature-loving masculinity.

Horned gods are by no means exclusively Celtic, but thanks to Cernunnos they have a firmly Celtic identity within neopaganism. Whereas little is known of Cernunnos's original identity and function, he appears to be a lord of the beasts and a giver of prosperity (he is sometimes shown with an overflowing bag of coins). His antlers may indicate virility and/or strength, and may also symbolize—by their being shed and regrown every year—the cycle of the seasons and/or death and rebirth.

> **Notes from the Otherworld**
>
> The Wiccan way of seeing Cernunnos as a horned god may not be the only way to approach this Celtic figure. In shamanic terms, Cernunnos can be viewed as a mythic "lord of the hunt" who merges shamanic energies with the spirit of the hunter to guide hunters to success in their quest for prey.

Among today's neopagans the generic horned god represents the wild dimension of masculinity, the connection between humanity and the untamed parts of nature, and primal energies of hunting as the means by which men secured food for their families and tribes.

Maiden, Mother, Crone

Brigid and the Morrígan are two examples of goddesses who appear in triple form. For the ancient Celts, such triple goddesses often represented three aspects of a similar function, three distinct faces who were grouped together within a single concept of a goddess (analogous to how three different persons comprise the single Christian God).

> **Notes from the Otherworld**
>
> The maiden/mother/crone is the single most popular depiction of the Goddess within many forms of Wicca. But it originated with a modern writer, Robert Graves, not in any ancient Celtic myth or symbol.

In modern terms, the triple goddess specifically represents three different stages in a woman's life: the maiden (youth/adolescence), the mother (young adulthood to middle age), and the crone (menopause to old age).

In classical myth, the story of Demeter and Persephone represents this triple goddess image: Demeter is the mother of the maiden Persephone; after Persephone is lost, the aged Hecate lends her cronish wisdom to Demeter's search for the girl. Some Wiccans and others also consider the maiden/mother/crone to be three different phases in a single woman/goddess's life. It's a tool for honoring the entire life span of the goddess (and the women who venerate her). Like the horned god, this isn't necessarily a uniquely Celtic spiritual concept, but rather a universal principle that fits in well with other Celtic concepts (such as the goddess's primal connection with nature and the land).

A Who's Who of Other Celtic Deities

There are so many deities who appear in sources other than medieval Irish and Welsh literature—in places such as archaeology, place names, and folklore—that a list of them could easily fill this entire book! Instead, here are a few examples of such spirit beings, to give you just a hint of how vast this tradition is. Truly, for the Celts, the world was full of the shimmering presence of divine beings.

- **Artio.** A Gaulish bear-goddess, known from a statue in which she is depicted offering food to a bear.

- **Belenus.** A Gaulish god of healing and the sun, whom the Romans equated with the Greco-Roman deity Apollo. He was depicted on numerous coins from Gaul. The festival of Beltane (May 1) is sometimes thought to be named for Belenus.

- **Cernunnos.** This mysterious figure has become one of the most popular of Celtic gods, especially among many Wiccans. His name, which appears on only one ancient carving, means "the horned one," signifying his most vivid attribute: a god of human form but sporting antlers or horns. Cernunnos is a god of animals and the wilderness, and is regarded as the patron of hunters and hunting. Cernunnos is a shamanic figure, clearly connected to the spiritual powers of animals and the wilderness.

- **Epona.** An extremely popular goddess associated with horses; her name literally means "horse" or "mare." One of the few Celtic deities who was widely venerated by Roman soldiers (particularly among those in the cavalry—not surprising, given their dependence on horses). The Welsh Goddess Rhiannon is generally thought to be a British version of Epona. Often depicted holding a cornucopia, she is also associated with abundance and prosperity.

> ### The Bard's Bookshelf
>
> Irish novelist Morgan Llywelyn has written a fictionalized account of the life of Epona called *The Horse Goddess* (Houghton Mifflin Company, 1982).

- **Esus.** Described by the Roman writer Lucan as a bloodthirsty god who required human sacrifice, although no archaeological evidence supports this. (Monuments to Esus show him peacefully pruning a tree.) His name may simply mean "lord" or could mean "good" in the sense of being competent.

◆ **Nantosuelta.** A water goddess venerated primarily in Gaul. Her name means "winding river"; she is also associated with domesticity. Nantosuelta typically is depicted with Sucellus.

◆ **Nemetona.** Goddess of the sacred grove (the "nemeton") who was particularly venerated by a tribe in modern-day Germany called the Nemetes.

◆ **Rosmerta.** British Goddess of abundance whose name means "great provider." On Romano-British reliefs she is generally paired with the Roman god Mercury.

◆ **Sirona.** The meaning of this central European goddess's name is uncertain, but could mean "divine star." Her emblem is a snake and she is associated with healing and fertility.

◆ **Sucellus.** A Gaulish hammer god, perhaps similar to the Norse god Thor. His *totem animals* are the dog and the snake and he is often depicted carrying a cask or a mug. He is sometimes called the "Good Striker." He is associated with harvest, cattle, and wine.

> **Druidspeak**
>
> A **totem animal** is an animal associated with, or symbolic of, a particular god, goddess, or tribe of people; often a totem is venerated and the god or goddess associated with it is seen as having qualities similar to the totem.

◆ **Taranis.** Mentioned in the writings of Lucan, Taranis was a Gaulish storm god. His name means "Thunderer."

◆ **Teutates.** This Gaulish god (also worshipped in Britain) has been linked to the Roman gods Mercury and Mars. His name means "god of the tribe," and scholars speculate that he may have been a protector-god who was invoked during times of war.

Comparative Mythology: The Ultimate Research Adventure

You've probably noticed that one of the frustrating themes of Celtic studies is how fragmentary it is. Because the druids were willfully nonliterate, and the myths were transcribed by Christian scribes who didn't always understand their inner meanings, what we have today are only shards of information about the spiritual wisdom of our Celtic ancestors.

While on the one hand many creative people have attempted to interpret the ancient evidence in ways that make sense for modern times, astute students of Celtic wisdom will get a nagging sense that even the best modern theory is little more than an educated guess. For this reason, many people interested in discovering the native wisdom of the ancient Celts have turned to the discipline of comparative mythology. This field, based on the work of a twentieth-century French scholar named Georges Dumézil, explores common themes and elements in different mythological traditions within the Indo-European family. Comparative mythology shows that, despite the many differences in myth and lore that separate different cultures, when those cultures come from the same ancient source, they share many similarities in terms of cosmology (way of seeing the world) and understanding of the spirit world.

Although the study of comparative mythology involves research into many different, non-Celtic traditions (think of it this way: Iceland, Ireland, Iran, and India all fall within the Indo-European world), it can help you "connect the dots" in the Celtic world and make sense of many themes and ideas in Celtic archaeology and myth that might otherwise be confounding.

 Geasa

Comparative mythology is an important academic tool for getting to know the Celtic traditions and how they relate to other Indo-European cultures. But it's not intended to reduce all legends and lore to a single unified mythology.

Where to Go for Further Study

Like the previous two chapters, the material presented in this chapter is little more than a teaser to introduce you to what's out there regarding Celtic archaeology and folklore. Here are a few ideas on how you can take your studies further.

An excellent starting point for learning about the riches of Celtic sacred archaeology would be Miranda Green's *Symbol and Image in Celtic Religious Art* (Routledge, 1989). Numerous photographs and drawings illustrate this in-depth discussion of the themes found in this scholarly work. Although technically a work of art history, it contains a lot of information that the modern wisdomseeker will find meaningful. Another interesting book, particularly if you're interested in pagan religion, is *The Archaeology of Ritual and Magic* by Ralph Merrifield (Guild Publishing, 1987). Although he covers more than just Celtic material, the scope of information Merrifield explores will help you understand the spiritual life of the ancient Celts.

Folklore is a vast field, with many anthologies and studies available for the wisdomseeker. Here are a few other interesting books to get you started:

◆ Janet and Colin Bord's *Earth Rites: Fertility Practices in Pre-Industrial Britain* (Granada Publishing, 1982), includes both Celtic and non-Celtic folklore practices from England and other parts of the British Isles.

◆ Scottish folklore has been chronicled by F. Marian McNeill in her dated, but still magisterial, four-volume set called *The Silver Bough* (William Maclellan, 1957, 1959, 1961, 1968). For a brief introduction to Scottish lore, read Joyce Miller's *Myth and Magic: Scotland's Ancient Beliefs and Sacred Places* (Goblinshead, 2000), Ann Ross's *Folklore of the Scottish Highlands* (Rowman and Littlefield, 1976), and Barbara Ker Wilson's *Scottish Folk-Tales and Legends* (Oxford University Press, 1954).

◆ Of the many anthologies of Irish folklore available, some of the most respected include Sean O'Sullivan's *Folktales of Ireland* (University of Chicago Press, 1966), Henry Glassie's *Irish Folk Tales* (Pantheon Books, 1985), and Séamas Ó Catháin's *Irish Life and Lore* (The Mercier Press, 1982).

Comparative mythology is an academic discipline, so expect the following books to be more technical than spiritual:

The Seer Says

Good books often go out of print, but because they're classics, they are worth hunting down. If you can't find a book through a used-book website online (such as www.abebooks.com or www.half.com), try your local library. If they don't have a copy of the book you're seeking, they can usually get it through an interlibrary loan.

◆ To get started, consult these excellent surveys: Jaan Puhvel's *Comparative Mythology* (Johns Hopkins, 1987) and C. Scott Littleton's *The New Comparative Mythology: An Anthropological Assessment of the Theories of Georges Dumézil* (University of California Press, 1982).

◆ If you want to explore further, you might enjoy Bruce Lincoln's *Myth, Cosmos, and Society: Indo-European Themes of Creation and Destruction* (Harvard University Press, 1986) and Wendy Doniger O'Flaherty's *Other People's Myths: The Cave of Echoes* (Macmillan, 1988).

The Least You Need to Know

◆ Archaeology provides insight into many deities who were never documented in written form.

◆ Folklore, although not a systematic source of wisdom, is still an important source of insight into the surviving tradition of ancient Celtic lore.

◆ New ways of understanding Celtic deities show that this is a living, growing tradition.

◆ The academic field of comparative mythology has helped many Celtic wisdom-seekers understand the tradition more fully.

Part 4

Further Steps Along the Path

There's no one right way to pursue Celtic wisdom. You may be drawn to the most primitive, shamanistic elements of Celtic spirituality, or you may prefer the glorious mysticism of Celtic Christianity or the quest for the grail. Or perhaps you are dedicated to the revival of Celtic paganism, whether that means the revival of the druids, the rebirth of Celtic forms of witchcraft, or simply the ongoing tradition of belief in the faeries. Whatever your particular path is in the Celtic world, you'll want to find ways to walk it with integrity, honor, and devotion.

The chapters in this part introduce you to a cornucopia of ideas and practices aimed at taking your quest for Celtic wisdom to its next level. Skip around and read the sections that appeal to you the most: Those are the ones that hold a promise for your continued growth. Have fun as you travel your path!

Chapter 16

Quest for a Disciplined Mind

In This Chapter

- ◆ Druid = smart
- ◆ The ingredients of an accomplished wisdomkeeper
- ◆ Good ol' fashioned druid virtues
- ◆ Meditation: It's not what you think
- ◆ Finding a community to pursue your path

This chapter, and the chapters that follow it, invite you deeper into the Celtic path. On occasion you'll find that this path takes you in the opposite direction of the values of mainstream modern society. Don't be afraid to walk in the other direction! It will enable you to truly grow into the subtle beauties of the Celtic path.

Please Pass the Elbow Grease

Now that you've gotten a taste of the riches of the Celtic world, you might feel tempted to go in any of a dozen directions. You might start reading all you can about the ancient druids, or learning the myths, or even studying a Celtic language. You could put hours of effort into learning the basics of shamanism, just so you can contact your ancestors or your spirit guides. And of course, there's the vast and mysterious world of magic to consider as well. Who knows where to begin?

Not so fast! Celtic spirituality isn't something that can be mastered in a weekend workshop (or by reading a single book like this one). Think in terms of the long haul. The proverbial "slow and steady wins the race" truly applies here: Making an effort to grow little by little into the mysteries of Celtic wisdom will, in the end, be the best way to embrace this ancient and beautiful tradition.

This may seem like a drag to you; after all, you live in the twenty-first century, where videogames define the pace of life and the Internet brings the entire world to within a mouse-click of your grasp. Ours is an age of instant gratification, where everything happens here and now—or else it's just not worth having.

Remember everything I've said about the bards being keepers of an alternative vision? This is where the rubber hits the road. The alternative vision that is at the heart of the Celtic tradition is a vision that leads us away from the hyperfrenetic, instantaneous, me-me-me energies of the modern world. In its place, the Celtic tradition offers a gentle pace where we can truly connect with nature, learn about ourselves (and one another), and find the space to truly connect with lasting joy—as opposed to the fleeting amusements of our buy-now-pay-later society.

The Seer Says

Our world is full of products like instant oatmeal, permanent-press fabric, fast food, and disposable diapers. The Celtic path is the opposite of such things. Instead of emphasizing your convenience, it stresses growth, excellence, and service, which all require old-fashioned hard work.

So to begin your journey into the more demanding dimension of the Celtic world, let's go back to our friends the druids, and look at one of the most striking features of their order. The druids valued and strove for, above all else, strong and keenly disciplined minds.

Geasa

The Celtic path is a path of balance, and everyone has room for improvement when it comes to living life in a balanced way. Do you spend too much time watching TV and too little time outdoors? Are you so caught up in books about magic and spirituality that you forget to exercise? Watch out for imbalances like these, and when you identify them, make it a part of your spiritual path to change.

The Disciplined Mind of the Druid

So how do we know that the druids were such big brains? We can find evidence of this in ancient writings. And then we can look at how modern Celtic wisdomseekers have adapted this important aspect of their spirituality.

Twenty Years?!?!

As noted previously, Julius Caesar (who was hardly a friend of the druids), reports that students pursuing a career as a druid would engage in a rigorous program of learning druidic lore, in poetic form, by heart. The druids prohibited the writing of their teachings; instead, students would spend up to 20 years memorizing the verses, which contained the knowledge of the lore.

Twenty years! It's a long time. It's equivalent to five U.S. presidential terms. Think back 20 years: Who was the president of the United States then? (Or the prime minister of Britain?) What was happening in the world? What technology was considered cutting edge? Where were you? In school? Were you even born yet?

In Caesar's day, 20 years was even more of a commitment than it is now, because the average life expectancy was much, much shorter than it is now. (Living to 50 would mean making it to a ripe old age.) Truly, to spend that much time studying meant two things: first, that the aspiring druid must have rock-solid commitment to his path, and second, that the knowledge required must have been truly considerable.

Notes from the Otherworld

It's likely that the 20 years of study required of apprentice druids began in childhood. Think of the modern educational process: 8 years of primary education, 4 years of high school, 4 years of college, and 4 years of graduate school equals 20 years. So it's not unreasonable to think of a druid as having the same level of education as a someone with a Ph.D.!

The Modern Druid Perspective

Of course, today's world is light-years away from that of the Iron Age Celts; no one becomes a professional druid anymore. But that's not to say that our society has no use for druidic knowledge; nor is it to imply that the modern variation of druidism (which is more of a private spiritual exercise than a public counselor/scientist position) no longer requires vigorous training. On the contrary …

◆ Modern "druids" (such as counselors, lawyers, scientists, and university professors) still require 20 (or more!) years of study in order to achieve their status as wisdomkeepers.

◆ Modern spiritual communities based on druidism often have rigorous and involved training programs; they might not last 20 years, but they're more than just a weekend workshop or two.

The mottoes of one of the largest American druid organizations, Ár nDraíocht Féin, demonstrate how modern druids retain a commitment to intellectual growth. Their first motto is "Why Not Excellence?" This speaks to the fact that becoming a druid requires high standards in every area of life, including intellectual development. Their second motto is "As Fast as a Speeding Oak Tree!" This points out that some things (like intellectual development, or the maturing of a hardwood tree) take a long, long time to accomplish. It's a recognition that the excellence they seek sometimes takes years to manifest—and it's worth the wait.

Why a Disciplined Mind Makes Sense Today

Here are two reasons why a disciplined mind is just as important today as ever:

- **Personal enjoyment.** Yes, sometimes it's challenging to study and learn. But the more we understand about history, science, technology, psychology, and other fields, the better we will be able to understand, interpret, and enjoy our spiritual experiences. A disciplined mind doesn't ruin spirituality; on the contrary, it enhances it.

- **Community service.** We live in a world that requires creative thinkers with innovative ideas. Environmental problems, economic issues, social inequality, and other issues can only be solved when our society becomes truly educated and uses our collective intelligence to make the world a better place. Even if you only want to be a small-town mail carrier and a weekend druid, you still have a vote to cast and an opinion that can influence those around you. Taking the time to discipline your mind makes you a better citizen.

The Seer Says

Read your daily newspaper! Remember, the druids of old were counselors to the kings. You can bet they kept up on current events. Keeping informed is a natural part of the wisdom path.

Elements of a Disciplined Mind

Okay, okay. You're probably grumbling to yourself, "So what did I sign up for, then? What does all this disciplined mind stuff entail?" So lighten up, already! Just because the druids stress excellence and hard work doesn't mean it has to be dreadful and agonizing. Indeed, most modern wisdomseekers would tend to believe that we need something that's pretty much the opposite of our current educational system, in order for druids (and others) to recapture the joy of a disciplined mind. Modern education, after all, is really just designed to make people into happy, submissive factory workers.

To followers of the Celtic path, the disciplined mind isn't something we develop in order to be happy drone workers, but is rather a way to flex our spiritual and intellectual muscles, much like playing sports or going backpacking is a way to hone our physical strength. The strength of a disciplined mind is then a source of personal joy, as well as a tool to use in making life better; both for ourselves and for others.

But what does the disciplined mind entail? Here are a few ideas.

Knowledge

You're reading a book right now. That's a good sign. Don't stop. To embody the spirit of the druids, become a voracious reader, if you aren't one already. And don't just read websites devoted to your favorite pop group, either. Make it a habit to always be reading at least one book on a topic you're not familiar with. From quantum physics to Byzantine art to postmodern literary criticism to corporate accounting, the world we live in is full of interesting and exciting fields of inquiry. (Okay, so corporate accounting isn't all that exciting. But it's an important part of modern life, so suck it in and start learning.)

Balance your inquiries between practical material that can directly benefit your life (like how to be a better manager) and "pure knowledge," which you acquire simply for the sake of developing your wisdom (like art history).

Meditation

Disciplining your mind is more than just cramming it full of facts. There's also the question of developing concentration, improving memory, sharpening the vividness of your imagination, and fostering the ability to think logically and creatively. All these "mental fitness" skills can benefit from the same basic practice: the practice of meditation.

No, I'm not trying to turn you into a Zen master. Meditation doesn't necessarily mean spending three hours a day chanting ancient Tibetan hymns. But it does mean taking the time on a regular basis to cultivate silence and relaxed, focused attention within your consciousness. Even though it appears to be the easiest thing in the world to do, meditation isn't a skill quickly or casually mastered. A meditation practice not only stretches your attention and focuses muscles, but it will give

> **The Bard's Bookshelf**
>
> Want to learn more about meditation? Check out *The Complete Idiot's Guide to Meditation,* now in its second edition, by Joan Budilovsky and Eve Adamson (Alpha Books, 2003). It provides a comprehensive overview of meditation practice, both in spiritual as well as health-benefit terms.

your commitment and discipline muscles a workout as well. Discipline, of course, is the point of this entire chapter, so any effort that improves your stick-to-it-iveness will ultimately serve your pursuit of the Celtic path.

Service

In their heyday, druids were public servants. Caesar says that they were exempt from military service (which might have been nothing more than his anti-druid propaganda). What may be closer to the truth is that they were so involved in matters of the mind that they couldn't be spared to wield a sword or a spear. Druids did engage in psychological warfare (classical writers talk about how members of the Roman military were frightened of the druids and their "dreadful imprecations"), and they provided counsel to the kings and chieftains in order to help them rule effectively.

But druidic service didn't stop with affairs of the state. They were healers and prophets and religious leaders who served all members of society, from the greatest to the least. It's fair to say that being a druid meant not only developing true knowledge and wisdom, but then pressing such skill into serving the greater good.

Today people are so focussed on getting and spending that concepts like "serving the public interest" seem quaint and old-fashioned. Yet that is the very heart of the druid path. As an aspiring seeker of Celtic wisdom, you may never counsel heads of state (but who says you *won't* someday serve in such a capacity?), but you can help others, whether that means serving your community as a whole or simply helping others out on a one-by-one basis. Here are some of the ways you can serve others:

♦ Volunteer in programs to help teach literacy skills to adults and immigrants.

♦ Participate in programs to feed the homeless.

♦ Here's an especially Celtic-appropriate service idea: Participate in environmental cleanup or tree-planting programs.

♦ Get involved politically! Fight for what you believe in, and support candidates who most closely reflect your views. Don't think just in terms of one or two "hot-button" issues, but rather educate yourself on several important issues and rate candidates for their overall performance.

The Seer Says

Volunteer work doesn't have to be anything heroic. Helping out at a local nursing home or getting involved in the PTA at your child's school are examples of simple ways to stretch the "service" section of your brain.

Judgment and Discernment

Just stuffing your mind full of facts is hardly a way to be disciplined. You could end up incapable of doing anything more momentous than winning at Trivial Pursuit. The key to wisdom is not merely great knowledge, but skill in interpreting and applying such knowledge in positive and helpful ways. This is the skill of discernment. It's the mark of sound and mature judgment.

Learning how to discern between right and wrong, or effective and ineffective, can hardly be taught in a book, or programmed into a computer. This is because every situation requiring judgment is different. Books and computers can help us understand the past, but only our imagination can truly envision the future. To learn how to make winning judgment calls, it's a good idea to find a mentor—an older person whose ability to make the right decision impresses you. Bounce important decisions off your mentor before making them, and over time, you'll become someone that people look up to for your decision-making skills as well.

Courage and Honor

The ancient Celts took pride in the valor of their great heroes like Cú Chulainn and Lugh. Their exploits have been immortalized forever in Celtic myth. What can we, modern wisdomseekers, learn from these ancient warriors? Here's where mental discipline isn't a matter of facts and figures, but of emotional focus and intent.

Courage isn't a matter of never being afraid, but rather a willingness to do what needs to be done, in spite of any fears. Courage is the discipline to put our principles first.

Honor is a value that doesn't get talked about much these days, and that's too bad. Honor is the place where personal pride and community ethics intersect. To be honorable is to do the right thing, both for the good of the community as a whole as well as for one's own self-respect. Thus, honor requires that even one's enemies be treated a certain way. Think of how qualities like treachery, deception, theft, and plain old-fashioned lying are lionized in movies and on television. A Celtic wisdomkeeper stands tall above such dishonorable ways of being.

> **The Bard's Bookshelf**
>
> Fostering a disciplined mind means developing emotional as well as intellectual skills. If you want to learn more about this, look into Daniel Goleman's *Emotional Intelligence* (Bantam Books, 1995).

Hospitality

Throughout Celtic myth, as well as the teachings of Celtic Christians, is a great emphasis on values such as hospitality, compassion, and charity. The old joke that Scotsmen are stingy is a deeply unfair (and unfounded) stereotype. The Celtic ideal is one of helping out the stranger, welcoming the visitor, feeding the poor and needy, and finding joy in generosity.

> **Notes from the Otherworld** _____
>
> Celtic hospitality is still very much alive. During my first trip to Ireland I drove into a small town where I couldn't find an inn or a bed and breakfast. I inquired at a pub to see if anyone could recommend lodging, and the pub manager insisted on driving me around town to find a place! The first place we went to was full for the evening, but the woman who owned it got on the phone and called around until my lodging was secured. Neither she nor the pub manager would take anything other than my gratitude, even though between the two of them they had spent over half an hour helping me find a room for the night. How many businesspeople in America are willing to take time out of their busy days to help out a total stranger?

Sacrifice

Related to courage, honor, and hospitality is the notion of sacrifice. We've already seen how sacrifice has a spiritual dimension of making offerings to the gods and goddesses, but any time we defer immediate gratification in order to achieve a larger, more worthy goal, the energies of sacrifice are at play. To the disciplined druid, sacrifice makes sense as a symbol of his or her ability to stay focussed on the highest and best goals, and continually work toward their fulfillment.

Humility

With all this talk about virtue, charity, sacrifice, and courage, one might think that a druid would be pretty self-satisfied and morally superior. But another important element of the disciplined mind is humility—not in the sense of having a low opinion of one's self, but in the original and best meaning of the word, which means having an accurate and balanced opinion of one's self! Humility means taking appropriate pride in one's strengths and accomplishments, but also being realistic about one's faults and foibles. It's so easy to fall in the trap of inflated pride, or its mirror image—inflated self-abnegation. The rigorous honesty of true humility requires a disciplined mind.

Serenity

Finally, a truly disciplined mind finds peace and equilibrium within itself. One doesn't need to have the utter placidity of a Zen monk, but a druid also learns not be triggered or upset by life's normal ups and downs. Rather, the wisdom that comes from intellectual development balanced by emotional maturity enables the druid to find, and maintain, his or her serene center.

Unleashing Your Inner Druid

Among the seven branches of Celtic wisdom (described in Chapter 4), the one most clearly aligned with the quality of the disciplined mind is, not surprisingly, the druid path. The rest of this chapter provides a bit more information about pursuing this specific form of Celtic wisdom.

The Two Types of Druids

If this chapter hasn't scared you off from the quest to explore the path of the wisdom-seeker, you might be interested in connecting with a druid teacher or grove to help you develop your knowledge and discipline as a follower of Celtic ways. Modern druids fall into two main categories:

◆ **Philosophical druids.** They tend to espouse religious freedom and diversity, seeing druidism as a pursuit that is easily adaptable to any positive form of spirituality and religion, whether Celtic in origin or not. Example: the Order of Bards, Ovates, and Druids (OBOD).

◆ **Religious druids.** They tend to see druidism as a pagan spiritual path, and attempt to practice their druidism in a manner that conforms as closely as possible to their understanding of pre-Christian Celtic spirituality. Example: Ár nDraíocht Féin (ADF).

Obviously, the path you choose to follow is a matter of personal preference. But regardless of which path you choose, participating in a grove or teaching program can foster growth in your life as a Celtic wisdomseeker.

What a Druid Grove Does

A druid grove is a small group of practicing druids. Groves meet on a regular basis for learning, fellowship, and rituals. Most groves have some sort of teaching program, and often provide opportunities for community service. But grove membership isn't just about work! It's a way to develop friendships with others who have similar interests in the Celtic path, and to find spiritual meaning through the grove's rituals.

The websites of the major druid groups (such as ADF and OBOD) feature lists of existing groves. It's also possible to start your own grove, although if you do so, remember that leading a group like this involves many hours of volunteer (nonpaid) work!

A Modern Druidry Who's Who

Here are a few of the leaders of the contemporary druid movement. Most of these people have written books on the subject, and are well known as leaders of one or more druid organizations.

- **Isaac Bonewits.** The founder of ADF, Bonewits is also the author of several books, including *Real Magic* (Weiser, 1989).

- **Philip Carr-Gomm and Stephanie Carr-Gomm.** Philip is the current Chosen Chief of OBOD. He's written a number of books. He and his wife Stephanie co-authored *The Druid Animal Oracle* (Simon & Schuster, 1994), a popular divination tool based on Celtic animal lore.

- **Ellen Evert Hopman.** Formerly a vice president with the Henge of Keltria, Hopman is the author of *A Druid's Herbal for the Sacred Earth Year* (Inner Traditions, 1994).

- **Emma Restall Orr.** Joint Chief of the British Druid Order, Orr is the author of *Spirits of the Sacred Grove: The World of a Druid Priestess* (Thorsons, 1998).

- **Philip Shallcrass.** Joint Chief of the British Druid Order, Shallcrass is the author of *Druidry: The Piatkus Guide* (Piatkus Books, 2000).

The Least You Need to Know

- Celtic spirituality is a rigorous, lifelong commitment to develop wisdom, not only of mystical matters, but of the mundane world as well.

- Because ancient druids functioned as judges, diplomats, counselors, scientists, doctors and psychologists, modern Celtic wisdomseekers can only benefit from learning as much as practical about these important fields of human knowledge.

- Values such as excellence, commitment, courage, and honor are important aspects of the Celtic path.

- One important way to foster a disciplined mind is through meditation.

Chapter 17

Reaching Out to the Otherworld

In This Chapter

- The spirituality of otherworld contact
- The shaman-Celtic connection
- Visualization as the doorway to the spiritual realm
- Benefits of shamanic work
- Meditation: a tree and the landscape

In Chapter 6 you learned about the many different ideas and images associated with the otherworld, also known as Faeryland or the spiritual dimension of the universe. As you walk the path of Celtic wisdom, you'll want to reach out to this mystical, magical realm. The otherworld is more than just a fun idea from Irish or Welsh myth: It's the inner dimension that forms the basis of Celtic spirituality.

Whether you accept the idea that the otherworld has a literal reality or you think it's "just a metaphor" for the inner universe of your soul, you'll find that entering the otherworld and seeking guidance from the spirits who live there is an essential part of your wisdom journey. It's in the otherworld that you will find guidance, intuitive insight, information for spiritual healing and personal direction, and training on how to more effectively serve the gods and the land.

The Path of the Celtic Shaman

Throughout this book I have talked about shamanism as an important element of the Celtic tradition. In this chapter we'll take a closer look at Celtic shamanism: What it is, what it isn't, and how it plays an important role in the pursuit of Celtic wisdom.

But first, it's important to clarify what is meant by the term "Celtic shamanism." In other words, you need to recognize that shamanism is not originally a Celtic concept. As I noted in the first part of this book, *shaman* is a word from Siberia that originally meant a very specific kind of spiritual healer/magician from one particular tribe—the Tungus people—in that region of the world. The word has, in the last 50 years or so, taken on a new meaning in the English language, referring to any kind of primitive, primal, indigenous spiritual practice that involves magic, healing, spirit contact, and ritual, usually in a tribal, nature-based, or pre-industrial setting.

> **The Bard's Bookshelf**
>
> Michael Harner's *The Way of the Shaman: A Guide to Power and Healing* (Bantam Books, 1982) is the essential guide to shamanic spirituality as practiced in the modern post-industrial world. Even though it doesn't discuss the Celtic dimension of shamanism, it's still a classic. To study general shamanism or learn more about Michael Harner's work, visit www.shamanism.org.

When we speak of "Celtic shamanism," it's important to remember that we're using the word in this newer, rather vague sense. In other words, Celtic shamanism really just means the most primal forms of Celtic spirituality that probably date back to the earliest centuries of Celtic civilization. This is the root of Celtic wisdom—the core from which all other forms of Celtic spirituality (druidism, the grail quest, faery faith, and even modern Celtic Wicca) originally evolved. And it is this general sense of Celtic shamanism that gives us insight into the role of the otherworld and spirit contact in Celtic mysticism.

What Is Shamanism?

To truly understand the otherworld and its role in Celtic wisdom, it's helpful to look at the key elements of shamanism (as a universal spiritual concept).

The Shaman Path from Around the World

Religious scholars like Mircea Eliade wrote about the fascinating and powerful spiritual practices of the original Tungus shamans, as well as documented similar practices among other indigenous and tribal cultures from around the world. Eventually, certain themes and patterns of primal spiritual activity became apparent. Some of these themes include the following:

- The experience of a major crisis or initiation process whereby a person would undergo a magical transformation from ordinary individual to magically powerful shaman.

- The use of trance, ritual, hypnotic music, or even mind-altering substances to establish a link between the human and spiritual worlds.

- The belief that certain spirits can be sources of power and knowledge, and that alliances can be formed with such spirits to benefit the shaman and his tribe.

- The use of ritual or other spiritually sourced healing practices to foster health and well-being and to cure the sick (both physically and psychologically).

Each of these core elements of shamanism exists in many traditional cultures from around the world. For this reason, the word *shamanism* has been loosely (and some would say inaccurately) applied to Native American, African, Australian, and Asian spiritual leaders/healers. And as the rest of this chapter will show, these core elements are all part of the Celtic tradition as well. By understanding that shamanic characteristics are part of Celtic wisdom, it helps us see what steps to take in order to establish and maintain contact with the ancestors, gods, goddesses, and faeries who reside in the Celtic otherworld.

How It Fits In with the Celtic Tradition

Why is shamanism important to the Celtic tradition? All the key elements of shamanism as described above are found in Celtic myth, lore, and tradition. Of course, the Celts never called it shamanism, but the lore shows that such practices were nevertheless part of the ancient wisdom.

After centuries of Christian and modern scientific rationalist influence, the hidden teachings at the core of the ancient Celtic myths and legends are largely forgotten by or invisible to the average person. This is why shamanism has become so helpful. By studying shamanism from cultures around the world, and experiencing shamanic trance journeys or healing, people in the Western world (Europe and places like North America and Australia where people of European descent have settled) have become much more consciously aware of the dynamics of shamanic spirituality. And with that awareness, we are much more capable of seeing the living tradition within the Celtic path.

Entering the Otherworld: The Quintessential Shamanic Activity

Correctly understood, shamanism is a path of healing. Much of the modern interest in shamanism has occurred among mental health professionals, who see in the ancient rituals and practices of the shaman a valuable adjunct to modern psychological therapy. And even if you are not a professional healer, you can practice a shamanic spirituality to bring healing energies into different dimensions of your life. Indeed, put in a single sentence, shamanism could be described as "reaching out to the otherworld to foster healing in our own world."

To the seeker of Celtic wisdom, therefore, the primary gift of shamanism (both as a dimension of Celtic spirituality and as a universal path) is that it shows a way to make contact with the realm of faery (that is to say, with the realm where we receive guidance from our ancestors and from the spiritual dimension of nature). By applying shamanic principles to your life, you can enjoy a much deeper sense of spirituality and foster healing in your life, all thanks to the guidance you receive from the otherworld.

The Benefits of a Disciplined Mind

Okay then: How do we reach across the divide separating this world from the other? Shamanic expert Michael Harner describes the "shamanic state of consciousness" as the doorway into the magical realm where the gods and goddesses and faeries dwell. Such an altered state of consciousness can be achieved in a number of different ways: Meditation, visualization, ritual, and myth are all tools that can be used to trigger heightened awareness. These are all key elements of the Celtic path. Chapter 16, for example, introduced you to the value of a disciplined mind, with meditation as an important technique for mental development. Here is a practical application of meditation skills: When you open your mind to higher levels of consciousness, you also open the doorway to the faery realm.

> **The Seer Says**
>
> Following a common practice throughout the world, many students of shamanism rely on drumming as a tool for entering the otherworld. The hypnotic rhythm of a single monotonous drumbeat entrains the mind to enter into a relaxed, higher awareness: the shamanic state of consciousness.

Visualizing the Otherworld Pathway

Meditation is a passive way to access the consciousness of the otherworld. Visualization, combined with meditation, is a way of directing the mind to reach across the worlds into the magical realm. Visualization is using the imagination's ability to create images (and other sensory data, like sounds or even touch and smell) within the mind, and focusing such inner sensations to access the soul's innate link to the spiritual realm. Such a link exists at a level higher/deeper than mere images. But images are helpful to us, in that they allow pure spiritual energies to connect with us on a level that seems familiar and understandable. Visualization, therefore, is using the faculties of the imagination to access a reality (the otherworld) that lies beyond the imagination. The only way the pure spiritual essence of the otherworld can make sense to us is through images and concepts that we can comprehend—in other words, that we can imagine.

Through visualization, we see the otherworld not only as a real "place" inhabited by real spirits, but we can also learn to find our way around the otherworld and even visualize doorways or pathways to and from the Land of Faery.

Contacting Otherworld Guides

Why visualize the otherworld? If you just want to exercise your imagination, can't you just do that by reading a good book? Of course. But the shamanic state of consciousness operates at a deeper, more profound level than mere imagination. Granted, using the imagination to visualize positive changes and spiritual growth in your life is important, but keep in mind that shamanism takes you to a higher/deeper level of consciousness, where you become open to the energies of the otherworld that reach you through visual and auditory imagery. This is why meditation (or trance induced by such stimuli as a steady drumbeat) is as important to shamanic work as visualization. Meditation or trance ushers you into the more receptive shamanic state of consciousness, where your visualization can help you connect with otherworld guides.

Remember, in spiritual work such things as meditation or visualization are means to an end—the end being personal growth, healing, and a sense of balance found through the support and guidance of spiritual entities and energies.

Spirit Guides

Shamans have found in their otherworldly travels many spirit beings who have worked with them, supported them, and guided them on their healing journeys. In Celtic terms, this means that among the gods, goddesses, faeries, and ancestors, we can find spiritual beings who take an interest in our life and who wish to help us along our way.

The Seer Says

When making a connection with an otherworld entity, whether a spirit guide, ancestor, or any other entity, use the same common sense you would use in meeting anyone for the first time. Take your time to get to know the spirit being. Your best guides will be the ones with whom you have an ongoing, trusting relationship.

Not every spirit we encounter in our otherworld travels will necessarily be a guide. Spirits, like physical beings, vary widely in their personality, character, and trustworthiness! If you trust your intuition, you will know when a spirit you encounter is truly your guide—a being you can rely on to support your spiritual growth and teach you of the magic and beauty of the faery realm.

Power Animals (and Plants)

Not all spirit guides appear in human or humanlike form. The Celtic tradition honors the wisdom qualities of many animals and plants, ranging from salmon to doves to boars and horses. Trees such as hazel, apple, willow, and yew embody principles such as wisdom, beauty, intuition, and transformation. When you journey to the otherworld, note carefully everything (and everyone) you encounter. Even the plants and animals may have something to share with you, on a symbolic or intuitive level.

What Is the Purpose of Shamanism?

Why is shamanism important? What gifts can you find when you undergo spiritual excursions into the Land of Faery? Here are a few of the benefits associated with Celtic shamanism (as well as shamanism in all its forms).

Personal Growth

Excursions into the faery world have the potential to transform your life. Your spirit guides and contacts can shed light on problems and issues facing your life; they sometimes offer confirmation when they support the choices you've made in life, but they also can offer a kick in the psychic butt if they think you deserve it. Either way, your efforts to seek out spiritual guidance and apply the wisdom you receive can be an enlightening doorway into emotional and spiritual growth.

> CAUTION
>
> **Geasa**
>
> Shamanism is a path of healing and service. It's not something to do just to get a spiritual kick. If you need more entertainment in your life, go to a movie. Save shamanic work for when you're ready to be of service to others.

Healing

A shaman is a "medicine man"—in other words, a healer whose spiritual abilities are used in practical ways to bring about health and well-being, both for individuals as well as for the community as a whole. Such healing might have a physical or a mental/spiritual dimension. Illness often is viewed as resulting from fragments of the sick person's soul trapped by unfriendly spirits; thus, the shaman might travel into the spiritual realm to retrieve one or more soul fragments for the afflicted person.

Irish myth tells of the god Dian Cécht, who was the chief healer among the Túatha Dé Danann. Dian Cécht symbolizes the importance of healing as a spiritual practice, and as a part of the shaman's role in society.

Balance

This might be a rather abstract principle, but balance, or equilibrium, is regarded as an essential quality for a shaman to maintain, not only on a personal level, but in cosmic terms as well.

How does a shaman maintain balance? Through ritual and through forming alliances with helping spirits that share an appropriate commitment to maintaining order in the cosmos. A shaman also supports balance on a grand scale by helping each individual to become balanced in his or her personal life. Balance includes balancing activity and rest, work and play, and engaging in environmentally friendly activities like recycling or organic gardening.

The Seer Says

Your spirit guides from the otherworld can be valuable allies in fostering balance in your life. Ask your guides to show you the areas in your life where you're out of balance, and to guide you in determining what needs to be done. Don't be surprised if they communicate to you in nonverbal ways. If a guide wants you to realize that your diet is out of balance, he or she might haunt you with images of overweight Americans and starving children from the third world!

Key Voices in Celtic Shamanism

If you want to explore the specifically shamanic part of the Celtic world, here are a few teachers and writers whose work you might want to get to know:

◆ **Tom Cowan.** Tom has written several accessible books on the spirituality of shamanism for twenty-first-century urban dwellers. But for seekers of Celtic wisdom, his don't-miss book is *Fire in the Head: Shamanism and the Celtic Spirit* (HarperSanFrancisco, 1993). This book lyrically weaves together the riches of the Celtic tradition with the key principles of core shamanism.

- **Frank MacEowen, M.A.** Frank is a shamanic counselor and practitioner/ teacher whose journey began with early life experiences and initiations with First Nations and other indigenous people. Today, his work involves applying global shamanic insights to his own ancestral Scottish and Irish background. He is the author of *The Mist-Filled Path: Celtic Wisdom for Exiles, Wanderers, and Seekers* (New World Library, 2002).

- **John and Caitlín Matthews.** Two of the most prolific authors on the Celtic spirituality scene, the Matthews approach the inner mysteries of the Celtic tradition from a variety of angles. Both have written interesting books on shamanism, and each has put together divination sets based on shaman wisdom principles. Among the many books they've co-authored is *The Encyclopedia of Celtic Wisdom: The Celtic Shaman's Sourcebook* (Element, 1994).

Tree and Landscape Meditation

Here is a *guided meditation* to help you experience a sense of connection with the otherworld. This meditation is based on a story from Irish myth. If possible, record the guided meditation or have a friend read it to you; that will enable you to focus more fully on entering an altered state.

> **Druidspeak**
>
> A **guided meditation** is an inner voyage that you read, or listen to, to inspire your visualization within the meditative/ shamanic state of consciousness.

Close your eyes and relax, sitting comfortably with both of your feet flat on the floor and your spine straight. Take several long, slow, deep breaths, allowing your heart rate and "mind rate" (the busy-ness of your conscious thought) to slow down gently. You do not need to force your sense of relaxation and peace, just allow it to flow. Allow your eyes to relax in the darkness of their closing.

Allowing your eyes to remain closed, envision with your inner eyes a point of light, as if far, far in the distance. See the point of light growing slowly, gradually, as if it were moving closer to you. As it grows, you can see it assume a round shape, as if it were the mouth of a tunnel. The light comes closer and closer, and in it you can begin to see the distinction between land and sky. Soon you reach "the end of the tunnel" and then, suddenly, you are standing in a strange and beautiful world. As far as you can see is beautiful green grass, with rolling hills in the distance. The horizon supports a lovely blue sky, luminous with the radiance of the sun and punctuated by brilliant, fluffy cumulus clouds.

Although most of this magical landscape seems empty and open, you notice that you are standing with your back to a tree. It's as if the tunnel you stepped out of was located in its trunk. Turn around and gaze at the tree. If you need to, you may have to step back a few paces so you can see it in its entirety. Notice every detail you can possibly see. Is the tree large or small? Does it appear to be a young sapling, or is it old beyond measure? Is it sturdy and windswept, or sagging under the abundance of its fruit? Is it an evergreen, or perhaps a hardwood, revealing the time of year by its appearance? If it is a hardwood, notice if it is bare, in bud, or covered with green or autumn-colored leaves.

Take time to enjoy the energy of the tree. Perhaps you may feel a telepathic bond, and can "talk" to the tree. If so, ask it a question, and listen for its answer. Or you might feel more aligned to communing wordlessly with the tree spirit. Relate to the tree in whatever way seems right. Spend as much time communing with the tree as you wish.

Now, notice how the horizon behind the tree appears to you. Never mind how open the horizon appeared when you first stepped out into the light; the horizon behind the tree will appear in whatever way is uniquely right for you. Is the tree on a windswept island, surrounded by the turbulent force of the Atlantic? Or is it at the edge of a lush and verdant forest? Perhaps there is a city behind the tree, or a desert, or a mountain range. Perhaps the tree stands alone, or perhaps it is in the company of other trees, or even animals or other beings. Take your time and notice the tree's habitat. Pay attention to as many details as you possibly can. Take all the time you need.

Eventually, it will be time for you to return to your ordinary consciousness in the physical world. When it seems time to leave, say goodbye to the tree and its environment in whatever way feels right. Then, envision your inner eyes "closing," so that the tree and its landscape fade into darkness. Allow yourself to rest in that dark space that is between your inner and outer worlds. While you rest there, allow your mind to focus awareness on your physical body: on your breathing, your bodily position, the sensation of the floor beneath you or your clothing covering your skin. Simply rest in whatever you are physically aware of experiencing. When you are ready, gently and slowly open your eyes. You may need to stretch, yawn, or engage in some gentle movement in order to feel sufficiently grounded in your body. Take time to do that, and then make notes of your experience with the tree and its environs.

The inspiration for this meditation comes from a legendary story about an ancient Irish king, Cathaoir Mór. Cathaoir was a high king of Ireland who ruled from the Hill of Tara. One night he had a strange and wondrous dream of a beautiful, magical tree. The tree was fragrant and heavily laden with fruit, and the very air surrounding the tree seemed filled with magical music. The king consulted his chief druid about the meaning of the dream; the druid divined that the tree symbolized Cathaoir himself. The music represented the king's eloquence, while the fruit symbolized his generous nature. The druid assured Cathaoir that this dream was an affirmation from the spirit world on the king's fitness as a ruler.

In your meditation, the tree likewise represents your own self. Consider how you envisioned yourself: Were you tall or short, ancient or young, barren or fruitful? Were you a big old shade tree, or a hardy little sapling? Reflect on how the symbolism of the tree represents who you are (or perhaps, how you see yourself). If you aren't happy with the kind of tree you are, ask yourself what it would take to "morph" into your ideal tree? If you experienced communication with the tree, what was its message? What did it teach you or share with you?

The landscape surrounding your tree represents your vision of the otherworld. Again, reflect on the meaning of the landscape you saw. Was it lush, abundant, and fruitful? Was it cold and dreary? Did you feel at home there, or could you envision others who would call this place home? How do you feel about spending time in this place? Is it possible that, were you to travel into this landscape, you would see and feel different regions with different characteristics?

Geasa

Don't get caught up in judging your meditation experience, or worrying that your tree wasn't "good enough"! Instead, try to understand both what you like and dislike about your tree, and resolve to strengthen the good parts and heal or transform the others.

Do you feel comfortable in this otherworldly landscape? Why or why not? If you saw animals or other beings, what were they like, and what message might they have for you? Make notes of what you remember, and any insights you might have about your relationship with the spiritual world.

You can return to your tree and its environment whenever you want. Try to make notes whenever you visit; as you may find that the tree and its surroundings change and evolve over time. And don't forget to record your insights in your journal.

The Least You Need to Know

◆ A core element of Celtic wisdom involves reaching out to the otherworld, a spiritual practice that can foster healing, personal growth, and balance.

◆ To help facilitate their connection with the otherworld, many Celtic wisdom-seekers rely on shamanic ideas and practices from around the world.

◆ One simple way to establish a link to the otherworld is to visualize an inner realm; spiritually speaking, your mental images are a "doorway" to the faery realm.

Chapter 18

Revering the Ancestors

In This Chapter

- ◆ Why our ancestors matter
- ◆ Biological forebears and ancestors of the heart
- ◆ How to honor your family tree
- ◆ Reconstructionism: Celtic wisdom with a scholarly twist

It's a universal spiritual principle, found on every continent and in virtually every wisdom tradition. "It" refers to the practice of worshiping, honoring, and venerating one's ancestors. Our ancestors are as close to us as mother and father—our most immediate forebears—extending backward in a line that stretches beyond the limits of human memory. To be human is to be the end product of untold generations; we carry the DNA of all our forebears in our living bodies. The Celtic tradition, like other wisdom traditions, links reverence for the ancestors with reverence for nature and for the gods and goddesses.

In this chapter, we'll look at what it means to honor ancestors from a Celtic perspective, including both biological and spiritual forebears. We'll also look at specific rituals and ceremonies you can perform to venerate your ancestors, and why such practices can be meaningful for you, today in the twenty-first century.

Honor Your Father(s) and Mother(s)

The scriptures of the Jewish and Christian traditions say it best, with the blunt mandate: "Honor your father and your mother." (Exodus 20:12) But this isn't unique to those paths. From Confucianism to Native American spirituality to various forms of paganism and shamanism the world over, religious and spiritual practices devoted to the spirits of the ancestors can be found just about everywhere.

> **Notes from the Otherworld**
>
> The Christian Church honors saints and martyrs (like Joan of Arc); nations honor their founders or great war leaders (like George Washington), and even corporations honor the people who originally founded the business (like Henry Ford). These are all forms of ancestor worship, for they all are ways to connect with the honor and virtue of key figures who have gone before us.

Why is this such an important practice? Start at the beginning: Loving one's mother and father is both a normal part of life, as well as a spiritually beneficial part, since our parents are the first ones who introduce us to the ways of the world. On a more abstract level, we honor our ancestors as a way of honoring ourselves and honoring who we are. For it is from our ancestors that we receive our DNA, the "computer program" that gives us our biological identity. Indeed, many spiritual traditions hold that the ancestors watch over us—and why wouldn't they, since we carry their DNA?

It Doesn't Matter Where Your Ancestors Are From ...

Remember that in Part 1 of this book I pointed out that there's no such thing as a "pure" Celtic identity or tradition. Well, the same holds true for biological ancestry. Chances are, you have ancestors from any different parts of the world. Especially if you are a member of the Celtic diaspora, it is likely that you have forebears of both Celtic and non-Celtic heritage. Even if you are a born-and-bred Irishman or citizen of one of the other Celtic nations, your land has had so many non-Celtic influences over the years (Romans, Vikings, Normans, and so forth) that in all probability you have ancestors from various different cultural backgrounds as well. People who come from regions that are not specifically thought of as Celtic (like England or Germany) in all probability have a few Celtic ancestors in their past, too!

Ten Generations, Thousands of Ancestors

Do the math: You have 2 biological parents, which means 4 grandparents, 8 great-grandparents, 16 great-great-grandparents ... go back 10 generations, and you have more than 1,000 ancestors! If the average generation is 25 years, that's only as far back as the mid-1700s. And yet, we human beings have been on planet Earth for tens of thousands of years now. All this means that innumerable souls have gone before us as our forebears.

Who were those thousands of people whose DNA we now carry? Were they kings? Commoners? Heroes? Thieves? Ordinary folks, or famous names of history? Chances are, each of us is an intricate mixture of all the above. When we revere our ancestors, we honor those who represent the entire sweep of humanity.

Herein lies an important part of reverence for the ancestors. When we honor our ancestors, we aren't just praising one particular heritage or ethnic group, or one particular type of human being. There's no such thing as a purebred human. All of us have ancestors from different backgrounds, different walks of life, different parts of the world. When we honor the ancestors, we rise above the petty differences of class and race and ethnicity that keep us divided, and we can more easily see that we are all truly one—one family of children, born of Mother Earth.

> **Notes from the Otherworld**
>
> Ancestor worship may have its roots in ancient times when tribes would keep alive the memory of particularly well-loved chiefs and warriors. These revered forebears may also have been the original inspiration for the heroes of myth and folklore.

Ancestors of Blood and Ancestors of the Heart

It's important to keep in mind that reverence for the ancestors extends beyond our biological predecessors. As important as the line of forebears are who gave us biological form through their DNA, every one of us also has innumerable "ancestors of the heart"—great teachers, leaders, and visionaries of the past whose words, ideas, and teachings have shaped who we are today. For those of us who walk the path of Celtic wisdom, such ancestors of the heart include the shamans, druids, and mystics of the Celtic past. Revering the ancestors means revering both those who gave shape to our bodies as well as those ancestors of the heart who helped give shape to our souls.

The Concept of Worship

Celtic spirituality, like other traditions from around the world, grew out of a primal spirituality of ancestor worship. Today, this notion may seem strange and perhaps even a bit unsavory to most people. If you grew up in a monotheistic religion (like Christianity, Islam, or Judaism), chances are you learned that worship should be reserved for God alone. But when we understand the true meaning of "worship," we can see how it's appropriate to worship our ancestors.

Geasa

Honoring the ancestors isn't just a sentimental way of thinking that your forebears were all pretty special people. On a deeper level, it means coming face to face with ancestors whose values or behavior may not be to your liking, such as Nazi sympathizers or slave traders or common criminals. Revering the ancestors also means healing whatever wounds may be carried in our line of DNA.

Worship comes from the old English word *weorth-scipe*, which means "worthiness." Even today in Great Britain, magistrates and other dignitaries are appropriately addressed as "Your Worship," a term of honor and respect. Thus, worship primarily means to offer honor and respect to those deemed worthy of such devotion.

Worshiping the ancestors isn't meant to replace or supplant the requirements of your religious beliefs. Rather, honoring the ancestors is a way to deepen your overall spirituality. In Celtic terms, this is especially appropriate, for the ancestors can be seen as connected to the old gods and goddesses.

The Gods and Goddesses Are Ancestors, Too

Remember the goddess Dana and the god called the Dagda? They represent the energies of motherhood and fatherhood, respectively. They represent the sacred union of the sun and the soil, out of which all life emerges and unfolds.

In other words, the god and the goddess are the ultimate ancestors! To offer reverence to our mortal ancestors and to honor the deities ultimately converges into a single act of worship. If we see the gods and the goddesses in nature, we realize that there is no gulf that separates us from the divine. Just as the land is part of Dana and the light of the sun is part of Lugh, so each of us is part of the divine nature. When we revere and love the gods and goddesses, we are also loving ourselves, as the children of those very deities. In a similar way, celebrating our ancestors as the wisdomkeepers of their day means honoring the biological link that connects us, back through time, to the earliest humans, who were the first generation of children of the divine.

Notes from the Otherworld

Exchanging gifts is a central part of human culture. We give gifts on birthdays, religious holidays like Christmas, and at rites of passage like graduation or retirement. It only makes sense that offering gifts would be a central part of relating to spiritual beings, whether gods, faeries, or ancestors.

Pwyll and Arawn: The Principle of Exchange

In the Welsh Mabinogi, an interesting point is made concerning two of the main characters, Arawn (the lord of the Underworld, Annwn) and Pwyll (the prince of the Welsh province of Dyfed). After Pwyll spends a year in Annwn helping Arawn defeat an enemy, the two become fast friends for life. Long after the good deed is performed, the story makes note that each one was continually sending gifts to the other. This is the spiritual foundation of sacrifice—of making offerings to the gods and goddesses. But it also applies to reverence for the ancestors as well. When we send "gifts" to the otherworld in honor of our forebears, they will return in kind with gifts for us. It is out of this exchange of gifts that the bonds between the living and the dead are strengthened.

Why Honoring Our Ancestors Serves the Cause of Wisdom

Revering the ancestors isn't just some sort of exercise to do because that's what ancient Celts used to do. It's a practical tool that can support us in our ongoing search for the deeper mysteries of Celtic wisdom. Here's why:

- ◆ **Ancestors are a source of wisdom.** So much of ancient wisdom has been lost—but once upon a time, our ancestors possessed the wisdom of their day, the wisdom that created Stonehenge and oriented Newgrange to the winter solstice. When we seek to connect with our ancestors, we make contact with spiritual guides who are interested in us and love us.

- ◆ **Ancestors help us know who we are.** To know who you are and where you're going, you need to start at the beginning. Befriending your forebears is a way to trace your identity back through time to the "beginning." Knowing your past empowers you to make wise choices about your future.

- ◆ **Ancestors unite us with all of humanity.** As I stressed earlier in this chapter, our many ancestors cut across all social, economic, and ethnic lines. And from our thousands of ancestors, we recognize that virtually all of the human family are, on some level, our "cousins"—our relatives, no matter how near or distant. Recognizing this common connection with all segments of the human family is a powerful doorway into the higher truths of not only Celtic wisdom, but universal wisdom. When we acknowledge our relatedness to the entire human family and we combine that with the Celtic virtue of hospitality, we realize that the key to true wisdom lies in treating all people as our kindred.

How to Honor the Ancestors

What's involved in paying homage to the ancestors? How do we do it?

To begin with, remember that "worship" in this sense means respect, honor, and acknowledgment of worthiness. You don't have to grovel in front of your ancestors or belittle yourself in order to magnify them. Quite the opposite! One way of honoring your ancestors is by loving and caring for yourself. Remember, you are the carrier of

The Seer Says

If it's too awkward for you to think about "paying homage to" or "worshipping" the ancestors, call it "honoring" instead. The words you use aren't as important as the intention of your heart.

the DNA that was originally theirs. Treating your body as a sacred temple (getting adequate rest and exercise, eating properly, meditating or practicing other stress-management techniques, and enjoying life to the fullest) is the first step toward showing love for your forebears.

Here are some other specific things you can do to say "I love you" to those who have gone before you.

Find Out Who They Are

If you live in America, you may know very little about your ancestors. So many Americans come from displaced families; our mothers and fathers or grandmothers and grandfathers often moved great distances. Unless you are entirely of Native American ancestry, then your ancestors immigrated across the ocean at some point over the last 500 years. Even today, many Americans live hundreds or thousands of miles from where they or their parents grew up. All this means knowing who our forebears really are (or were) is far less likely for us than for someone who comes from a long line of people who have lived in the same part of Cornwall for the last 1,000 years.

The Bard's Bookshelf

Want some help getting started on climbing your Celtic family tree? Here's a book worth checking out: *In Search of Your British and Irish Roots: A Complete Guide to Tracing Your English, Welsh, Scottish, and Irish Ancestors* by Angus Baxter (Genealogical Publishing Company, 2000).

To get to know who your ancestors are, try the following:

◆ **Genealogical research.** Yes, climb your family tree! This isn't just for Mormons or candidates for the Daughters of the American Revolution. For Celtic wisdomseekers, tracing your genealogy means repairing the roots that have been broken by the travel that your parents and grandparents took in order to find a better life. Unless you are 100 percent Native American or Australian Aboriginal, this tracing will eventually take you across the water and back to your ancient homeland, thereby giving you a real, solid connection with the Celtic (or other) lands.

◆ **Get to know your clan and tartan.** If you have Scottish ancestry, one easy way to begin connecting to your family history is through clan and tartan identity. If you or a maternal ancestor have a Scottish name, you can use it to find your clan. For example, my surname (McColman) is a *sept* of the Clan Buchanan. Numerous books exist on the Scottish clan system, many of which list clan septs. Once you've discovered your clan, you can research its history, as well as its tartan—a unique textile pattern consisting of stripes of different widths and colors, crossed at right angles against a solid color. Tartan fabrics are used for kilts and other articles of clothing. Each clan has one or more tartans that, when worn, identify the wearer with the clan. In addition to the tartans, each clan also has a clan crest, coat of arms, and motto. Familiarizing yourself with these elements of your clan identity are all ways to forge a sense of connection with your ancestors. Many clans also have organizations, both in Scotland and around the world, where you can connect with your "cousins" who share a common clan heritage.

◆ **Cherish your family heirlooms.**
Often, our best connection with our recent ancestors includes heirlooms, valuable or sentimental objects that belonged to our forebears. Whether jewelry, diaries, military medals, or other keepsakes, heirlooms are powerful symbols of the beating heart that once cherished those items; when we cherish them today, we reach over the years to connect with those who came before us.

Druidspeak

A **sept** is a branch of a family. It especially refers to branches of Scottish clans that have different surnames from the clan name, but are still considered members of that clan.

Visiting Ancestral Homes or Grave Sites

Many people strengthen their connection to the ancestors by traveling to their homeland and visiting their graves. In Celtic terms, this ultimately means returning to the Celtic nation(s) where your ancestors dwelled. While it can be a spiritually powerful experience to visit Ireland or Scotland merely as a tourist, combining a pleasure trip with a research-oriented project to connect with ancestors can truly make the journey come alive as a profound search for your soul.

For many people, visiting ancient grave sites is itself an "ancestral" journey, even when we have no certain evidence that blood ancestors were buried at the site. Prehistoric tombs in Ireland such as *dolmens* or cairns or passage graves like Newgrange were once the graves of kings or chieftains or great warriors of old—figures who we can claim, at the very least, as ancestors of the heart.

Druidspeak

A **dolmen** is a specific prehistoric monument, consisting of two or more standing stones, which support a capstone. Dolmens usually were burial sites.

The Brownshill Dolmen, in County Carlow, Ireland, is a remarkable dolmen because of its huge capstone.

Dolmens and other ancient burial sights are meaningful on several levels. Because of their connection with the pagan past, many modern Celtic wisdomseekers see them as great silent witnesses to the wisdom of long ago. Celtic myth and folklore assert that most ancient burial sites were doorways to the otherworld and portals where faery contact was more possible. And given that the otherworld is the natural abode of the soul after death, it makes sense that an ancient grave (where we can go to revere our ancestors) be understood in such a way.

Knowth, near Newgrange in eastern Ireland, features a number of burial mounds both large and small.

Ancestor Worship in the Home

As meaningful as it can be to travel back to your ancestral home, you don't have to do so in order to make meaningful veneration of the ancestors' part of your regular spiritual practice. Indeed, following the idea that the ancestors and the old gods and goddesses are ultimately connected, one practical way to honor your forebears is by creating an altar specifically for them.

An ancestral altar can consist of the same elements as an altar for gods and goddesses—candles, incense, offerings, and symbols of nature are all appropriate. But what sets an ancestral altar apart are the symbols that connect you to your specific ancestral lineage. These may include heirlooms, photographs, articles of clothing, or anything else that has an actual or symbolic connection to your forebears, whether of the recent or ancient past.

Your ancestor altar can be a place for meditation and reflection. You can make token offerings to your ancestors, just as you make such offerings to the gods or the faeries. But remember, the main thing your ancestors want isn't so much a bowl filled with herbs or fruit, but rather a heart that remembers them and tries to live in a way that honors their memory.

Samhain: The Holiday of the Ancestors

One particularly appropriate (and Celtic) way to pay homage to your ancestors involves the observance of Samhain (also spelled Samhuinn), the Celtic new year that occurs at the end of the harvest time (and in modern times corresponds with Halloween). For the ancient Celts, Samhain was a time of ending one cycle and beginning another: The harvest is over, but a new year (seen as beginning with the darkness of winter) is about to begin. Celtic lore holds that the veil separating the manifest world from the otherworld is especially thin at Samhain, which means that it is an especially auspicious time to psychically reach out to departed ancestors.

For more about Samhain, see Chapter 24.

Celtic Reconstruction: One Way to Honor the Ancestors

In the modern Celtic pagan movement, a small but dedicated group of scholars and seekers have been engaged in a project known as Celtic reconstruction. This is an effort to re-create, as best and accurately as possible, a Celtic pagan worldview and spirituality based on what we know of the ancient, Iron Age Celts.

Celtic reconstructionists draw on a wide variety of sources, including Indo-European studies, comparative mythology, archaeology, anthropology, and cross-cultural religious studies to develop their working model of revived Celtic paganism. Typically, the reconstructionist community relies much more heavily on scholarship and academic material than on personal inspiration or psychically derived ideas of Celtic spirituality. Indeed, the reconstructionists often reject anything that seems to blend Celtic and non-Celtic source material, including Christianity, Wicca, the grail tradition, as well as more esoteric theories (such as the idea, popular among some Celtic mystics, that the druids originally came from Atlantis).

Celtic reconstructionists are admirable for the purity of their intent, but that purity can also be a liability when the focus on "getting it right" becomes more important than the values of spirituality (like hospitality or compassion). Still, if you feel drawn to revere your forebears in as authentic a way as is reasonably possible, connecting with Celtic reconstructionists may be the path for you.

See Appendix B for several websites managed by Celtic reconstructionists.

The Ultimate Honor: Living an Honorable Life

Among our thousands of ancestors are figures of virtue and integrity, but every one of us can count on there being a few skeletons in our ancestral closet as well! Although it's spiritually beneficial to honor all our ancestors, regardless of their moral rectitude, one important way to put that veneration into practice is to carefully choose to emulate the most praiseworthy figures in our lineage.

As a Celtic wisdomkeeper, you have the choice to live a life that is selfish, isolated, and ungenerous—or you can conduct your life according to the highest ideals of hospitality, virtue, honor, compassion, and love. When you choose the higher road, you give all your ancestors something to be proud of. You'll also take your place as a truly praiseworthy ancestor for all those who come after you!

The Least You Need to Know

- Reverence for ancestors is a part of nearly every culture and religion, including the Celtic tradition.

- Ancestor worship is a way to feel connected with all aspects of human society.

- Genealogical research and setting up an ancestor's altar are two practical ways to honor your forebears.

- The best way to revere the ancestors is by living an honorable and virtuous life.

Chapter 19

Befriending the Good People

In This Chapter

- The origins of the Good People
- The faery-nature connection
- A history of faery contact
- Where to find the faeries
- How to treat the faeries

Faeries are hot! Go into any metaphysical bookstore or New Age gift shop and you'll find it literally infested with faeries. From books on how to contact faeries, to oh-so-cute little faery figurines, to jewelry emblazoned with winged critters of all shapes and sizes, the faeries are truly out in force. Faeries, like angels or spirit guides, are not unique to the Celtic world: People from all walks of life and all corners of the world see and contact faeries (even though the language and symbolism used to describe such otherworldly beings might be quite different in Hawaii or Africa than in Ireland or Wales). But there are some ways in which the faeries of the Celtic world are unique. This chapter will introduce you to the specifically Celtic world of faeries, along with ways to make a connection with the Gentry yourself. (Traditional lore suggests that one way to show respect to the faeries is by calling them names of respect, such as "the Fair Folk," "the Good People" or "the Gentry.")

Where Do Faeries Come From?

What does the Celtic tradition teach us about the origin of the faery race? Here are two theories, both from Ireland.

How the Túatha Dé Danann Became the Faeries

Once upon a time, the faeries weren't faeries. They were gods and goddesses.

The Seer Says

The contradictory myths presented here, linking the faeries with the Irish gods or with the neutral angels, are not the only way of thinking about who the faeries are. They are presented here to give you a glimpse into the many different ways of approaching spirituality in the Celtic tradition. As always, trust your intuition rather than looking for the "ultimate truth" in Celtic spirituality.

In other words, the spiritual beings that we normally think of as faeries were, in the Celtic world at least, originally seen not as just some sort of cuddly sprites who like to hang out in gardens, but were actually the powerful and awe-inspiring beings our ancient ancestors regarded as divine. When the Christian spiritual revolution occurred and declared that there was only one god, all the old goddesses and gods were gradually "demoted" until they were seen in the eyes of most people as spiritual beings without much more power than ordinary mortals. These ex-deities might be somewhat worthy of our respect, in the sense that they could cause us trouble if we didn't treat them properly, but the kind of deep awe that you might associate with a full-fledged god was simply no longer part of the faery picture.

Notes from the Otherworld

Many people think of the faeries as the "little people." But archaeology suggests that the inhabitants of the British Isles prior to the coming of the Celts were short in stature. Perhaps the concept of "the little people" is nothing more than the ancient memory of those diminutive natives. Another concept associated with faeries—the "hill dwellers" —might come from the fact that the pre-Celts built cairns and passage-grave mounds in which the dead were interred; to subsequent inhabitants of the Celtic lands, these mounds appeared like magical hills where otherworldly beings could dwell.

But in some ways, the old godliness did survive in the Celtic world, and this is important in understanding how Celtic faeries are different from other ideas regarding the spirits of the natural world. The faeries were not usually seen as small, but if anything actually towered above human beings, appearing seven or eight feet tall (if not taller)! This isn't to say that faeries never appeared in tiny forms, for faeries could appear in any shape or size they chose. And as might be expected from such sizable spiritual beings, the faeries of the Celtic world are not "cute" and "cuddly" like the ones depicted in your local New Age store—on the contrary, Celtic faeries appear as powerful entities, some of whom are helpful, others almost scary, and all of whom are worthy of respect.

An Alternative Theory: The Neutral Angels

The idea that the faeries were originally the old gods and goddesses (such as the Túatha Dé Danann) isn't the only theory you'll run into regarding the origin of the faeries. Another idea, which I first heard from an old storyteller in County Galway, is that the faeries were originally angels. When there was war in heaven and Lucifer and his followers rebelled against God, God and his archangels cast the rebel angels into the Underworld (hell). But some angels had been neutral, neither supporting God nor Lucifer. These neutral angels didn't deserve to be punished in the Underworld, but God decided they didn't exactly deserve to stay in heaven, either. So they were banished to the earth itself, where they would exist throughout eternity as faeries, spirits neither good nor evil, but who behaved pretty much in the same manner by which they were treated.

What's Unique About Celtic Faeries

Perhaps the most important point to bear in mind about Celtic faeries is that they are a different breed of spiritual being altogether from the better known faeries which, for lack of a better term, I'll call "Victorian faeries," since they resemble the concept of faeries that was popular in England in the nineteenth and early twentieth centuries. The Victorian faeries are the type that you are likely to see adorning cute little books or statues at your local New Age bookstore. They are very small, cherubic creatures with dragonfly wings and attire that could have come out of a pre-Raphaelite painting. They are cute, sweet, and adorable. They are utterly nonthreatening, not least because of how small they are. They are the kind of wee sprite that anyone would hope to have living in their garden.

> **CAUTION**
>
> **Geasa**
>
> People often mistakenly regard faeries as either purely good, sweet, and nonthreatening or as completely dangerous and untrustworthy. The truth is in the middle: Faeries come in all shapes, sizes, and moral perspectives. Don't think of them as one-dimensional.

Celtic faeries could, in theory, choose to appear as small beings, but they are far more than just sugary little creatures of Victorian romanticism. Rather, the faeries of the Celtic lands often appear as larger-than-mortal-humans, with an awe-inspiring radiance that explains why they are sometimes called "the shining ones." They might well be beautiful, but they are hardly cute and cuddly. Rather, the Gentry are more likely to evoke a sense of awe or even terror within those who come across them. These are powerful spiritual beings worthy of our respect, not trivial little thoughtforms incapable of any harm!

Another interesting concept found in the Celtic tradition is the concept of the fey (pronounced *fay*), which refers to an out-of-the-ordinary feeling or energy, sometimes associated with a particular place. Such fey energy occurs in places or situations where the faery and human realms intersect. Like anything else concerned with the faeries, it can be benevolent and healing, or spooky and unsettling.

Why Faeries Are Considered Nature Spirits

Faeries have a reputation for being spirits of nature. Some of this may in fact stem from the Victorian "garden sprite" image of faeries. But even in the Celtic tradition, faeries are creatures of the outdoors and the wild. Their habitat—the otherworld—isn't removed from the physical universe, but rather closely interwoven with it. Traditional teachings suggest that, on at least one level, the otherworld closely mirrors the features and dimensions of the physical universe. Therefore, the inhabitants of the otherworld have a natural connection to whatever location in our material world corresponds with their home in the faery realm. Some faeries may have particular connections with specific features of the natural world, such as rivers, wells, or stones. Traditional stories often depict faeries as congregating in stone circles, or forest glens, or even at desolate crossroads. Faeries, it seems, usually have some sort of connection to a particular place. That is what "anchors" them in the natural world.

The Implication of the Faery-Nature Connection

What difference does it make, to see the world as filled with faeries, or to see faeries as having a profound link to nature? Simply put, if nature and faeries are closely related, then a spiritual path that honors and appreciates one must naturally honor and appreciate the other. In other words, interest in faeries naturally implies a need to honor, respect, and care for nature. (How can we truly respect the faeries if we are trashing their home?) Meanwhile, any attempt to care for the natural world, even just for strictly ethical or philosophical reasons, would be much more effective and efficient if it included a spiritual component of respecting the spirits of nature.

The History of Faery Contact

How do we know faeries exist? Many people have extraordinary experiences of spiritual "presences" in the everyday world. But how do we know that these are the Gentry, and not just some figment of the imagination? To answer this question, let's turn to the history of faery contact. You see, faeries are not just some New Age fad that a marketing guru thought up in the 1980s to make lots of money. No, faeries have been with us for centuries. And interactions with the Good People have been documented in folklore and folk song, as well as in books, for hundreds of years.

> **Notes from the Otherworld** _____
>
> What's the difference between an elf and a faery? Mostly, it's a difference of language. *Elf* comes from an old German word for "white being," implying a shining entity from the otherworld. *Faery* comes from the French and Latin words for "fate," suggesting entities who originate outside the normal bounds of space and time. Although the Irish tradition rarely refers to otherworld beings as elves, this word does appear in the Scottish tradition.

An interesting glimpse into the world of the faeries can be found in traditional ballads, including two from Scotland: *Tam Lin* and *Thomas the Rhymer*. But as early as the seventeenth century, actual people were recording their experience in Fairyland (including a Christian minister named Robert Kirk). Today, faery spirituality is more popular than ever, with teachers like R. J. Stewart helping a new generation of seekers find the authentic faery tradition.

Thomas the Rhymer

Thomas of Erceldoune, also known as "True Thomas" or "Thomas the Rhymer," is celebrated in medieval manuscripts as the father of Scottish poetry and a prophet on a par with Merlin or Taliesin. He is said to have lived in the thirteenth century. Celebrated in poetry and song, Thomas experienced a profound vision one day of a beautiful woman riding toward him on a majestic steed. He assumed she was Mary, Queen of Heaven, and addressed her so, to which she replied that she was queen of another country. Thomas declared his devotion for the queen; and after they made love, she took him back to her underworldly kingdom, passing the roads to heaven and to hell and instead taking a third road, "to Fair Elfland," where his love was queen. Once in her country, Thomas enjoyed feasting and merrymaking for what seemed to be only a few days. But when he returned to the mundane world, he found that seven years had passed by. As a parting gift, the queen bestowed him not only with the gift of eloquent poetry, but also the gift of unalterable truth—in other words, Thomas could never tell a lie from that day forward!

Many stories grew around the figure of True Thomas following his return from the Land of Faery. Not only could he speak only the truth, but he also enjoyed the gift of prophecy, especially regarding Scottish politics. Medieval stories of Thomas recount him predicting many of the events related to Scottish-English conflict in the fourteenth century.

Eventually Thomas the Rhymer became a folk hero, and has been immortalized in traditional songs that can still be heard performed by folk musicians today.

Tam Lin

The ballad of Tam Lin presents a darker, more sinister glimpse into the world of faery-human contact. It is an *eldritch* story of a young woman named Janet who encounters a faery being named Tam Lin. The two become lovers and Janet is soon pregnant with his child. She learns, however, that Tam Lin is not faery-born, but rather a mortal man who is held captive by the queen of faeries, and who is an intended sacrifice to the lord of the Underworld.

Druidspeak

Eldritch means "weird" or "eerie." Scottish literature includes a number of so-called eldritch poems, which are filled with bizarre, unusual, or fantastic imagery.

Tam Lin explains how Janet can save him, by rescuing him from a wild faery hunt that occurs on the night of Halloween (Samhain). On that fateful night, she pulls him from his horse and holds him tightly while the faery queen shapeshifts him into a series of fearsome shapes. Finally Tam Lin assumes his own, naked form, and by clothing him, Janet succeeds in setting him free.

This story offers several insights into the faery tradition. Not only are the faeries shown as magical beings with shapeshifting abilities and the power to cross between the worlds (in the ballad, Janet herself never visits the otherworld), but are also depicted as amoral beings against whom one must be protected. In this sense, the ballad shows the influence of Christianity as a religion that has generally depicted the faeries at best as neutral beings, and often as demonic.

Robert Kirk

In 1691 (in other words, just a year before the Salem Witch Trials), a Scottish minister named Robert Kirk wrote a fascinating book called *The Secret Commonwealth of*

Elves, Fauns and Fairies. This book recounts his experiences with the inhabitants of the otherworld, along with a wealth of traditional Scottish folklore about the second sight and otherworld journeying. Among other interesting points, Kirk argues that it is perfectly valid to believe in faeries and make contact with them, and still be a good, practicing Christian.

> **The Bard's Bookshelf**
>
> Want a glimpse into the Scottish dimension of faery belief? Check out Lizanne Henderson's and Edward J. Cowan's *Scottish Fairy Belief* (Tuckwell Press, 2001).

Turlough O'Carolan

Turlough O'Carolan, the blind Irish bard whom you learned about in Chapter 8, was said to have learned some of his harp tunes from the Fair Folk. Nor was he the only musician to have had a traditional connection with the faeries—an entire family of pipers on the Isle of Skye were said to have received their talent as a gift from the faeries! Indeed, the Gentry have a reputation for their love of dancing and music, and many stories are told of how they will seek mortal musicians to play for them or other mortals to join in their dances.

R. J. Stewart

Here's an example of a living person with a profound connection to the faery realm. R. J. Stewart is a Scottish musician and spiritual teacher who has written a number of books on magical and mystical topics, including *The Living World of Faery* and *Celtic Gods, Celtic Goddesses.* (He also translated Kirk's *The Secret Commonwealth* into a modern English edition published as *Robert Kirk: Walker Between Worlds.*) Stewart teaches methods for establishing contact with otherworldly beings, faeries as well as ancestors.

From Thomas the Rhymer to R. J. Stewart, the Celtic faery tradition has existed virtually unchanged for centuries. Again and again, those who have established contact with the otherworld teach that such contact is possible for the ordinary person, and that the relationships formed with beings there can have profound, life-altering experiences, usually for the good (although Tam Lin's story is a reminder that not all faeries are necessarily "nice").

Sites Associated with the Faeries

Where does a person go to contact the faeries? Well, insofar as they are spirits of nature, they are everywhere (for nature is everywhere, too—even in the middle of a glass/steel/concrete city). But some places, especially in the British Isles, have legendary reputations for being centers of faery activity. Visit these places, and you just might encounter the Gentry yourself!

Places with traditional faery associations often have names like "Faery Glen" or "Faery Hill" that reveal how such places are considered to be connected with the otherworld in a powerful way. What's also interesting to keep in mind is how so much of the faery tradition regards the fey folk as living in a subterranean realm. This could be seen as a metaphor for the shamanic way of understanding the cosmos, with upper and lower worlds existing alongside the "normal" physical world. This, in turn, can be viewed as a symbolic way of understanding human consciousness, where "higher" and "lower" forms of unconsciousness co-exist with normal waking awareness. Perhaps the traditions that insist that the Gentry live beneath the land are symbolically reminding us that the key to contacting these otherworldly beings lies in an altered state of consciousness (such as shamans find through drumming or deep meditation).

Dolmens

Found throughout western Europe, dolmens or *cromlechs* are prehistoric graves. The name is a Breton word that means "table stone," and indeed, that's what a typical dolmen looks like—most consist of three or more stones standing upright, with a capstone laid across them, like a tabletop above its legs. Dolmens can be large or small—the largest one in Ireland, the Brownshill Dolmen in County Carlow, has a capstone as large as an automobile!

> **Druidspeak**
>
> **Cromlech** is the Welsh term for dolmen. It literally means "bent stone."

The Poulnabrone Dolmen, located in the west of Ireland.

Many dolmens feel like miniature chambers or human-made caves. Sitting inside a dolmen, it's easy to get a sense of timelessness and a feeling of awe as you consider the lives and fates of the people who erected it, so many thousands of years ago. Dolmens (like cairns, discussed in the next section) are not only traditionally associated with the faeries, but also are excellent locations for seeking contact with ancestral spirits.

Cairns

Like dolmens, cairns are pre-Celtic graves or monuments found throughout the British Isles. They consist of mounds of stones that can range in size from just a few feet to well over 10 feet high. Some cairns are located on the tops of hills and mountains where they are dramatically visible for miles around. This has led archaeologists to conclude that only great leaders and warriors were interred in such tombs. Many cairns have become associated with Celtic myth; for example, the large cairn at the summit of Knocknarea to the west of Sligo in Ireland is known as Queen Maeve's tomb, associated with the legendary Queen of Connacht who plays a prominent role in the Irish epic *The Táin*. Other cairns may not have such a famous figure attached with them, but are associated in a general way with faeries.

The Poulawack cairn, located in County Clare, Ireland, is an example of the pre-Celtic graves or monuments traditionally associated with faeries.

Passage Tombs

The most famous type of prehistoric grave is the passage tomb, such as Newgrange or Knowth in eastern central Ireland. These structures are essentially human-made hills with carefully constructed corridors leading to an open room in the center, where the ashes and bones of the dead were interred. The greatest passage tombs, like

Newgrange, are filled with beautifully cut stones decorated with spirals and other abstract shapes. Several of the passage tombs are oriented so that sunlight shines into the tomb at important times of the year: Newgrange, for example, is filled with sunlight for several minutes on the morning of the winter solstice. This suggests that the pre-Celtic builders of these structures not only had a precise understanding of the sun's movement in the sky, but also associated the sun with resurrection or safe passage to the otherworld so that the souls of the dead could rest prior to reincarnation.

Notes from the Otherworld

Newgrange is an amazing archaeological site. It's approximately 5,000 years old, and yet there is no evidence that rainwater has *ever* leaked into the central passage. This is due to a brilliantly engineered corbelled ceiling. Think about that the next time you're in a modern building with a leaky roof!

Although passage tombs, dolmens, and cairns are structurally quite different, their folkloric association with faeries is essentially the same. To the modern seeker, these ancient gravesites can serve as powerful markers for undertaking the inner journey to contact the spirits of nature as well as the spirits of the honored dead.

Ringforts

In many locations throughout the traditional Celtic lands, you'll find raths, or ringforts. Little is left of these ancient sites other than earthwork, often in a circular shape; but these silent remains have been fertile ground for faery lore to develop, and over the years, many ringforts developed reputations as faery haunts.

Stone Circles

From the famous ones like Stonehenge or Avebury in England and Callanish in Scotland, to lesser-known but still beautiful circles like Grange or Drombeg in Ireland, the circle of stones is perhaps the most obvious symbol associated with the earth-centered spirituality of pre-Christian Europe. Because the circles date back centuries before the arrival of Celtic culture, their true meaning and purpose are lost in the mists of time, although we can assume they served both scientific/astronomical and religious functions. But even after the original uses of stone circles were lost to history, they remained associated with the spirit world in the popular mind. It's easy to imagine stepping through two tall standing stones into the middle of a circle and slipping into the magical realm where faeries feast and dance.

Could ancient stone circles like this one in Co. Sligo be the habitat for faery folk?

Holy Wells

Water sources have probably been venerated for so long because they are seen as portals between our world and the faery realm. If the faeries lived beneath the ground (whether in hills, cairns, or a more remote Underworld), and water comes up from under the ground … you get the idea. This explains also why the waters of sacred wells are seen as having curative powers. Since the faery realm is the origin point of spiritual healing, water that flows from that magical world would naturally carry its own holistic power.

Sacred Trees

Often, particular trees will develop a reputation as being favored by the faeries or as situated on a gateway to the otherworld. Hawthorne and yew trees have particular magical associations, and when a particular tree is regarded as a faery tree, it is considered foolhardy to cut it or harm it in any way, for fear of bad luck or reprisal from the Gentry. Indeed, a popular Irish legend maintains that a faery tree was cut down to build the factory for the DeLorean automobile—resulting in the prompt bankruptcy of the company!

Anything Natural, Wild, Untamed

Finally, perhaps the places where contact with the faeries might be most easily made are those that are untouched by human hands. In other words, the closer you are to the wilderness, the closer you are to a place where the veil separating this world from the otherworld is naturally thin. If you've ever felt a sense of magic and wonder while walking through the woods or enjoying a majestic view of mountains, then you have a sense of how close you are to Faeryland in such places.

The Seer Says

It's interesting to learn about all the traditional sites considered to be favorable for faery contact. But just as all of the world is part of nature (even a concrete-covered urban landscape), so, too, the faeries can be reached from just about anywhere. If you are willing to go within yourself and seek that place where your imagination opens up into the spiritual world, then you've found a place to make a connection with the fey folk. But be sure to read the section on faery protocol at the end of this chapter; better yet, find an experienced Celtic shaman or druid practitioner to teach you how to enter the faery realm safely.

What's So Wise About the Faeries?

From myth to folklore to entertaining folk ballads, faeries are an essential element within Celtic culture. But why should you, as a seeker of Celtic wisdom, pay any attention to the faeries?

It's not the purpose of this book to speculate about how "real" the faeries are (in other words, whether faery existence might ever be scientifically measured). Faeries are certainly real on some level, even if it is just in our imagination. But anyone who takes the time to explore contact with the faery realm will quickly discover that how "real" the faeries are is ultimately inconsequential. For all questions of science aside, the experience of faeries can be profoundly meaningful in the following ways:

◆ Because faeries are associated with nature, interacting with them can help you feel more respectful of, and connected to, nature.

◆ Faeries can function as guides and allies (as described in Chapter 17)—in other words, they provide support to your exploration of the shamanic dimension of Celtic spirituality.

◆ Faeries can be profound teachers. True faeries (not the cute little sprites that show up in gift shops) command respect. Among other things, faeries expect humans to treat other beings with respect and kindness—a message that, alas, we don't always get from the rest of society!

◆ Finally, faeries will remind you that there's more to life than just the mundane world as experienced in ordinary consciousness. No matter what you might believe about faeries, experiencing them on your inner journeys can help you more fully appreciate the spiritual dimension to ordinary existence.

Faery Protocol

You may wish to seek out your own contacts in the faery realm, to improve your knowledge of faery ways and seek their guidance in your quest for wisdom. The following list provides a brief rundown of some traditional and common-sense guidelines for contacting and relating to the faeries.

Remember, faeries may vary widely in their personality or friendliness. Some may be very open to positive dealings with humans, but others are more like tricksters or can be unreliable and unhelpful. Some may actually be hostile to humans. When doing inner work related to the faeries, use common sense and discretion. As a seeker of wisdom, your job is to contact only helpful, friendly faery spirits; if you should bump into any of the less-pleasant types of faeries in your travels, respectfully but firmly tell them you're not interested in dealing with them.

◆ Contacting the faeries is no more difficult or momentous than reaching out to ancestors or to the otherworld in general (see Chapters 17 and 18). Remember that not all spirits in the otherworld are necessarily faeries—some may be ancestors, some may be gods and goddesses, and some may identify themselves in some other way (such as elves or angels).

◆ Be polite when approaching faeries. They are not your servants to command at will! Approach a spirit like you would approach any other new acquaintance—with respect and good manners. If the entity you approach responds in a like manner, you can take time to get to know him or her; but if the spirit brushes you off or in any way indicates you're not welcome, move on and look for a more hospitable contact.

◆ Offer a gift to the faeries you encounter. Such gifts can be imaginal offerings from the inner realm, or can be actual gifts of oil, herbs, or food left in small amounts beneath a tree or in a forest setting. Remember your manners: If you're going to ask the faery for help, or guidance, or just for friendship, it's polite to offer a token of your gratitude.

◆ Accept gifts graciously, with one exception: Don't eat or drink any faery food. But even then, be gracious in declining.

The Seer Says

Tradition holds that it's dangerous to eat food in the otherworld—doing so might trap you there! In respect for the tradition, it's best to politely decline any food that might be offered to you when traveling in the otherworld.

◆ Live your life in a way that respects the faeries. First and foremost, this means respecting nature. Because faeries are so strongly associated with the natural world, you'll want to show them your interest in them by demonstrating care for our mundane environment. The Gentry are not stupid: They'll be impressed by your environmental sensitivity, and will be much more inclined to welcome you as an ally.

The Least You Need to Know

◆ Far from being just a marketing fad, faeries have long been respected (and feared) in the Celtic lands as powerful nature spirits.

◆ Evidence of belief in faeries and faery contact stretches from the Middle Ages to the present day.

◆ Folklore suggests that ancient sacred sites and natural settings are powerful places for faery contact.

◆ Treating faeries—and nature—with respect and good manners is essential for anyone wishing to explore this part of the Celtic tradition.

◆ Although taking inner journeys to make faery contact can be meaningful, it's important not to be superstitious about faery existence or influence.

Chapter 20

Celtic Spirituality and Christianity: Cultivating the Heart of Holiness

In This Chapter

- ◆ Introducing Celtic Christianity
- ◆ Why Celtic Christianity is unique
- ◆ Brigid: saint or goddess? Or both?
- ◆ The *Carmina Gadelica:* a manual of Celtic Christianity
- ◆ Integrating Christianity with Celtic paganism

Most of the material covered in this book is based on the indigenous pagan spirituality and religion of the Celts. The distinctively Celtic form of wisdom originated within the pagan treasures of the past, which are preserved in archaeology, mythology, and traditional spiritual practices. Meanwhile, many modern Celtic wisdomseekers turn to the ancient Celtic pagans for guidance and inspiration.

But it's a mistake to assume that only pagan forms of spirituality can express the timeless wisdom of the Celts. As we have seen, the Celts were always interacting with other cultures, and this included adopting spiritual beliefs and religious practices from other lands. The supreme example of this was the coming of Christianity. In regard to Ireland, historians have noted that what the Roman Empire and the Vikings could never do, the Christian Church did handily—that is to say, conquered Eire. To this day, Christianity remains the most widely practiced religion worldwide among Celts and their descendents.

This chapter takes a closer look at the sometimes turbulent relationship between the Celts and Christianity, including some beautiful parts of the Celtic Christian story—in the earliest centuries of Celtic Christianity, beautiful art and literature flowed from the pens of the Christian monks. But there's also a dark side to Christianity in the Celtic land. (You need look no farther than Northern Ireland to know what I mean.) By understanding what makes Celtic Christianity unique, you'll learn more about the nature of Celtic wisdom.

The Story of the Coming of Christianity

After the death of Christ in approximately 30 C.E., it didn't take long for Christianity to make it to the British Isles (which, by then, was the last stronghold of independent Celtic nations). According to legend, Joseph of Arimathea, the wealthy businessman whose grave was used as Christ's tomb, had a trading relationship with the British Celts and Joseph is even said to have brought the boy Jesus to England where he studied under the druids at the Isle of Avalon (modern Glastonbury). Joseph is then said to have come to England with a small band of Christians in the years directly following Christ's death.

Notes from the Otherworld

The English poet William Blake (1757–1827) wrote a poem that commemorates the idea of Jesus studying under druids in England:

> And did those feet in ancient time
> Walk upon England's mountains green;
> And was the holy Lamb of God,
> On England's pleasant pastures seen!

Blake, incidentally, is believed to have been a druid chief and is recognized as such by the Order of Bards, Ovates, and Druids.

Although there's no independent evidence to support the Joseph of Arimathea-Glastonbury connection, it's an electrifying concept, for two important reasons:

◆ If Jesus actually studied under the druids, that would imply that Jesus' message had been influenced by druidic thought. It also suggests that there may be a basic harmony between at least some parts of Jesus' teaching and at least some parts of druidic teaching.

◆ Legend states that when Joseph returned to Glastonbury following the death of Christ, he brought with him the cup that Jesus used at the Last Supper. This cup was the Holy Grail (see Chapter 22).

If the Glastonbury legends are true, then Christianity may have arrived in Britain even before the Roman conquest that began in 43 C.E. Even if Joseph of Arimathea never came to England, we can still assume that Christianity came with the Romans or some other missionaries from the ancient world (one tradition holds that Egyptian Christians first brought the Gospel to the British Isles), meaning that at some point within the first two centuries C.E. there was a Christian presence in Britain.

Christianity and Ireland

One of the most popular and well-known Christian saints is Patrick, the apostle to the Irish. Patrick is said to have converted the Irish, driven the snakes (a code word for the druids) out of Ireland, and used the shamrock to explain the Christian Trinitarian concept of God. To this day, his March 17 feast day is celebrated boisterously by the Irish and their descendents and friends the world over.

But Patrick, like so many early figures, is a mysterious character about whom we know little. Some historians have suggested that there may have in fact been more than one "Patrick." Others suggest that Christianity probably had made it to Ireland through trade and the normal travels of people, even before Patrick launched his missionary efforts. But we do know that a figure named Patrick was born in a Christian family in Britain toward the end of the fourth century. In his autobiography, Patrick recounts being captured by Irish pirates and sent to Ireland as a slave; eventually he escaped and made his way back to England, where he studied for the priesthood. Around the year 431 C.E. he returned to Ireland as a missionary. Many legends and folk tales grew up around the figure of Patrick; what we do know is that he probably spent the rest of his life traveling around Ireland, preaching the Christian religion and establishing churches and monasteries.

Patrick's mission to Ireland was successful, and the land embraced Christianity with a devotion that remains to this day. Ireland produced many saints besides Patrick, the two most famous being Brigid and Columba.

Christianity and Scotland

The earliest recorded Christian missionary to Scotland was Ninian, who established churches in the late fourth century (even before Patrick's mission to Ireland). But the figure to have the most lasting impact on the establishment of Celtic Christianity in Scotland was Columba (Colum Kille) in the sixth century.

Saint Columba was born to a wealthy Irish family about the year 521 C.E. He received a monastic education and became a priest and monk himself, founding several monasteries in Eire. About the year 563, he took a small band of monks and set sail for Scotland. They landed on the island of Iona and established a monastery there, from which he and his followers spread Christianity throughout Scotland, converting kings and commoners alike.

> ### Notes from the Otherworld
>
> Here's a bit of Celtic trivia for you: The patron saints of Ireland and Wales were missionaries to those countries—Patrick in Ireland and David in Wales. It would logically follow, then, that Scotland's patron saint would be Ninian or Columba. But instead, Scotland chose one of the 12 apostles, Andrew, to be its patron.

Iona became an important center for Christianity in the Celtic lands. Kings came there to be consecrated and after death were buried there. The monastery at Iona remained a powerful and important part of Scottish Christianity until the sixteenth century, a time when monasteries were being closed throughout the British Isles. In the twentieth century, Iona has become the home to a progressive community dedicated to Christian spirituality and social justice.

Some Important Celtic Christians

Here are a few of the key figures in Celtic Christianity, aside from Patrick and Columba (just discussed) and Brigid (discussed later in this chapter):

- **Aidan.** A monk from Iona who founded a major Celtic Christian center on the northeast coast of Britain, at the holy island of Lindisfarne. He died in 651 C.E.

- **Brendan.** The sixth-century founder of an important monastery in western Ireland, Brendan is called "the Navigator" because of a legendary voyage that he and several of his monks took over the Atlantic, visiting a number of islands. Scholars believe he may have traveled all the way to Iceland, Greenland, or even possibly North America.

- **Columbanus.** This sixth-century Irish monk spread the ideals of Irish Christianity to Gaul, establishing a number of monasteries there. He died in 615 C.E.

- **Cuthbert.** A monk of Lindisfarne who adopted the life of a solitary hermit. Later, he accepted the position of Bishop of Lindisfarne, but only after much cajoling. He had a reputation for being a kind and gentle spiritual leader. He died in 687 C.E.

- **David.** Little is known about this figure who died in 601 C.E.; he was a missionary to the Welsh and is now the patron saint of Wales.

- **Kevin.** Kevin founded an important monastery at Glendalough in Ireland. According to his biography, he lived to be 120! He died in 618 C.E.

> **The Bard's Bookshelf**
>
> If you're interested in learning more about a variety of Celtic saints, check out John Matthews's *Drinking from the Sacred Well: Personal Voyages of Discovery with the Celtic Saints* (Harper-SanFrancisco, 1998).

How Celtic Wisdom + Christianity = Celtic Christianity

You might recall that in Chapter 2 you learned that the Roman Empire pulled out of Great Britain around the year 410 C.E. At that time, Christianity was already a thriving religion in the British Isles. But with the loss of Roman rule, the church (like the rest of Britain) was left to fend for itself. Official ties with the church in Rome would not return to Britain for nearly 200 years, until a Roman-authorized bishop set up a cathedral in Canterbury England in 597. It would be another 70 years until most of the Celtic Christians would recognize Roman authority.

During that 200- to 250-year period, Celtic Christianity flourished as a unique and independent form of the Christian religion. Today, many people of Celtic heritage wish that Celtic Christianity had become the dominant form of Christianity, rather than the Roman (and later Protestant) versions that so often seem to operate almost at odds with the teachings of Jesus. This is because Celtic Christianity, as preserved in the writings and beautiful art of the period, was deeply mystical, nature loving, and optimistic. In other words, the emphasis was not on "sin" or "judgment," but rather on divine love and the beauty of creation. The Christians of the Celtic lands incorporated the central ideas of Celtic wisdom into their expression of Christianity, creating a powerful and beautiful religious synthesis.

Let's look at these key elements of Celtic Christianity.

Mysticism

In Christian terms, mysticism is defined as experiencing the direct presence of God. Mystical Christianity celebrates the closeness of God's love, instead of worrying about such things as God's wrath or judgment. Many of the ancient Celtic Christian writings express in beautiful poetic form a sense of the closeness of God—setting the Celtic Christians in stark contrast to many other corners of the Christian world, where God was increasingly being seen as a remote kinglike figure whose only interest in humanity was to judge us.

Love of Nature

Celtic Christian poetry is literally drenched with nature imagery. Many of the stories about the old Celtic monks speak of their close ties to the natural world, of how animals would come to pray with them. One story tells how Saint Columba used to wade out into the sea up to his neck (!) to pray, and that otters would come and pray with him while he stood there in the cold water.

Emphasis on Family Rather Than Celibacy

You may have noticed that most of the great Celtic monks founded monasteries. But these were generally not like monasteries in the rest of Christendom. Although most nuns and monks were celibate, in the Celtic world married persons as well as singles could become monks (that is to say, live within an intentional community of other Christians). Meanwhile, Celtic Christians permitted their priests to marry.

Beautiful Art

Perhaps the greatest enduring legacy of the Celtic Christians is their intricately designed artwork, which appeared both in sacred religious art (such as church decorations or ritual tools) and vividly illustrated hand-drawn manuscripts. The most famous of these is the Book of Kells, which probably was created at Iona but eventually was hidden in a monastery in Kells, Ireland for safekeeping. The Book of Kells is a hand-made book of the four Christian gospels. Each page not only contains carefully scripted Latin text, but is ornately decorated with Celtic knotwork, drawings of animals, saints, and other illustrated motifs. It was created sometime around the beginning of the ninth century.

> **The Bard's Bookshelf**
>
> Facsimile copies of the Book of Kells are expensive, but if you want to enjoy the beautiful artwork of this ancient Celtic masterpiece, consider getting it on CD-ROM. Trinity College Dublin (where the original manuscript is located) has produced a disc with all the images from the Book of Kells included. To learn more, visit www.bookofkells.com.

Other illustrated manuscripts exist as well, from such monasteries as Lindisfarne in England or Armagh and Durrow in Ireland. The sheer beauty of these texts indicates a spirituality that is based not on self-denial and rejection of the world, but on a deep appreciation for the many blessings of creation.

Brigid: Christian Saint, or Goddess Makeover?

One of the most interesting figures within Celtic Christianity is at the center of a complex web of connections between the Celtic church and its pagan forebears. That figure is Saint Brigid. Along with Patrick and Columba, she is considered one of the three foremost saints of Ireland—yet scholars are divided as to whether she ever even existed. Some historians believe she was never anything more than the pagan goddess Brigid (who you met in Chapter 13) after receiving a Christian "makeover."

The Story of Brigid

Brigid (you'll see her name spelled a number of different ways, including Bridget, Brighid, Brigit, and Bride) was supposed to have been born around the year 450 C.E. and died in 523 C.E. She is said to have been born of an interfaith marriage—her father was a druid and her mother a Christian. As a girl, Brigid was taught by druids, but embraced the faith of her mother and chose to become a nun, eventually founding the first convent in Ireland at Cill-Dara (the Church of the Oak), which is today the town of Kildare. One ancient source says that Brigid was consecrated a bishop—pretty remarkable, when you consider that to this day women aren't even allowed to be priests in the Catholic Church!

Many stories associated with Brigid attest to her holiness and generosity. She is said to have been deeply concerned about the needs of the poor; on one occasion as a girl she took butter from a churn in her druid master's house and gave it to wandering beggars who had happened by. When the druid found out, he grew angry and instructed Brigid never to give away food without his permission again. Of course, the very next time beggars showed up, Brigid gave away more butter, but this time prayed for God's blessing over the churn. When the druid checked the churn, even after Brigid's charity, it was always overflowing with butter!

Another story recounts a time when Brigid was looking for pasture land for the cows of her convent. She appealed to the king of Leinster (eastern Ireland) to ask if her convent could have just enough land that her cloak could cover. The king, thinking this a rather silly request, agreed. When Brigid threw her cloak to the ground, it spread, and spread, and spread, until almost 5,000 acres were covered! And although this land was then granted to the convent, it was common land where anyone could graze their sheep or horses, and it remains so to this day.

Yet another fascinating tale describes Brigid's father as wealthy, and Brigid as having the habit of giving her father's belongings away, either to the poor directly or selling them and then giving the money to the needy. One time, she even gave her father's sword away! Frustrated, her father tried to sell her off as a slave, but the potential buyer recognized Brigid's holiness (or independent mind!) and refused to buy her.

Legend has it that Brigid died early in the sixth century, leaving behind a convent in Kildare town. This convent became famous, not only for its historical association with the holy woman, but for an unusual practice: For centuries, the nuns of Kildare tended a sacred fire in a temple that was dedicated to Saint Brigid. No men were allowed to tend the fire, which was watched over by 19 nuns, each tending the flame for a day at a time; on the twentieth day, the flame was left in Brigid's own care. The flame was kept lit perpetually long after Brigid's death. This apparently wasn't something that began with the coming of Christianity, but was rather the survival of a pre-Christian sacred fire dedicated to the goddess Brigid. For this reason, several Bishops in the Catholic (and later, Anglican) Church attempted to extinguish the flame. After the Protestant Reformation, the flame was finally extinguished in the sixteenth century, only to be relit in the twentieth. To this day, a small community of nuns in Kildare carefully tend the flame that burns in honor of this goddess/saint.

> ### Notes from the Otherworld
>
> The legends about Brigid the saint reveal her connection to the goddess of the same name. For example, the goddess Brigid was associated with cows and milk; and so, Brigid the saint had the ability to make butter appear miraculously and secured free land where cows (and other livestock) could safely graze.

The site of Brigid's fire temple, outside the Cathedral of St. Brigid in Kildare, Ireland.

Brigid as a Wisdomkeeper

The many legends about Brigid are charming folk tales, but they also carry insights into Brigid's role as a wisdomkeeper. She is depicted again and again as a woman who cares for the poor, who loves the natural world, who believes in living simply, and who embodies a spirit of compassion. You might think that these are natural qualities for a "saint" to possess, but note also that each of these is a value central to the Celtic path.

The Seer Says

In Kildare (Brigid's hometown) there is a wonderful holy well dedicated to the saint. In front of the well are five stones. According to local custom, these stones represent five virtues associated with Brigid: care for the earth, peacemaking, generosity to the poor, hospitality, and contemplation. Even if you live nowhere near Ireland, find five stones and put them on your altar; when you see the stones, meditate on the Brigidine virtues.

Christianity and Hostility

One of the tragedies of the Christian religion has been how it hasn't always lived up to the vision of peace and harmony proclaimed by its founder, Jesus. In the Celtic lands (as well as in other parts of the world), Christianity has sometimes been a force of hostility rather than a force for love and reconciliation.

Hostility Between Christian and Pagan

It's important to acknowledge that, even with all the ways in which Celtic Christianity has adopted elements of paganism, there actually was considerable enmity between pagans and Christians in the early years of the new religion. Although there are some reasons to believe that the ancient encounter between Christians and pagans was harmonious (for example, there is no evidence that the earliest Christians were persecuted or martyred by the pagan Celts), it's also important to acknowledge that some of the ancient written sources paint a picture of enmity between the two faiths, an enmity that began with the Christian assumption that it was the "one true way" and the paganism was therefore evil. Unfortunately, this perspective still exists today among some of the more conservative elements of the Christian faith.

Hostility Between Catholic and Protestant

What is perhaps more familiar to most people is the tragic, ongoing troubles between Catholics and Protestants in Northern Ireland. Although there is clearly a political as well as a spiritual dimension to this conflict (generally speaking, Catholics support Irish independence while Protestants are loyal to the government of the United Kingdom), the battle lines usually are drawn along religious lines. Violence in Northern Ireland has erupted intermittently since the 1960s, and despite occasional cease fires and attempts to negotiate agreements between the parties, extremism and terrorism have haunted the process and kept the fires of enmity fanned.

The Antidote to Hostility

It seems ironic that a religion that lauds its leader as the "Prince of Peace" should have such a violent heritage (again, not only in the Celtic lands but in many other parts of the world). The traditional Christian explanation for such hostility would be sin, the notion that human beings rebel against God and therefore do ungodly things. The pagan view would suggest that Christianity, as a monotheistic religion imported from the Middle East, is inherently hostile to (and inappropriate for) the Celtic temperament.

Rather than get mired in that conflict, let's look at ways to envision harmony, rather than hostility, when it comes to the Celtic experience of religion. No matter what your personal religious view may be—Catholic, Protestant, Wiccan, neopagan, shamanic, or whatever—as a Celtic wisdomseeker, you can make the choice to live your own life in a way that respects and honors differences in religion. You can be faithful to your personal beliefs and still accept the fact that others see things differently. You don't have to convert others or change them in order to be faithful to your own position. As more and more Celtic wisdomseekers adopt this position, we slowly are healing the centuries-old wounds of religious intolerance that still trouble the people of Northern Ireland today. And while easing tensions between Catholics and Protestants in Northern Ireland might not directly solve the complex political problems in the region (that ultimately has to do with Irish sovereignty, not religion), improving relations between the different factions of Christianity can only help the overall quest for peace.

> **Notes from the Otherworld**
>
> A nonprofit organization called the Ulster Project is working hard to create a better future for Northern Ireland. Each summer the Ulster Project sponsors trips for Catholic and Protestant youth to different locations in North America, where the kids can encounter each other—and a society where Catholics and Protestants generally get along—in a spirit of cooperation and trust. For more information, visit www.ulsterproject.org.

Christopaganism: A Celtic Possibility

Healing the wounds of religious hostilities can involve more than just respect and tolerance, however. For some people, the ultimate majesty of Celtic spirituality lies in the way it transcends all religious boundaries. Think of how this theme has appeared again and again in this book: the holy wells where Christians follow in the footsteps of their pagan ancestors in venerating healing waters ... the lorica, the incantation of protection that has been used by pagans as well as Christians ... the druids, that ancient pagan order of scholars/priests who inspired centuries of Christians seeking the wisdom of their land ... and Brigid, the goddess who became a saint, whose nuns kept her fire burning whether they identified themselves as pagans or Christians.

For some Celtic wisdomseekers, it makes sense to acknowledge Celtic wisdom as encompassing both pagan and Christian streams of wisdom. Rather than try to put one stream down in favor of another, perhaps the true Celtic way is one of hospitality and honor, where all spiritual and religious perspectives are welcome, provided they share with one another in a spirit of respect and goodwill.

The technical term for this religious cross-breeding is *Christopaganism*. Although Christopaganism is not a movement per se (you won't find any Christopagan churches or associations listed in your phone book), it has attracted a small but fervent community online.

Like other forms of Christian-based spirituality, Christopaganism isn't necessarily Celtic. But for many people who wish to integrate the path of Christ with the path of nature, Celtic spirituality is an obvious inspiration. Christo-paganism is a spiritual perspective that says "Yes!" to both love for Mother Earth and love for the Heavenly Father.

As you continue to walk your journey into the wisdom of the Celts, you may find this Christopagan model attractive to you. Even if you are a dedicated and devout practitioner of Christianity (or, for that matter, of paganism), if there are elements of the other path that you find appealing and attractive, there's no

Druidspeak

Christopaganism is a word that first was used among neopagans to signify anyone who identifies as a pagan but maintains some ties to Christianity. Usage of the word has expanded, however, to include anyone (of either religion, both, or none) who seeks to integrate elements of the two faiths.

Geasa

Chances are, the more you explore Celtic spirituality, the more impatient you will become with the religious boundaries that separate Christians from pagans from other religions. Just remember that most people remain mired in a worldview that sees one religion as "right" and all others as "wrong"—and it's not your job to make others see the light.

reason why you can't integrate the two on a personal, individual level. Just remember that, for most people, religion involves clear boundaries that separate what is acceptable from what isn't. This means that if you enjoy blending Christian and pagan spirituality, you may not find many other people who support your position. When trying to deconstruct the walls that have separated earth-based spirituality from traditional monotheistic religion, you will face opposition from both sides of the wall.

Carmina Gadelica—a Manual of Christopaganism

In Chapter 1 you learned about the *Carmina Gadelica*, a large anthology of chants, spells, runes, and poems collected in rural Scotland at the turn of the twentieth century. Much of the material published in the *Carmina Gadelica* had been translated from the Gaelic. Thus, this collection represented a powerful and authentic glimpse into the average person's experience of Celtic spirituality about a century ago.

The Seer Says

The *Carmina Gadelica* is more than just an old collection of folklore. It's still in print, and can be used as a prayer book or ritual manual. Just flipping through it will inspire you as well as give you a glimpse of life in rural Scotland a century ago.

Naturally, given how powerful the Christian religion is to this day in the Celtic nations, most of the material recorded in the *Carmina Gadelica* has a clearly Christian feel. The collection includes hymns, chants, and spells dedicated to Jesus, to Mary, to Brigid, and to other saints and figures from the Christian tradition. But this is not your garden-variety anthology of church hymns. Indeed, much of the material in this anthology has an unmistakably pagan feel, even though it contains plenty of Christian imagery as well. Consider this prayer, in which both saints and nature are invoked for blessing:

The love of the Mary Mother be thine,
The love of the Brigit of flocks be thine,
The love of Michael victorious be thine,
With their arm each hour surrounding thee.

The great bounty of the sea be thine,
The great bounty of earth be thine,
The great bounty of heaven be thine,
Thy life be hale and fruitful.

The mild grace of the Father be thine,
The loving grace of the Son be thine,
The loving grace of the Spirit be thine,
Laving thee with the graces.

—*Carmina Gadelica*, 290

The *Carmina Gadelica* includes prayers and invocations for healing, protection, blessing, and abundance. It includes charms to ward off sickness in livestock, and hymns of praise to both moon and sun. It's a veritable feast of Celtic spirituality—encompassing both Christian and pagan dimensions.

Putting Christopaganism into Practice for Yourself

If you find that your heart is tugging you in the direction of Christopaganism, it may well be the only way for you to embrace the fullness of Celtic wisdom. Practically speaking, you may still "officially" be either a Christian or a pagan, especially if you are involved in a Christian church or pagan circle. But if your heart offers prayers both to the father in heaven and the mother who is the earth, if you turn to both pagan myth and Christian scripture for guidance, or if you believe that Celtic hospitality demands a spirit of respect and goodwill toward those whose faith is different from your own, then congratulations! You are well on your way toward embodying the fullness of Celtic wisdom.

Key Voices in Celtic Christianity

In this chapter I've concentrated mainly on Celtic Christians from ancient times, such as Brigid or Patrick. But it is truly a living tradition. Here are some writers whose work may be nourishing to you if you wish to walk the path of the Celtic saints:

♦ **John O'Donohue.** This Irish Catholic priest wrote a bestseller called *Anam Cara: A Book of Celtic Wisdom* (HarperCollins, 1997), which celebrates the place where Christianity and Celtic spirituality converge (and yes, "anam cara" means the same thing as "anamchara").

♦ **Noel Dermot O'Donoghue.** Irish priest who was the first Catholic to teach at the University of Edinburgh in Scotland, and the author of *Mountain Behind the Mountain: Aspects of the Celtic Tradition* (T & T Clark, 1996) and *Heaven in Ordinarie: Some Radical Considerations* (Templegate, 1979).

♦ **Iona Community.** Mentioned earlier in this chapter, the Iona Community is a modern expression of Celtic Christianity, in which urban clergy and at-risk youth find community together on the mystical island of Iona. Several books have been published about Iona or documenting the community's common prayer, including *The Pattern of Our Days: Worship in the Celtic Tradition from the Iona Community* (Paulist Press, 1999).

CAUTION

Geasa

Don't assume that the only way to explore Celtic Christianity is by reading books. This is an experiential form of Christian spirituality—to truly live the Celtic Christian spirit, you need to do two things: pray and spend time in nature!

◆ **Esther Dewaal.** This popular Christian writer has released several books that celebrate the Celtic spirit, including *The Celtic Way of Prayer* (Image Books, 1999) and *Every Earthly Blessing: Rediscovering the Celtic Tradition* (Morehouse Publishing, 1999).

Cultivating the Heart of Holiness as a Celtic Wisdomseeker

In writing this book, at first I wasn't sure if I should include a section on Christianity. After all, the elements that make Celtic Christianity distinctive are all present in the native tradition, and I didn't want to introduce a divisive element into the book. That said, it's important to honor the role that Christianity has played (and continues to play) in the hearts of most Celts. I believe that Celtic wisdom calls us to rise above the troubles in Northern Ireland or the antipathy that exists between pagans and Christians, and instead simply see the best in Christianity, which is a religion dedicated to values like holiness, charity, compassion, forgiveness, and love. Such values form the heart of Celtic spirituality, whether pagan or Christian. They are values to be celebrated and cultivated—no matter what your religious preference may be.

The Least You Need to Know

◆ Christianity has long been part of Celtic spirituality, and remains the most widely practiced religion among the Celts.

◆ The Celtic form of Christianity is unique in its optimism and its deep mysticism and love for nature.

◆ One of the most interesting of Celtic saints is Brigid, who may be simply a Christianized version of the goddess with the same name.

◆ Celtic spirituality as a blend of pagan and Christian elements is preserved in a large anthology of folklore called the *Carmina Gadelica*.

◆ The enduring gift of Christianity to the Celtic world is a deep love for mysticism, holiness, and charity—values that accord well with the old pagan virtues of honor and hospitality.

Chapter 21

Mastering the Magical Arts

In This Chapter

◆ Magic: It's not for everyone

◆ Which witch is a Wiccan witch?

◆ Why Wicca is (and isn't) Celtic

◆ How to get started on a magical path

◆ The ethics of magic

This chapter will give you an introductory glimpse into the mysterious world where Celtic wisdom and magic intersect. If your religious beliefs prevent you from practicing magic, you might still want to read this chapter strictly for information's sake. If your beliefs and interests call you to embrace the magic of the Celtic path, then the pages that follow can help you get started.

The Controversial Concept of Magic

In the modern Irish and Scots Gaelic languages, the word for magic is *draíocht* and *drúidheachd*, respectively. You don't have to be a linguist to see the connection between these words and *druid*. This shows as simply as anything the powerful and age-old connection between Celtic wisdom and the pursuit of magic, or spiritual, power.

Here's a basic definition of magic:

> Magic involves the tools, traditions, ideas, symbols, and rituals available to anyone who wishes to find spiritual means for achieving personal growth, happiness, healing, or any other goal. Magic is the technology of the spiritual world; and in the Celtic tradition, it has always been a legitimate area of inquiry.

That last statement is important because many religious traditions from around the world prohibit magic—including Christianity, which has been the most dominant religion in the Celtic world for the past 1,500 years. For this reason, there is a certain ambiguity to Celtic magic. For some people who follow Christian teaching closely, magic is simply an off-limits topic. Others, who do not feel any particular allegiance to the Christian faith, may embrace magic with gusto, often choosing to embrace paganism or witchcraft as a framework for their magical studies. Many others may choose a middle ground, appreciating Christianity for its tradition of holiness and devotion to the spiritual world, but recognizing that even among many devout Christians, Celtic mysticism has always included a strong element of faith in spiritual healing and magical power that arises out of the natural world.

> **The Seer Says**
>
> Remember, druids were the wisdomkeepers of the ancient Celts. They were also the magicians. Whether or not you are interested in magic yourself, it's important to consider that the Celts regarded wisdom as an important quality for those empowered to work with magic.

Understanding Celtic Magic

Is Celtic magic the same thing as druidism, or shamanism? Certainly these three arenas of Celtic wisdom overlap. The differences between them are more differences of degree than of kind. Celtic shamanism, druidism, and magic all involve accessing spiritual power or guidance for positive change. But at least for the purposes of this book, the difference between these three aspects of Celtic wisdom has to do with their basic source of inspiration. Celtic shamanism draws inspiration from the most primal forms of Celtic wisdom, illuminated by shamanic practices from other cultures. Meanwhile, druidism draws inspiration from the Iron Age druids or the myths of gods and goddesses as recorded in the Middle Ages. Celtic magic (as practiced today) draws from more modern sources, particularly esoteric magical traditions like the Golden Dawn or Wicca, which aren't Celtic but can easily be adapted to Celtic spirituality.

Here's an example of how a druid, a Celtic shaman, and a Celtic magician might differ from one another in today's world:

◆ A Celtic shaman might focus his or her energies on contacting spirit guides and power animals, on attaining shamanic states of consciousness through meditation or trance, and on using information gleaned from such inner journeys for the healing of self or others.

♦ A student of druidism might focus instead on learning about the ancient gods and goddesses, and applying that wisdom to his or her life. Meanwhile, the aspiring druid is more likely to focus on observing Celtic holidays and performing rituals to honor the spiritual world.

♦ The Celtic magician combines his or her love of the Celtic world with the study of universal magical principles, learned through the study of Wicca or participation in an organization dedicated to magic.

Notes from the Otherworld

One of the most influential of modern organizations dedicated to the study and practice of magic, the Hermetic Order of the Golden Dawn (commonly called the Golden Dawn) was formed in England in the late nineteenth century and still exists in a number of different organizational forms today. The Golden Dawn studied magic from many different cultures and so isn't properly considered a Celtic group. But as a system of universal magic, it certainly could appeal to Celtic wisdomseekers (such as William Butler Yeats, who was a member of the Golden Dawn).

Keep in mind that these distinctions are somewhat artificial, meant to help you understand that there can be differences in the ways that different people put the Celtic way into practice. At the same time, it's important to remember the overlap, and that many people might integrate elements of shamanism, druidism, Wicca, or other forms of magic into their own unique way of seeking Celtic wisdom. Remember, there's no single right way to master Celtic wisdom, nor are there any rules saying that if you're interested in shamanism you can't master the principles of Wicca (or vice versa).

Celtic Magic 101

What exactly is Celtic-inspired magic?

The answer to this question is twofold. First, in getting to know the Celtic tradition, we can find (in myth and lore) many insights into what the elements of ancient Celtic magic must have been like. Second, anyone serious about Celtic magic in the twenty-first century will need to acknowledge that their studies will include non-Celtic as well as Celtic theories and exercises. Basically, the Celtic magician of today is a student of magic who seeks to incorporate the universal principles of magic into a Celtic form of spirituality.

From Ancient Myth to Modern Practice

We know that the druids were said to be accomplished magicians, and the words for magic in modern Irish and Gaelic reflect this druid-magic connection. Meanwhile, because the druids never wrote down their teachings, none of their ancient wisdom has survived in any clearly defined way. Thus, to get a glimpse into Celtic magic, our best strategy is to study the myths, see how magic was understood there, and relate it to modern magical studies, a discipline that (like Wicca) draws on lore from around the world.

Looking at the myths and other sources such as the *Carmina Gadelica*, here are a few basic principles of the Celtic approach to magic:

◆ **Shapeshifting.** At its root, Celtic magic is essentially Celtic "shamanism." From Amergin to Taliesin to Arawn's transformation of himself and Pwyll, the myths are filled with stories of beings who could transform themselves in order to achieve a goal.

◆ **Use of charms (words of power).** The *Carmina Gadelica* is filled with songs, poems, and incantations used for practical purposes: to call forth psychic protection, to heal a sick farm animal, or to ensure a safe journey. Some of these spells involved the use of herbs believed to have curative properties, but many of them relied simply on the power of the words themselves. These "words of power" are reminiscent of a popular modern practice with magical overtones: the use of *affirmations*.

◆ **Divination/prophecy.** The seers and druids were said to be gifted at prognostication, or foretelling the future; in the myths, some figures such as Cathbad (the most prominent druid in the Ulster Cycle) likewise have a talent for unlocking the mysteries of what is yet to come.

◆ **Use of magical tools.** The four treasures of the Túatha Dé Danann were imbued with magical power, from weapons that could not fail in battle to the cauldron that never ran dry. Cú Chulainn likewise benefited from weapons with supernatural power.

Notes from the Otherworld

In the popular children's book *Harry Potter and the Chamber of Secrets,* Harry and his friends drink a magic potion that temporarily changes their appearance. Although it might be fun to try a potion like that, magical shape-shifting is more of an inside job. By experiencing transformation within your consciousness, you can find insight to improve your life, inside and out.

Druidspeak

Affirmations consist of positively worded phrases or sentences used to encourage the mind to envision (and subconsciously work to create) a desired result. For example, someone trying to improve their diet might use this affirmation: "I eat only healthy, natural foods."

◆ **Erotic power.** Perhaps most mysterious of all is the hidden theme in Celtic myth that sexuality or erotic power has magical implications. From Niall's kiss of the hag of sovereignty that transformed her into a beautiful goddess to the practice among ancient Irish kings of ritually mating with the goddess of the land as a way to promote fertility and abundance, sexuality is regarded not just as an instrument of loving pleasure or procreation, but as a powerful conduit of magical energy.

How to Become a (Celtic) Magician

Learning about magic from the ancient myths and folklore can be an interesting academic exercise, but how do you put such knowledge into practice? In other words, knowing that the ancient Celtic magicians were shapeshifters, diviners, or enchanters is one thing. But what does it take to manifest such powers in our day and age?

This is where Wicca, or other programs for magical study like the Golden Dawn, come into play. Given that the druids left no written instructions as to how an aspiring Celtic magician would learn their skills, today's wisdomseeker must approach magic not as a Celtic discipline, but as a universal spiritual tool. Thankfully, other ancient cultures were not as willfully secretive as the druids, and many seekers of magical ability from around the world have left their teachings to us in books or organizations dedicated to promoting their work.

You can devote a lifetime of study to mastering a school of magical thought such as the esoteric *Qabalah*, or you can join a magical order such as the Golden Dawn (which included William Butler Yeats among its early members). You can study the lore associated with ancient magical cultures like the Egyptians. And of course, you can study Wicca, probably the most accessible venue for magical training in the modern world. None of these paths will make you a distinctly *Celtic* magician. Your task, as a seeker of Celtic ways, will be to learn universal principles of magic and then use them in the context of your devotion to the Celtic tradition. Magic, like Celtic lore, is adaptable.

Naturally, some aspects of the Celtic tradition lend themselves well to magic. For example, the Ogham, an ancient Irish alphabet, can be used as a tool for divination (see Chapter 23 for more on this). Meanwhile, the *Carmina Gadelica* is a treasure trove of authentic affirmations and incantations. And naturally, calling on the Celtic gods and goddesses for magical aid would be a way to give your magical work a Celtic focus.

Druidspeak

The **Qabalah** originated in Jewish mysticism, but beginning during the Renaissance became popular among occultists and magicians because it provides a useful map of the flow of magical energy in creation.

Being Magic

The Vietnamese Buddhist writer Thich Nhat Hanh wrote about "being peace," suggesting that peace isn't just an abstract concept that one thinks about, but rather a way of life. I think the same holds true for magic. In his book *Sunday After the War*, writer Henry Miller comments that the goal of life should not be to possess power, but to radiate it. This is certainly true in the world of magic, which can be seen as spiritual power.

Magic isn't just an intellectual concept to understand, but a way of living that is based on belief in the spiritual power of healing and transformation. To be a magical person today is to integrate your spirituality with your mind's ability to visualize and put into words your desires for positive change. In the world of magic, such change always begins with an inner change. Living a magical life means believing in your own abilities to access spiritual power (whether through ritual, meditation, prayer, or whatever tools work for you) and applying it in your life to bring about beneficial results. It also means taking responsibility for everything in your life, good or bad, and taking steps to change whatever isn't working for you. And incidentally, such steps are not just limited to spiritual work like affirmations or meditation. Good magicians realize that magic relies on good old-fashioned hard work to make changes happen!

Applying Magic in Your Life Today

Remember, Celtic magic isn't exactly the same thing as Celtic wisdom. Magic involves spiritual disciplines, tools, or principles used to create change in life, by spiritual means, for the purposes of healing, growth or happiness. Wisdom, by contrast, covers a larger terrain. Wisdom includes the knowledge necessary to be an effective magician, the discernment to know when it's time to work for a change and when it's best to let things be, and the ethics to know when it's appropriate to work magic and when such action would cause more harm than good. You don't have to be a magician to be wise. But you must develop wisdom if you wish to pursue the study of magic.

The way I see it, the true making of a Celtic magician that any ancient druid would be proud of consists of this: the dedicated pursuit of wisdom, both in terms of the teachings of the Celts as well as the pursuit of universal knowledge and discernment. The study and use of magic would then be an aspect of this overall dedication to wisdom. Applying universal magical principles within your overall Celtic approach to spirituality and life would make you as much a Celtic magician as anyone could hope to be.

One other point worth noting: The magicians of the ancient myths typically used their spiritual power not for selfish gain, but in ways that often served others or the community at large. It's a subtle point, but one worth considering. If you're interested in studying Celtic magic, know your motivations. If you're looking for spiritual power just as a way of improving your self-esteem or making purely selfish dreams come true, you've begun to veer away from the heart of Celtic magic. But if your interest in magic is motivated by a genuine desire to help others to heal and grow (in addition to your own positive transformation), then you're more truly walking along the Celtic path.

The Bard's Bookshelf

Here's an interesting book that looks at the Celtic tradition from a specifically magical perspective: Murry Hope's *The Ancient Wisdom of the Celts* (Thorsons, 1999).

Celtic Witchcraft?!

In the landscape of modern spirituality (whether Celtic or general), magic is a concept that inevitably leads to another, even more controversial topic: witchcraft. Although witchcraft has been part of the collective human psyche for thousands of years, in the last 50 or so years it has increasingly become visible in the western world, as more and more people embrace the pursuit of magic as a viable, legitimate, and ethical spiritual activity. In modern parlance, "witchcraft" refers to the pure pursuit of magical ability, which may or may not have a spiritual or religious component. Meanwhile, many people who place their interest in magic in a religious context (based on the worship of the earth and the Goddess) follow the spiritual path of Wicca (an archaic English word for "witch").

Although witchcraft is an ancient practice, Wicca as a religion is basically a new phenomenon created in England in the early- to mid-twentieth century. One Wiccan priestess I know says she likes to think of Wicca as the "reincarnation" of the old religion: "same soul, different form, new personality incorporating the lessons of the past." That's a lovely (and intellectually honest) way of thinking about this modern form of religious witchcraft.

An Often-Misunderstood Topic

Magic, Wicca, and witchcraft are all frequently misunderstood topics. In many parts of the world, including those where Christianity is prevalent, magic and witchcraft have historically been feared as dangerous or evil powers. In the modern world, Wicca, along with magic and witchcraft, is sometimes denounced by outsiders as being forms of "devil worship." This is a misconception; in truth Wiccans practice a spirituality very similar to ancient Celtic wisdom, in which the earth is regarded as sacred, and the supreme Spirit is revered as both masculine and feminine (in other words, as the God and the Goddess). Wiccans hardly could worship the devil—they don't even believe he exists!

The Bard's Bookshelf
If you're interested in Wicca and witchcraft, be sure to read Ronald Hutton's *The Triumph of the Moon* (Oxford University Press, 1999). It explains the overwhelming evidence that shows that Wicca is a modern, not an ancient, religion.

Witchcraft and magic, meanwhile, are spiritual tools, not systems of belief or worship. Like any tool, they can be used for good or bad purposes; but there is nothing *inherently* malevolent in them. Perhaps the reason why religions like Christianity disapprove of magic is because in ancient times it was regarded as a dangerous tool (just like a jackhammer or dynamite are dangerous tools). In fact, in much of Christian history, elite priests or scholars would practice magical spirituality, even though witchcraft was frowned upon for the general population.

A Brief History of Wicca

Wicca began in England in the first half of the twentieth century, basically created by people who were studying magic, witchcraft, and pre-Christian European religion. Some scholars of the time, most notably Margaret Murray, theorized that the European women who had been killed for practicing witchcraft in the fifteenth through eighteenth centuries were actually practicing the vestigial remnants of the ancient, pre-Christian religion of the great Goddess that was believed to be widespread throughout ancient Europe. (This theory is not widely accepted in our day, but 75 years ago it was all the rage.)

In the 1950s, an elderly Englishman named Gerald Gardner claimed to be the member of a surviving underground "witch cult." He said he had been sworn to secrecy when he joined the cult, but he was so worried that witchcraft was dying out that he felt compelled to publicize it, in hopes that other witches would come forward and that interested young people would choose to embrace witchcraft, thereby keeping it alive.

Notes from the Otherworld

Was Gerald Gardner a fraud? His critics think so, and even many people who practice Wicca doubt his story. Some people trust his good intentions, but believe he may have been deceived by his associates, who claimed to be practicing an "ancient religion" but were in fact simply creating something new. But even if Gardner fabricated his story, he still drew on symbolism and ideas that were inspired by pre-Christian spirituality. Thus, it's fair to say that Wicca is a modern re-creation of an ancient spiritual path.

Gardner's claims electrified a society that was still reeling from the horrors of World War II and looking for meaning in an increasingly alienated modern world. Shortly after his books were published, the hippie/counterculture era was in full swing, and thousands of people eagerly sought personal enlightenment through occultism, meditation, and witchcraft. By the 1970s, leading Wiccan writers were making the case that Wicca was a religion especially well suited for feminists and environmentalists.

Despite Gardner's claims, today the evidence indicates that Gardner and his associates created Wicca over the course of many years by blending together elements taken from the history of magic, folklore, secret societies (like the Freemasons), elements of eastern mysticism, and even the rituals of the Church of England! Still, for many people (current estimates suggest that hundreds of thousands of people may be practicing Wicca or some other form of witchcraft), Gardner's spiritual path has become a meaningful part of their lives.

Wicca and Celtic Magic

Wicca has been a mixed blessing to Celtic wisdomseekers. On the one hand, it has popularized elements of the Celtic tradition, and helped spark a new interest in both magic and ancient mythology (Celtic and otherwise). But many people mistakenly think of Wicca as a Celtic religion. Although Wicca can be an effective tool for studying magic and gives its practitioners the freedom to use their magic within a Celtic mythological framework, it's important to understand that, strictly speaking, Wicca is no more inherently Celtic than Christianity or Buddhism.

The Wicca-Celtic Connection

From the beginning, Wicca's practitioners have seen a powerful link between their religion and the ancient Celtic ways. Indeed, many Wiccans and Wiccan groups describe their tradition as "Celtic." What does this mean? What connection is there between Wicca and Celtic spirituality?

> **CAUTION**
>
> **Geasa**
>
> For some reason, the Celtic world has attracted many dreamers and romantics who don't always treat the heritage of the Celts with the respect it deserves. Plenty of books have been published over the years on the subjects of Celtic witchcraft or druidism that are based more on fantasy than on fact. Remember this, especially when reading about Celtic magic. Read all you can: The more knowledgeable you are, the more easily you will separate the fantasy from authentic wisdom.

The answer isn't simple. Briefly put, Wicca does incorporate some important Celtic symbolism and material into its culture, including reverence for old Celtic gods and goddesses and the celebration of old Celtic holy days. But there's plenty of elements in the Wiccan world that are not "Celtic," and that instead reflect English, Italian, or Egyptian forms of spirituality.

The Celtic Dimension of Wicca

There are basically two reasons why Wicca has a reputation as a Celtic spiritual path:

- **Wicca uses Celtic holidays.** As you'll see in Chapter 24, the holidays of Samhain, Imbolc, Beltaine, and Lughnasadh all originate in the Celtic tradition (these are Gaelic names, but forms of these holidays can be found throughout the Celtic world). These are four of the eight main holidays now observed by Wicca. (The other four are the solstices and the equinoxes.) Naturally, because the holidays are Celtic, much of the lore surrounding each day also can be traced back to Celtic sources.

- **Wicca encourages the veneration of Celtic deities.** Several of the deities popular among Wiccans, such as Ceridwen with her cauldron of inspiration, Brigid with her magical, healing, and poetic energy, and Cernunnos, the horned one of the wild forest, have been warmly embraced by many of the practitioners of Wicca. In honoring these old Celtic goddesses and gods, naturally many Wiccans have also taken to studying Celtic myth, using many of its symbols in Wiccan ritual. However, it should be pointed out that nothing in Wicca requires practitioners to venerate the Celtic deities (or deities from any other tradition), so while many Wiccans honor Celtic goddesses and gods, others may not.

These two elements—Celtic holidays and Celtic deities—are the primary ways in which Wicca can be considered a Celtic spiritual path. Meanwhile, it's just as important to acknowledge that, in some significant ways, Wicca does *not* qualify as a Celtic religion.

Why Wicca Isn't Really a Celtic Religion

Here are a few reasons why Wicca, although it contains some elements of Celtic wisdom, doesn't truly deserve to be called a Celtic path:

- **Wicca is largely a multicultural path.** For most Wiccans, it's permissible to perform rituals involving gods and goddesses from virtually any culture the world over. Celtic spirituality, by definition, is limited to the mythic figures from Irish, Welsh, or other Celtic traditions. This doesn't mean that a Celtic wisdomseeker cannot explore the spiritual gifts and lessons associated with non-Celtic spirituality; it's just a recognition that a religion where non-Celtic deities are routinely honored is multicultural, rather than Celtic, in focus. Incidentally, there are some Wiccan groups that are exclusively focused on one spiritual culture or tradition (including Celtic forms of Wicca), but there's nothing inherent to Wicca that requires such a cultural focus.

Notes from the Otherworld

Remember, the culture of England is based on many different sources, including Celtic, Roman, Norman, Scandinavian, and (primarily) Anglo-Saxon cultures. Meanwhile, the originators of Wicca (including Gerald Gardner and other figures like Doreen Valiente) drew on a variety of world sources to develop this new spiritual tradition. All this means that Wicca is, properly speaking, a truly multicultural spiritual path that doesn't have any one cultural identity (Celtic or otherwise).

♦ **Wicca originated in England, not in a Celtic region.** Although witchcraft is a universal phenomenon found in cultures the world over, Wicca (as a modern religious expression of witchcraft) is a distinctly multicultural path with English roots. All its major early spokespersons were English, and to this day it isn't nearly as popular in Ireland or Scotland as it is in England, America, or Australia. The word *Wicca* itself comes from a medieval English word for "witch."

♦ **Many elements of Wicca come from non-Celtic sources.** The four elements used in Wiccan ceremonies (earth, air, fire, and water) came out of Greek philosophy; many of the practices found in Wiccan ritual are based on French or English traditions of magic and occultism. Italian folklore and eastern mysticism also were stirred into Wicca's cauldron. Meanwhile, the degrees of initiation as practiced in many Wiccan groups come out of Freemasonry. Many of the tools used in Wicca, such as the athame (ritual dagger) or the Book of Shadows (a handwritten anthology of spells and rituals), come from sources other than the Celtic tradition.

For these reasons, it's best to see Wicca as a Celtic-*influenced* spiritual path rather than a Celtic path per se.

"Celtic" Wicca: A Balanced Approach

My insistence that Wicca is not a Celtic religion isn't meant to be a repudiation of Wicca. Frankly, I think it's just as important to bear in mind that Christianity isn't an inherently Celtic religion, either! Christianity and Wicca are both non-Celtic religious traditions that have been embraced by (at least some) Celts, and have (at least on some levels) incorporated Celtic imagery into their spirituality in beautiful ways. Some people, though, who explore Celtic paganism find Wicca frustrating, since so many Wiccans erroneously believe their path to be more Celtic than it really is.

Part of the beauty of Celtic wisdom lies in its adaptability. You can walk the path of Celtic wisdom and follow any positive, ethical spiritual path, whether Christianity, Wicca, Buddhism—even Judaism or Islam!

It's best to have a balanced approach to the Celtic-Wicca question. Since so many people find beauty in a spirituality that blends religious witchcraft with Celtic wisdom, it's entirely appropriate to embrace Celtic Wicca as a *variety* of Wicca, just as Celtic Christianity is a variety of Christianity. But it's also important to remember that Wicca, like Christianity, is not inherently Celtic. There's nothing wrong with being interested in both Wicca and Celtic wisdom, but do your homework and understand that there's a difference between the two.

Magic, Wicca, and Celtic Wisdom: A Summary

Here are some basic principles to keep in mind as you explore the relationships between Celtic wisdom, magic, and Wicca/witchcraft:

> **The Seer Says**
>
> Is it okay for Christians to explore magic? This is a question where personal conscience must dictate the choices you make. Traditionally, Christianity has opposed magic; but then again, Christianity traditionally supported the subjugation of women. Christians, like anyone else, must be true to themselves, even when it means going against the majority opinion.

- The druids were said to be accomplished magicians, so magic is an appropriate element within Celtic wisdom.

- Christianity, however, has historically discouraged the practice of magic; therefore, ancient Celtic magic is essentially a lost art.

- Because Wicca (a modern religion based on magic and witchcraft) is a popular vehicle for studying magic, many seekers of Celtic magic find Wicca to be an appropriate framework for their magical studies.

- However, because Wicca is not inherently Celtic, one doesn't need to be Wiccan in order to practice Celtic-inspired magic.

Magical Ethics: The Wiccan Rede and the Law of Three

From the perspective of Celtic wisdom, magic is only worth pursuing for ethical, responsible, positive reasons. Here's another important principle associated with magic: It's a power that can be used for good or evil. And truth be told, who hasn't at some point or another wanted to turn an ex-boyfriend into a toad, or use magic as a shortcut to an "A" in that organic chemistry class, or figure out a way to get the head cheerleader to fall hopelessly in love with you? Okay, so there's an adolescent part of each and every person who would love to possess magical powers just so that life could be easy.

But real Celtic magic—or, better put, magic performed in the context of Celtic wisdom—doesn't work that way.

Just because authentic spiritual power exists doesn't mean we have the freedom to use it any old selfish way we choose. That would be like saying that, because nuclear power exists, countries would get to bomb each other every time there is an international dispute. Just as heads of state must use restraint in exercising the terrible force of nuclear power, so, too, does Celtic spirituality involve some pretty significant restraints on the use of magic.

The ethics of magic are best summed up in two teachings from Wicca, the "Law of Three" and the "Wiccan Rede." Although as Wiccan teachings these are not necessarily Celtic in origin, they summarize the wisdom of using magic only for positive reasons.

> **Geasa**
>
> If you're interested in magic because you want to make someone fall in love with you or you're trying to get even with someone, you are studying magic for the wrong reasons. Such interests are not only a violation of magical ethics, they are not consistent with the overall message of Celtic wisdom, either.

The Wiccan Rede states that as long as you're harming none, you may do what you will. The Law of Three states that whatever energies you send out into the world will, sooner or later, come back to you, three times as powerful as what you sent out. What do these teachings mean?

 ♦ The Wiccan Rede says you can use magic for whatever purpose you intend—as long as you harm no one. In other words, no revenge. Also, it's a no-no to use magic that interferes with the free will of another (so love spells are out). Finally, remember that "harm none" includes yourself. So you can't do any magic that would hurt you, either. And as the Law of Three points out, any magic you do that would hurt someone else will eventually hurt you, too.

◆ The Law of Three is basically the law of investment. If you invest your energy in good things (like healing magic), you'll find good energy coming back to you, three times what you've sent out. But if you invest your energy in harmful or vengeful magic, then look out! That energy, times three, will eventually come back to you as well (some Wiccans don't take this law literally, but see it as a general reminder that our actions can have exponential consequences, for good or ill).

The bottom line is this: If you want to do magic, keep your focus on healing or helping people in positive ways. That's the best approach to using spiritual power responsibly.

Key Voices in Celtic Wicca

If you want to make magic a part of your Celtic studies, you might enjoy pursuing a Celtic form of Wicca (although some druid groups do teach magic as well). Here are two writers who have produced interesting books on Celtic-flavored Wicca:

◆ **Jane Raeburn.** Author of *Celtic Wicca: Ancient Wisdom for the 21st Century*, Raeburn takes an honest and responsible approach to the ways in which Wicca and Celtic tradition do (and don't) mesh.

◆ **Katherine Clark.** While Raeburn's approach to Celtic culture focuses primarily on the Roman Celtic world, Clark's *An Irish Book of Shadows: Tuatha De Danaan* presents Wicca from the perspective of the Irish tradition.

The Least You Need to Know

◆ Magic is a universal concept, but the evidence suggests that the druids were magicians, so it's an important part of the Celtic path.

◆ One of the most popular forms of modern magical spirituality is called Wicca, from an archaic English word for "witch."

◆ Wicca is not a Celtic religion, but rather an eclectic religion that incorporates some Celtic elements.

◆ Although the Wiccan Rede and the Law of Three may not be Celtic in origin, they are important universal principles that anyone interested in magic needs to remember.

Chapter 22

The Quest for the Grail

In This Chapter

- ◆ The best-known Celtic symbol
- ◆ Uncovering the Celtic roots of the grail
- ◆ Celtic myth meets Christian mysticism
- ◆ How the grail symbolizes enlightenment and consciousness
- ◆ Embarking on your own grail quest

If there's one symbol with roots in the Celtic tradition that has most firmly made its way into mainstream culture, it's the grail. In the motion picture industry, for example, the grail has shown up in comedy films (*Monty Python and the Holy Grail*) as well as action movies (*Indiana Jones and the Last Crusade*). The quest for the grail is most closely associated with the cycle of legends related to King Arthur, but it also is linked to Christian mysticism, to Freemasonry, and to ceremonial magic. But the earliest symbols and themes related to the grail quest can all be found within Celtic (or Celtic-inspired) myth. The idea of searching for a lost object of inestimable value is something that just about anyone can identify with, and people who have almost no knowledge of Celtic myth or Arthurian legend will still speak of "the grail" as a code word for "the ultimate prize."

This chapter will give you a basic overview of the grail tradition, from its murkiest Celtic beginnings to the encounter between pagan symbolism and Christian mysticism that yielded this mysterious and beautiful symbol. Rather than leave the grail as an artifact of history, you'll also discover how the grail can be relevant to wisdomseekers and aspiring mystics here in the twenty-first century.

The Grail Tradition

At its most basic level, the grail is little more than a symbol that appears in literature. A variety of legends and tales dating back to the Middle Ages, many of which are connected to the lore associated with King Arthur, speak of knights or other seekers involved in a quest for the mysterious grail. But the quest for the grail isn't just an entertaining story. For one thing, the legends themselves are filled with contradictions and inconsistencies. Close examination of the many grail stories reveals that these legends encode a symbolic mystical quest. The grail, it seems, is important not for what it is, but for what it symbolizes.

What Is the Grail?

Perhaps the most basic, challenging question is this: What exactly *is* the grail? The word itself is obscure, but appears to mean "dish" or "cup" or perhaps even "platter." But over the years it has been depicted in many different ways, including as the following:

♦ A cauldron

♦ A chalice

♦ A cup

♦ A dish

♦ A jewel

♦ A stone

♦ Even a severed head!

> **The Bard's Bookshelf**
>
> Perhaps the best single book for beginning your studies of the grail legend is the anthology *Sources of the Grail*, selected and introduced by John Matthews (Lindisfarne Press, 1996). Matthews's introduction clearly expresses the spiritual value of the grail, while the text itself combines both ancient writings on the grail with a selection of interpretive essays.

> **Notes from the Otherworld**
>
> For the purposes of this book, I'm using the following distinction: The "Holy Grail" refers to the grail specifically as the cup used by Jesus at the Last Supper, while just speaking of the "grail" refers to the larger tradition of a valuable object worth surmounting any obstacle to attain—which doesn't necessarily have any connection to Christianity or any other religion.

In the Middle Ages, the grail took on its best-known quality: It became the Holy Grail, that is to say, the cup used by Christ when he instituted the Holy Eucharist at the Last Supper, the night before his crucifixion. This explains much of the mystique surrounding the grail, for it seems reasonable, at least within a Christian worldview, that the actual cup used by Jesus himself would be an object of unlimited spiritual power.

From Celtic Beginnings to Universal Myth

Strictly speaking, the grail is not a Celtic symbol. As it appears in medieval romance, it is an object that blends Celtic with Christian symbolism. Many of the grail writings were penned by French or German writers, with little or no connection to the Celtic world. Why, then, should it be considered a Celtic symbol? Because the origins of the grail myth are Celtic in nature.

Even a casual reading of the earliest legends associated with the grail point to a tradition that actually predates the life of Christ (even though the earliest surviving written records about it only date from the Middle Ages). The grail may have found its greatest renown as a symbol of Christian mysticism, but its origins go back to the wisdom of the Celts. Indeed, all the major themes of the grail legend—the wasteland, the wounded king, the mysterious grail itself, and the innocent fool who seeks it—can be found in Celtic myth.

The Earliest Grail Story

The two earliest stories in the grail tradition are *Perceval* by the medieval French writer Chrétien de Troyes and "Peredur the Son of Efrawc," a Welsh tale from *The Mabinogion*. The tales are quite similar, and scholars are divided over which one came first, whether one influenced the other, or if both are retellings of an even older tale. Both tales involve a foolish young knight (Perceval/Peredur) who is essentially on a quest to "find himself" and prove his worthiness as a knight.

Perceval's tale recounts how, while on his adventures, our hero discovers a mysterious castle that is the home of a king who has suffered a wound that will not heal. While in the castle, a strange procession appears, in

> **Notes from the Otherworld**
>
> Scholars have dated the French manuscript *Perceval* at circa 1180, making it about a hundred years older than the oldest existing copy of *Peredur*. But many authorities believe that the story of Peredur is actually the older story, because it has more obviously pagan elements in it (like the veneration of the severed head).

which Perceval sees people carrying such objects as a spear, a dish, candelabras, and the grail itself. But he had been counseled by an elder knight not to ask lots of questions, and so Perceval, while curious about the grail and its procession, says nothing to his host. Later, he learns that if he had only asked about the grail, he would have enabled the wounded king to be healed and to return to his rightful place as guardian of the land.

Peredur's story is similar, but with a few important differences. While in the king's castle, Peredur sees a procession with a spear from which blood is dripping and a platter with a severed head. He does not ask the important question, and later learns that his failure to do so will cause great distress throughout the land.

While there are real differences between the two tales (most notably the severed head), the tale of Peredur is so similar to the tale of Perceval that it appears to be an earlier, more explicitly pagan version of the same story. And the key symbols from both tales—the spear, the cup/dish/platter, and the severed head—all point to Celtic myth as the source of information about the grail.

Even Earlier Still ...

Although the tales of Perceval and Peredur are the first actual tales of the grail quest, an obscure and mysterious poem from ninth-century Wales might hold a clue to the earliest origin of the grail quest. This poem, attributed to the great bard Taliesin, is called "Preiddeu Annwn," or "The Spoils of the Underworld." It tells, in enigmatic imagery, of a quest led into the otherworld itself by a hero named Arthur to obtain treasures, including a magical cauldron. The poem doesn't say if the treasures are ever won, but does say that of three shiploads of warriors, only seven warriors survive the journey!

This poem represents the earliest story in which a quest was undertaken for a grail-like object (because a cauldron, like a grail, is a bowl-shape object). The story involves a magical, mystical adventure, in which the ill-prepared quester may lose his life. The hero of the quest is Arthur (who at this point may not have even been seen as a king, but only as a heroic adventurer).

The Seer Says

The connection between Arthur and the grail goes back to the ninth century, before most of the Arthurian literature we are familiar with today was written. For wisdomseekers, the grail is the primary element that makes Arthurian lore more than just an entertaining story, but actually an allegory of the spiritual life. But you don't need to be a fan of King Arthur in order to incorporate grail symbolism into your spiritual life.

Back to the Pagan Myth

"The Spoils of the Underworld" suggests that there is a link between the grail and the Celtic symbol of the cauldron. Indeed, the cauldron is one of the most important of Celtic symbols.

Remember the four treasures of the Túatha Dé Danann, discussed in Chapter 11? They include the sword, the stone, the spear, and the cauldron. That is hardly the only occurrence of cauldrons in Celtic myth. Here are some of the main occurrences of the cauldron as a mythic symbol:

◆ The cauldron of the Dagda, one of the four treasures, is a source of limitless food.

◆ The cauldron of Ceridwen (see Chapter 8) was a source of wisdom and inspiration.

◆ A third cauldron that appears in the Second Branch of the Mabinogi had the magical ability to revive the dead (although without the ability to speak).

◆ And the otherworldly cauldron that Arthur and company seek to plunder from Annwyn in "The Spoils of the Underworld."

Clearly, cauldrons in Celtic myth are associated with magic and with abundance of some form or another. The cauldron is also often seen as a symbol of feminine energy, in contrast to the spear, which is traditionally masculine.

Notes from the Otherworld

In *The Encyclopedia of Celtic Wisdom,* Caitlín Matthews describes a tradition of the "cauldrons of inspiration" found within the body. These cauldrons, similar to chakras, are power centers related to health and well-being. They include the cauldron of warming (located at the solar plexus), which governs physical health; the cauldron of vocation (located at the heart), which governs mental health; and the cauldron of knowledge (located at the head), which governs spiritual health.

But what about the severed head? The story of Bran, the mighty giant-god who appears in the Second Branch of the Mabinogi, tells of how he was mortally wounded during an epic battle between the British and the Irish; he instructed his followers to remove his head from his body; the head continued to live for many years. When Bran's head finally dies, it is buried in London as an object providing magical protection to prevent Britain from invasion.

Among the Celtic warriors of the classical era, headhunting was an acceptable (if grisly) pursuit. The Celts believed that the soul resided in the head, and so keeping the head of a legendary opponent was a mark of honor.

Thus, Peredur's vision of the severed head, like Perceval's vision of the grail (and the spear that appears in both their stories) all harken back to powerful magical symbolism from the Celtic tradition. At its heart, the grail seems linked to the abundance and magic of the Celtic cauldron.

From Severed Head to Wounded King

Bran's importance to the grail story extends beyond how his magical cauldron or his severed head contributed to the formation of the grail symbol. Bran is also important because, according to the Mabinogi, he was the king of Britain. Of course, given the magic associated with him (as well as his head's ability to survive for years after decapitation), it's apparent that he was a god-king. Nevertheless, as a king wounded in battle, he represents the first occurrence of the symbol of the wounded king, the monarch in whose care the grail is entrusted but who has suffered some sort of debilitating wound that not only prevents him from ruling but also causes the land to go to waste. In some of the high grail legends, the wounded king is named Bron, suggesting another connection with the Celtic Bran.

The Wasteland

The grail legends speak of the wounded king ruling over a ruinous wasteland. The lack of fertility in the land is analogous to the wound of the king. (The legends often hint that the wound suffered by the king is in his thighs or genitals.) But the origin of the wasteland motif may also lie in the Celtic past. A medieval French manuscript called *The Elucidation* is believed to be based on ancient Celtic themes, and may shed light on the origin of the wasteland.

According to *The Elucidation*, once upon a time the land was covered by holy wells, each of which was tended by a lovely maiden, who would offer hospitality of food and drink to anyone who traveled by the wells. These maidens of the wells were both protectresses of the sacred waters and the voice of the wells, for they would sing and speak according to the sacred energies associated with their water source. Eventually, there came an evil king, Amangons, who lusted after one of the well maidens. One day he raped her and stole the golden chalice she used when offering her hospitality to travelers. Soon, all his knights were raping the maidens of the wells, stealing their chalices; this resulted in the wells drying up and the voices of the wells going silent. According to *The Elucidation*, it was only with the coming of King Arthur and his noble knights that an effort was made to rescue the well maidens from their oppressors.

Even though the manuscript of *The Elucidation* was written in the early fourteenth century, the story echoes the themes of a much more ancient sensibility. The maidens of the wells are clearly land goddesses, and their rape is a symbol of a world where human greed overpowers the ordinary abundance of nature. This evil throws all things out of balance, resulting in the distress of the maidens and the silencing of the wells—in other words, a land gone to waste.

> **The Bard's Bookshelf**
>
> T. S. Eliot's poem "The Wasteland," considered to be one of the greatest of twentieth-century English poems, took its titular theme from the grail tradition. Wasteland imagery also appears in F. Scott Fitzgerald's *The Great Gatsby*.

The key to healing both the wounded king and the wasted land is the mysterious object of spiritual power and light called the grail.

The Flowering of the Grail Legends

The grail legends are an excellent case study of how fragmented and incomplete ancient Celtic mysticism is, even when preserved in medieval myths or in folklore. The symbols of the wounded king, the wasteland, the magical cauldron, the severed head, and the perilous quest are all present in Celtic tradition, but it would only be in the hands of non-Celtic medieval writers like Chrétien de Troyes or Sir Thomas Malory that the grail would achieve its exalted status as the supreme goal of the ultimate quest. In the late twelfth and early thirteenth centuries, the grail became a popular subject of medieval writings; it was during this time that the Celtic symbolism became grafted on to the dominant religion of the age: Christianity.

Much of the mystical dimension of Christianity centers on devotion to the Holy Eucharist—the ritual consumption of bread and wine blessed in accordance to instructions given by Christ the night before he was crucified. Christ said of the bread and wine "This is my body" and "This is my blood," suggesting that the bread and wine themselves are, once consecrated, holy and filled with Christ's grace. Thus, much popular spirituality (from the Middle Ages to the present day) centers on devotion to the Eucharist as a palpable means to access divine presence.

The Eucharistic Cup as the Holy Grail

If the wine consecrated in the Holy Eucharist is sacred, wouldn't the very cup that Jesus used during the first Eucharist be, itself, supremely holy? Numerous legends had developed in Europe regarding the cup used by Christ in the Last Supper. One tradition held that Mary Magdalene brought the cup with her to France.

Notes from the Otherworld

One strand of the grail tradition holds that Mary Magdalene was Christ's consort, and brought not only the grail with her to Europe, but something even more precious: Christ's child in her pregnant body. In fact, one mystical way to view Mary was that she herself was a "holy grail"—a vessel containing the sacred child!

As noted in Chapter 20, another tradition traced the Holy Grail to Joseph of Arimathea, the wealthy businessman whose grave was used for Christ's body after the crucifixion. According to legend, Joseph was a wealthy tradesman who did business with the Celts of southwest Britain. He is said to have moved to Avalon (modern Glastonbury), bringing the grail with him.

By identifying the otherworldly cauldron of Celtic lore with the must-be-real Holy Grail of Christian symbolism, the legend took on a fascinating level of believability. Not only was the grail the goal of the ultimate quest, but it symbolized the highest mystical energies of the Christian religion. And—if legends were to be believed—it actually was hidden somewhere in Europe!

Key Themes of the Grail Quest

One way to approach the grail story is on this real-world level of speculation that the actual cup used by Christ exists somewhere, carefully hidden if not forgotten. Indeed, this was the backstory to the movie *Indiana Jones and the Temple of Doom*. Many theories exist about the whereabouts of the "real" grail: from Glastonbury, to Rosslyn Chapel in Scotland, to various other sites in the British Isles and throughout Europe. For that matter, other theories hold that the grail remains in the Middle East.

Chalice Well, in Glastonbury, England. According to local tradition, the Holy Grail was hidden in this well for safekeeping.

It is not the purpose of this chapter to exhaust all the various theories and ideas surrounding the whereabouts of the "real" grail. After all, the Christian Holy Grail is an outgrowth of the mythical Celtic grail. Whether or not the actual cup used by Jesus does exist and is located somewhere is a fascinating enigma, but it isn't our focus as Celtic wisdomseekers.

The Celtic tradition, with its rich otherwordly myth and symbolism, is less concerned with what the grail *is* than what the grail *means*. In other words, the most important "grail" isn't a physical object at all, but rather a mystical symbol that represents the crowning glory of the spiritual life.

The Quest for the Grail as a Metaphor for the Mystical Quest

From the ninth century to the present day, one of the most important characteristics of the grail is its hidden-ness. One can't just waltz down to the corner discount store and buy a grail! Whether the grail is hidden in the Welsh Underworld, in a perilous forest, at the heart of a mystical wasteland, or merely in the vast uncharted realm of your own unconscious mind, part of what makes the grail so valuable is its elusiveness.

In this sense, the grail corresponds to the goal of spiritual traditions the world over. From the Buddhist quest for enlightenment to the Christian desire for holiness or the Wiccan quest for the magic of the Goddess, spirituality—like the grail quest—always beckons the seeker to pursue a goal that is difficult to attain. It is precisely that difficulty that makes the goal so worthy.

In the grail legends, knights and fools and adventurers never give up on their quest, even when faced with terrifying dangers or insurmountable obstacles. The grail quest is a powerful metaphor. It symbolizes the value of seeking something so valuable that one's life could be spent in the pursuit—and then being so loyal and dedicated to the quest as to never give up, no matter what the cost.

> **The Seer Says**
>
> We live in a world where everything is valued according to how "practical" or "cost effective" it is. But the grail quest reminds us that some things are so valuable that merely seeking them is a worthy pursuit—even if the goal itself is never (or only partially) attained.

Quest for the Grail, Quest for Healing

Part of what makes the grail legend so rich is the symbolism of the wasteland and the wounded king. The successful grail-seeker will ask the right question that will unleash the power of the grail—a power that will serve to heal both the king and the land.

The land is symbolic not only of nature, but also of the goddess. Likewise, the king symbolizes human society, but also represents the god. To heal the king and the land means to bring harmony and balance back to the relationships between goddess and god, or between humankind and nature.

Such harmony and balance may have purely practical applications (the attainment of the grail would mean a world where despoiling of the environment no longer occurs), but it also has a spiritual dimension (this would be a world where human beings clearly hear the "singing of the land").

If such visions as "a world without environmental despoiling" or "a world where humanity can hear the singing of the land" seem impossible to you, remember: *The grail is not easily attained.* Here's the most important question: Do you have what it takes to begin the quest?

As a symbol of supreme spiritual value, the grail has nothing to do with selfishness or personal gain. We seek the grail only to find the spiritual power of service. This is the true message behind the question, "Whom does the grail serve?" In asking this question, the grail-seeker acknowledges the ultimate value of service. Service, incidentally, doesn't mean being in submission to other human beings (as in a servant-master relationship), but rather being of service to the spiritual world; such service is performed through a life dedicated to healing and balance.

The Consciousness of the Grail

Here's a final thought about the grail quest. Perhaps, in addition to the grail as a symbol of mystical attainment, it also symbolizes the forward thrust of human evolution. Perhaps that which we seek ("the grail") is to be found at the next stage of human development.

Many leaders of both the spiritual and scientific community speculate that the next frontier in human evolution is defined by advances in consciousness. Sure, the human body will probably continue to improve in a variety of ways with each succeeding generation. But what's really exciting is to consider the ways in which the human mind and soul are evolving. Growth in intuition, in compassion, in psychic awareness, in the ability to attain shamanic states of consciousness, and in skills such as creativity and innovation mark the most exciting frontier of evolution. Perhaps the best way to think about the grail is to see it as the future of human consciousness itself.

This way of thinking about the grail has implications on several levels. On one level, it invites every person to seek his or her own maximum potential, through personal development and spiritual growth. On another level, it also encourages us to invest in tomorrow, through careful love, nurture, and education of our children. Perhaps it is in the next generation that lies our best hope for attaining the grail.

Embarking on Your Own Grail Quest

If you feel a fascination for the symbol of the grail, or the long tradition of legends and stories surrounding the quest for this transcendent prize, here are some ways you can incorporate your own grail quest into your larger quest for Celtic wisdom.

The Historical Grail

As mentioned previously, the search for the physical grail is beyond the scope of this book, because that is more of an esoteric Christian than Celtic matter. But if you feel so inclined, researching the history of the grail tradition or visiting legendary grail sites like Glastonbury or Rosslyn Chapel, can be an enjoyable and interesting pastime. Such a research project is most meaningful when combined with the inner dimension of the grail quest.

The Inner Grail Quest

The inner grail quest combines elements of shamanism, meditation, personal growth, and knowledge of tradition to nurture your personal quest for spiritual growth and development. One simple way to embark on the inner grail quest would be to read the legends associated with the grail and use grail-related imagery in your rituals, meditations, and shamanic visualizations. Meditate on your own commitment to the quest. Would you ever give up, regardless of the challenges you face? What would you do if you reached the castle or chapel where the grail was hidden? What would you expect the grail to do for you? For the earth? For the community of humankind? Merely reflecting on questions like these can further your own quest, not just for the grail, but for your growth in wisdom.

Using the Grail as a Metaphor for Reaching Goals

Because the grail symbolizes the difficult-to-attain goal, it can be a powerful tool for any significant undertaking, even if it doesn't have a "spiritual" component. Completing a Ph.D., financing a trip around the world, building a dream house, or starting a charitable nonprofit organization are examples of goals that can appear daunting. The grail quest teaches that any goal worth reaching requires commitment, dedication, hard work, willingness to ask questions, reliance on others, willingness to make sacrifices, and perseverance. Imagine how you can relate the spiritual lessons of the grail to your own nearly impossible goal. Perhaps the grail can serve as an inspiration to help you achieve far beyond your dreams!

Key Voices in the Grail Quest

If you are interested in exploring the symbolism of the grail for your own spiritual quest, several capable guides are available to you. Here are several authors whose works are particularly helpful for the twenty-first-century grail-seeker:

♦ **Dion Fortune.** Fortune was a leading occultist and magical theorist in the early twentieth century. A number of her books are now considered esoteric classics. For her insights into the grail tradition, check out *Glastonbury: Avalon of the Heart* (Samuel Weiser, 2000).

♦ **Shadwynn.** Author of *The Crafted Cup*, an intriguing attempt at synthesizing Christian mysticism and Wiccan/Goddess spirituality, centered on the image of the grail. A great resource for anyone interested in Christopagan spirituality. *The Crafted Cup* includes a series of rituals for creating your own community of grail mystics.

♦ **Gareth Knight.** One of the leading voices in contemporary occultism and ceremonial magic, Knight's writing is dense and multilayered, reflecting the profound spirituality of the inner path. Several of his works explore Arthurian or grail-related themes, including *The Secret Tradition in Arthurian Legend* (Samuel Weiser, 1983) and *Merlin and the Grail Tradition* (Sunchalice Books, 1999).

♦ **John Matthews.** Probably the leading voice in the contemporary grail quest, Matthews has written numerous books on Arthurian, grail, and general Celtic mysteries. To get a taste of his guidance for grail-seekers, read *Healing the Wounded King: Soul Work and the Quest for the Grail* (Element, 1997) or *The Elements of the Grail Tradition* (Element, 1990).

The Least You Need to Know

♦ The grail is the most recognizable symbol of the Celtic tradition, even though in its popular form it also includes non-Celtic elements.

♦ The root of the grail tradition lies in Celtic traditions of the cauldron of abundance, the wounded king, and the wasteland.

♦ In the Middle Ages, when the quest for the Celtic cauldron was united with popular interest in the cup used at the Last Supper, the result was the richly layered symbolism of the Holy Grail.

♦ For modern wisdomseekers, the grail's main value lies in what it symbolizes.

♦ The grail tradition can inspire dedication to the attainment of any worthy, if difficult, goal.

Part 5

Applied Celtic Wisdom

Wisdom can't really be all that wise if it's just a collection of abstract ideas and theories that only make sense on the printed page. For Celtic wisdom to truly make a difference in our lives, we need to find real ways to apply it to our everyday world.

Celtic wisdom isn't like a computer program—you can't master it after reading a book or two. It's a journey that can take you throughout an eternity of wonders. Hopefully, the ideas presented in this part of the book will support you as you take your quest far beyond these pages. Blessings to you as you continue along your way!

Chapter 23

Divination: The Theory and Practice of Spiritual Guidance

In This Chapter

◆ Seeking knowledge spiritually

◆ Nature: the heart of Celtic divinations

◆ The Celtic tree alphabet

◆ Using the Ogham

◆ Divination sets to get you started

A significant part of the quest for wisdom involves the desire for knowledge. While much knowledge may be learned through books or websites or interacting with other people, other aspects of life are shrouded in mystery. From the silent unknown that is the future, to the spiritual principles at the heart of the universe, life includes many treasures hidden behind a veil of unknowing. To be human includes seeking ways to pierce the veil, and for spiritual seekers of any culture, divination is the key to such a quest for knowledge.

This chapter surveys different Celtic methods of divination, with attention focused on the Ogham, an ancient Celtic alphabet that can be used as a tool for accessing spiritual knowledge. If you're looking for Celtic methods of accessing information beyond what is physically available to you, the material covered here will help you get started.

The History of Celtic Divination

As long as there have been Celts, there have been seekers of spiritual knowledge among them. We know from classical writers that the seers were gifted in prophecy and divination. By the Middle Ages, several methods of divination were codified enough to be described by writers. What these methods of divination all shared was a common quest for divine knowledge, or *fios*.

Quest for the Fios

Divination is, in essence, a quest for spiritual knowledge. This is slightly different from the quest for wisdom. Remember, wisdom is the ability to use knowledge effectively, and so one can be wise without necessarily having knowledge; conversely, you can gain all the knowledge in the world and not necessarily be wise. That said, there is certainly a long history of seeking spiritual knowledge within the Celtic tradition, so any Celtic wisdomseeker may also wish to employ a method of seeking knowledge from the spiritual world. Such knowledge can be called fios or imbas (a concept you first encountered in Chapter 8).

Druidspeak

Fios is the old Irish word for "ascertaining." It was a word used to describe spiritually derived knowledge, and in modern Irish is the word for the second sight. Incidentally, *fios* in Scots Gaelic means "knowledge" and the *fiosaiche*, or "knower," is a type of seer gifted at divination.

Both written sources and folklore describe different ways in which Celtic druids and diviners would seek spiritual knowledge. Here are a few of those ancient divination methods:

◆ *Imbas forosnai.* This literally means "the poetic talent/knowledge that illuminates." Described in a medieval text called *Cormac's Glossary*, imbas forosnai involved a diviner chewing a piece of dog, cat, or pig flesh, setting the chewed meat on a ceremonial stone, chanting incantations to his helping spirits, and then chanting another spell over the palms of his hands. He would then lie down to sleep, placing the palms of his hands on his cheeks. Someone would guard his body while he slept so that no one would disturb him in any way; within three days he would receive the gift of clairvoyant knowledge, which might come to him in a dream.

Notes from the Otherworld

Related to the imbas forosnai is the *tarbfheis*, or "bull feast." This method of divination was employed at Tara (traditional seat of the Irish high kings) to select a new king. A bull would be sacrificed and a chosen diviner would eat his fill of the meat, drink the broth, and then lay down to sleep. Druids would perform a ritual incantation over the man as he slept, so that he would dream of the person who was the rightful new king.

- ◆ *Teinm laída,* **or chewing the thumb of knowledge.** This method of divination was particularly associated with Fionn mac Cumhaill, although it may have been practiced by others. In Fenian legends, it is said that Fionn (whose thumb has been blistered by juices from the salmon of knowledge when it was cooked) could receive divinatory wisdom by chanting and sucking or chewing on that thumb.

- ◆ *Díchetal do chennaib.* This obscure old Irish term means "extemporaneous incantation." It involved a druid literally improvising a poem in which his or her clairvoyant impressions would be conveyed to the listener. This practice not only required the practitioner to be a gifted psychic, but also be eloquent enough to compose verse on the spot! It was a skill that had to be mastered before a person could achieve the highest rank of the fili, or Irish seers/bards. Interestingly, although St. Patrick condemned several forms of divination as being wicked, he tolerated díchetal do chennaib.

- ◆ *Neladoracht.* The Scottish Highland practice of "divination by clouds" involved interpreting omens in the patterns and formation of clouds.

- ◆ *Slinneanachd.* Another form of divination through natural omens, this old Highland method of divining involved burning a sheep's shoulder blade and interpreting the cracks in the bone.

- ◆ In more recent eras, Celtic diviners have relied on methods of attaining knowledge that most certainly were not "Celtic" in origin, such as the *Tealeughadh chupaichean,* or reading of the tea leaves, which was practiced in the Highlands of Scotland in the eighteenth century.

Celtic Divination Today

The ancient methods of divination described in the preceding section are by no means the only ways to access the fios. If you seek to access spiritual knowledge as part of your quest for Celtic wisdom, you have several options for divination: mainstream methods of divination (such as astrology or Tarot), working with the Ogham or other specifically Celtic divination tools, or mastering a form of divination related to a traditional Celtic practice, such as reading omens found in the natural world, shamanic trance, or dream interpretation.

Mainstream Divination Tools

It's beyond the scope of this book to introduce you to astrology, Tarot, the *I Ching*, or other well-known methods of divination. A visit to your local metaphysical bookstore will connect you with a lifetime's worth of information on any one of these tools. Although such tools come from cultures other than the Celtic nations (for example, the *I Ching* is Chinese and astrology comes from the Middle East), there's no reason why you can't use them if you so choose. Any divination tool involves a set of symbols, images, or correspondences that form a pattern, either at random (such as the random drawing of Tarot cards or runes) or in accordance with the rhythms of nature (as in astrology, which is based on the various cycles of planets in our solar system).

> CAUTION
> **Geasa**
>
> Divination is meant to help you, not make your life more complicated. Beware the temptation to rely too heavily on divinatory guidance. An astrologer friend of mine once told me of her experience becoming dependent on astrology: She got to the point where she consulted her horoscope to determine what was the best day to go the grocery store! Think of divination as a consultant. It can give you information helpful for making decisions, but the buck always stops with you.

Learning the meanings of the various symbols in any divination tool is enough to get you started, for your subconscious mind will guide you in putting those various meanings together in a coherent pattern of knowledge. To truly be gifted at divination, ultimately you'll want to balance your familiarity with the symbols of divination with an ability to listen to your intuition—for it is truly there that spiritual knowledge/information is ultimately accessed (and ultimately, the symbols in any divination tool are useful primarily in how they inspire your intuition).

Reading Omens in Nature

To really give your divination work a Celtic spin, look for hints of spiritual information in the natural world. This is not unique to the Celts—indeed, shamans the world over develop a facility for reading signs and omens in the natural world. But we know from the tradition that such nature-based divination was indeed part of the Celtic tradition.

There's no one "right way" to read the omens of nature: Seeing an owl in flight in the late afternoon does not have a fixed, unchanging meaning. What makes omen-reading a powerful tool for divination is the combination of seeing a sign in the natural world and your intuitive sense of what that sign means for you at this particular moment in time.

Here's an amusing story from a friend of mine that illustrates how reading the omens of nature can be a way to access divine knowledge. My friend recounts, "I had a dual major in writing and music in college, and I was taking voice lessons in hope of some-day being an opera singer." As it turned out, she chose a successful writing career instead of pursuing opera. She goes on, "One night this past year I was driving home by myself. I was listening to public radio, and they started playing one of my favorite arias, so I started to sing along. I was having a splendid time, and then I got to won-dering what would have happened if I had gone on with my vocal studies and had tried to sing professionally. Barely a moment after I finished the thought, a skunk ran out and crossed the road ahead of me—how much more forcefully could I have been told that I would have stunk as an opera singer! I laughed, let go of my lingering regrets, and gave thanks that I chose a career in literature instead! And I still sing opera in the car for fun."

The Bard's Bookshelf

No book can teach how to read the signs and omens of nature, because nature is so vast and something extraordinary could mean different things in different contexts. But if you'd like some ideas about traditional lore (from many cultures) on animals, check out Ted Andrews's books *Animal Speak: The Spiritual and Magical Powers of Creatures Great and Small* (Llewellyn, 1993) and *Animal Wise: The Spirit Language and Signs of Nature* (Dragonhawk Publishing, 1999).

Celtic Divination Tools

Given that reading the signs of nature requires almost total dependence on your intu-ition, you might feel more comfortable working with a divination tool. In addition to the well-known but non-Celtic tools like astrology, several items are available that draw on the wisdom of the Celtic tradition. Some of these (like the Druid Animal Oracle or the Silver Branch Cards) are cards, similar to the Tarot but based entirely on Celtic myth and lore. The other tool is the Ogham, to which most of the rest of this chapter is devoted.

The Tree Ogham: A Modern Celtic Oracle

Perhaps the single most popular form of divination that's based on the Celtic tradition is the Tree Ogham (pronounced *o-em* or *oh-gim*). The Ogham is an ancient alphabet used by the Irish and other Celts.

The Controversial History of the Ogham

Like any other part of the Celtic tradition, the Ogham has changed and evolved over time. While it can be a powerful and useful tool for divination, it's important to understand that it is a *modern* tool, only *based* on an ancient alphabet. We have no evidence that the ancient druids or bards ever used the Ogham for anything other than mundane, practical forms of communication. This does not mean that the Ogham has no power as a divination tool. Remember, even if it did go back 2,000 years, once upon a time it would have been new. The power of the Ogham does not derive from how old a system it is, but rather from how it takes Celtic symbolism and mythology, connected with nature, and applies it in a way that a person with real-world problems can seek (and receive) guidance.

If the Ogham isn't an ancient mystical tool, then what is it? We do know that the alphabet itself is ancient. It appears on approximately 300 stones in various locations throughout the British Isles, mostly in southern Ireland and Wales, and most of these stones were carved sometime between 300 and 700 C.E. Often, the inscription on the stone is entirely mundane—the stones functioned as gravestones or marked property lines. Such ordinary inscriptions are hardly the stuff of myth and legend! But some of the power of the Ogham lies simply in the fact that the alphabet itself is so old, and so it gives us a link, however tenuous, with the ancient Celts.

The Seer Says

Just because the Ogham is essentially a modern divination tool doesn't make it any less useful. After all, much of the technology we use on a daily basis is less than a hundred years old! Ogham divination is an example of how Celtic wisdom is a living, evolving tradition.

An Irish medieval manuscript, *The Book of Ballymote*, provides an overview of the Ogham characters and explains their meanings. It suggests that each character can be related to a tree (with the concept of "tree" understood loosely—vine, ivy, reed, and several shrubs are considered "trees" for this purpose). It also includes several mysterious diagrams designed with the Ogham characters, with puzzling names like "Fionn's Wheel" and the "Stream Strand of Fechertne."

Some writers have speculated that these diagrams are hints of a lost ancient system where the Ogham was used for magic and divination. According to this idea, by the time the Christian monks were writing their manuscripts in the thirteenth century, the ancient lore was all but lost and only fragments of the wisdom could be preserved for posterity. It's a fascinating idea, but it can only remain a speculation, because we have no evidence to support such claims.

From Robert Graves to Today

The Ogham came to prominence in the twentieth century thanks largely to Robert Graves, author of *The White Goddess: A Historical Grammar of Poetic Myth* (Farrar, Straus and Giroux, 1948). This book is a poetic celebration of the mythic origins of the divine feminine, and includes two chapters on the spiritual meaning of the Ogham. Most critics today dismiss Graves's work as more imaginative than factual, but regardless of Graves's sources, his ideas helped spark the development of modern goddess spirituality (such as Wicca) and also inspired a new wave of interest in the Ogham.

Following Graves, a number of other writers and teachers have continued to explore the Ogham as a tool for accessing and transmitting spiritual knowledge. Even if Ogham cannot be traced back to ancient wisdomkeepers, it is emerging as a valid and useful tool for seekers here in the twenty-first century.

The Ogham as a Divination Tool

How does the Ogham work as a tool for accessing intuition and guidance? In practice, it is actually quite similar to a well-known divination tool, the *runes*. Each of the 20 characters in the Ogham corresponds to a sacred tree or plant and also corresponds to a set of meanings associated with that tree or plant. To perform divination with the Ogham, you need to buy or make a set of 20 sticks or cards, with each Ogham character inscribed on it. You will then use these to randomly select the characters that will provide insight into your divination.

To use the Ogham as a divination tool, you'll first want to memorize the 20 *fid* or characters, their tree/plant associations, and the meanings assigned to each one. The following table will help you become familiar with the Ogham.

> **Druidspeak**
>
> The **runes** are an alphabet from Germanic culture, now used as a divination tool, where each character, or letter, of the runes has its own unique meaning.

Divination with the Ogham

Fid	Letter	Gaelic/English Name	Divinatory Guidance
├	B	Beith/Birch	Make a new start. Clear your clutter.
╞	L	Luis/Rowan	Trust in spiritual protection.
╞	F	Fearn/Alder	Lay a strong foundation for achieving your goals.
╞	S	Saille/Willow	Tune in to your dreams, intuition, imagination, but beware of deception.
╞	N	Nuin/Ash	Put your inner guidance into action. Walk your talk.
┤	H	Huathe/Hawthorn	Clean up your act. Be disciplined and restrain yourself.
╡	D	Duir/Oak	Rely on your strength. Your strength is your spiritual doorway.
╡	T	Tinne/Holly	Be balanced and direct. Fight for what is right.
╡	C	Coll/Hazel	Seek knowledge through meditation and inner guidance.
╡	Q	Quert/Apple	Choose wisely. Appreciate beauty. Be aware of eternity. Feel the wonder.
┼	M	Muin/Vine	Speak your truth, even if your voice shakes.
╪	G	Gort/Ivy	Be persistent. You have the power to succeed.
╪	NG	Ngetal/Reed	Find the eye of the storm. Work for harmony, unity, and reconciliation.
╪	SS	Straif/Blackthorn	Persevere. Take charge of your destiny with singleness of purpose.
╪	R	Ruis/Elder	Flow with universal energies to manifest healing and transformation.
┼	A	Ailim/Fir	Take the high road. Look at the big picture.
╪	O	Ohn/Gorse	Be generous. Enough abundance will come to you so that you can share.

Fid	Letter	Gaelic/English Name	Divinatory Guidance
≢	U	Ur/Heather	Open up to love, dreams and passion.
≣	E	Eadha/Aspen	Be courageous. You can endure and overcome obstacles.
≣	I	Ioho/Yew	Embrace change. Every ending is a new beginning.

How the Ogham Relates to Nature

One of the ways in which the Ogham is especially suited as a Celtic method of divination has to do with its connection to nature. In identifying the spiritual meaning of each Ogham character, it's helpful to get to know the personalities of the Ogham trees and other plants. Here's another table, providing a little bit of lore connected with each fid (character). As you read this, see if you can see the connections between the lore and the divinatory guidance as detailed in the previous table.

Nature Lore and the Ogham

Fid	Letter	Gaelic/English Name	A Bit About the Tree
├	B	Beith/Birch	According to myth, the first use of Ogham was on birch wood.
├	L	Luis/Rowan	Rowan has long been used as a wood to protect against psychic attack.
├	F	Fearn/Alder	Alders were used in Venice and other places to form waterproof foundations.
├	S	Saille/Willow	Willows require lots of water, hence this tree's connection with water and intuition.
├	N	Nuin/Ash	Associated with shamanism, the ash is linked to integrating the cosmos.
┤	H	Huathe/Hawthorn	Hawthorn was associated with the passing of winter: "winter's restraint."

continues

Nature Lore and the Ogham   (continued)

Fid	Letter	Gaelic/English Name	A Bit About the Tree
⊣	D	Duir/Oak	The oak is considered the king of trees, mighty and strong.
⊣	T	Tinne/Holly	Evergreen yet prickly, holly stood for balance; its wood was used to make spears.
⊣	C	Coll/Hazel	The hazel has long associations with knowledge and spiritual wisdom.
⊣	Q	Quert/Apple	In Celtic myth, the apple has long been associated with immortality.
⊢	M	Muin/Vine	Not native to British Isles, the vine is linked to intoxication and loss of inhibition.
⊢	G	Gort/Ivy	Ivy is aggressive, persistent, difficult to destroy, and can be dangerous.
⊢	NG	Ngetal/Reed	Reed was used to make writing instruments, hence its link to poetry and history.
⊢	SS	Straif/Blackthorn	Historically, the blackthorn was linked with the forces of fate.
⊢	R	Ruis/Elder	Elder was considered to be a faery tree, hence the link with universal energies.
+	A	Ailim/Fir	One of the tallest of British trees, hence the "high-perspective" quality.
+	O	Ohn/Gorse	Abundant growth makes this shrub the perfect symbol for generosity.
+	U	Ur/Heather	Heather was seen as a healing plant, and thus a plant of beauty and harmony.
+	E	Eadha/Aspen	A hardy, resistant plant that lends those characteristics to the Ogham interpretation.
+	I	Ioho/Yew	Yews can live to be 2,000 years old, and are often found in graveyards in the British Isles.

And finally, here is a pronunciation guide to the Gaelic names of the Ogham trees:

Pronunciation Guide

Fid	Letter	Gaelic	English	Fid	Letter	Gaelic	English
├	B	*beith*	*be'yeh*	┼	M	*muin*	*min'ye*
├	L	*luis*	*loo'sh*	╪	G	*gort*	*gort*
├	F	*fearn*	*fyarn*	╪	NG	*ngetal*	*nyayt'l*
├	S	*saille*	*sal'ye*	╪	SS	*straif*	*straf*
├	N	*nuin*	*nyin*	╪	R	*ruis*	*reesh*
┤	H	*huathe*	*OO'a-huh*	┼	A	*ailim*	*al'yem*
┤	D	*duir*	*doo'er*	╪	O	*ohn*	*on*
┤	T	*tinne*	*tyin'uh*	╪	U	*ur*	*oor*
┤	C	*coll*	*coll*	╪	E	*eadha*	*ayda*
┤	Q	*quert*	*kyert*	╪	I	*ioho*	*yoho*

How to Consult the Ogham

The Ogham can be used in a number of ways to access sacred guidance. Here are a few ideas:

◆ Put your Ogham sticks into a bag, concentrate on a question or problem where you need guidance, and without looking pull one stick. Reflect on how the divinatory meaning or the energy of the tree/plant associated with that Ogham character could provide guidance to your situation.

◆ Same as above, only pull three sticks; the first one signifies the past (energies leading up to the current situation); the second represents the present (energies now impacting the situation); and the third pointing to the future (likely direction the energy of the situation will take).

♦ This method is based on ancient Irish concepts regarding the energies of the north, east, south, west, and center of the land. Traditional lore associates the east with farming or abundance, the south with bardic arts or harmony, the west with the druids or learning, and the north with warriors or conflict. The center, meanwhile, was associated with the king and with the maintaining of social and cosmic order. This divination method draws from these traditional correspondences to interpret your reading. Pull five sticks from your bag, laying them out as follows:

	Four	
Three	One	Five
	Two	

The first character represents *Sovereignty*, or the energies governing the situation you're facing.

The second character represents *Harmony*, or energies supporting you as you deal with your situation.

The third character represents *Learning*, or the lessons you are grappling with as you work on your situation.

The fourth character represents *Conflict*, or the challenges you face in the current situation.

And the fifth character represents *Manifestation*, or the likely outcome to your current situation.

The Seer Says

Like any other divination method, the Ogham is best learned through practice. Try doing a reading for yourself on a regular basis (no more than once a day); or read for friends. Experiment with the one-, three-, and five-character method to see which one works best for you. If you feel inspired to do so, create your own method of using the Ogham for divination. Remember, the most important part of the divination process is your intuition!

Commercially Available Celtic Divination Systems

Given the popular interest in divination (and in Celtic spirituality), it's no surprise that several interesting divination sets are available for purchase. These tools range from Celtic-inspired Tarot cards, to Ogham-based sets, to items inspired by Celtic myth and lore.

Celtic Tarot Decks

One of the most popular divination tools is the Tarot, a set of 78 cards that originated in medieval Italy. Many different types of Tarot decks have been created, including several with Celtic themes:

- ◆ *The Celtic Tarot* by Courtney Davis and Helena Paterson (Thorsons, 1991). Beautifully designed images based on intricate Celtic knotwork design.

- ◆ *The Celtic Wisdom Tarot* by Caitlín Matthews with illustrations by Olivia Raynor (Destiny Books, 1999). Replaces traditional Tarot suits with categories based on Celtic cosmology.

- ◆ *The Merlin Tarot* by Miranda Gray and R. J. Stewart (Aquarian Press, 1992). Uses themes and imagery based on the life and lore of Merlin.

Other Celtic Divination Tools

Some writers and artists have chosen not to adapt the Tarot to Celtic wisdom, but rather create an entirely new divination set based on their interpretation of the tradition and how it applies to the quest for spiritual knowledge:

- ◆ *The Celtic Book of the Dead: A Guide for Your Voyage to the Celtic Otherworld* by Caitlín Matthews, illustrated by Danuta Mayer (St. Martin's Press, 1992). Based on the mythical voyage of Maelduin, this 42-card set provides a spiritual atlas of the many wonders awaiting the otherworld explorer.

- ◆ *The Celtic Shaman's Pack: Exploring the Inner Worlds* by John Matthews, illustrated by Chesca Potter (Element, 1995). A popular author and artist teamed up to create this colorful, impressionistic deck of otherworldly images.

- ◆ *The Druid Animal Oracle* by Philip and Stephanie Carr-Gomm, illustrated by Bill Worthington (Simon & Schuster, 1994). Featuring exquisitely beautiful cards, this 33-card set draws on the wisdom and lore of animals that appear in Celtic myth.

- ◆ *The Silver Branch Cards* by Nicholas Mann (Druidways, 2000); elegant set of 52 black-and-white cards, featuring scenes from Irish and Welsh myth.

> **The Seer Says**
>
> Celtic-based divination tools are useful in more ways than just for actual divination. All of the sets listed here include beautifully designed decks (or sticks) with insightful companion books. Reading the books and becoming familiar with the cards is, in itself, a valuable step toward getting to know the Celtic tradition. These sets can be used to inspire meditation, visualization, or simply to be enjoyed for their unique perspective on the tradition.

Ogham Sets

The Ogham is relatively challenging, as divination tools go: It only consists of 20 symbols (compared with the 78 images of the Tarot), meaning that you must rely heavily on your intuition to provide accurate readings. Still, the beauty and simplicity of the Ogham system make it a favorite among Celtic wisdomkeepers. If you lack the time or resources to create your own Ogham set, these tools can help you get started:

- *Ogham: Druidic Oracle of the Trees* by Matthew Flesch (Dragon Torque Press, 1997). Nicely made set of Ogham sticks with a 72-page booklet.

- *The Voice of the Woods* by Amanda Fisher (Pixelations, Inc., 2000). This gorgeous set includes beautifully designed fids made of alder, with an interpretive booklet; they can be ordered online at www.electriccelt.com.

- *The Celtic Tree Oracle: A System of Divination* by Liz and Colin Murray; illustrated by Vanessa Card (St. Martin's, 1988). If you'd rather work with cards than with sticks, this attractive deck is based on the Ogham, with illustrations that will help you recognize the tree associated with each few. Recommended as a learning tool, even if you choose to work with traditional fids.

The Least You Need to Know

- Divination is a universal process for accessing spiritual knowledge.

- The ancient Celts had several methods of divination, including seeking information through trance state or in dreams.

- A simple and effective tool for divination is the Ogham, an ancient alphabet where every letter corresponds to a tree or other plant.

- Different divination tools based on Celtic wisdom are commercially available.

Chapter 24

The Cycles of Time

In This Chapter

- ◆ It's time to rethink your view of time
- ◆ The Wheel of the Year
- ◆ A quick tour through the four Celtic festivals
- ◆ The solstices and the equinoxes
- ◆ The Celtic view of time … and life after death

Does time move in a line … or in a circle?

Sure, it's the kind of question that college undergrads love to argue about while they're waiting for the pizza to arrive. But it also speaks to one of the ways in which Celtic wisdom differs from the mainstream perspective of Western culture.

This chapter examines the Celtic understanding of time, exploring the yearly cycle of great holidays celebrated by Celts in ancient times—holy days that are undergoing a spiritual revival today.

The Real Reason Why Clocks Are Round!

Okay, so I'm joking about clocks. But the round face of a clock does give us an important hint about the Celtic view of time.

In the parts of the world where Christianity has had a profound influence, time has historically been depicted as a line, moving steadily from "beginning" to "end." Read the Bible, probably the single most influential book in the Western Hemisphere, and you'll see just this model of time: The book of Genesis begins at the beginning of time, while the Revelation to John concludes with the completion of time. Every moment of existence is simply another dot on the line.

The linear concept of time may make sense, especially given that we human beings experience life as a sequential process that begins at birth and ends at death. But there can be another way of understanding time. Think about how modern physics depicts the universe: Current thinking holds that space is curved, which means if a projectile moving in an absolutely straight line at a fixed, unchanging rate of velocity were fired at one point in the universe, eventually it would return to its point of origin. That could only be possible if the very structure of the universe were curved, rather than linear.

Apply this to time. What if time moves not in a line, but in a grand cycle? What implications would this have for the attainment of wisdom?

Notes from the Otherworld

As a religion that sees time as linear, Christianity's most important holidays are based on events from the linear life experience of Jesus. Christmas marks the beginning of Jesus' linear time (his birth), while Good Friday and Easter mark the events that occurred at the end of Jesus' linear time (his death and resurrection).

Okay, let's reduce our perspective: The Celts didn't worry about the rise and fall of the entire universe. But they did have a way of understanding time that was based not on the birth-life-death linear sequence of human experience, but rather on the cycles of nature, such as fall-winter-spring-summer-fall or dusk-night-dawn-day-dusk.

Such cycles meant that the spiritual holidays of the Celtic people were not based on events in linear time (such as the birth and death of a great leader), but were rather based on recurring events in cyclical time (such as the changing of the seasons).

The Wheel of the Year

Imagine that a year could be charted as a circle. The top of the circle would represent winter and the bottom would mark summer. If time progressed in a clockwise fashion, the right side of the circle would signify spring; the left would correspond to autumn.

In the Celtic world, the ancients celebrated a major festival that corresponded, roughly, with the beginning of each season. Those festivals were as follows:

◆ **Samhain (or Samhuinn)** (literally "summer's end"). Marked the onset of the winter months. Other names for this holiday include *Trinoux Samonia*, "Three Nights of the End of Summer" (ancient Gaul); *Calan Gaeaf* (Welsh); *Calan Gwaf* (Cornish); and *Kala-Goañv* (Breton), all of which mean "first day of winter."

◆ **Imbolc (or Oímealg)** (meaning "in the belly" or "ewe's milk"). Corresponds to the time when pregnant livestock would begin lactating, thus signifying the onset of spring. Particularly sacred to Brigid. Other names for this holiday include *Gwyl Mair Dechrau'r Gwanwyn* ("Feast of Mary of the Beginning of Spring") or *Gwyl Ffraed* ("Brigid's Feast") in Welsh; *Gouel Varia ar Goulou* ("Feast of Mary of the Light") in Breton; *Lá Fheile Bri[as]de* in Gaelic; and *Laa'l Breeshey* ("Brigid's Feast") in Manx.

◆ **Beltaine (or Bealtinne)** (literally "bright fire"). Celebrated the return of the sun and the onset of the hottest time of the year. Other names for the holiday all translate as the "First Day of May": *Calan Mai* (Welsh), *Calan Me* (Cornish), or *Kala-Mae* (Breton).

◆ **Lughnasa (or Lughnasadh)** ("the festival of Lugh"). Marked the beginning of the autumn harvest period, which would continue through to the next Samhain.

Now Appearing at a Wiccan Circle Near You!

The four great Celtic festivals are well documented in Celtic myth and folklore, and in many places in the Celtic world, these holidays are still observed in some form or fashion. But thanks to the influence of Christianity, the holiday observances are but a shadow of what they must have been in the pagan past. Although folklore dies slowly and many customs surrounding these four holidays persist to the present day, for many people they are just quaint little customs held over from a superstitious past.

Notes from the Otherworld _____

The play *Dancing at Lughnasa* by Brian Friel (and the movie starring Meryl Streep), set in rural 1930s Ireland, explores how ancient Celtic rituals had transformed with the passage of time: Lughnasa, once a major harvest festival, had become little more than a wild party by the early twentieth century. But with the rise of neopaganism in the second half of the twentieth century, new life was breathed into the old ceremonies.

But what brought the festivals to a much larger segment of the population (both in the Celtic lands and, especially, throughout the world) was the Celtic-Wiccan connection. When Wicca exploded on the spiritual scene of the 1950s and 1960s, one of the defining elements of the religion was its focus on nature-based holidays. These included the monthly full moons (which makes sense, as witchcraft has been associated with the full moon since time immemorial), and eight annual holidays that collectively became known as the "Wheel of the Year." These holidays included the four Celtic holidays, along with four holidays based on the solstices and equinoxes:

♦ **Ostara** (named for a Teutonic goddess of spring). The spring equinox.

♦ **Midsummer.** The summer solstice.

♦ **Mabon** (named for the Welsh "young god"). The fall equinox.

♦ **Yule.** The winter solstice.

The Wheel of the Year.

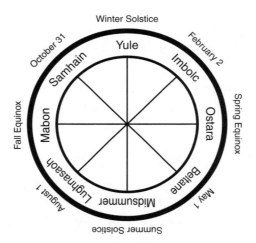

The idea that these eight holidays fit together in a "Wheel of the Year" (as shown in the illustration) is essentially a new concept, popular among Wiccans and other neo-pagans. There's no evidence that any ancient culture (Celtic or otherwise) had a systematic annual cycle of eight holidays. But while it may be a new method of marking the passage of time, it has become firmly connected with the modern revival of Celtic wisdom.

How Celtic Is the Wheel of the Year?

Although the four festivals are clearly of Celtic origin, the solstices and equinoxes are more problematic. Medieval literary sources such as Irish and Welsh myth don't mention the solstices and equinoxes, and folklore practices connected with them are not necessarily Celtic in origin (for example, Scottish customs related to Yule are clearly Norse in origin). On the other hand, evidence points to a recognition even in pre-Celtic times that these dates were significant. From Stonehenge's alignment with the summer solstice to Newgrange's alignment with the winter solstice, it is clear that the ancient people who built these monuments possessed astronomical knowledge as impressive as their engineering ability. Other ancient monuments (such as the Knowth tomb, which is located near Newgrange) are aligned to the equinoxes, although there is even less evidence that they were celebrated in ancient times.

Granted, just because Newgrange and Stonehenge were constructed in astronomically significant ways doesn't mean that the pagan Celts (or even their pre-Celtic predecessors) had ceremonies to mark these days. Remember, Stonehenge and Newgrange existed for centuries before Celtic culture first arrived in the British Isles; by that time, whatever astronomically based practices associated with these monuments may have long fallen into disuse. But bearing in mind that the Celtic tradition is a living tradition—and that nature-based spirituality throughout the world today observes the solstices and equinoxes—for modern Celtic wisdomseekers, the astronomical dates have become nearly as important holidays as the actual ancient festivals.

The Importance of the Wheel

Why is the Wheel of the Year important? For several reasons:

♦ It celebrates the relationship between humanity and nature, as expressed through the drama of the changing seasons.

♦ The ancient Celts may have relied on their four festivals as a sort of "yearly planner" that helped the tribe organize agricultural work such as sowing, harvest, and slaughter of livestock.

> **The Seer Says**
>
> The dates for the holidays given here are based on the Northern Hemisphere, which is after all where the Celtic nations are located. If you happen to live in the Southern Hemisphere, you'll invert the dates: thus, in Australia Samhain occurs at the end of April, not October; Imbolc is in August rather than February, and so forth.

◆ In modern times, when so few of us are involved in the production of our own food, the Wheel of the Year is a symbolic reminder of how dependent we remain on the abundance of Mother Earth.

Here's a closer look at the four great Celtic festivals, followed by a look at the solstices and equinoxes.

Samhain: Roaming Spirits and the Chill of Death

In the ancient Celtic mind, a day began not at midnight or at sunrise, but actually at sundown. Night precedes the light, and together they form a single unit of time.

In a similar way, the Celtic year began not with the coming of midwinter or the new spring, but with the end of the harvest time. Thus, Samhain ("summer's end"), celebrated on or near October 31, marked not only the end of autumn and the onset of winter, but it was also the Celtic new year.

The Lore of Samhain

Samhain is a time when fearsome beasts and monsters could walk the earth. Because it marks the end of an old year and beginning of the new, it means a break in the flow of time; this break means that the veil separating our world from the otherworld was temporarily opened. But more than just ghoulies and beasties could come visit from the other side: to the Celts, this is a solemn and reverent holiday, filled with transformational magic. It's the best night of the year to make contact with the spirits of loved ones who have passed to the otherworld—the ancestors, from whom we received our life and our DNA.

> **The Seer Says**
>
> Traditionally, Samhain is the best night for divination. So next October 31, get out your Tarot cards (or better yet, Ogham sticks) and dare to gaze into the future!

The children's customs of Halloween are rooted in Samhain traditions. Kids wear masks to frighten and confuse the scary entities from the spiritual realm, while a jack-o-lantern (originally a turnip, before North Americans started to use pumpkins) is lit to show friendly spirits the way home.

A Ritual for Today

To celebrate Samhain, set up a "dumb supper." This is a meal that you and your family or friends eat in silence. Set an extra place at the table and put small portions of food on the plate at this setting. This is the meal for the ancestors. As you eat in silence, reflect on your loved ones who have crossed over to the other side, and pay attention: You just might feel their presence!

Imbolc: Bridget's Milk and Pregnant Ewes

Imbolc is the festival marking the coming of spring. It is particularly sacred to the goddess Brigid. Folklore associated with Imbolc places it at February 1, which is also the festival of St. Brigid in the Christian year. Although it might seem odd to mark the beginning of spring at a time when winter is still raging throughout much of the Northern Hem-isphere, consider the pregnancy imagery associated with this festival. New life grows for nine months in the womb prior to birth; Imbolc represents the "womb" of spring, where it is not yet manifest but clearly on its way. In some areas, agricultural tools were blessed at this holiday, and it signaled the time to begin the first plowing.

The Lore of Imbolc

More than any other holiday, Imbolc is connected to a specific figure: Brigid, the goddess/saint whose name means "exalted one." Many of the traditions associated with this day involve seeking the goddess's blessing. In the Scottish Highlands, women would make a corn dolly to represent Brigid, that would be then placed in a basket to symbolize a bed/crib. In this way, Brigid represents both mother and daughter, both the giving of life and new life itself.

A Brigid's corn dolly, set in her basket for a Wiccan Imbolc celebration.

A Ritual for Today

In the Christian tradition, Brigid's festival became associated with Candlemas, a festival for blessing the candles used at the church. Given Brigid the goddess's association with a sacred fire, this is not an inappropriate connection. You can honor Imbolc by lighting a series of candles (nine would be an appropriate number), giving thanks for the goddess's blessing in your life, and meditating on your plans for a productive and fruitful year to come.

Beltaine: Blossoming Hawthorn and Nighttime Revels

Beltaine is the sexiest of the Celtic holidays, although much of the erotic lore connected with it seems to be more modern in origin. It is the opposite of Samhain, occurring on or about May 1. In the natural world, it is the time when the hawthorn tree is in bloom. It signifies the beginning of summer and the time of sowing.

The folklore associated with Beltaine, or May Day, suggests that it is a festival of fertility, when magical rituals would be performed to ensure a healthy crop and bountiful harvest later that year. What better way to promote agricultural fertility than for young men and women to spend the night in the woods, doing what comes naturally?

Alas, it's a titillating thought, but there's very little evidence to support the idea that Beltaine was a time for sexual licentiousness, at least among the Celts (Beltaine got its sexy reputation in Britain, actually, probably in the late Middle Ages or early modern period). Although we can't know for sure exactly how the ancients celebrated this day, in the modern neopagan world this celebration of life and the beginning of summer has a distinctively erotic element (which is appropriate, for after all, eroticism is the heart of fertility, and part of celebrating life is celebrating fertility).

> **Notes from the Otherworld**
>
> Fire plays an important role in each of the four Celtic festivals. Bonfires are traditionally associated with Samhain and Beltaine; candles (or the hearth fire) are associated with Imbolc, and the fires of the oven baking bread are associated with Lughnasa. For this reason, many Wiccans and other neopagans refer to these holidays as the four fire festivals.

The Lore of Beltaine

As the opposite of Samhain, Beltaine is the second most "open" day of the year, that is to say, the time when the veil separating our world from the otherworld is nearly as open as at the beginning of the Celtic year. For this reason, much of the traditional lore connected with Beltaine involves protection against mischievous faeries. Many elaborate ceremonies and festivals have grown up around this holiday, not only in the

Celtic lands but in other areas. (England, for example, has many lovely May Day festivities, including the Maypole, a tall pole from which ribbons are draped and men and women dance in a way that weaves the ribbons on the pole.)

One old rural Beltaine tradition involved building two bonfires and driving livestock between them; the fire was considered to be a form of purification. A modern variant, especially popular in Wicca, is to build a small bonfire and jump over it, the jump seen as fostering positive fertile energy.

> **CAUTION**   **Geasa**
>
> Jumping over a bonfire can be dangerous! The fire must be small, and no one should jump over it if wearing a long skirt or any other item that could catch fire. Children should never do this without parental supervision.

A Ritual for Today

Just as Samhain celebrates the coming of darkness and winter, so Beltaine is a celebration of new life. The best way to mark it would be with a sensuous evening making love with your partner. If that's not possible, find some sort of way to pamper yourself: a bubble bath, a massage, or filling your living space with fragrant flowers. Do something to celebrate being alive on this day!

Lughnasa: Sporting Games and a Harvest of Grain

Today Lughnasa is celebrated on or near August 1. Originally, it wasn't a single event, but rather a month-long festival to mark the first fruits of the harvest. Occurring at the opposite end of the wheel from Imbolc, here is when the hopes and wishes from six months ago begin to come to fruition.

In its original form, Lughnasa was a social event, when marriages would take place, legal proceedings would be decided upon, and young people would test their skill against one another in a variety of contests and sporting events. Indeed, the ancient festival of Lughnasa was like the Olympics of the Celtic world!

The Lore of Lughnasa

As its name implies, this is a festival sacred to Lugh, the many-skilled god of light. Occurring at a time of year when the sun's power is greatest, it only seems appropriate to honor a solar deity. But the theme of this festival is sacrifice. The days are growing shorter, meaning that the solar deity must soon yield to the encroaching dark. Traditionally, the harvest of wheat and grain at this time of year suggests that the spirit of vegetation must be cut down: in the words of the English ballad, "John

Barleycorn must die." So Lughnasa is also a time when the god lovingly lays down his life so that others may live, by enjoying the fruits of his sacrificial harvest.

In some parts of Ireland, Lughnasa customs indicated that the drama of the festival centered around Lugh defending the harvest against the hostile forces of nature (perhaps echoing Lugh's battling the Fomorians in Celtic myth). With the coming of Christianity, in many communities Lugh's role was taken over by Saint Patrick or the archangel Michael.

A Ritual for Today

Lughnasa was a festival similar to our modern Thanksgiving. It included sporting events and feasting (just like our college football on TV followed by a turkey dinner!). Thus, a great way to honor this old festival would be to gather with friends for good-natured competition of some sort (whether athletic or even just indoor games), followed by a feast. If possible, include homemade bread.

Solstices and Equinoxes

Part of the beauty of the Wheel of the Year lies in how evenly spaced the four Celtic festivals are in relation to the astronomical dates of the solstices and equinoxes. Today, it is possible to honor the passage of time with these eight holidays, each one occurring every six to seven weeks.

The Bard's Bookshelf

Here are three great books for learning more about the Wheel of the Year: Ronald Hutton's *The Stations of the Sun: A History of the Ritual Year in Britain* (Oxford University Press, 1996) looks at seasonal traditions with a critical eye, while Alexei Kondratiev's *The Apple Branch: A Path to Celtic Ritual* (The Collins Press, 1998) tells how a modern Celtic spirituality group can draw on ancient traditions to honor the eight holidays. For children, check out Clare Walker Leslie and Frank E. Gerace's *The Ancient Celtic Festivals and How We Celebrate Them Today* (Inner Traditions, 2000).

Are They Celtic?

As mentioned earlier in this chapter, there are no ancient holidays, recorded in medieval Celtic writings, to correspond with the solstices and equinoxes. This has led some neopagans to the conclusion that it isn't really "Celtic" to observe the astronomical days. Yule, for example, is a Norse holiday, while the main observances connected with the fall equinox come from the Christian festival of Michaelmas. To some modern Celtic wisdomseekers, the seasonal celebrations nevertheless fit in beautifully with the ancient Celtic holidays, so that even if the early inhabitants of Ireland and Wales never observed these days, they can still be an important part of twenty-first century Celtic spirituality.

Ways to Honor Them

Because there isn't the same depth of tradition associated with the solstices and equinoxes as is connected with the four ancient festivals, these days are more of a "blank slate" where you can create your own ways of honoring the cycle of the seasons. I've included a few ideas for you to consider. You'll notice that they are based on customary ways of honoring the season in which the holiday occurs. We know that the summer solstice falls near the Fourth of July and the winter solstice falls near Christmas and Hanukah. There's nothing wrong with integrating your observance of the seasons with the existing customs by which our society marks the passage of time:

- ◆ You can celebrate the spring equinox with colored eggs hidden in the yard for the children of your neighborhood to find.

- ◆ Mark the summer solstice with a cookout and plenty of water to keep cool. (Ideally, a trip to the beach works best.)

- ◆ Enjoy the fall equinox with a drive in the country to see the changing colors of the leaves.

- ◆ And the winter solstice is a great time to exchange gifts and sing songs to stay warm (and invite the sun back for another year!).

The Dark Comes First: The Symbolism of the Cycle

Earlier in the chapter I mentioned how, in the Celtic view of time, a unit of time began with the dark, before moving to the light. In other words, a day begins at sundown the night before.

This is an interesting spiritual metaphor. It suggests that the dark precedes the light. To the ancients, when the sun set on the western horizon, it must have seemed as if the sun were entering the Underworld—the home of the gods, goddesses, and ancestors. Their "day" would then correspond with our night, and vice versa. This also suggests that our world—the physical universe—precedes from the otherworld (a concept that is often taught in modern metaphysics holds that the physical world is little more than a projection of the spiritual world).

The darkness of night corresponds with the darkness of soil—that is to say, with the goddess. Meanwhile, the light of the sun corresponds with the radiance of "shining ones" like Lugh or the Dagda. Thus, in the cycles of time, the ancient Celts may well have envisioned a symbolic template of the universe as the abode of the Goddess and the God. And certainly in our modern quest for Celtic knowledge, we can see the great polarity of divine masculine and divine feminine at the heart of everything—even the rhythm of day and night.

The Cycles of Time and the Nature of Human Existence

Finally, the Celtic understanding of time is important for the wisdomseeker because it can affect the way you understand life, the universe, and everything.

Here's a question to ponder: From the perspective of a single human life, time seems to move in a line (such as from birth to death). But in nature, time appears to move in a cycle (such as the cycle of the seasons). Does it make more sense to project the human linear experience of time onto the universe (suggesting that the universe, like human life, moves strictly in a line from beginning to end), or does it make more sense to assume that human life is like the rest of nature, existing in a cycle—which would imply that our experience of birth-life-death is only one part of a larger whole?

Traditionally, Celtic wisdom favors the latter view. Why should human beings assume the entire universe functions according to our experience of time and life? Isn't it more reasonable to assume that, because the universe as a whole is curved and everything moves in cycles, then so, too, does human experience? This, of course, is the foundation of belief in reincarnation. Just as day alternates with night, so, too, does human life alternate between existence in this physical world, followed by a period in the otherworld.

Naturally, you'll never know for sure what comes after death until your own time comes. But to the Celtic mind, reincarnation seems the most natural way of understanding the mysteries of life, death, and time.

The Least You Need to Know

◆ Celtic wisdom includes the ability to see time as cyclical, rather than linear.

◆ In Celtic spirituality, holy days (holidays) are based on the rhythms of nature, not on historical events.

◆ The four great Celtic holidays are Samhain, Imbolc, Beltaine, and Lughnasa.

◆ The four Celtic holidays, combined with the solstices and equinoxes, make up a cycle of eight holidays known as the Wheel of the Year.

◆ To Celts, the cyclical nature of time suggests that all things move in cycles—even human life.

Chapter 25

Practical Celtic Wisdom: Living the Celtic Life Today

In This Chapter

◆ The 24/7 wisdomkeeper

◆ Solitary spirituality or Celtic community?

◆ Practical steps on the path to wisdom

◆ From death to rebirth

◆ The ground you walk on

Our journey together is nearing its end, but the quest for Celtic wisdom and spirituality goes on forever. From the misty Irish landscape to the congested suburbs of America, people from many different corners of the globe and many different walks of life seek guidance from this tradition, each and every day. Having gone through this book doesn't make you an expert on things Celtic. If anything, it has simply given you enough information to begin on your own lifelong quest.

This chapter looks at ways to make the Celtic path your own, 24 hours a day, 7 days a week. Celtic wisdom isn't something you keep tucked away in a box somewhere, to take out on Sundays or on the full moon or whenever you feel like "being Celtic." On the contrary, this wisdom tradition is challenging

The Seer Says

Just a reminder: The material in this chapter represents one perspective on the Celtic path. Always remember, there are many other ways to approach the riches of this tradition!

and demanding. It challenges us to hold the alternative vision of a world where earth and humanity live in balance, and where spiritual wisdom weaves together with down-to-earth knowledge (like science and technology) to help make the world a better place. In other words, this is no mere hobby. Celtic spirituality is a way of life. Walk a ways along this path, and you will find your entire life transformed forever.

A Nine-Step Process to Living the Celtic Life

But where to begin with living a Celtic life? Sure, various chapters throughout this book have offered practical suggestions for your own spiritual growth, from keeping a journal to practicing visualization to creating your own personal altar. But now it's time to see how all these activities can be woven together into an integrated practice of Celtic wisdom. This section provides nine steps you can take to make the Celtic spirit come alive in your life on a daily basis.

1. Through the Telling of Stories, We Learn the Ways of Our Ancestors

When all is said and done, Celtic wisdom begins and ends with storytelling. From the bards of ancient times to the shanachies of rural Ireland to webmasters creating magical websites filled with Celtic lore, recounting tales has always been (and always will be) the single most important way that Celtic wisdom is collected, celebrated, learned, and transmitted. These don't have to be fantastic, grand stories, like something Tolkien would have written. Any story, no matter how short, simple, or humble, can be a repository of wisdom.

Why is storytelling so important to this path? Because it's been a part of the tradition since the beginning, but also because it's a down-to-earth, ordinary way of communicating. Storytelling doesn't require a college degree or a computer with lots of special effects software. Even the act of storytelling itself contains wisdom: the wisdom that the most ordinary, everyday, and humble parts of life can be tools for accessing spiritual insight.

Find ways to tell your own story. You can do this privately through keeping a journal; if you want to share it with others, you can do so online through websites like www. livejournal.com. Or you can learn the art of storytelling, where you can entertain others with your yarn-spinning skills. Just remember: When you tell a story, look for the moral (the wisdom contained within it). And remember that your storytelling is part of a long and glorious Celtic tradition.

2. Through Tales of Magic and Mysticism, We Learn About Worlds Beyond Our Imagination

Sure, by keeping a journal you'll be telling your own story, but Celtic storytelling is more than just autobiography. You'll find great pleasure (and more than just a few life lessons) in the stories of Celtic poetry, myths, and legends from down the ages. So in addition to telling stories, take the time to learn the stories of others. Learn the stories of the gods and goddesses, or of the early Celtic Christian saints, or of the hapless farmers over the years who have had fortunate (or unfortunate) dealing with the faeries.

If you're lucky enough to know a gifted storyteller or two, you can learn the Celtic tales the way they're meant to be shared: by listening to stories told. If that's not possible, get your hands on as many books containing Celtic stories as you can. Listen to or read the stories, and learn them. Try to find the nugget of wisdom contained in each tale. And once you get to know the stories well, you may find yourself being asked to share a tale while sitting around a campfire or in front of a fireplace on a cold winter's night!

> **The Bard's Bookshelf**
>
> Want to dive into the legends and myths of the Celts? Here's a fun book to get you started: *One Hundred and One Read-Aloud Celtic Myths and Legends* by Joan C. Verniero (Black Dog & Leventhal, 2000). It's filled with simple retellings of myth and legend that you can read aloud (or better yet, memorize and tell) to your family and friends.

3. Through the Silent Witness of Archaeology, We Find Clues of How an Ancient Culture Managed Their Life Differently, and in Some Ways Better, Than We Do Today

Okay, you probably don't have the freedom to just run off to Cornwall or Brittany and become a full-time archaeologist. But that doesn't mean that you can't explore archaeology; you'll just have to do it through books or websites or classes at your local college. I'm using the word *archaeology* in the broadest sense of including all historical information about the way our ancestors and forebears lived their lives and interacted with their environment. Through archaeology we gain information on how society was organized, what was considered artistic or beautiful, and what tools were used to conduct spiritual services or make offerings to the gods and goddesses.

Remember, many of the sites commonly thought of as "Celtic" (such as Stonehenge or Newgrange) actually are pre-Celtic, having been built hundreds or thousands of years before the coming of Celtic culture to western Europe. But it's still appropriate to explore such ancient pre-Celtic archaeology under the banner of Celtic wisdom, because Celtic mythology and lore were influenced by traditions surrounding such ancient sacred sites.

The Seer Says

One doesn't have to literally apply the wisdom of the past (whether gained through archaeology, history, or mythology) to the present to be a wisdomkeeper. In other words, we don't all have to live like Iron Age warriors in order to walk the Celtic path! We study the past not to conform to it, but to have wisdom of ancient times shed light on our modern world. For example, we know the Iron Age Celts lived in close-knit tribes. Perhaps the modern Celtic wisdomseeker would naturally look for ways to build community spirit in the modern world, even for those who live urban or suburban lives.

4. Through Mythology and Personal Experience, We Discover Principles for Relating to the Spiritual Realms

Mythology begins with the great tales of Irish and Welsh gods, goddesses, and heroes from ancient writings like *The Táin* or *The Mabinogion*—but it doesn't end there. It's best to think of mythology as a living tradition of information about how we can relate to the inhabitants of the otherworld. These inhabitants run the gamut from the greatest of deities, through to ancestors and others who can be called "the mighty dead," to the countless spirits of nature known as the faeries.

Myths are simply the stories through which we learn about the inhabitants of the otherworld and discover what others who have gone before us have learned about relating to that magical realm. But as a living tradition, mythology depends on us to contribute to it and move it forward. Every time you encounter the spiritual world for yourself, through meditation, dreams, or ritual, you increase your own wisdom on a practical level. This wisdom is now available to serve you as you continue on your journey, and, if you share your story with others, you make your wisdom available to support their journey as well.

5. Through the Forces of Nature, We Discover That Spirituality Has a Body as Well as a Soul

The Goddess isn't just an abstract idea, but rather is embodied in the land herself. Many Celtic spiritual personalities have strong ties to one or more aspects of nature, from Brigid's connection with fire, to Manannán's connection with the sea, to Epona's connection with horses. Celtic spirituality teaches us that nature is holy, but this process works in reverse as well: the natural holiness that we can find in our environment if we only look for it serves to remind us that spirituality isn't just a "head trip" but actually is part of the material world.

So one of the simplest and most effective ways to live a daily practice of Celtic spirituality is to connect with nature, in some form or fashion, each and every day. Depending on your life situation, "nature" may mean something as vast as the wilderness of Montana or something as small and immediate as a potted African violet in your urban apartment. Do whatever works for you to get close to nature—just be sure to do it, whatever it is, and to make it a normal part of your daily life. When encountering the natural world, approach it spiritually: Enter into a meditative space and listen to your inner guidance for insight into what nature may have to teach you. Remember, in the Celtic world, all of nature is part of the Goddess, so even that little African violet may have a sacred insight to offer you!

> **The Bard's Bookshelf**
>
> Check out the book *Sacred Land Sacred Sex: Rapture of the Deep* by Dolores LaChappelle (Kivaki Press, 1988) for ideas about living in closer harmony with nature. It's not a specifically "Celtic" book, but its approach is in harmony with Celtic wisdom.

6. Through Ritual, We Find Ways That Our Spirits Can Be Transformed

Like mythology, ritual needs to be understood in as broad a way as possible. Perhaps for you ritual means a structured ceremony of religious observance, such as a Wiccan circle or a Christian Holy Communion service. Or maybe you're more comfortable with a shaman's improvisational style of using dance, trance, music, and meditation to create an impromptu ritual of spirit contact. Or maybe for you, your daily walks in nature and regular forays into studying myth and archaeology are your personal rituals of observance. These are all valid and useful ways to weave ritual into your life.

Think of ritual as a "planned spiritual activity." Whether it's highly structured (like the Catholic mass) or loosely organized (like the shaman's ceremony) doesn't matter so much as the simple fact that you're doing something to initiate spiritual transformation. Ritual takes us out of our heads (or out of our books) and puts us in a place where we make our spirituality come alive in our bodies. Since the body is part of the earth (and therefore part of the Goddess), this is an integral part of the Celtic path—and something you can do, in elaborate or simple ways, on a regular basis.

7. Through Omens and the Ogham, We Are Given Knowledge That Can Help Make Us Wise

Let's face it: We live in a big, scary world, filled with risk and danger and uncertainty. Disease, suffering, and death are nonnegotiable realities. Everyone who has any shred of faith in the spiritual world sooner or later looks to it for guidance.

As a Celtic wisdomseeker, there are tools available to you for accessing this kind of spiritual guidance, both for your benefit and in service to others. Whether your interest lies in a structured divination tool like the Ogham, or the intuition-by-the-seat-of-the-pants method of looking into the natural world to discover meaningful omens, you can walk the path of the great seers of old and learn to rely on your intuition as a trustworthy doorway into the world of spiritual guidance.

8. Through Language, We Can Discover a Way of Life in Which Prayer Never Ceases

Celtic spirituality is a path of poetry, song, and prayer. Just as the seers of old inspire our efforts to master intuition, so the long tradition of bards reminds us that beauty and creativity are just as important to wisdom as spiritual guidance or divination. Several times in this book I've spoken of the value of the traditional Celtic languages. While it may not be practical for everyone to learn Gaelic or Welsh, we can still become familiar with the poetry and prayers of such languages, even in translation (such as the *Carmina Gadelica*).

Notes from the Otherworld

Celtic spirituality places importance on the language of poetry and prayer to create beauty and spiritual blessings in life.

In their traditional language, the Celts are people who speak poetically and prayerfully. No matter what language you speak, you can cultivate a sense of poetry and prayer in your communication. Writing poetry doesn't mean you have to be the next Shakespeare—it simply means learning to communicate beautifully, lyrically, and imaginatively. And prayerful communication simply means that your spiritual values are constantly kept front and center in your words. That's not about being heavy-handed with your spirituality. (People get tired of hearing lots of God-talk.) But it does mean less cursing and more giving thanks; less complaining and more optimism.

How does this relate to wisdom? Well, maybe injecting a sense of poetry and prayer into your patterns of communication won't make you any smarter. But I believe they'll make you happier and more in tune with the Goddess. And that's wise indeed!

9. By Fostering Celtic Wisdom in Our Lives, We Become Custodians of a Powerful Vision

At several points in this book I've talked about how the Celtic path, the druid path, or the bardic path are all paths of an "alternative vision." Just as the druids of old resisted the tyranny of the Roman Empire, so today's Celtic wisdomseekers need to resist forces that would destroy our environment, erode freedom and civil liberties, or diminish the quality of life under ever more stressful and materialistic conditions. This "resistance" can occur on many levels—it can be a personal matter of making choices to safeguard your individual life as a healer and wisdomkeeper, but it can also involve becoming active in social and political ways to benefit not only yourself, but your entire community (and indeed, the entire earth).

Whatever social and political choices you make I will leave to the dictates of your own conscience. But whether you are conservative or liberal, Christian or pagan, religious or secular, you will find that the path of Celtic wisdom is a social path. In other words, it's not some private little hobby where you can feel cozy with your spirit guides. Sure, Celtic spirituality will be meaningful and joyful on a strictly private level. But much of the meaning and joy will come from how you relate to others out of a deeply lived, deeply felt spirituality. In that you will find true happiness—and transformational wisdom.

Geasa

When considering the social dimension of Celtic wisdom, beware of these two traps. First, don't ignore it. Celtic spirituality isn't a path of apathy. But just as important, don't assume that Celtic spirituality is consistent with only one political view. Just as there are many ways to express Celtic spirituality, so are there different ways to apply Celtic wisdom to politics and society.

In Summary ...

You may have looked at the preceding nine steps for living the Celtic life and thought, "Eek! It's a lot of work!" Well, yes, that's true. The path of Celtic wisdom requires commitment, study, and effort. Remember that one of the sources of wisdom is knowledge, and that one of the characteristics of the ancient bards and druids is that they studied for up to 20 years before they were considered masters of their craft.

Follow your heart and your interests when studying the Celtic path. Perhaps you enjoy languages, and find the thought of learning Cornish or Manx fascinating. Or perhaps you're drawn to shamanism, and want to develop your skills of intuition, inner journeying, and work with spirit guides and power animals. Or maybe you're like a classical druid, wanting your spiritual knowledge to be grounded in the "real world" of science, psychology, and current events. There is no single right way to be a seeker of wisdom or a keeper of knowledge. What is important is that you take the time to know for yourself where your interests lie, and you pursue them.

By Yourself or with Others: Living the Life of a Wisdomkeeper

An important question you'll want to explore as part of your life as a Celtic wisdom-keeper is whether to express your spirituality in a solitary manner or through a connection with other spiritual seekers. The Celtic tradition doesn't mandate that you go it alone, or that you join any kind of group or church or circle. As a Celtic seeker, you get to decide what format your spiritual practice will take.

The Path of the Lone Wisdomkeeper

In today's world, people sometimes perceive a difference between religion and spirituality in this way: Religion is something that happens with other people, as in a church, synagogue, or mosque; whereas spirituality is a very personal, private, and solitary matter, just between the individual soul and the spirit world.

As in so many other ways, in the Celtic world distinctions like this get a little blurry. Many Celtic Christian monks lived as hermits—both highly religious *and* completely solitary. And all forms of Celtic religion, from druidism to Christianity to Wicca, have a powerful element of personal spiritual experience. So in terms of Celtic spirituality, it's not useful to talk about religion versus spirituality, but rather to see all forms of Celtic wisdom as embodying both religious and spiritual qualities, with some branches of the tradition being more naturally group oriented and others being more naturally solitary oriented.

Here, then, are a few examples of how the Celtic tradition can fit within a solitary path:

- **The shaman.** Traditionally, shamans worked alone or with one or two students/assistants. They found community not in other shamans, but in their spiritual guides and allies.

- **The witch.** In modern Wicca, witches convene in religious organizations known as covens, circles, or groves. But the traditional witch is actually much closer in practice to a shaman: a self-employed spiritual entrepreneur, who might offer her or his skills to others for healing, but who is self-reliant in terms of dealing with the spirit world.

- **The hermit.** Among ancient Celtic Christians, one model for spiritual holiness was the life of the hermit who lived alone (or with just a few animal companions) in his or her quest for union with God.

- **The grailseeker.** Dedicated entirely to the quest for the grail (spiritual attainment), the grailseeker relies not on other people, but only on the urgency of the prize, for inspiration.

Pros and Cons of Solitary Spirituality

We live in an individualistic society, and therefore an individualistic spirituality kind of fits in with our mainstream culture. Not having to deal with the problems associated with group dynamics or others' expectations can be liberating when focusing on personal spiritual growth. But on the downside, a lone ranger approach to spirituality can be difficult to sustain, or can leave you feeling unfulfilled. The human heart, after all, was made to relate with other people. Finally, solo spirituality means you have only your own resources to count on: No one will ever disappoint you (but yourself), and no one will ever lend you a helping hand (but yourself).

The main thing you need as a solo practitioner of Celtic wisdom is your own will to proceed. You'll still need the disciplined mind of a druid, so study is important. (See Appendix A for a list of books to get you started.) Some sort of access to nature is important, as is a regular block of time set aside for study, meditation, and personal ritual. With these essentials, you have what it takes to pursue the path!

> **The Seer Says**
>
> Unless you live as a hermit in a remote wilderness, you are never fully alone in terms of wisdom and spirituality. Even if you are the only person you know with an interest in Celtic matters, keep in mind that every person with whom you interact is a potential teacher, companion, or student in the spiritual lessons of life!

Celtic Spirituality in a Group Setting

If you're thinking, "Well I'm not *sure* that I have the discipline, or the commitment, or the rugged self-reliance necessary to walk the path of the spiritual hermit or shaman," then you might best serve your interest in the Celtic world in a group setting. This isn't always easy to do, as relatively few groups specifically devoted to Celtic wisdom are available. Your primary choices include joining a druid group, a Wiccan or other pagan group with a Celtic focus, or finding a Christian church with others interested in the Celtic path.

Druidism

Modern druidism is the most explicitly "Celtic" of spiritual paths available. Fortunately, many druid groups are very liberal and accept members even when they practice another religion, so you don't have to renounce anything to become a druid. In Appendix B you'll find listings of websites for several prominent druid groups, including OBOD, ADF, and the Tuatha de Brighid. While some druid groups conduct their affairs mainly online, others have a variety of groves and study groups, one of which may be near you; if not, most druid groups have guidelines for starting your own local chapter.

Christianity

Still the most widely practiced religion among the Celts, Christianity when combined with Celtic wisdom is especially lovely. Your best bet here is trying to find a priest or pastor with an interest in Celtic matters; he or she might even be willing to lead a Celtic spirituality prayer/study group. The Roman Catholic, Presbyterian, Methodist, and Anglican churches are all prominent in Celtic lands; these churches are often the ones most likely to include clergy or members with an interest in Celtic matters.

There are also a few very small Christian denominations that are specifically "Celtic" churches. Such groups can be found online and may have congregations in your city. Christian sects are a mixed bag; while small religious groups can be intimate and friendly, they may also reflect an extreme political or theological viewpoint. Make sure you are comfortable with their perspective before signing on.

Paganism

There are so many different options for Celtic spirituality in the world of Wicca and neopaganism that an entire book could be written on this subject alone! Many pagan groups are wonderful, supportive environments for personal growth; others can be like any dysfunctional family, filled with emotional drama, internal conflict, and one-upmanship. As with the small Christian groups, do your homework before joining a group and make sure it feels comfortable to you.

If you live in a remote area, or even a small to medium-size city without a large Celtic community, you may not have many options for participating in a Celtic spiritual organization of any religious persuasion. If that's the case, you may find online resources such as bulletin boards, newsgroups, and e-mail lists to be particularly supportive of your journey. Literally thousands of websites exist on every imaginable perspective of the Celtic tradition, and many of these sites are linked to interactive resources where you can "meet" and converse with others whose interests are similar to yours.

Pros and Cons of Communal Spirituality

The advantages and liabilities of connecting with other people to express your quest for wisdom are basically the inverse of the pros and cons connected with solitary spirituality. You'll benefit from making friends and finding emotional and intellectual support from others as you pursue your path. On the downside, a group (and all its members) will have expectations of you that you may not always want to meet. It's important to make sure that any group you participate in or join truly reflects your personality and approach to the Celtic tradition.

Honoring the Path of Wisdom: Celtic Ethics

Whether you walk the Celtic path as a solitary course of personal study, or through becoming active in a druid group or some other communal expression of Celtic wisdom, you'll want to put enough energy into your quest that it truly makes a difference in your life. But what does that look like?

Celtic wisdom invites you to live according to certain ethical principles that can enable you to find happiness and a sense of fulfillment. It's important to remember that Celtic ethics are not ploys to please an angry God (or Goddess), but rather are time-tested principles that should be adhered to simply because they make life flow more smoothly and joyously.

> **CAUTION**
>
> **Geasa**
>
> Cultural stereotypes equate holiness and humility with self-effacing behavior. That's not the Celtic way. Celtic spirituality avoids the extremes of both excessive pride *and* excessive self-negation. In Celtic terms, true humility involves a balanced sense of self.

Here are a few ethical principles that you'll encounter again and again in the myth, lore, and contemporary landscape of the Celts. You'll see how each of these, when properly embraced, can foster happiness, healing, and a better life.

- **Holiness (rather than arrogance).** Although primarily expressed in Christian terms, this value is one that all Celts can embrace. It's the path of finding personal value through connection with the spirit, rather than through self-aggrandizement or egotism. Holiness is related to humility, a splendid word that comes from a root meaning "earth." A holy person is an earthy person.

- **Hospitality (rather than hostility).** The Celts always have been (and still are) masters at the art of hospitality, which includes welcoming the stranger and being available to those who are in need. Hospitality is more important to the Celtic world than purity, in which persons are so concerned with protecting themselves that they never reach out to others.

- **Honor (rather than oath-breaking).** The warriors who appear throughout Celtic legend were men and women of honor. The lived by their word, and they took pride in their personal integrity. A person of honor would never cheat or deceive others, or even "cut corners" in his or her personal conduct, not only because they consider such behavior wrong, but because they believe they (and all their relations) would be shamed by such behavior, whether discovered or not. Our modern world is so focused on cutting costs (corners) and taking the easy way out that for most of us, learning the path of honor would be difficult indeed—but as seekers of Celtic wisdom, it is truly the only path worth taking.

◆ **Heroism (rather than spinelessness).** Balancing the immaculate honor of the warrior is his or her valiant courage. It is a core part of the Celtic identity to be people of valor. Heroism means that we make choices in life based on courage, hope, and faith, rather than fear, cowardly self-protection, or cynicism.

The Virtues of Brigid as a Template for Honor

In the town of Kildare, southwest of Dublin, a wonderful holy well dedicated to the saint/goddess Brigid has a row of five standing stones leading to the water source. These stones, according to local custom, symbolize five virtues associated with Brigid. I believe these virtues actually represent the heart of Celtic honor, and so I'd like to close this book with a celebration of these eternal values.

The five sacred stones at Brigid's Well in Kildare.

Protecting the Earth

The first stone symbolizes care for the natural world and living in balanced harmony with our environment. As a goddess and as a saint, Brigid stands for appropriate ways of interacting with the natural world. This means practical matters (like conservation, recycling, and reducing our levels of consumption) as well as spiritually relating to the earth as a gift from the Goddess.

Peacemaking

Brigid represents the energy of peace. This may seem a contradiction to the warrior energy that is found throughout Celtic myth, but not really. A true warrior is a defender of the peace. He or she fights only as a last resort. Brigid reminds us that, even when we must fight, to keep in mind what we are fighting for—that peace in which all beings may thrive.

Befriending the Poor

Many tales are told of how Brigid would take valuables from the wealthy and sell them to buy food for the poor—she mastered Robin Hood's calling centuries before he appeared in Sherwood Forest! Today's practitioner of Celtic honor does more than just repeat New Age mantras about prosperity and abundance: The path of Celtic wisdom means extending a helping hand to those who have less than we do, both in literal ways (such as the truly needy) and in social ways (such as those who are victims of discrimination or prejudice).

Sheltering the Stranger

The fourth stone is where the Celtic virtue of hospitality really kicks into action. It's one thing to extend a helping hand to others (the virtue of the third stone), but this virtue calls us to make our home a sanctuary where others can find peace, quiet, and love. This virtue doesn't mean that you should turn your home into a homeless shelter, but it does mean that your home ought to be a place where Celtic spirituality isn't just talked about, but lived. The Celtic path is one where the home becomes a place of renewal, not only for you but for others as well.

Meditation

Finally, the last stone at Brigid's Well stands for meditation. Again, this can mean contemplation, or prayer, or Zenlike silence, or deep shamanic trance. But on whatever level you understand it, meditation means a serious engagement with practical spirituality. Celtic wisdom isn't just something you think about or read about or talk about. It's something you do. And meditation represents the most basic foundation of all spiritual work.

Conclusion

Obviously, the values and ethics associated with Brigid, or with Celtic wisdom in general, are not mastered overnight—or even in a year or two. This is not a quick-fix program of feel-good spirituality, but rather a deep, profound, and beautiful path that will reward but also challenge you. Because you've read this far, you clearly have enough of an interest to accept that challenge and allow the poetry and magic of the Celtic path to truly transform your life.

May your journey be filled with blessings! In parting, here is a blessing based on the wisdom of the Ogham:

> By the initiation of the birch,
> the protection of the rowan,
> the foundation of the alder,
> the vision of the willow,
> the guidance of the ash,
> the restraint of the hawthorn,
> the strength of the oak,
> the justice of the holly,
> the wisdom of the hazel,
> the beauty of the apple,
> the truth of the vine,
> the perseverance of ivy,
> the harmony of the reed,
> the magic of the blackthorn,
> the healing of the elder,
> the height of the fir,
> the abundance of gorse,
> the passion of heather,
> the courage of the poplar,
> and the silence of the yew:
> May the trees of the forest of the faery realm take root within your heart, that you may grow in wisdom, joy, and love for all who live in the earth's embrace.

The Least You Need to Know

- The ultimate goal of Celtic wisdom is to help us live happier, healthier, more fulfilled lives, where all things are held in a sacred balance.

- Celtic wisdom can be effectively pursued alone or within a supportive group such as a grove of druids or Celtic Christian prayer group.

- Ethical values like holiness, hospitality, honor, and heroism are central to the life of Celtic wisdom.

- Protecting the earth, peacemaking, care for the poor, spirituality in the home, and meditation epitomize the heart of the Celtic path.

Appendix A

Bibliography

Adam, David. *The Cry of the Deer: Meditations on the Hymn of St. Patrick.* Harrisburg, PA: Morehouse Publishing, 1989.

Blake, William. *Poetry and Designs.* Edited by Mary Lynn Johnson and John E. Grant. New York: W.W. Norton & Company, 1979.

Blamires, Steve. *Celtic Tree Mysteries: Secrets of the Ogham.* St. Paul, MN: Llewellyn Publications, 1997.

Bord, Janet, and Colin Bord. *Earth Rites: Fertility Practices in Pre-Pre-Industrial Britain.* London: Granada Publishing, 1982.

Brake, Julia, and Christine Jones. *Teach Yourself Welsh.* Chicago: NTC Publishing Group, 2001.

Brennan, Éilis. *Heritage: A Visitor's Guide.* Dublin: The Office of Public Works, 1995.

Brenneman, Walter L. Jr., and Mary G. Brenneman. *Crossing the Circle at the Holy Wells of Ireland.* Charlottesville: University Press of Virginia, 1995.

Caesar, Julius (translated by S. A. Hanford). *The Conquest of Gaul.* London: Penguin Books, 1976.

Caldecott, Moyra. *Women in Celtic Myth: Tales of Extraordinary Women from the Ancient Celtic Tradition.* Rochester, VT: Destiny Books, 1992.

Carmichael, Alexander. *Carmina Gadelica: Hymns and Incantations Collected in the Highlands and Islands of Scotland in the Last Century.* Hudson, NY: Lindisfarne Press, 1992.

Carr-Gomm, Philip, ed. *The Druid Renaissance: The Voice of Druidry Today.* London: Thorsons, 1996.

Carr-Gomm, Philip. *The Druid Way*. Shaftesbury, Dorset: Element, 1993.

———. *Druidcraft: The Magic of Wicca and Druidry*. London: Thorsons, 2002.

———. *The Elements of the Druid Tradition*. Shaftesbury, Dorset: Element, 1991.

———. *In the Grove of the Druids: The Druid Teachings of Ross Nichols*. London: Watkins, 2002.

Carr-Gomm, Philip, and Stephanie Carr-Gomm. *The Druid Animal Oracle: Working with the Sacred Animals of the Druid Tradition*. New York: Simon & Schuster, 1994.

Chadwick, Nora. *The Celts: A Lucid and Fascinating History*. London: Penguin Books, 1971.

Cherici, Peter. *Celtic Sexuality: Power, Paradigms, and Passion*. Hampton, CT: Tyrone Press, 1994.

Clancy, Padraigín, ed. *Celtic Threads: Exploring the Wisdom of Our Heritage*. Dublin: Veritas Publications, 1999.

Clark, Katharine. *An Irish Book of Shadows: Tuatha De Danaan*. Lakeville, MN: Galde Press, 2001.

Clarke, David, with Andy Roberts. *Twilight of the Celtic Gods: An Exploration of Britain's Hidden Pagan Traditions*. London: Blandford, 1996.

Condren, Mary. *The Serpent and the Goddess: Women, Religion and Power in Celtic Ireland*. San Francisco: HarperSanFrancisco, 1989.

Cowan, Tom. *Fire in the Head: Shamanism and the Celtic Spirit*. San Francisco: HarperSanFrancisco, 1993.

Cunliffe, Barry. *The Ancient Celts*. Oxford: Oxford University Press, 1997.

———. *The Celtic World*. New York: McGraw-Hill, 1979.

Dames, Michael. *Mythic Ireland*. London: Thames & Hudson, 1992.

Davies, Oliver, and Fiona Bowie. *Celtic Christian Spirituality: An Anthology of Medieval and Modern Sources*. New York: Continuum Publishing Company, 1995.

Davidson, H. R. Ellis. *Myths and Symbols in Pagan Europe: Early Scandinavian and Celtic Religions*. Syracuse, NY: Syracuse University Press, 1988.

Davidson, Hilda Ellis, ed. *The Seer in Celtic and Other Traditions*. Edinburgh: John Donald Publishers, 1989.

Delaney, Frank. *Legends of the Celts*. New York: Sterling Publishing Co., Inc., 1992.

Dillon, Myles, and Nora Chadwick. *The Celtic Realms: The History and Culture of the Celtic Peoples from Pre-History to the Norman Invasion*. London: Phoenix Press, 2000.

Drabble, Margaret, ed. *The Oxford Companion to English Literature, Sixth Edition*. Oxford: Oxford University Press, 2000.

du Maurier, Daphne. *Vanishing Cornwall: The Spirit and History of Cornwall*. Harmondsworth, Middlesex: Penguin Books, 1972.

Dwelly, Edward, comp. *The Illustrated Gaelic-English Dictionary (Faclair Gaidhlig Gubeurla Le Dealbhan)*. Glasgow: Gairm Publications, 1977.

Dyer, James. *The Penguin Guide to Prehistoric England and Wales*. London: Penguin, 1981.

Eliade, Mircea. *Shamanism: Archaic Techniques of Ecstasy*. New York: Pantheon Books, 1951.

Ellis, Peter Berresford. *The Celtic Empire: The First Millennium of Celtic History 1000 B.C.–A.D. 51*. London: Constable and Company, 1990.

———. *Celtic Women: Women in Celtic Society and Literature*. London: Constable and Company, 1995.

———. *The Chronicles of the Celts: New Tellings of their Myths and Legends*. New York: Carroll & Graf Publishers, Inc., 1999.

———. *A Dictionary of Celtic Mythology*. London: Constable, 1992.

———. *A Dictionary of Irish Mythology*. London: Constable, 1987.

———. *The Druids*. London: Constable and Company, 1994.

Evans-Wentz, W. Y. *The Fairy Faith in Celtic Countries*. New York: Carol Publishing Group, 1994.

Farrar, Janet, and Stewart Farrar. *A Witches Bible: The Complete Witches' Handbook*. Custer, WA: Phoenix Publishing, 1984.

Fleming, Fergus, Shahrukh Husain, C. Scott Littleton, and Linda A. Malcor. *Heroes of the Dawn: Celtic Myth*. Amsterdam: Time Life Books, 1996.

Ford, Patrick K. *The Celtic Poets: Songs and Tales from Early Ireland and Wales*. Belmont, MA: Ford and Bailie, 1999.

Ford, Patrick K., ed. and trans. *The Mabinogi and Other Medieval Welsh Tales*. Berkeley: University of California Press, 1977.

Fortune, Dion. *Glastonbury: Avalon of the Heart*. York Beach, ME: Samuel Weiser, 2000.

French, Claire. *The Celtic Goddess: Great Queen or Demon Witch?* Edinburgh: Floris Books, 2001.

Fritz, Jean. *Brendan the Navigator: A History Mystery About the Discovery of America*. New York: Coward-McCann, 1979.

Galloway, Kathy, ed. *The Pattern of Our Days: Worship in the Celtic Tradition from the Iona Community*. Mahwah, NJ: Paulist Press, 1999.

Gantz, Jeffrey, trans. *Early Irish Myths and Sagas*. London: Penguin Books, 1981.

Glassie, Henry, ed. *Irish Folk Tales*. New York: Pantheon Books, 1985.

Graves, Robert. *The White Goddess: Amended and Enlarged Edition*. New York: Farrar, Straus and Giroux, 1966.

Green, Miranda J. *Animals in Celtic Life and Myth*. London: Routledge, 1992.

———. *Celtic Art: Symbols and Imagery*. New York: Sterling Publishing, 1997.

———. *Celtic Goddesses: Warriors, Virgins and Mothers*. New York: George Braziller, 1996.

———. *Dictionary of Celtic Myth and Legend*. London: Thames and Hudson, 1992.

———. *The Gods of the Celts*. Phoenix Mill, Stroud, Gloucestershire: Sutton Publishing, 1986.

———. *Symbol and Image in Celtic Religious Art.* London: Routledge, 1989.

———. *The World of the Druids.* London: Thames and Hudson, 1997.

Green, Miranda J., ed. *The Celtic World.* London and New York: Routledge, 1995.

Gregory, Lady. *The Blessed Trinity of Ireland.* Gerrards Cross, Buckinghamshire: Colin Smythe Limited, 1985.

———. *Irish Myths and Legends.* London: Running Press, 1998.

———. *Visions and Beliefs in the West of Ireland.* Gerrards Cross, Buckinghamshire: Colin Smythe, 1970.

Guest, Lady Charlotte, trans. *The Mabinogion.* Mineoloa, NY: Dover Publications, 1997.

Hale, Amy, and Philip Payton, eds. *New Directions in Celtic Studies.* Exeter: University of Exeter Press, 2000.

Harbison, Peter. *Pre-Christian Ireland: From the First Settlers to the Early Celts.* London: Thames and Hudson, 1988.

Hardman, Charlotte, and Graham Harvey. *Paganism Today: Wiccans, Druid, the Goddess, and Ancient Earth Traditions for the Twenty-First Century.* San Francisco: HarperSanFrancisco, 1996.

Harner, Michael. *The Way of the Shaman: A Guide to Power and Healing.* New York: Bantam Books, 1982.

Harris, Mike. *Awen: The Quest of the Celtic Mysteries.* Oceanside, CA: Sunchalice Books, 1999.

Haywood, John. *Atlas of the Celtic World.* London: Thames & Hudson, Ltd., 2001.

Hinds, Kathryn. *The Celts of Northern Europe.* New York: Marshall Cavendish, 1997.

Hope, Murry. *The Ancient Wisdom of the Celts.* London: Thorsons, 1999.

Hopman, Ellen Evert. *A Druid's Herbal for the Sacred Earth Year.* Rochester, VT: Inner Traditions, 1994.

Hutton, Ronald. *The Pagan Religions of the Ancient British Isles: Their Nature and Legacy.* Oxford: Blackwell, 1993.

———. *The Stations of the Sun: A History of the Ritual Year in Britain.* Oxford: Oxford University Press, 1996.

———. *The Triumph of the Moon: A History of Modern Pagan Witchcraft.* Oxford: Oxford University Press, 1999.

Iona Community. *The Iona Community Worship Book.* Glasgow: Wild Goose Publications, 1988.

Jackson, Kenneth Hurlstone, trans. *A Celtic Miscellany: Translations from the Celtic Literatures.* London: Penguin Books, 1971.

James, Simon. *The World of the Celts.* London: Thames and Hudson, 1993.

Jones, Leslie Ellen. *Druid Shaman Priest: Metaphors of Celtic Paganism.* Enfield Lock, Middlesex: Hisarlik Press, 1998.

Joyce, James. *Finnegans Wake.* New York: The Viking Press, 1939.

———. *Ulysses.* London: The Bodley Head, 1992.

Keightley, Thomas. *The Fairy Mythology, Illustrative of the Romance and Superstition of Various Counties.* London: Bell & Daldy, 1873.

Kindred, Glennie. *The Tree Ogham.* Derbyshire, England: Apple Tree Cottage, 1997.

King, John. *The Celtic Druids' Year: Seasonal Cycles of the Ancient Celts.* London: Blandford, 1994.

Kinsella, Thomas, trans. *The Tain.* Philadelphia: University of Pennsylvania Press, 1985.

Knight, Gareth. *Merlin and the Grail Tradition.* Oceanside, CA: Sunchalice Books, 1999.

———. *The Secret Tradition in Arthurian Legend.* York Beach, ME: Samuel Weiser, 1983.

Kondratiev, Alexei. *The Apple Branch: A Path to Celtic Ritual.* Cork: The Collins Press, 1998.

Laurie, Erynn Rowan. *A Circle of Stones: Journeys & Meditations for Modern Celts.* Chicago: Eschaton Productions, 1995.

Lavin, Patrick. *The Celtic World: An Illustrated History 700 B.C. to the Present.* New York: Hippocrene Books, 1999.

Leech, Kenneth. *Soul Friend: Spiritual Direction in the Modern World.* Harrisburg, PA: Morehouse Publishing, 2001.

Leslie, Clare Walker, and Frank E. Gerace. *The Ancient Celtic Festivals and How We Celebrate Them Today.* Rochester, VT: Inner Traditions, 2000.

Litton, Helen. *The Celts: An Illustrated History.* Dublin: Wolfhound Press, 1997.

Llywellyn, Morgan. *Bard: The Odyssey of the Irish.* Boston: Houghton Mifflin Company, 1984.

———. *Druids: A Novel.* New York: William Morrow and Company, 1991.

———. *The Horse Goddess.* Boston: Houghton Mifflin Company, 1982.

———. *Red Branch.* New York: William Morrow and Company, 1989.

Logan, Patrick. *The Holy Wells of Ireland.* Buckinghamshire: Colin Smythe Limited, 1980.

———. *The Old Gods: The Facts About Irish Fairies.* Belfast: Appletree Press, 1981.

MacCana, Proinsias. *Celtic Mythology.* New York: Peter Bedrick Books, 1983.

MacEowen, Frank. *The Mist-Filled Path: Celtic Wisdom for Exiles, Wanderers, and Seekers.* Novato, CA: New World Library, 2002.

Mackey, James P., ed. *An Introduction to Celtic Christianity.* Edinburgh: T&T Clark, 1989.

MacKillop, James. *Dictionary of Celtic Mythology.* Oxford: Oxford University Press, 1998.

MacLennan, Malcolm. *Gaelic Dictionary: Gaelic-English, English-Gaelic.* Stornoway, Isle of Lewis, Scotland: Acair, 1979.

MacManus, Dermot. *The Middle Kingdom: The Faerie World of Ireland.* Gerrards Cross, Buckinghamshire: Colin Smythe, 1973.

MacNeill, Máire. *The Festival of Lughnasa: A Study of the Survival of the Celtic Festival of the Beginning of Harvest*. Oxford: Oxford University Press, 1962.

Maier, Bernhard, and Cyril Edwards, trans. and cont. *Dictionary of Celtic Myth and Culture*. Suffolk: Boydell & Brewer, 1997.

Markale, Jean. *The Celts: Uncovering the Mythic and Historic Origins of Western Culture*. Rochester, VT: Inner Traditions International, 1993.

———. *The Druids: Celtic Priests of Nature*. Rochester, VT: Inner Traditions International, 1999.

———. *Women of the Celts*. Rochester, VT: Inner Traditions International, 1986.

Matarasso, P. M., trans. *The Quest of the Holy Grail*. Harmondsworth, Middlesex: Penguin Books, 1969.

Matthews, Caitlín. *Arthur and the Sovereignty of Britain: King and Goddess in the Mabinogion*. London and New York: Arkana, 1989.

———. *The Celtic Book of the Dead*. New York: St. Martin's Press, 1992.

———. *Celtic Devotional*. New York: Harmony Books, 1996.

———. *The Elements of the Celtic Tradition*. Boston: Element Books, 1989.

———. *Mabon and the Mysteries of Britain: An Exploration of the Mabinogion*. London and New York: Arkana, 1987.

Matthews, Caitlín, and John Matthews. *The Encyclopedia of Celtic Wisdom: The Celtic Shaman's Sourcebook*. Rockport, Massachusetts: Element, 1994.

Matthews, John. *Taliesin: The Last Celtic Shaman*. Rochester, Vermont: Inner Traditions, 2002.

———. *The Celtic Shaman: A Handbook*. Shaftesbury, Dorset: Element Books, 1991.

———. *The Elements of the Grail Tradition*. Rockport, MA: Element, 1990.

———. *Healing the Wounded King: Soul Work and the Quest for the Grail*. Rockport, MA: Element, 1997.

———. *King Arthur and the Grail Quest: Myth and Vision from Celtic Times to the Present*. London: Blandford, 1994.

———. *The Song of Taliesin: Tales from King Arthur's Bard*. Wheaton, IL: Quest Publishing, 2001.

———. *Tales of the Celtic Otherworld*. London: Blandford, 1998.

Matthews, John, ed. *The Bardic Source Book*. London: Blandford, 1998.

———. *The Celtic Seers' Sourcebook: Vision and Magic in the Druid Tradition*. London: Blandford, 1999.

———. *The Druid Source Book*. London: Blandford, 1996.

———. *Sources of the Grail*. Hudson, NY: Lindisfarne Press, 1996.

Matthews, John, and Marian Green. *The Grail Seeker's Companion*. Wellingborough, Northamptonshire: The Aquarian Press, 1986.

McAnally, D. R. Jr. *Irish Wonders: The Ghosts, Giants, Pookas, Demons, Leprechawns, Banshees, Fairies, Witches, Widows, Old Maids, and Other Marvels of the Emerald Isle.* New York: Weathervane Books, 1888.

McColman, Carl. *The Complete Idiot's Guide to Paganism.* Indianapolis: Alpha Books, 2002.

McMahon, Joanne, and Jack Roberts. *The Sheela-Na-Gigs of Ireland and Britain: The Divine Hag of the Christian Celts: An Illustrated Guide.* Cork, Ireland: Mercier Press, 2000.

McNeill, F. Marion. *The Silver Bough, Volume One: Scottish Folklore and Folk-Belief.* Glasgow: William Maclellan, 1957.

————. *The Silver Bough, Volume Two: A Calendar of Scottish National Festivals: Candlemas to Harvest Home.* Glasgow: William Maclellan, 1959.

————. *The Silver Bough, Volume Three: A Calendar of Scottish National Festivals: Hallowe'en to Yule.* Glasgow: William Maclellan, 1961.

————. *The Silver Bough, Volume Four: The Local Festivals of Scotland.* Glasgow: William Maclellan, 1968.

Merrifield, Ralph. *The Archaeology of Ritual and Magic.* London: Guild Publishing, 1987.

Miller, Joyce. *Myth and Magic: Scotland's Ancient Beliefs and Sacred Places.* Musselburgh, Scotland: Goblinshead, 2000.

Minehan, Rita, CSB. *Rekindling the Flame: A Pilgrimage in the Footsteps of Brigid of Kildare.* Kildare, Ireland: Solas Bhríde Community, 1999.

Monaghan, Patricia. *The Red-Haired Girl from the Bog: The Landscape of Celtic Myth and Spirit.* Novato, CA: New World Library, 2003.

Monaghan, Patricia, ed. *Irish Spirit: Pagan, Celtic, Christian, Global.* Dublin: Wolfhound Press, 2001.

Murray, Liz, and Colin Murray. *The Celtic Tree Oracle: A System of Divination.* New York: St. Martin's Press, 1988.

Nichols, Ross. *The Book of Druidry: History, Sites and Wisdom.* London: Thorsons, 1990.

Ó Catháin, Séamas. *The Festival of Brigit: Celtic Goddess and Holy Woman.* Dublin: DBA Publications, 1995.

O'Donoghue, Noel Dermot. *Heaven in Ordinarie: Some Radical Considerations.* Springfield, IL: Templegate, 1979.

————. *Mountain Behind the Mountain: Aspects of the Celtic Tradition.* Edinburgh: T & T Clark, 1996.

O'Donohue, John. *Anam Cara: A Book of Celtic Wisdom.* New York: HarperCollins, 1997.

Ó Duinn, Seán, OSB. *Where Three Streams Meet: Celtic Spirituality.* Dublin: The Columba Press, 2000.

Ó hÓgáin, Dáithí. *Myth, Legend and Romance: An Encyclopedia of the Irish Folk Tradition*. New York: Prentice Hall Press, 1991.

———.*The Sacred Isle: Belief and Religion in Pre-Christian Ireland*. Woodbridge, Suffolk: Boydell Press, 1999.

Ó Maoildhia, Dara. *Legends in the Landscape: Pocket Guide to Árainn: Inis Mór, Aran Islands*. Árainn, Co. na Gaillimhe: Aisling Árann, 1998.

Orr, Emma Restall. *Principles of Druidry*. London: Thorsons, 1998.

———. *Ritual: A Guide to Life, Love and Inspiration*. London: Thorsons, 2000.

———. *Spirits of the Sacred Grove: The World of a Druid Priestess*. London: Thorsons, 1998.

O'Se, Diarmuid, and Joseph Sheils. *Teach Yourself Irish*. Chicago: NTC Publishing Group, 2002.

Ó Siadhail, Mícheál. *Learning Irish: An Introductory Self-Tutor*. Dublin: Dublin Institute for Advanced Studies, 1980.

O'Sullivan, Sean, ed. and trans. *Folktales of Ireland*. Chicago: University of Chicago Press, 1966.

Owen, Trefor M. *A Pocket Guide: The Customs and Traditions of Wales*. Cardiff: University of Wales Press, 1991.

Perera, Sylvia Brinton. *Queen Maeve and Her Lovers: A Celtic Archetype of Ecstasy, Addiction and Healing*. New York: Carrowmore Books, 1999.

Piggot, Stuart. *The Druids*. New York: Thames and Hudson, 1975.

Pollard, Mary E. *In Search of St. Brigid, Foundress of Kildare*. Kildare, Ireland: St. Brigid's Cathedral, 1988.

Rackard, Anna, and Liam O'Callaghan. *Fishstonewater: Holy Wells of Ireland*. Cork, Ireland: Atrium, 2001.

Raeburn, Jane. *Celtic Wicca: Ancient Wisdom for the 21st Century*. New York: Citadel Press, 2001.

Raftery, Barry. *Pagan Celtic Ireland: The Enigma of the Iron Age*. London: Thames and Hudson, 1994.

Rees, Alwyn, and Brinley Rees. *Celtic Heritage: Ancient Tradition in Ireland and Wales*. New York: Grove Press, Inc., 1961.

Richards, Monica. *The Book of Annwyn*. Hollywood, CA: Neue Äesthetik Multimedia, 1998.

Robertson, Boyd, and Iain Taylor. *Teach Yourself Gaelic*. Chicago: NTC Publishing Group, 1993.

Rolleston, T. W. *Celtic Myths and Legends*. New York: Dover Publications, 1990.

Ross, Anne. *Everyday Life of the Pagan Celts*. London: B. T. Batsford, Ltd., 1970.

———. *Folklore of the Scottish Highlands*. Totowa, NJ: Rowman and Littlefield, 1976.

———. *Pagan Celtic Britain*. London: Routledge & Kegan Paul, 1967.

Ross, Anne, and Don Robins. *The Life and Death of a Druid Prince: The Story of Lindow Man, an Archaeological Sensation*. New York: Summit Books, 1989.

Rutherford, Ward. *Celtic Mythology: The Nature and Influence of Celtic Myth—from Druidism to Arthurian Legend*. London: Thorsons, 1995.

Sellner, Edward. *The Celtic Soul Friend: A Trusted Guide for Today*. Notre Dame, IN: Ave Maria Press, 2002.

Shadwynn. *The Crafted Cup: Ritual Mysteries of the Goddess and the Grail*. St. Paul, MN: Llewellyn Publications, 1994.

Shallcross, Philip. *Druidry*. London: Piatkus Books, 2000.

Sharkey, John. *Celtic Mysteries: The Ancient Religion*. New York: Crossroad, 1975.

Sheldrake, Philip. *Living Between Worlds: Place and Journey in Celtic Spirituality*. Cambridge, MA: Cowley Publications.

Sjoestedt, Marie-Louise. *Celtic Gods and Heroes*. Mineola, NY: Dover Publications, 2000.

Snyder, Christopher. *The World of King Arthur*. London: Thames and Hudson, 2000.

Squire, Charles. *Celtic Myth and Legend*. Franklin Lakes, NJ: New Page Books, 2001.

Stephens, James. *The Crock of Gold*. New York: The Macmillan Company, 1912.

Stewart, R. J. *Celtic Gods, Celtic Goddesses*. London: Blandford, 1990.

———. *Celtic Myths, Celtic Legends*. London: Blandford, 1994.

———. *Earth Light: The Ancient Path to Transformation, Rediscovering the Wisdom of Celtic and Faery Lore*. Lake Toxaway, NC: Mercury Publishing, 1998.

———. *The Living World of Faery*. Glastonbury, Somerset: Gothic Image Publications, 1995.

———. *Power Within the Land: The Roots of Celtic and Underworld Traditions Awakening the Sleepers and Regenerating the Earth*. Lake Toxaway, NC: Mercury Publishing, 1998.

———. *The Underworld Initiation: The Authentic Core of the Western Mysteries Revealed Through Oral Traditions, Celtic Myth and Legend*. Lake Toxaway, NC: Mercury Publishing, 1998.

Stewart, R. J., ed. *The Book of Merlin: Insights from the Merlin Conference*. London: Blandford, 1987.

Stewart, R. J., and Robin Williamson. *Celtic Bards, Celtic Druids*. London: Blandford, 1996.

Sutherland, Elizabeth. *Ravens and Black Rain: The Story of Highland Second Sight*. London: Constable and Company, 1985.

Thomas, Charles. *Celtic Britain*. London: Thames and Hudson, 1986.

Thomas, Dylan. *Collected Poems, Revised Edition*. New York: New Directions, 1956.

Thorsson, Edred. *The Book of Ogham: The Celtic Tree Oracle*. St. Paul, MN: Llewellyn Publications, 1992.

Tolstoy, Nikolai. *The Quest for Merlin*. Boston: Little, Brown and Company, 1985.

Van de Weyer, Robert, ed. *Celtic Fire: The Passionate Religious Vision of Ancient Britain and Ireland*. New York: Doubleday, 1990.

Verniero, Joan C. *One Hundred and One Read-Aloud Celtic Myths and Legends.* New York: Black Dog and Leventhal, 2000.

Walton, Evangeline. *The Mabinogion Tetralogy: The Prince of Annwn; The Children of Llyr; The Song of Rhiannon; The Island of the Mighty.* Woodstock, NY: The Overlook Press, 2002.

Webster, Graham. *The British Celts and Their Gods Under Rome.* London: B.T. Batsford Ltd., 1986.

Wilson, Barbara Ker. *Scottish Folk-Tales and Legends.* Oxford: Oxford University Press, 1954.

Wooding, Jonathan M., ed. *The Otherworld Voyage in Early Irish Literature: An Anthology of Criticism.* Dublin, Four Courts Press, 2000.

Yeats, William Butler. *Mythologies.* New York: Macmillan, 1959.

———. *The Poems.* Revised. edited by Richard J. Finneran. (*The Collected Works of W. B. Yeats, Vol. 1.*) New York: Macmillan, 1989.

Young, Ella. *Celtic Wonder Tales and Other Stories.* Edinburgh: Floris Books, 1988.

Zaczek, Iain. *Chronicles of the Celts.* New York: Sterling Publishing Company, 1997.

Appendix B

Online Resources

From the many cybercafés in Dublin where you can get online for two euros an hour, to the public libraries across America where Internet access is free for the asking, it's getting easier every day to access the world's largest computer network. Celtic wisdomseekers of all religious stripes and spiritual persuasions have found their way online, meaning that seemingly endless resources are available for you, only a mouse click away. The following pages list enough websites to get you started.

In developing this list, I've given preference to sites managed by established organizations with their own URL, so that hopefully this list will still be useful three weeks (or even two years) after publication. *Hint:* If a site you're interested in doesn't appear when you use the URL I've provided, go to a web search engine (like www.google.com) and search for the name of the website. Often websites migrate to new URLs, and can be accessed via the search engine. And if all else fails, conducting a search for keywords like "druid" and "Celtic shaman" is likely to turn up some interesting sites for you to visit.

Please note: Given the diversity of the Celtic world, the websites listed here represent a variety of political, philosophical, cultural, and religious perspectives. As a wisdomseeker, you need to research any group or community carefully to ensure that the group's values are compatible with your own.

Ár nDraííocht Féin: A Druid Fellowship
www.adf.org

The largest neopagan druid organization in the United States; it has more than 40 active groves in the United States and Canada. ADF emphasizes a pan-Indo-European approach to neopaganism, so it incorporates not only druidism but other pagan cultures, such as Norse or Hellenic traditions. The website includes a wealth of information on ritual, study, and the philosophy of neopagan druidism.

Brigit's Forge

www.brigitsforge.co.uk

Hilaire Wood's personal website, with information about Brigit the goddess, Brigit the saint, and various poems and meditations for exploring the spirituality of this key Celtic figure.

Carl McColman

www.carlmccolman.com

Home page for the author of this book. The site includes several essays of interest to Celtic wisdomseekers.

Celtic Studies Resources from an Opinionated Digital Medievalist

www.digitalmedievalist.com

The home page of Lisa L. Spangenberg, Celtic scholar and self-described "digital medievalist;" it includes a number of interesting and intelligent articles on Celtic culture and history.

Chalice Center for Celtic Spirituality

www.celticspirit.org

The home page of Mara Freeman, author of *Kindling the Celtic Spirit*. The website includes articles and rituals, along with information on Freeman's tours of Celtic lands and her anamchara practice.

Clannada

www.clannada.org

Clannada was a Celtic reconstructionist community based in Chattanooga, Tennessee, but by 2002 the organization was inactive. However, its website remains online, with a wealth of intelligent information on Celtic history, art, philosophy, culture, and spirituality.

Dalriada Celtic Heritage Trust

www.dalriada.co.uk

A website dedicated to the preservation of Celtic culture. In its own words, "This site is dedicated to the preservation of the Celtic Cultures within the British Isles, focusing mainly on Alba and Erin. On this site you can find articles on History, Mythology, Folklore, Culture, Customs, Poetry, Traditional Crafts, Celtic Languages and much more."

Draoidana: The Home Page of Frank MacEowen

www.celticwisdom.org

Author of *The Mist-Filled Path*, MacEowen is a shamanic practitioner and Celtic wisdomkeeper who leads workshops and retreats based on the Celtic tradition. His work is particularly oriented toward honoring the ancestors.

Hallowquest: John and Caitlín Matthews's Home Page

www.hallowquest.org.uk

Information, news, and workshop schedules for two of the most popular and prolific of Celtic wisdom writers.

Henge of Keltria
www.keltria.org

The Henge of Keltria is a neopagan druid organization that split off from ADF in the early years of that organization's existence. Keltria has several active groves in different regions of the United States. The website includes a variety of articles and essays.

Gaeltalk.net: Gaeltacht-Based Online Irish Course
www.gaeltalk.net

Exciting new multimedia online Irish language course featuring audio dialogues, sound pattern sentences, multimedia demonstrations, and easy-to-follow lesson plans.

National Eisteddfod of Wales
www.eisteddfod.org.uk

The National Eisteddfod is the largest and oldest celebration of Welsh culture. Held each year in a different location in Wales, the Eisteddfod provides poets, musicians, and other artists opportunities to compete for recognition for prizes and recognition.

Order of Bards, Ovates, and Druids
www.druidry.org

Large and useful website managed by one of the world's largest and oldest druid organizations. OBOD has groves and seed groups in both North America and Europe, but the primary resource the organization offers is a comprehensive, three-year self-study correspondence course in druidism. The website includes ordering information for the course, along with information on OBOD's many activities.

Tuatha de Brighid
www.tuathadebrighid.org

This relatively small Druid organization is remarkable for its intentional commitment to serve inclusively Christian and pagan druids (as well as druids of any other religious stripe). Like the ADF website, this site features a lovely anthology of poetry, articles, and sample rituals. If you're interested in getting to know the TdB folks, the site includes information on how to subscribe to the community's e-mail lists.

British Druid Order
www.druidorder.demon.co.uk

Home page of a relatively young (founded in 1979) British druid group under the leadership of authors Emma Restall Orr and Philip Shallcrass. Although explicitly pagan, the BDO advocates interfaith cooperation and promotes a vision of druidry that is inclusive of both Irish and British sources.

Ellen Payne Odom Genealogy Library
www.electricscotland.com/familytree

One of the largest resources for Scottish genealogy, the Odom Library is located in Moultrie, Georgia, USA, and contains archival and genealogical information for approximately 120 Scottish clans.

Geo Cameron

www.celticshamanism.com

Cameron is a contemporary shamanic practitioner based in Scotland. Her website includes information on the wisdom tradition as she understands it.

Guide to the Druids and Celtic Spirituality

www.wildideas.net/cathbad/druid.html

An intelligent, thoughtful, and literate collection of essays, articles, and opinions by a young Canadian philosopher-druid, Brendan Cathbad Myers. Excellent resource for anyone interested in the political and philosophical (in contrast to the magical or mystical) dimensions of contemporary druidism.

Imbas

www.imbas.org

Imbas describes itself as "an organization that promotes the spiritual path of Senistrognata (pronounced *SEN-iss-trog-NAH-tah*), the ancestral customs of the Celtic peoples. It is a path open to Pagans, Christians, and Agnostics alike." As of late 2002 the organization appeared to be inactive, but its website remained available, with numerous links to articles and essays on the Celtic tradition.

Isaac Bonewits's Home Page

www.neopagan.net

One of the best Celtic/druidic sites on the web. Bonewits is the founder of ADF and brings a high level of scholarly excellence to his work. The website not only explores the many permutations of druidism, but also includes plenty of information on Wicca and general neopaganism.

Order of Whiteoak

technovate.org/web/whiteoak

According to the website, Whiteoak is "a loose collection of Celtic Reconstructionists, philosophers, and students of Druidry who are concerned with the matter of ethics in the Druidical community." Followers of any druid path are welcome to participate in their ongoing conversation about ethics in the druid world.

Reformed Druids of North America

www.geocities.com/mikerdna/index.html

Founded in 1963, the Reformed Druids of North America began as little more than a joke—the organization was created to protest a chapel requirement at a private college in Minnesota. Students could only get an exemption from having to attend chapel if they were members of an alternative religion. Thus, a number of creative students founded a "druid grove" mainly as an excuse to get out of chapel and spend some time in nature. The following year the college dropped its chapel requirement, but interest in the druid organization continued. The RDNA website includes information on the order along with links to other druid sites.

Riverdrum: Tom Cowan's Website

www.riverdrum.com

According to the website, "Tom Cowan is a shamanic practitioner specializing in Celtic vision-ary and healing techniques. He combines universal core shamanism with traditional European spirit lore to create spiritual practices that can heal and enrich one's own life and the lives of others." The website gives you information about his workshop and retreat schedule.

Society of Celtic Shamans

www.faeryshaman.org

This organization provides a series of correspondence courses designed to train those inter-ested in pursuing shamanic spirituality within a Celtic framework.

Scottish Gaelic Learners' Materials Online

www.smo.uhi.ac.uk/gaidhlig/ionnsachadh/

Website with many links to online resources for learning Scots Gaelic. Includes online lessons, dictionaries, useful expressions, and links to purchase study materials.

When Is a Celt Not a Celt?

www.cyberwitch.com/wychwood/Library/whenIsACeltNotACelt.htm

Joanna Hautin-Mayer's article reprinted on this website should be required reading for anyone interested in Celtic wisdom, especially from a Wiccan or neopagan perspective. The article explores how some contemporary authors rely too heavily on poor scholarship or misinforma-tion when presenting their "Celtic" teachings. The article also recommends several books and authors who provide careful scholarship in their presentation of Celtic material.

Why Wicca Is Not Celtic

sophiagroup.org/clanwicca.html

This influential article by Iain MacAnTsaoir and Dawn O'Laoghaire explains why Wicca isn't properly considered a Celtic religion, even though it can involve reverence for Celtic gods and goddesses and observance of Celtic holidays. Several versions of this essay exist; at press time for this book, the most current version was 3.2.

Willow's Grove: The Home Page of Ellen Evert Hopman

www.geocities.com/gaias_song/willow.html

Home page of a popular druid author and herbalist. Includes information on her speaking and workshop schedule.

The Work of R. J. Stewart

www.dreampower.com/

R. J. (Bob) Stewart is the author of numerous books on paganism, magic, and Celtic wisdom, including *The Underworld Initiation* and *The Living World of Faery*. He leads a variety of work-shops on spiritual topics at numerous locations each year. The website gives you details about his work, along with suggestions for reading and practical spiritual work.

Appendix C

Timeline of Celtic History

Note: Many of the dates from early to medieval times are approximate.

Date	Event
circa 3100 B.C.E.	Newgrange constructed in pre-Celtic Ireland
circa 2800 B.C.E.	Construction begins on Stonehenge in pre-Celtic Britain; it reaches its present form circa 1100 B.C.E.—500 years before the arrival of Celtic cultures
circa 2500 B.C.E.	Dolmens (such as the Poulnabrone Dolmen) constructed
circa 2000 B.C.E.	Passage grave constructed at the site later known as Tara
circa 1200 to 750 B.C.E.	Emergence of Celtic culture in the Rhine/Danube area of Europe
circa 750 to 450 B.C.E.	Golden age of Halstatt culture
circa 600 B.C.E.	Approximate arrival of Celtic culture in Britain
circa 450 to 0 B.C.E.	La Tène culture
387 B.C.E.	Celts sack Rome
280 B.C.E.	Celts settle in Galatia (modern central Turkey)
279 B.C.E.	Celts unsuccessfully attack Delphi, Greece
225 B.C.E.	Celts unsuccessfully march on Rome
circa 150 B.C.E.	Expansion of trade between Celtic and Roman merchants

continues

continued

Date	Event
circa 125 B.C.E.	Roman military presence in southern Gaul
58 B.C.E.	Caesar begins the conquest of Gaul
55 B.C.E.	Gaul fully under Roman authority; Julius Caesar's first expedition into Britain
54 B.C.E.	Julius Caesar's second expedition into Britain
52 B.C.E.	Defeat of Vercingetorix
43 B.C.E. to 84 C.E.	Conquest of southern and central Britain
19 B.C.E.	Roman conquest of Galicia
60	Romans destroy the Druid community at Anglesey (in what is now Wales)
61	Uprising of British Celts led by Queen Boudicca
122	Construction of Hadrian's Wall to protect Roman Britain from the Celtic Picts to the north (what is now Scotland)
143	Antonine Wall built north of Hadrian's Wall to protect Roman Britain from the Celtic Picts to the north
163	Antonine Wall abandoned by Romans
circa 200	Christians in Britain
circa 300 to 1022	Tara serves as the seat of the High Kings of Ireland
circa 379 to 405	Legendary dates for the reign of Niall of the Nine Hostages
390 to 461	Life of St. Patrick, Apostle to Ireland
410	Romans withdraw from Britain
432	St. Patrick's mission to Ireland begins
circa 450 to 523	Life of St. Brigid, Abbess of Kildare
circa 450 to 650	Saxons, Angles, and Jutes invade and transform England
circa 484 to 577	Life of St. Brendan, "the Navigator"
circa 540 to 550	Possible dates for the reign of Arthur (Celtic chieftain or warlord who fought against the invading Saxons)
563	St. Columba (Colum Cille) leaves Ireland to found a monastery on the Island of Iona off the coast of Scotland
circa 575	St. David establishes Christian monasteries in Wales
597	Death of St. Columba; establishment of Roman-approved Christianity in Canterbury, England
circa 800	Scribes begin to illustrate *The Book of Kells*
circa 840 to 1000	Viking communities established throughout Celtic world

Date	Event
circa 900	"Preiddeu Annwn" ("The Spoils of the Underworld") early Arthurian/Grail poem legendarily attributed to Taliesin
936	Bank of the Tamar River established as the boundary separating Saxon England from Celtic Cornwall
1002	Brian Boru becomes High King of Ireland
1066	Norman invasion of England
circa 1100	*The Book of the Dun Cow* (Irish manuscript)
circa 1160	*The Book of Leinster* (Irish manuscript)
1170	Norman Richard Strongbow leads an invasion of Ireland
circa 1180	*Perceval* by Chrétien de Troyes, an early grail legend
1190	*The Speckled Book* (Irish manuscript)
circa 1220 to circa 1297	Life of Thomas of Erceldoune (Thomas Rhymer)
1250	*The Book of Aneirin* (Welsh manuscript); *The Black Book of Carmarthen* (Welsh manuscript)
1263	Scots defeat the Norse at the Battle of Largs
1297	Under the leadership of William Wallace, Scots defeat the English at the Battle of Stirling Bridge
circa 1300	*The White Book of Rhydderch* and *The Book of Taliesin* (Welsh manuscripts)
1320	Signing of the Scottish Declaration of Arbroath, which proclaims that liberty is worth defending, even with one's life
circa 1325	*The Book of Taliesin* (Welsh manuscript)
circa 1390	*Yellow Book of Lecan* (Irish manuscript)
circa 1391	*The Book of Ballymote* (Irish manuscript)
circa 1400	*The Red Book of Hergest* (Welsh manuscript)
1540	Brigid's flame extinguished in Kildare
1670 to 1738	Life of Irish harpist Turlough O'Carolan
1691	Robert Kirk writes *The Secret Commonwealth of Elves, Fauns, and Fairies*
1745 to 1746	Bonnie Prince Charlie leads an unsuccessful Scottish rebellion against English rule
1781	Foundation of the Ancient Order of Druids
1790 to 1860	The Highland Clearances, in which many Scottish tenant farmers and their families were forced off the land, many of whom emigrated to North America or Australia

continues

continued

Date	Event
1792	Iolo Morgannwg convened the first Gorsedd, or gathering, of the Bards of the Isle of Britain at Primrose Hill in London
1798 to 1874	Life of Irish wisewoman Biddy Early
1825	Publication of Thomas Croker's *Fairy Legends and Traditions of the South of Ireland*
1845 to 1850	Irish Potato Famine ("The Hunger") leads both to widespread death and emigration
1852 to 1932	Life of Irish playwright and folklorist Lady Augusta Gregory
1861	Establishment of the annual National Eisteddfod in Wales
late 1800s	Folklorist Alexander Carmichael begins collecting Gaelic prayers, chants, and songs, which he published as the *Carmina Gadelica*
1890	W. B. Yeats joins the Golden Dawn
1898	Lady Gregory and W. B. Yeats found the Abbey Theatre in Dublin, which helped spark the Irish literary revival
1908	Winston Churchill initiated into the Ancient Druid Order
1914 to 1953	Life of Welsh poet Dylan Thomas
1916	Easter Rising, a turning point in the Irish struggle for independence
1919 to 1921	Irish war for independence against Britain
1922 to 1923	Irish Civil War
1923	W. B. Yeats wins the Nobel Prize for Literature
1926	An Cumann le Béaloideas Éireann (the Folklore of Ireland Society) created
1939	Publication of James Joyce's *Finnegans Wake*
1949	Formation of the Republic of Ireland
1954	Publication of Gerald Gardner's *Witchcraft Today*
1962 to 1975	Archaeological excavations and restoration of Newgrange
1963	Founding of Reformed Druids of North America (RDNA)
1964	Formation of the Order of Bards, Ovates, and Druids (OBOD)
1976	Northern Irish Peace Activists Mairead Corrigan and Betty Williams win the Nobel Peace Prize
1976 to 1977	English explorers led by Timothy Severin successfully sail from Ireland to Newfoundland in primitive boats similar to those Brendan would have used in the sixth century
1979	Formation of the British Druid Order (BDO)
1983	Ár nDraíocht Féin (ADF) founded by Isaac Bonewits

Date	Event
1993	Brigid's flame relit in Kildare, Ireland
1995	Seamus Heaney wins the Nobel Prize for Literature
1999	Scottish Parlaiment convenes for the first time since 1707
2001	Beltane fires lit on the Hill of Uisneach in Ireland to celebrate Irish unity
2002	Rowan Williams, future Anglican Archbishop of Canterbury, is made a druid of the Welsh Gorsedd of Bards; International Gathering of Shamans held in Ireland

Index